1789: THE FRENCH REVO

M000237458

The French Revolution marks the beginning of modern politics. Using a diverse range of sources, Robert H. Blackman reconstructs key constitutional debates, from the initial convocation of the Estates General in Versailles in May 1789, to the National Assembly placing the wealth of the Catholic Church at the disposal of the nation that November, revealing their nuances through close readings of participant and witness accounts. This comprehensive and accessible study analyses the most important debates and events through which the French National Assembly became a sovereign body and explores the process by which the massive political transformation of the French Revolution took place. Blackman's narrative-driven approach creates a new path through the complex politics of the early French Revolution, mapping the changes that took place and revealing how a new political order was created during the chaotic first months of the Revolution.

ROBERT H. BLACKMAN is Elliott Professor of History at Hampden-Sydney College, where he won the J. B. Fuqua Award for excellence in teaching. He is the author of articles in *French History* and *French Historical Studies*, regularly presenting his research at the Western Society for French History and the Society for French Historical Studies. He is also co-editor of "Becoming Revolutionaries: Papers in Honor of Timothy Tackett" with Micah Alpaugh and Ian Coller.

NEW STUDIES IN EUROPEAN HISTORY

Edited by
PETER BALDWIN, University of California, Los Angeles
CHRISTOPHER CLARK, University of Cambridge
JAMES B. COLLINS, Georgetown University
MIA RODRÍGUEZ-SALGADO, London School of Economics and Political Science
LYNDAL ROPER, University of Oxford
TIMOTHY SNYDER, Yale University

The aim of this series in early modern and modern European history is to publish outstanding works of research, addressed to important themes across a wide geographical range, from southern and central Europe, to Scandinavia and Russia, from the time of the Renaissance to the present. As it develops, the series will comprise focused works of wide contextual range and intellectual ambition.

A full list of titles published in the series can be found at www.cambridge.org/newstudiesineuropeanhistory

1789: THE FRENCH REVOLUTION BEGINS

ROBERT H. BLACKMAN

Hampden-Sydney College

CAMBRIDGE
UNIVERSITY PRESS

CAMBRIDGE
UNIVERSITY PRESS

University Printing House, Cambridge CB2 8BS, United Kingdom

One Liberty Plaza, 20th Floor, New York, NY 10006, USA

477 Williamstown Road, Port Melbourne, VIC 3207, Australia

314-321, 3rd Floor, Plot 3, Splendor Forum, Jasola District Centre, New Delhi - 110025, India

79 Anson Road, #06-04/06, Singapore 079906

Cambridge University Press is part of the University of Cambridge.

It furthers the University's mission by disseminating knowledge in the pursuit of
education, learning and research at the highest international levels of excellence.

www.cambridge.org
Information on this title: www.cambridge.org/9781108716673
DOI: 10.1017/9781108591447

First published 2019
First paperback edition 2020

A catalogue record for this publication is available from the British Library

Library of Congress Cataloging in Publication data
NAMES: Blackman, Robert H., 1967– author.
TITLE: 1789 : the French Revolution begins / Robert H. Blackman.
OTHER TITLES: French Revolution begins
DESCRIPTION: New York, NY : Cambridge University Press, 2019. | Series: New studies in
European history | Includes bibliographical references and index.
IDENTIFIERS: LCCN 2019008017 | ISBN 9781108492447 (hardback)
SUBJECTS: LCSH: France – History – Revolution, 1789–1799. | France – Politics and
government – 1789–1799. | France – History – Revolution, 1789–1799 – Causes. |
BISAC: HISTORY / Europe / General.
CLASSIFICATION: LCC DC163 .B55 2019 | DDC 944.04/1–dc23
LC record available at https://lccn.loc.gov/2019008017

ISBN 978-1-108-49244-7 Hardback
ISBN 978-1-108-71667-3 Paperback

Contents

Tables

Acknowledgments

Over the years, I have had wonderful conversations about my work with too many people to count. Those who have given me great ideas and useful feedback include Micah Alpaugh, Elizabeth Bond Andrews, James Arieti, Eric Arnold, Keith Baker, David Bell, Michel Biard, Gail Bossenga, Jack Censer, Helen Chenut, Suzanne Desan, Eric Dinmore, Annelien de Dijn, Caroline Emmons, Jim Friguglietti, Bob Hall, Paul Hanson, Mette Harder, Carol Harrison, Shaunna Hunter, Katie Jarvis, Annie Jourdan, Danna Kostroun, Ted Margadant, Laura Mason, Mary Miller, Jim Munson, Adrian O'Connor, Jeremy Popkin, Sophia Rosenfeld, Lynn Sharp, Noah Shusterman, Rebecca Spang, Jim Stinchcomb, Don Sutherland, David Troyansky, Mike Utzinger, Steven Vincent, Michel Vovelle, Charles Walton, Bill Weber, Kent Wright, Joseph Zizek, and many more.

Judy Coffin helped me find my way to being an historian of France. Mark Poster, Wolfgang Iser, and Marjorie Beale taught me how to read texts in new ways, and Marjorie sparked my interest in the French Revolution. Barry Shapiro read work of mine related to Chapter 5 and provided useful documents. Jeff Horn read an early version of Chapter 6; Marisa Linton and Malcolm Crook each read the entire book. All three gave me critical feedback that improved the book immensely. Marisa in particular has given me encouragement all along and gently pushed me to get this book finished. Jim Arieti gave me great help in compiling the index, and Ursula Acton did a wonderful job as copy editor. I thank my editors at Cambridge University Press, Liz Friend-Smith, Michael Watson, and Jim Collins, as well as Abigail Walkington and Natasha Whelan, for their help in getting this project to fruition. Jim Collins has been a very supportive series editor, reading numerous drafts and giving me lots of advice and assistance along the way. I also thank my anonymous readers. Their comments made this a better book. Timothy Tackett deserves special thanks for all the encouragement and support he has given me over the years and for the many conversations we have had about this work in particular and the French Revolution in general. Without his help, encouragement, and example, I would never have completed this project.

I thank Hampden-Sydney College for generous research support from the Office of the Provost and Dean of Faculty, from the Professional Development Committee, and from the Department of History. I could never have collected all the sources I needed without the help of the ILL staff at the Bortz Library. I also thank the Virginia Foundation of Independent Colleges for a Mednick Research Fellowship that helped fund a trip to Paris in the summer of 2014. The people at the Uptown Café generously let me use a table there while I wrote this book.

I have been fortunate enough to present my work at the conferences of the Western Society for French History, the Society for French Historical Studies, the Consortium on the Revolutionary Era, the Society for the Study of French History, and the American Historical Association. Portions of this book draw on my articles "Representation without Revolution: Political Representation as Defined in the General *Cahiers de doléances* of 1789," *French History* 15:2 (2001), 159–85; and "What's in a Name? Possible Names for a Legislative Body and the Birth of National Sovereignty during the French Revolution, 15–16 June 1789," *French History* 21:1 (2007), 22–43. I gratefully acknowledge Oxford University Press for permission to build on that work here. I also used revised material from "What Does a Deputy to the National Assembly Owe His Constituents? Coming to an Agreement on the Meaning of Electoral Mandates in 1789," *French Historical Studies* 34:2 (Spring 2011), 205–41, with permission from Duke University Press. Finally, I drew material from "What was 'absolute' about the 'absolute veto'? Ideas of national sovereignty and royal power in September 1789," *Proceedings of the Western Society for French History* 32 (2004), 123–39. In all cases, I updated material taken from these articles with new research and revised my conclusions.

Finally, I wish to thank my wife, Kelly Nelson, our son, Allen Blackman, and my father, Donald Blackman. These three have been very understanding and supportive as this project took over my life during the last five years. It is to them that I dedicate this book.

24 January 2019
Hampden-Sydney, Virginia

Abbreviations

AHR	*American Historical Review*
AHRF	*Annales historiques de la Révolution française*
AP	*Archives Parlementaires*
AN	Archives Nationales (France)
BNF	Bibliothèque nationale de France
FHS	*French Historical Studies*
FH	*French History*
JMH	*Journal of Modern History*

Introduction: Building a National Assembly

The French Revolution (1789–99) marked the beginning of modern politics. For the first time, a major European state moved from traditional monarchical rule to a more democratic, participatory political system, creating its own institutions as it went. The French Revolution erupted from a stalemate that had developed between the French Crown and traditional political and social elites over how to reform the way in which the state financed itself. The old system could not keep up with the demands placed on it by generations of war. It was hamstrung by the woefully unfair imposition and inefficient collection of taxes. By the time Louis XVI (r. 1774–92) asked his subjects for assistance and advice in the winter of 1787, the system was already under considerable strain. But the French elites refused to accept the plan proposed by their king without being granted a large and permanent role in the kingdom's political system. The king would not give it to them. The resulting struggle pushed the state to the edge of bankruptcy and led to a political crisis. To resolve the crisis, the king summoned the only nationwide representative body available to the French, the long-defunct Estates General.

No longer would political decisions be made in secret by Court factions gathered around the king or by the king's ministers, meeting in rooms far from the public eye. Instead, from the very beginning of the Revolution, questions of policy and constitutional reform were discussed openly by men elected for that very purpose. The deputies of the Estates General of 1789 quickly adapted to the circumstances of political and public disorder that surrounded them and turned their attention to writing a constitution meant to prevent future crises. The questions the deputies faced are still relevant today: How can major changes be made in a failing political system? How can a legitimate government be established in the ruins of a previous political order? Can a new constitutional system be crafted in the face of opposition from those who long to keep their privileged position in society? The struggles of the French deputies and the solutions they crafted to complicated financial, economic, and political problems speak to us in the twenty-first century, as we grapple with the ramifications of collapsed states in North Africa and the Middle East and the rise of illiberal political movements in Europe and the United States. Study of the first attempt by a major European state to reorganize itself on modern foundations gives us examples we can use to guide our own policy decisions.

This book is about how the deputies elected to the Estates General of 1789 created a new political culture and constitutional order during the first seven months of the French Revolution, May–November 1789. These deputies took what had once been a purely consultative body, the Estates General, and transformed it into a modern representative body with the power to write a constitution, the National Constituent Assembly. This book explains how this change came to pass and lays out the implications of their work for the course of the French Revolution as a whole. As we explore the transformation of French politics, we focus on the period from the initial convocation of the Estates General in Versailles at the beginning of May 1789 to the Assembly's decision to put the vast wealth of the French Catholic Church at the disposal of the nation the following November, with additional discussion of the period leading up to the convocation of the Estates General. In this, we cover roughly the same period as did Georges Lefebvre in his masterful *The Coming of the French Revolution*.[1] This is when the deputies and the king lived and worked near each other in Versailles and in which king and deputies determined how they would relate to each other and to the nation at large. In effect, despite the declaration by commoner deputies (known as the "Third Estate") and some deputies from the order of the Clergy on 17 June 1789 that they were a "National Assembly," a political body capable of acting on its own, this was a period in which the political legitimacy of the Assembly was still nascent. Only in the weeks following the removal of the king to Paris on 6 October did the deputies secure their role as the main government power in France.

In this book, we study how the deputies created the National Assembly as the legitimate representative body of the French nation, able to change constitution, state, and society to better rule the French.[2] The deputies elected in 1789 to help the king reform the French state were not the first

[1] G. Lefebvre, *The Coming of the French Revolution*, trans. by R. R. Palmer, with an introduction by T. Tackett (Princeton, 2005). The original work in French was published in 1939, with Palmer's translation appearing in 1947.

[2] We use the term "National Assembly" here to refer to the body first formed on 17 June 1789, largely from the Third Estate, and to the National Constituent Assembly, the name taken by the combined

men to discuss political reform in the long eighteenth century. Like the British Members of Parliament in 1688–89 or the American Founding Fathers, the deputies to the Estates General of 1789 had to craft a constitutional settlement that would enable their state to weather the terrible storms of political revolution. But the French deputies faced the additional necessity of crafting reform in the largest and most powerful monarchy in Europe while the state was too weak to enforce its will.[3] They had to create and direct a consensus in the nation behind policies that required major changes, even as the institutions that could implement change collapsed. Of necessity, the deputies had to explain their own legitimacy and convince the French to follow their lead in reform. Looking carefully at the speeches and actions of the deputies who directed these changes allows us to see how they crafted a new political order in response to the crises they faced. We see how they hoped to form consensus around a modern political system based on free elections, the principle of majority rule within the resulting elected bodies, and strong constitutional protections for individual rights, all while trying to find a way to deal with increasingly strident political opposition, as well as a collapse of order in the countryside and in many cities. As we will see, the French struggled mightily with the concept of a loyal opposition in their system, but during our period they did not seek to erase opposition, merely overcome it.

When studying the development of a new political culture in France, there are many choices to be made. Here we have chosen to focus on the deputies who sat in the early assemblies because of the outsized impact their decisions had on the course of events. The deputies decided during summer and early fall 1789 how the branches of government would relate to each other and what the boundaries of their powers would be. They also determined the way in which the broader public would be able to influence political affairs. In doing this, they set the rules by which the national political game would be played in subsequent years. While regional

orders on 7 July 1789. We prefer "National Assembly" for the period before 2 November 1789, as the Assembly's constituent role was contested before that date.

[3] The Americans also faced the problem of how to enforce order with a weak federal state, though in a much smaller and more isolated nation. See D. Andress, "Atlantic entanglements: Comparing the French and American Revolutions," in A. Forrest and M. Middell, eds., *The Routledge Companion to the French Revolution in World History* (London and New York, 2016), 164–65. On Polish attempts at constitutional reform during the Four-Year Sejm of 1788–92, see S. Fiszman, ed., *Constitution and Reform in Eighteenth-Century Poland: The Constitution of 3 May 1791* (Bloomington and Indianapolis, 1997); R. Butterwick, "Political Discourses of the Polish Revolution, 1788–92," *The English Historical Review* 120: 487 (June 2005), 695–73; Jerzy Lukowski, "'Machines of Government': Replacing the Liberum Veto in the Eighteenth-Century Polish-Lithuanian Commonwealth," *The Slavonic and East European Review* 90: 1 (January 2012), 65–97.

developments, such as the resistance to the Revolution that developed in western parts of France, had strong influence over the course of events from 1789–99, these regional developments were often caused by actions taken at the center. In order to better understand how and why the Revolution took the course it did, we need to understand how the deputies came to see themselves as having the power to legislate the broad reforms they did.

Throughout this work, we address the question of whether or not the constitutional project embarked on in the earliest months of the French Revolution was a viable one. By the summer of 1789, the French political system had been fatally destabilized and the absolute monarchy was quickly falling to ruin. The deputies elected to the Estates General had to find a form of political representation that would work while the state collapsed around them. We show how the deputies of the Third Estate and their allies in the Noble and Clerical orders worked together to create a new political system during a time of widespread public disorder, improvising as necessary when circumstances shifted, and with little or no direction from Louis XVI or his ministers. Through the summer and fall of 1789, the deputies acted with great deliberation and caution. They chose to make their arguments and decisions in front of an audience in the assembly chamber. They wrestled publicly with their own consciences as they tried to understand to what extent they were bound by the conditions of their election. They worried openly about whether or not they would be able to satisfy the demands of their constituents to create a system in which the will of the nation would be taken into account by the king as he ruled.

In order to show the how the ideas and practices of political representation changed over the summer of 1789, we analyze several key debates held in the assemblies, using a broad array of primary sources to reconstruct them in unprecedented detail. Given the depth with which we examine each debate, it would be impossible to cover the long summer of 1789 in a book of readable length. Instead, we focus on those debates crucial to the development of the National Assembly as a sovereign political body. Our work has led us to novel claims about the course of these early debates. We show that throughout the spring, summer, and fall of 1789, moderate deputies routinely pushed back against radical proposals and led their colleagues to compromise solutions. We show the influence of moderate deputies on the naming of the National Assembly itself on 15–17 June, on the response to the king's reluctance to accept the formation of a National Assembly (in the Tennis Court Oath of 20 June and their response to the Royal Session of 23 June) and how the deputies welcomed the arrival of their more conservative colleagues in the common hall in late June and early July. We also show the impact of center-left and center-right deputies' speeches on the decision to grant the king a suspensive veto power over legislation (11 and 21 September), and over the means the deputies used to resolve disagreements between the king and the Assembly in general. Finally, we show that it was necessary to compromise with moderates in order to pass a decree putting the properties of the Church at the disposal of the nation (2 November). These discoveries alone necessitate a revision of the political narrative of 1789, overturning previous claims that radical deputies drove the agenda of the National Assembly during the early Revolution and showing just how complex the interplay was among radical, moderate, and conservative ideas.

We also demonstrate how Louis XVI's reluctance to work with the National Assembly pushed the deputies to change their view of how future legislatures would relate to the executive power. As the king resisted their efforts at reform and unrest intensified throughout France, the deputies slowly broadened their role in crafting a new constitution. They had to create a political system that would be safe from royal resistance, but would also be safe from the kind of popular upheaval that had resulted from the king's dismissal of his reforming minister, Jacques Necker, in mid-July 1789. Over time, they came to realize that the king was not a good-faith partner in reform. Only then did they abandon their plan of writing a constitution in cooperation with the king and write one that would protect the French from the malfeasance of the old political elites and, if necessary, from the king himself. The constitution they wrote over the summer of 1789 was a clear statement that the deputies would do what they had to in order to save the monarchy and satisfy the demands of their constituents.

By focusing on the actions of the deputies, their caution, and their willingness to compromise with each other and with the king, we show that many scholars who have studied these events have misread them. Through a careful reconstruction of the debates over the boundaries between royal executive power and national legislative power in the new constitution, we demonstrate that the deputies gave the king a powerful role but established formal checks so that the king could not abuse his authority. The deputies envisioned the king and Assembly as partners in reform but made it clear that the Assembly would not allow the king to thwart the will of the nation. In showing how important the contribution of moderates was to the constitutional project, we challenge historians' claims that the deputies of 1789 broke definitively with the wishes of their constituents and created a political culture that shunned compromise, crafting a new political order that could only spiral into the violence of the Terror (1793–94).

Finally, we discuss how the rising political awareness and activism of ordinary Parisians upset the careful compromise the deputies pursued. We show that the October Days, when thousands of Parisian women marched to Versailles pursuing their own particular demands, caused the Assembly to act to defend its new role in national affairs. The deputies did this by taking the king under their protection, declaring that the National Assembly and the king were inseparable until the constitution had been written. In doing this, they showed to all that the unit of government in France was the king *and* the National Assembly. They then set about solving the problems of public order that the collapse of the king's authority had caused, so that events like the taking of the Bastille on 14 July or the march on Versailles would no longer be necessary. It was only by taking the king under their protection that the deputies assumed a dominant role in the national state. After 6 October, they found themselves leading France, tasked to reframe the constitution to protect France against its enemies, foreign and domestic.

In writing this book, we use contemporary and retrospective accounts of the early Revolution in new ways, opening up new insights into the political culture of the French Revolution. In order to chart the transformation of the Estates General into a National Constituent Assembly, we have reconstructed several key debates held by the deputies over how they related to their constituents and to the king. In this work, we have solved a major problem with interpreting the early Revolution. Strictly speaking, prior to our work there has been no reliable record of what the deputies said during the debates held in the early French Revolution. No official record was kept of the debates in the Estates General or the National Assembly from May to November 1789. For close to 150 years, historians writing about the speeches deputies made during this period have relied on the *Archives Parlementaires*, occasionally supplemented by well-known memoirs written long after the events had occurred.[4] Both types of sources are best used with caution. The *Archives Parlementaires* is not a contemporary record written by the deputies themselves. It is a mid-nineteenth-century attempt to create a real parliamentary record of the debates and decrees of the representative bodies of the Revolution. For the first months of the Revolution, the record the editors constructed is incomplete at best and misleading at worst. Many important speeches do not appear or only appear in summary, and entire debates do not appear at all. Worse,

---

[4] J. Madival and E. Laurent, eds., *Archives parlementaires de 1787 à 1860, Première série (1787–1799)*, 82 vols. (Paris, 1867–1913). Henceforth abbreviated as "AP."

many speeches appear only in the polished and complete versions that were later published by the speakers. Likewise, memoirs by deputy participants were published decades after the events they report and often rely on printed versions of deputy speeches when recounting major debates. To properly analyze the debates of the early Revolution we found it necessary to broaden the source base substantially to include material from a variety of contemporary sources. This allows us to give a much better account of what happened, what was said, and what was decided than has previously been possible.

We supplement the *Archives Parlementaires* and published deputy memoirs with a broad range of sources from the time of the Revolution itself. We rely by preference on accounts of the debates written by deputies who sat in the assemblies and witnessed or gave the speeches they recount, using where possible accounts written immediately after the events themselves. These retellings of the debates appear in the many letters deputies wrote to their friends, families, and constituents. They appear in the contemporary diaries of deputies, several of whom kept detailed records of what happened in the assemblies. In addition, we used detailed accounts of the debates written by journalists who were deputies themselves, accounts that are particularly valuable as the journalists analyzed the speeches and explained them to their readers. Finally, we use accounts from eyewitnesses who were not deputies, but who attended sessions of the Estates General and the National Assembly at different points during the spring, summer, and fall of 1789 and left us records of what they saw and heard.

These sources give us a rich and complex picture of what happened in the early Estates General and the National Assembly. Gone are the certainties found by relying on speeches recounted in the *Archives Parlementaires* to understand the debates of the early Revolution. When we look at a broader array of sources, we find that multiple versions of the speeches exist, many of which contain clear evidence of improvised comments and, most importantly, the ebb and flow of particular ideas and proposals. Relying on a much broader variety of sources shows us that the deputies took into account the objections of their opponents and modified their proposals on the fly. They worked to create an inclusive political process. They followed the traditional norms of political speech, seeking arguments to support their positions rather than simply embodying ideological movements. They tried to craft motions that would rally the largest number of votes possible. Our work shows that reliance on the *Archives Parlementaires* and a narrow base of sources has led historians to misinterpret the key debates of the early Revolution, giving us a misleading

understanding of the political culture of the deputies. Far from coming to
Versailles in May 1789 intending to destroy the monarchy and set up a new
system, the deputies found themselves pushed to take ever more aggressive
actions designed to keep the National Assembly in existence. Faced with
resistance to reform, the deputies sought to create a constitutional order
that would preserve the role of a representative legislative assembly in the
future.

Reconstructing the debates from 1789 is a difficult task. Conditions in
the main assembly hall made it difficult for the deputies to hear what
other deputies were saying. The main hall the deputies used in Versailles
had not been laid out for debate. It had all of its seats on the same level
and there was no obvious line marking off deputies from the large and
unruly audience that listened to their every word. The deputies had the
experience of trying to speak in the midst of a great crowd. It was not
until after 21 July, more than two months after the deputies first met in
Versailles, that the hall was reworked into a kind of auditorium so the
deputies could easily see who was speaking.[5] Even after the seating had
been changed, the body suffered from long and slow debates and interference from spectators. Disorder in the hall only grew over time, even
after the Assembly relocated to Paris, peaking in November 1789.[6]
Records of the debates in contemporary newspapers reflect these difficulties, with speeches reported in partial or mangled form, or in an
idealized form far from what the deputies could have heard when the
speech was given.[7] Observers and participants alike had trouble following
what was going on.

Early in the Revolution, speeches were misattributed in newspapers,
letters, and diaries, and the names of deputies spelled in creative ways.
Since most of the deputies read from prepared texts, journalists could ask
for copies of the speeches in order to accurately report them. But reports
based on the written texts left out the give-and-take of the debates,
interruptions from the floor or the audience, and the many times deputies
improvised responses to previous speakers. Journalists who relied on brief
notes taken during the speeches captured more of the vibrancy of the

[5] E. H. Lemay, *La Vie quotidienne des députés aux États Généraux, 1789* (Paris, 1987), 196. Tackett notes
that 4,000 spectators watched the deputies declare themselves the National Assembly on
17 June 1789. T. Tackett, *Becoming a Revolutionary: The Deputies of the French National Assembly
and the Emergence of a Revolutionary Culture (1789–1790)* (Princeton, 1996), 147.

[6] One debate, that of 11 September, ran eleven hours, from 9:00 am to 8:00 pm. It was hardly unique.
Lemay, *La Vie quotidienne*, 201, 205, 208.

[7] Lemay, *La Vie quotidienne*, 206; M. Linton, *Choosing Terror: Virtue, Friendship, and Authenticity in
the French Revolution* (Oxford, 2013), 15.

debates.[8] This practice had its limitations, though, as they could hear no better than anyone else and certainly missed much of what was said. In just one of many examples we could give, the Third Estate deputy Paul-Victor de Sèze wrote to the *Journal de Paris* on 7 September 1789 claiming that two other newspapers had misquoted his speech of 4 September in a way that completely changed the thrust of his argument. He worried that the misleading versions would reach his constituents long before he could send them a printed text and he hoped that the *Journal* could print a correction. It took until 17 September for this letter to be published, leaving plenty of time for an incorrect impression of his speech to spread.[9] His speech was hardly the only one misheard, misunderstood, or misrepresented.

Given the conditions in the hall, it seems almost miraculous that work could be done at all. Despite the chaos, the deputies managed to make persuasive speeches that led to constructive compromises. When one looks at the responses deputies and eyewitnesses had to the speeches, recorded soon after the debates took place, one sees what the deputies themselves found persuasive. We get insight into the mood of the Assembly in a way that simply reading the printed versions of the deputies' speeches can never give us. Though we cannot say for certain what the deputies listening to their peers speak felt or thought – after all, their accounts were written down with an audience in mind – we can explore how the deputies perceived the events they lived through and seek to better understand interaction between their experiences and the outcomes of the debates.[10] Only a small minority of the deputies who attended the Estates General of 1789 left any record of their thoughts. Our attempt at reconstructing the experience of the debates allows us to fruitfully imagine how the vast majority of the deputies – those who never or seldom spoke – understood events, how they were persuaded, how they came to be educated by the Revolutionary process, even as they made the decisions that shaped it.[11]

---

[8] Lemay, *La Vie quotidienne*, 202–3; H. Gough, *The Newspaper Press in the French Revolution* (London and New York, 1988), 55; J. Popkin, *Revolutionary News: The Press in France, 1789–1799* (Durham and London, 1990), 58–59.

[9] *Journal de Paris*, 17 September 1789.

[10] Tackett, *Becoming a Revolutionary*, 11–12; Linton, *Choosing Terror*, 21–22. Though Linton deals primarily with deputies of the left later in the Revolution, we can generalize this claim to include the accounts from deputy-witnesses we have for 1789.

[11] On the topic of experience in the French Revolution, see especially Tackett, *Becoming a Revolutionary*, ch. 5, "The Experience of Revolution"; D. Andress, ed., *Experiencing the French Revolution* (Oxford, 2013), especially, "Introduction: Revolutionary Historiography, Adrift of at Large," 1–15; See also Linton, *Choosing Terror*; T. Tackett, *The Coming of the Terror in the French*

Reading the debates in this way allows us to show the impact political speeches and contemporary events had on the decisions made by the deputies and to gain insight into their experience of the political process as it unfolded. Discussing the experience of the Revolution also gives us the opportunity to explore the way in which the deputies' emotions impacted the decisions they made.[12] After all, these debates did not unfold in a void. Long before the deputies met in Versailles in May of 1789, France had begun to experience civil disorder. The political Revolution that took place in Paris and Versailles ran in parallel with a popular revolution coming out of the increase in urban and rural unrest that occurred in the second half of the eighteenth century, popular unrest that intensified in 1789. For the elites meeting in Versailles, this widespread unrest indicated the possibility of a real breakdown of public order throughout France.[13] This parallel, popular revolution combined with a counter-revolution originating in the king's Court in the earliest stages of the Revolution to create an atmosphere of unease, even fear, in the minds of the reformers. As the premier historian of the long summer of 1789, Timothy Tackett, warns us, "we must avoid seeing the deputies' Revolutionary itinerary . . . as a series of calculated decisions based on careful deliberation and foresight." Though the speeches made in the assemblies seemed to direct events, "for the most part, all of the deputies found themselves swept along by circumstances over which they had only limited control. There was an erratic, unpredictable, chaotic quality to political action, action born as much of passion, fear, and uncertainty as of reason and premeditation."[14] As Marisa Linton reminds us, the deputies were real individuals making real choices based on their own experiences. Their political decisions arose out of their choices, and these choices were made according to the information the deputies had and the emotional impact the events had on them, coloring their decisions with joy, solidarity, fear, despair, and hope.[15]

Tackett, Linton, and Annie Jourdan all argue that an ambient feeling of unease and fear was an important spur that pushed the deputies to take increasingly serious, even violent actions as the Revolution progressed. Nevertheless, we must remember that during the early Revolution this

Revolution (Cambridge, Massachusetts, 2015); and A. Jourdan, *Nouvelle histoire de la Révolution* (Paris, 2018).
[12] For a discussion of recent works on emotion in the French Revolution, see Linton, *Choosing Terror*, 17–20.
[13] Jourdan, *Nouvelle histoire*, 31; M. Biard and P. Dupuy, *La Révolution française: 1787–1804*, 3rd ed. (Paris, 2016), 45; P. M. Jones, *Reform and Revolution in France* (Cambridge, 1995), 166–74. See Jones p. 169 for a table indicating the frequency of incidents of unrest.
[14] Tackett, *Becoming a Revolutionary*, 151.   [15] Linton, *Choosing Terror*, 4.

fear did not lead to violence on the part of the deputies against their peers, nothing like the "politicians' terror" that Linton identifies in 1793–94, which led to the deaths of scores of deputies.[16] In this work, we will see that the deputies gathered in Versailles felt a wide variety of emotions. While fear and anxiety were important in pushing the deputies to make their decisions, they also acted out of hope, joy, anger, solidarity, and even, on occasion, despair. We will see how the deputies hoped for a better world, how they defended their constituents with a sense of duty, and how they reacted to the actions of the deputies of the Nobles and Clergy and the king with a sense of wounded pride, even righteous anger. Though these emotional responses did not determine the deputies' actions, at key points they influenced their decisions, making them more likely to take the dramatic actions that pushed the Revolution forward.

The literature on the French Revolution is vast and here we limit ourselves to discussing those works that primarily focus on the deputies to the Estates General and National Assembly during the memorable spring, summer, and fall of 1789.[17] The most recent books that do this are those of Barry Shapiro and David Andress.[18] Shapiro looks carefully at the deputies' speeches and analyses their content. He also uses a broad array of sources to reach his conclusions. He approaches the debates from the perspective of psychological theory, coming to the conclusion that the deputies made their choices post–14 July under the influence of repressive denial. Using similar sources, we show that their behavior was broadly consistent over the summer but that they definitely acted to rein in the

---

[16] Jourdan, *Nouvelle histoire*, 82, 534–35; Linton, *Choosing Terror*, 4, 12, 158, 256; Tackett, *Becoming a Revolutionary*, 149–50; Tackett, *Coming of the Terror*, 5–7, 212–22. On the deaths of deputies during the French Revolution, see M. Biard, *La Liberté ou la morte: Mourir en député*, 1792–1795 (Paris, 2015); M. Harder, "A Second Terror: The Purges of French Revolutionary Legislators after Thermidor," *FHS* 38: 1 (February 2015), 33–60.

[17] Recent overviews of the Revolution include Jourdan, *Nouvelle histoire*; P. McPhee, *Liberty or Death: The French Revolution* (New Haven, 2017); Biard and Dupuy, *La Révolution française*, 3rd ed.; Tackett, *The Coming of the Terror*; N. Shusterman, *The French Revolution: Faith, Desire and Politics* (London and New York, 2014); S. Desan et al., eds., *The French Revolution in Global Perspective* (Ithaca, New York, 2013); J.-C. Martin, *Nouvelle histoire de la Révolution française* (Paris, 2012); M. Biard, ed. *La Révolution française: une histoire toujours vivante* (Paris, 2010). See also D. M. G. Sutherland, *The French Revolution and Empire* (Oxford, 2003); W. Doyle, *The Oxford History of the French Revolution*, 2nd ed. (Oxford, 2002); F. Furet, *Revolutionary France, 1770–1880*, trans. by A. Nevill (Oxford, 1992). For the historiography of the Revolution, see the special issue of French Historical Studies, "89: Then and Now," 34:4 (Fall 2009); H-France Salon 1:1, D. K. Smith, ed. (2009), www.h-france.net/Salon/Volumes1-3.html; P. Hanson, *Contesting the French Revolution* (Chichester, 2009).

[18] B. Shapiro, *Traumatic Politics: The Deputies and the King in the Early French Revolution* (University Park, PA, 2009). D. Andress, 1789: *T xhe Threshold of the Modern Age* (New York, 2009). See also W. Doyle, *Aristocracy and Its Enemies in the Time of the French Revolution* (Oxford, 2009).

king's powers after the taking of the Bastille. In short, we argue that his theory of repressive denial is not necessary to explain the deputies' behavior and underestimates their political sophistication. Before the mid-July crisis, the deputies had assumed the king was on their side, though misled by corrupt counselors. After 14 July, they increasingly acted to limit the king's ability to thwart reform. Andress's work is a comparative analysis of the American and French Revolutions, alongside analysis of British politics. While he covers the main events of 1789, he does not analyze the way in which the deputies constructed a new system of political representation, nor does he show how the dynamic between the king and the Assembly shifted over the summer of 1789. Micah Alpaugh's *Non-Violence and the French Revolution* is excellent on the early Revolution, but his focus is on political protest outside the Estates General and National Assembly. As such, our book acts as a complement to his work, not a challenge. The two together give a much richer view of the beginnings of the Revolution.[19]

Other works that analyze deputy behavior and thought in the summer of 1789 are much older. Paul Friedland provides a remarkable history of how theories of representation shifted in French theater during the eighteenth century. He argues that over the course of the century, the audience was gradually excluded from active participation in theater productions, removed from the stage and reduced to being a passive observer. Friedland then attempts to show that this same transformation happened in the Estates General and National Assembly over the summer of 1789, with deputies like the abbé Emmanuel Sieyès theorizing that representatives had to use their own best reason and were not beholden to the opinions of those who had elected them. Friedland argues that this new form of political representation required the people of France to be passive observers ruled by those who acted for them. He also argues that this form

---

[19] M. Alpaugh, *Non-Violence and the French Revolution* (Cambridge, 2014). Important essays on the summer of 1789 appear in P. McPhee, ed., *A Companion to the French Revolution* (New York, 2013); D. Andress, ed., *The Oxford Handbook of the French Revolution* (Oxford, 2015); and P. Campbell, ed., *The Origins of the French Revolution* (New York, 2006). Other works that cover the summer of 1789 include L. Boroumand, *La Guerre des principes* (Paris, 1999); E. H. Lemay and A. Patrick: *Revolutionaries at Work: The Constituent Assembly, 1789–1791* (Oxford, 1996); P. Brasart, *Paroles de la Révolution* (Paris, 1988); R. Halévi, "La révolution constituante: les ambiguités politiques," in C. Lucas, ed., *The Political Culture of the French Revolution*, vol. 2 of *The French Revolution and the Creation of Modern Political Culture* (Oxford, 1988), 233–57; P. Gueniffey, "Les assemblées et la représentation," ibid., 233–57; D. Richet, "L'esprit de la constitution, 1789–1791," ibid., 63–68; G. Chaussinand-Nogaret, *The French Nobility in the Eighteenth Century*, trans. W. Doyle (Cambridge, 1985); J. Égret, *The French Prerevolution, 1787–88*, trans. W. Camp (Chicago, 1977; the French original dates from 1962); and, *La révolution des notables: Mounier et les Monarchiens, 1789* (Paris, 1950); Lefebvre, *Coming of the French Revolution*.

of representation led directly to the Terror of 1793–94, as it became necessary for the state (his theater producers) to silence the unruly people (the audience) so that their representatives (the actors on stage) could act without constraint (that is, get on with the show).[20] Friedland's work is impressive when he deals with theater and theory, but he uses a narrow research base when discussing the debates of 1789 and focuses tightly on speeches by deputies who lost the debates rather than those who carried their motions. Nevertheless, his analysis of the speeches is careful and his attempt to understand the models of representation used by the deputies is a worthy, if ultimately flawed, effort.

The landmark work on the deputies to the National Assembly is that of Timothy Tackett. Tackett uncovered and used the writings of 129 deputies in order to chart the way in which they became Revolutionaries, creating new institutions and interpretations of their own role as they responded to the extraordinary events unspooling around them. Tackett uses a careful reconstruction of deputy opinion about the Revolution to show how their ideas concerning sovereignty and political reform were driven more by contingent events than by some predetermined ideology. As he puts it, the deputies came to see themselves as representatives of the French through a "school of Revolution," as they heard many different claims about what their role was and came to a collective understanding of what their work would be. Their ideas evolved into coherence during the process of revolution as they faced and tried to solve the many problems caused by the collapse of the monarchy around them. Combining his study of deputy opinions with the results of a careful collective biography of the National Assembly, Tackett challenges claims by previous historians that the Revolution of the mind had happened before the deputies arrived in Versailles and undermines claims that deputies from the different Estates were part of a "convergent elite," a group of men who had broadly similar backgrounds and ideas. Kenneth Margerison builds on Tackett's analysis to show how deputies envisioned strategies for reform before the Revolution and during its early months. He also carefully reconstructs events from a broad source base. Both emphasize the political weakness of radical deputies during the summer of 1789 and the persistence of a powerful centrist platform. While both works provide a necessary

---

[20] P. Friedland, *Political Actors: Representative Bodies and Theatricality in the Age of the French Revolution* (Ithaca, NY, 2002). See also Friedland, "Parallel Stages: Theatrical and Political Representation in Early Modern and Revolutionary France," in C. Jones and D. Wahrman, eds., *The Age of Cultural Revolutions* (Berkeley and Los Angeles, 2002), 218–50.

framework for any study of the early Revolution, neither work looks at the fine texture of the debates themselves.[21]

Michael Fitzsimmons's work focuses on the creation of a new polity in Revolutionary France, in part by examining the actions of the deputies to the Estates General and National Assembly. Fitzsimmons argues that the key moment in the creation of a new French political system was the night of 4 August 1789, when the deputies decided to eliminate the old system of privilege that had undergirded the social and political structures of the absolute monarchy.[22] While we agree with many of his findings, we show that the optimism of events like 4 August was sharply tempered by concerns that Louis XVI was not willing to engage in good-faith negotiations about reform with the Assembly. Fitzsimmons emphasizes the deputies' desire to craft a constitution that would establish and defend the new society envisioned in the August decrees. We argue that the deputies began setting up a defensive constitution much earlier than he claims, as early as mid-July, motivated by the Assembly's duty to protect the nation from a relapse into ministerial despotism and by doubts about the king's good will.[23]

The most important work that analyzes the speeches given by the deputies in the National Assembly is that of Keith Michael Baker. In a series of brilliant articles published during the 1980s, Baker explored the debates of the early Revolution as part of the long-term development of concepts concerning sovereignty, constitutionalism, political representation, and public opinion in early modern France. In particular, he ties the creation and self-legitimation of the National Assembly back to ideas about politics that arose in the last years of the Old Regime, roughly 1750 to 1789. He identifies three specific discourses derived from traditional aspects of the king's rule. These discourses came from groups who challenged the king's traditional role in different ways. The discourse of *justice* came from

---

[21] Tackett, *Becoming a Revolutionary*. See also Tackett, *Priest and Parish in Eighteenth-Century France* (Princeton, 1977) and *Religion, Revolution and Regional Culture in Eighteenth Century France* (Princeton, 1986). K. Margerison, *Pamphlets and Public Opinion: The Campaign for a Union of Orders in the Early French Revolution* (Lafayette, IN, 1998). See also B. M. Shapiro, *Revolutionary Justice in Paris, 1789–1790* (Cambridge, 2002). For the convergence of elites, see G. V. Taylor, "Non-Capitalist Wealth and the Origins of the French Revolution," *AHR* 72 (1967), 469–96; F. Furet, *Interpreting the French Revolution*, trans. E. Forster (Cambridge, 1981); H. Applewhite, *Political Alignment in the French National Assembly, 1789–1791* (Baton Rouge, LA, 1993); Chaussinand-Nogaret, *French Nobility*.

[22] M. Fitzsimmons, *The Remaking of France: The National Assembly and the Constitution of 1791* (Cambridge, 1994), and *The Night the Old Regime Ended: August 4, 1789 and the French Revolution* (University Park, PA, 2003).

[23] See also J. Guilhaumou, *L'avènement des porte-parole de la Republique (1789–1792)* (Paris, 1998).

the constitutional ideas of the great law courts of Old Regime France. That of *reason* came from the administrative ideas of the Physiocratic school of economic thought, and that of *will* from the writings of Jean-Jacques Rousseau and his followers in France. Baker argues that when the deputies set about working to solve the monarchy's financial and political problems they drew on these discourses to articulate possible lines of reform. For Baker, the ensuing clash of discourses caused the Revolutionaries to abandon their ties to history and an ancient monarchical constitution. To show this, Baker carefully examines speeches given in the National Assembly during the summer of 1789 in order to determine how the competing discourses played out. In the end, he argues, the decisions the deputies made during the summer of 1789 necessarily led to an unstable constitutional project. For Baker, the way in which the deputies tried to blend and refine the discourses they had inherited led them to abandon the discourses of justice and reason in favor of that of will, "in the long run . . . opting for the Terror" of 1793–94.[24]

We bring to the table a new approach to studying the important debates held in the Estates General and National Assembly from May to November of 1789. We focus on the analysis of the deputies' speeches, much as Baker and Friedland have, but we seek to expand the resource base, as Tackett has, and to put the debates into the context of the events that developed around them, as Tackett, Margerison, and Shapiro do with such force. This allows us to demonstrate that the way in which the deputies arrived at their decisions was much more complex than Baker and Friedland propose. In particular, our method differs from that of Baker and Friedland in that we consult far more accounts of the debates than they do, reconstructing little known and frequently ignored speeches and debates from the long summer of 1789. We also pay much more attention to the outcome of the debates, showing which speakers influenced the text of the final decrees and putting their decisions into a broader political context, including the actions of the king and his Court and of Parisian activists. This new method allows us to show that the political culture developed by the deputies of the National Assembly was much more inclusive and given to political compromise than historians have previously understood. Far from treating the debates of 1789 as a "prelude to Terror," as Norman Hampson once did, we have to view them as events

---

[24] K. M. Baker, *Inventing the French Revolution* (Cambridge, 1990). The quotation may be found on page 305. See also Baker, "Transformations of Classical Republicanism in Eighteenth-Century France," *JMH* 73: 1 (March 2001), 32–53. For a critique see M. Linton, "The Intellectual Origins of the French Revolution," in Campbell, ed. *Origins of the French Revolution*, 139–59.

in their own right, exploring the richness and texture of the deputies' words and the events that surrounded them.[25]

In this book, we show that the speeches given by radical deputies had less impact on the decisions made in the Assembly than many historians have claimed. Our detailed examination of the speeches, combined with careful analysis of the political context in which they were made, reveals two important and new things about the summer of 1789. First, the deputies quickly found themselves reacting to the events developing around them much more than driving them. The behavior of deputies from the upper orders changed the options available to the deputies of the Third Estate, making things that were previously unimaginable to the majority of the deputies suddenly possible. Second, the actions taken by Louis XVI, his Royal Council, and Court in the summer of 1789 pushed the deputies to take actions that few would have considered wise in the early weeks of the Estates General. From a body summoned by the king to assist him in saving the state, the Estates General transformed itself into a National Constituent Assembly intent on defending itself and its prerogatives from royal interference. This profound transformation came out of the interaction of the unsettled political culture the deputies inherited from the struggle between the great law courts of the realm, known as *parlements*, and the king in the eighteenth century, and the unprecedented political and social upheaval that surrounded them in 1789.

The book that follows examines how the National Assembly came into being, how it gained recognition by the king, and how its deputies struggled to press their reforms forward in the face of resistance from the king and many of the traditional elites of the realm. The transformation from Estates General to National Constituent Assembly came in stages during the first ten months of 1789. Constitutional debates carried out in the pamphlet press during 1787–89 had posed the Estates General as a body that superseded the great law courts of France, the parlements, as a check on royal power and the only body capable of discussing and approving the king's proposed reforms. Nevertheless, the Estates General had not been called since 1614. There was no settled understanding of how the Estates General would be formed, beyond the certainty that the deputies would be called from the three traditional orders of the realm, the Clergy, the Nobles, and a catchall category, the Third Estate, that in 1789 included commoner elites and poor peasants alike. The first stage of the political

---

[25] N. Hampson, *Prelude to Terror: The Constituent Assembly and the Failure of Consensus, 1789–1791* (Oxford, 1988). See also Applewhite, *Political Alignment*.

transformation from Estates General to legislative and constituent body happened during the election of deputies to the Estates General, which mobilized unprecedented numbers of voters and allowed men (and women, who could not vote but were often present at rural assemblies) to express their desire for change. The transformation can be seen in the *cahiers de doléances* that the deputies carried with them to Versailles, then the capital of France. These documents, literally "notebooks of grievances," were written by the electoral assemblies that sent deputies to the Estates General. They contained a statement of what each electoral district (known as a "bailliage" or a "sénéchausée") thought the Estates General needed to accomplish, compiled and generalized from the lesser *cahiers* drawn up in each district's parishes, religious houses, and by urban guilds and corporations. In the district-level *cahiers* we see the outlines of a new system of political representation, one in which the kingdom would have a regular, periodical and freely elected assembly to advise the king and perhaps to act as a legislative body. We discuss this stage in Chapter 1 and learn what the basic outlines of a new constitutional settlement were.

The second stage occurred after the Estates General met in early May 1789. The king and his ministers had not issued a clear statement of how the deputies would meet or vote once they arrived in Versailles. For a variety of reasons, the Crown decided to leave the matter up to the Estates General itself. But the three Estates could not agree on how to meet and vote. Third Estate deputies, along with a minority of the deputies from the privileged orders, as the Clergy and Nobles were known, wished to meet as one body with a vote by head. The majority of the deputies from the Nobles and the Clergy wished to meet and vote by separately by order, ensuring that they could block any reforms that targeted their privileges. A stalemate ensued that lasted until 17 June, when the deputies of the Third Estate (along with nineteen deputies from the Clergy) declared themselves a "National Assembly" capable of acting on behalf of the Estates General. They declared themselves able to take this step because they represented both the majority of the deputies who had been elected to the Estates General and almost the entirety of the French population. Having invited the rest of the deputies to attend, they moved on to provisionally accept existing taxes only through the current session. The process by which the deputies of the Third Estate came to take this momentous step is the subject of Chapter 2.

The declaration of the National Assembly triggered a reaction on the part of the Crown. The king announced on 20 June 1789 that the deputies of all three orders would have to attend a forthcoming meeting called a "Royal Session" at which the king would explain what forms the Estates General would use and what matters it would discuss. The king then suspended meetings of the Estates General until after this special session had taken place. But the suspension of the meetings caused the deputies of the National Assembly to formally declare, on that same day, in what we know as the Tennis Court Oath, that they did not recognize the king's right to suspend their meetings or dismiss the Assembly. At the Royal Session on 23 June, the king made a formal statement explaining how he expected the deputies to behave and what reforms he expected them to suggest. He then ordered the deputies to disperse and meet the following day according to the rules he had given them. The deputies of the National Assembly defied the king's order that they leave the hall. They reaffirmed their decisions of 17 and 20 June. The National Assembly had decided that it was a coequal part of the government with the king. Discussion of this momentous decision and the events leading up to it form the third stage of the development of a legitimate constituent assembly and are the topic of Chapter 3.

Though the king subsequently agreed to allow the orders to meet and deliberate in common, he did not accept the existence of a National Assembly. Neither did a substantial number of deputies from the upper orders. On 30 June, when the united orders met for the first time, these recalcitrant deputies protested against the activity of the National Assembly, if not its very existence. These protests led to a remarkable debate in early July during which the deputies explored the duties they had to faithfully represent their constituents and the effect that this obedience could have on the functioning of the Assembly. In the end, the majority of the deputies voted to reconfirm the principles adopted when they declared themselves the National Assembly on 17 June, specifically that no electoral district or part of a district could halt the work of the majority of the duly elected deputies sitting together in the common meeting hall. They also decided not to attack the links deputies had to their constituents or their obligation to act in their interest. The Assembly recommended instead that deputies who felt bound by their constituents not to participate seek new powers, much as the king had ordered on 23 June.

But while the deputies argued over whether or not the wishes of a particular constituency could halt the activity of the entire Assembly, fresh royal troops gathered around Paris and Versailles. When asked by the deputies what his intentions were in gathering troops near the capital, the king replied laconically that he intended to maintain order. Recently, historians have argued that the king intended to enforce the settlement he had declared in the Royal Session.[26] Whatever the king had hoped to accomplish, events quickly took on their own life. Louis's dismissal of Necker and other reforming ministers on the Royal Council late on 11 July triggered a massive uprising in Paris, one that was well beyond the ability of the Crown to manage. The city of Paris slipped entirely out of royal control, with the electors of Paris taking control of city hall and the king's army proving unable or unwilling to maintain order. Supported by soldiers who had deserted their units, the people of Paris seized the Bastille, a medieval fortress on the east side of Paris that symbolized royal control of the city. The king found himself worse off than before. He had to face the hard reality that he could not control the National Assembly and that without its help he could not restore order in Paris. On 15 July, the king came to the Assembly hall and pledged that he would work with the deputies to restore order and to solve France's problems. With recognition by the king and the nation alike, the National Assembly definitively became a power coequal with the king. This forms the fourth stage of the transformation from Estates General to legislative and constituent body, and from this point forward the Assembly held the initiative in crafting a new constitution. The final acceptance by the privileged deputies of the National Assembly and the capitulation of the king form the topics of Chapter 4.

It remained necessary, though, to establish the correct relationship between the powers of government in the new constitution. The events of May–July 1789 had convinced the deputies that the main source of unrest in France was the lack of an orderly constitutional government. From late July on, the deputies set themselves to work rewriting the basic rules of the monarchy. In order to calm Paris and to tamp down disorder that word of Necker's dismissal had caused through much of France, the deputies acted on the night of 4 August to abolish the old system of social inequality and inequality before the law. Later that month, they issued the Declaration of the Rights of Man and Citizen, ensuring that the people of France would know their rights and demonstrating their plan to write a constitution that would defend these rights. The deputies believed that the disorder in Paris and in the provinces had resulted from a disagreement between the king and the Assembly over how to proceed in reforming the constitution. It was clear to them that if the powers of the government

[26] J. Hardman, *Louis XVI* (New Haven, 1992); and, *Louis XVI: The Silent King* (London, 2000); M. Price, *The Road from Versailles* (New York, 2003).

continued to disagree, there would be continued or even growing disorder. In order to avoid causing further unrest, the deputies had to forge a path forward that avoided antagonizing or humiliating the king. They had to achieve a new constitutional settlement without highlighting the ongoing disagreement between the Assembly and king about how to proceed. Thus, from 31 August to 21 September the deputies went through the fifth stage of the transformation from Estates General to a truly national assembly. They worked to establish the proper relationship between the king, the legislative body, and the French people. This mainly took the form of a discussion of what kind of veto power the king would be granted, who by this power would act as a brake on the actions of the legislative body and thus ensure that the rights of the people would not be violated. But the veto power would also only be suspensive, ensuring that the nation would have the final say in any dispute between its representatives without needing to resort to the levels of violence seen in Paris.

The deputies crafted an elegant solution to a very difficult set of problems. The king would be able to delay the implementation of any legislation he disagreed with, necessitating further discussion of the issue by the broader public. When sufficient time had passed (and tempers had cooled), following regularly scheduled elections, future deputies would have the opportunity to pass the legislation again. After they had gone through this cycle twice, the law would come into effect without the king's signature. In doing this, the deputies signaled that they wanted a constitutional monarchy in which the king had a strong role in determining what kinds of laws would be made. All laws would have to pass the muster of the king, the deputies, and the broad literate public that could participate in debates over laws in the press. Such a calm and deliberative treatment of disagreement between the executive and legislative powers was meant to prevent popular unrest by ensuring that the will of the nation would always be followed. But let there be no mistake: by allowing the future assemblies to override the king's will concerning legislation, the Assembly made it clear that the king would not be able to halt constitutional reform or turn the clock back to the Old Regime. The discussion of this veto power and the way in which it typified the new constitutional arrangement forms the topic of Chapter 5 and the first part of Chapter 6.

It is not with this elegant solution that we end our inquiry. Throughout the summer, the king had resisted the depth of reform demanded by the National Assembly. In Chapter 6, we show that by mid September it was clear to the deputies that Louis would not easily accept the August decrees or the Declaration of Rights, let alone constitutional revisions that substantially diminished royal power. But no showdown between the Assembly and the king happened. Instead, in October 1789, disagreement between the king and the Assembly over the constitution dovetailed with an ongoing subsistence crisis in Paris to trigger a march on Versailles by tens of thousands of Parisians. They demanded first bread, then the return of the king to Paris, where his beloved people could keep him safe and watch over him to ensure that he acted on the will of the people, not on the advice of perfidious advisors. Louis's weakness was exposed for all to see and Louis himself was personally humiliated. This event led to the king's definitive withdrawal from good-faith participation in the Revolutionary experiment. The intervention of the people of Paris also led the Assembly to make a remarkable decree in which they swore never to separate from the king and led them to relocate the Assembly to Paris, to remain near him. With this decree, the Assembly established itself as something more than coequal with the king in the new constitutional system. It publicly put the king under its protection and irrevocably tied itself to the king, and thus tied the Revolution to the monarchy.

We finish the book by showing how and when the National Assembly achieved fully active status as a constituent assembly, moving beyond asserting this status to actually enjoying it. After the October Days, the Assembly addressed how to handle the still-worsening financial problems the government faced. The same problems that had undermined the absolute monarchy threatened to overwhelm the new system under construction. The deputies of the National Assembly had decided on 17 June 1789 to nationalize the royal debt and had firmly declared that there would be no royal bankruptcy. But over the summer the financial situation worsened as the king and the Assembly struggled over the mechanism by which reforms could be made. In October, the Assembly discussed how to revive the state's access to credit markets. After an extended debate, they declared on 2 November that the vast properties of the Catholic Church in France were at the disposal of the nation, a somewhat ambiguous phrase made necessary by many deputies' refusal to order the simple seizure of the Church's wealth. This declaration made manifest what most deputies from all three orders had assumed, that the Church would have to sacrifice much if not all of its property in order to prevent a royal bankruptcy. The previous reorganization of vast amounts of property, the August decrees that followed the night of 4 August, had been based on the voluntary renunciation of privileges and rights. Placing Church property at the disposition of the nation came despite the opposition of most of the Clerical deputies. With this decision, which some deputies protested went against the guarantees for property in the recently enacted Declaration of the Rights of Man and Citizen, the deputies completed their transition from a body summoned by the king to help him reform France into the only body that had sufficient legitimacy to craft a constitution and the pass the laws necessary to bring order back to the kingdom. Passing a law that dealt with the rights and privileges of the Clergy by a simple majority vote showed that the Old Regime society of orders was well and truly dead. It had been replaced by a new regime still under construction, led by a truly national, truly constituent assembly.

CHAPTER I

The Long Slumber of the Estates General

The forms of political representation in France before 1789 were nothing like political representation in our modern sense of the term. There were no elected representative bodies at the national level and the provinces had systems that varied greatly. The *pays d'états* had provincial estates that had some elective elements, but the *pays d'élection* had no province-wide representative bodies at all. The Catholic Church had its own assembly, but this assembly did not represent the church to the king, as the king was nominally its leader. There were only three political bodies that had any pretension to being "representative" and none functioned in a way that we moderns would recognize as representative government. First and foremost was the king himself. Though he was not elected or accountable in any way to those he represented, he did function as a symbol of France and it was only through the king that there was any unity among the diverse peoples, provinces and corporations that made up the kingdom. But since he was accountable only to God for his actions, there was no way for the people of France to ensure that he acted on their interests.

The second body that had some pretense to being representative was the Estates General, a long-defunct body that had once been a candidate in France for a role like that of Parliament in England. The Estates General had been an *ad hoc* body summoned by the monarch whenever the realm faced extraordinary problems, normally financial in nature. Because of its *ad hoc* nature, the body did not have regular structure for meeting or deliberating and was not convoked in a predictable way. Its only stable feature was that its deputies came from each of the traditional three orders or estates of the realm, the Clergy, the Nobles, and the Third Estate, a category that in 1789 included everyone from the rich, educated men of the cities to the poorest of peasants in the countryside.[1] Nevertheless, the

---

[1] In provincial estates and in some delegations – like that of Brittany to the Estates General – the Third Estate had not represented common people of the countryside before 1789. J. B. Collins, *The State in Early Modern France*, 2nd ed. (Cambridge, 2009), 356 n. 16.

Estates General was a consultative body, meant to deliver information to the Crown, not to legislate or to craft royal policy. It had been summoned last in 1614 when the queen regent, Marie de Medici, resorted to it in her efforts to overcome defiance and rebellion by some of the great nobles of the realm.

Finally, during the eighteenth century, the sovereign courts known as the parlements began to claim for themselves a kind of representative function within the kingdom. These courts existed in the *pays d'état* and had both judicial and administrative functions. An additional court, the powerful and prestigious Parlement of Paris, had jurisdiction over the *pays d'élection*, which together contained over one third of the population of France. These courts had a representative role in that they acted on behalf of the king, administering justice as if the king himself were present. Over the course of the eighteenth century, these great courts began to claim a fundamental legislative role in the kingdom. They claimed that in the absence of the Estates General they represented the French nation to the king and the king to the nation. These magistrates were a curious kind of representative by modern standards, though. They were neither elected by their supposed constituents nor could they easily be removed from office. They held their offices as private property, the legacy of earlier attempts by the Crown to raise money.[2] We will briefly discuss these three pretenders to representative status before moving on to the political and financial crisis that faced the monarchy in 1787–89. We will see how this crisis forced the Crown to resurrect the Estates General in a new form, one that retained its traditional role as a consultative body and bearer of information to the Crown but took on the pretenses of representative status and legislative power claimed by the sovereign courts. This overview will help us understand the basic ideas about how to reform the state and constitution the deputies carried with them to the Estates General that met in May 1789, giving us a necessary background for the tremendous changes that occurred during the long summer of that year.

The French monarchy had functioned in very different ways at different times since Hugh Capet, Louis XVI's distant ancestor, had taken the throne in 987 CE. Nevertheless, the monarchy had several central features. By the time Louis XVI became king in June of 1774, the monarchy had pursued a generations-long attempt to centralize power and authority. Louis XIV (r. 1643–715) had been particularly successful in this quest, establishing during his reign the basic forms of the absolute monarchy.

[2] W. Doyle, *Venality: The Sale of Offices in Eighteenth-Century France* (Oxford, 1996).

Though there has been spirited discussion among historians over what this "absolute monarchy" consisted of, there is a broad consensus that the Crown was more powerful at the end of Louis XIV's reign in 1715 than it had been on the accession of Henry IV, the first Bourbon king, in 1589.[3] Despite recent evidence that the monarchy had failed to establish a strong bureaucracy, we can still use historian Russell Major's classic definition of an "absolute monarchy" as

> one in which there were no theoretical limitations on the king's authority other than those imposed by divine, natural, and a few fundamental laws, and in which the king controlled the vertical ties necessary to hold society together and had an obedient army and bureaucracy of sufficient size to enable him to impose his will under ordinary circumstances.[4]

Nevertheless, "absolute monarchy" never meant "monarchy without limits." Louis XIV had only been able to establish his authority by cooperating with traditional elites in France rather than marginalizing or destroying them.[5] One of the more important practical checks on the king's authority was the traditional requirement that he seek counsel before acting. While the king could never be commanded, his subjects asked that he rely on them to provide counsel, so that the preservation of the common good, the goal and ground of the monarchy, might be better obtained.[6] This role had traditionally been filled by the Royal Council and by summoning representative bodies like the Estates General or Assemblies of Notables on an *ad hoc* basis in order to manufacture consent during times of exceptional need.[7] But

---

[3] S. Kettering, *French Society, 1589–1715* (London and New York, 2001), 90.

[4] J. R. Major, *From Renaissance Monarchy to Absolute Monarchy* (Baltimore, 1994), xxi. On whether or not "absolute monarchy" ever existed, see Kettering, *French Society*, 81–91; J. Swann, *Provincial Power and Absolute Monarchy: The Estates General of Burgundy, 1661–1790* (Cambridge, 2003), 1–25; Y.-M. Bercé, *The Birth of Absolutism*, trans. R. Rex (New York, 1996); R. Bonney, "Absolutism: What's in a Name?" *FH* 1:1 (March 1987), 93–117; R. Mousnier, *La monarchie absolue en Europe de ve siècle à nos jours* (Paris, 1982); Collins, *State in Early Modern France*, 2nd ed., 1–10; N. Henshall, *The Myth of Absolutism: Change and Continuity in Early Modern European Monarchy* (London and New York, 1992); P. R. Campbell, *Power and Politics in Old Regime France, 1720–1745* (London and New York, 1996), 10–35 and 296–318.

[5] Major, *From Renaissance Monarchy to Absolute Monarchy*, 375. Other historians have shown how the king used traditional elites and local bodies to achieve his goals. Collins, *State in Early Modern France*, 2nd ed., 6; Kettering, *French Society*, 81–91; Campbell, *Power and Politics*.

[6] W. Doyle, *Origins of the French Revolution*, 2nd ed. (Oxford, 1990), 55. Daniel Gordon sees the change from a monarchy that sought the counsel of its subjects to one based on bureaucratic, indirect rule occurring after 1680. D. Gordon, *Citizens without Sovereignty* (Princeton, 1994), 203. Other historians deny that this process of bureaucratization happened at all during the Old Regime. See Henshall, *The Myth of Absolutism*; Campbell, *Power and Politics*.

[7] For a history of the Estates General that overstates its ideal character, see Friedland, *Political Actors*, 29–51. For the character of the Estates General in 1614–15, see R. Mousnier, *The Institutions of France under the Absolute Monarchy, 1598–1789*, 2 vols. (Chicago, 1979–1984), 2: 216–27.

during his reign, Louis XIV refused to summon such bodies and developed new methods of gathering information from the governed with the intention of bypassing their predictable resistance to his policies. After 1661, Louis XIV chose his own counsel rather than accepting traditional, hereditary members on the Royal Council. Where he could not gain cooperation through traditional means of patronage and co-optation, he replaced elected local and provincial officials with those appointed from the center. He stripped the parlements of their right to suggest changes to new laws and delay their implementation (called the right of "remonstrance") when those laws fell into areas traditionally within the realm of the king's prerogatives. By these actions and through the deft management of political elites, the monarchy established for itself unprecedented authority to govern France.

Where he had bypassed traditional sources of information, Louis XIV relied on a variety of appointed or venal officials, from royal ministers in Paris to minor office holders in each parish, to gather the information necessary to rule and transmit it to Versailles. Nevertheless, gathering information was not the same as asking the governed to present their grievances and in the absence of the Estates General there was no legally recognized way to send information to the monarch. Short of asking the monarch's appointed agents or those traditional elites who cooperated with the monarchy for help or submitting unsolicited petitions, there were few legitimate ways to transmit one's opinions to the monarch. Louis XIV's successors, Louis XV (r. 1715–74) and Louis XVI managed to keep their predecessor's system of information gathering and control more or less intact, and even expanded the powers of the monarchy in some areas, making it ever more difficult for political interests to be expressed.[8]

The suppression of alternate forms of authority meant that throughout the eighteenth century, the most important political actor in France was the king himself. The king also acted as a political representative, though how the king "represented" the French is not self-evident to the modern reader. In order to understand how an unelected and unaccountable monarch could function as a political representative one must begin with Keith Baker's important and influential explanation of the ideas of political representation available to the French in the years leading up to the French Revolution. Relying on the work of Jacques-Bénigne Bossuet, tutor to Louis XIV's son and heir and an influential political theorist, Baker argues

---

[8] Under Louis XIV, the Regency, and Louis XV, there had been a consistent policy of "minimizing the possibilities for public expressions of resentment." F. Ford, *Robe and Sword* (Cambridge, MA, 1962), 191.

that the king was a representative only in the sense that he represented the Christian God to his people. As God's representative on earth, the king was accountable only to God, and this made the king a sacred figure, one whose words were those of God Himself. The king was a political representative in the sense that he derived his legitimacy from his sacral ability to manifest God's will on earth. But the king was also representative in a symbolic way in that "the realm [was] re-presented, or made visible to the people as a whole, in his very person." France of the eighteenth century was made up of many provinces that had entered the kingdom at different times and under different circumstances and all of them had separate cultural, legal, and political traditions. This diverse group of peoples and territories only became a kingdom because the king, in his person, unified them. Without the king, there was no "France" to represent. There was only a "people" when they submitted to their "sovereign magistrate," trading their individual force for the unified force wielded by him.[9] In this form of monarchy, the king alone had the authority to make decisions that impacted the whole and no one had the right to dispute his judgment or disobey his will.

Over the course of the eighteenth century, difficulties with this system became apparent. The information by which the king governed was only as good as the sources from which he drew it. By the reign of Louis XVI, the king no longer entirely controlled the process by which he chose his counsel. Because of developments in Court politics under Louis XV, Louis XVI needed to choose his ministers carefully to avoid giving one faction at Court too much power, regardless of the abilities of the candidates in question. Worse, because there were by tradition only six seats for royal ministers on the Council, there was no institutionalized way to represent the interests of different groups or factions in society to the king.[10] Despite the traditional claim that the king had knowledge of the realm that no other man did and that he thus represented the realm to itself, his ability to act was constrained by the imperfections of the system by which he gained information.[11] Nevertheless, though Louis XVI ruled

---

[9] Baker, *Inventing the French Revolution*, 225–26. In contrast, Collins argues that Louis XIV had done more than anyone to create a state independent of the individual monarch's body, notably saying on his deathbed that "I am going, but the state remains forever." J. B. Collins, *From Tribes to Nation: The Making of France 500–1799* (New York, 2002), 403.

[10] J. Hardman, "Decision-Making," in P. R. Campbell, ed., *Origins of the French Revolution*, 66. Hardman, *Overture to Revolution: The 1787 Assembly of Notables and the Crisis of France's Old Regime* (Oxford, 2010), 15–17. Louis XV had undermined the ability of the king to select his councillors by inviting titled nobles to serve as his ministers of war and of the navy. Collins, *Tribes to Nation*, 485.

[11] Under Louis XV, an extensive network of police informers was set up in Paris to gather information on public sentiments. Attempts by individuals to transmit information to the king could be seen as

indirectly through his ministers, his government remained theoretically based on the system developed by Louis XIV. The clash between the theoretical strength of the monarchy and the reality of imperfect management and even more imperfect information gathering was to lead to great difficulties during the financial and political crisis of 1787–88, when the Crown had to seek advice from outside its traditional channels in order to solve a crisis almost entirely of its own making.

Despite Louis XIV's suppression and bypassing of traditional representative bodies and his claim to absolute power, corporate bodies of many kinds had retained a kind of political existence and their members had kept a voice through the medium of their corporation.[12] Foremost among the powerful corporations in France were the dozen or so sovereign courts commonly called the parlements, charged by the king not only to administer justice but also to handle routine administrative matters in their jurisdictions. These courts had limited executive abilities, always subject to the approval of the king, but they held by tradition the right to remonstrate against laws that they felt infringed on the customs and privileges of their territorial jurisdiction. This right to remonstrate amounted to a weak negative legislative ability, used to protect the traditional rights and privileges of the provinces and the corporations found in them. It was weak because the parlement issuing a remonstrance could only delay the acceptance of a royal decree, not veto it. The monarch could take the court's objections into account and revise edicts and decrees they questioned or disputed if he so desired. But if he wished to enact the decree as written, he could force a parlement to accept it in a ceremony known as the "lit de justice," at which the king personally, or through his agent, commanded the court to write his decree into its law books.[13]

As part of his quest to center power on the king, Louis XIV had removed from the courts their right of remonstrance, but after his death this right was quickly restored. The courts were eager to use their restored power and

---

lèse-majesté. See A. Farge, *Subversive Words: Public Opinion in Eighteenth-Century France*, trans. by R. Morris (University Park, PA, 1995), 18–20, 151–95.

[12] Corporate privilege was a fundamental feature of Old Regime society, and individuals had rights largely by virtue of belonging to corporate bodies, such as the church, the guilds, legal residence in a city, or noble status. See M. Fitzsimmons, "Privilege and the Polity in France, 1786–1791," *AHR* XCII (1987), 269–95. See also Mousnier, *Institutions of France under the Absolute Monarchy*, 1: 429–76.

[13] On the powers of the parlements, see Ford, *Robe and Sword*; B. Stone, *The French Parlements and the Crisis of the Old Regime* (Chapel Hill, 1986), esp. 16–20; P. R. Campbell, "The Paris Parlement in the 1780s," in Campbell, ed., *Origins of the French Revolution*, 87–111. Collins, *State in Early Modern France*, 2nd ed., 17–20.

during the eighteenth century they argued that, in the absence of the Estates General, the sovereign courts had inherited its functions. They claimed the ability to speak for the dispersed people of the kingdom on their behalf, as well as claiming the right to speak to the nation on behalf of the king. As early as 1718, the Parlement of Paris argued that it had inherited the function of the Estates General as the means by which the monarchy could seek approval of extraordinary actions.[14] By mid century, the parlements increasingly saw the practice of free registration of laws by the courts as national consent to legislation, claiming for themselves a power that the Estates General had never had.[15] By the end of Louis XV's reign, the regional parlements, following the lead of Paris, also declared that, in the absence of the Estates General, the parlements of the realm were the sole representatives of the nation.[16] Moreover, they crafted a new and more modern theory of how they represented the nation. Rather than acting as the Estates General, bringing together the grievances of the kingdom in documents to be presented to the king and discussing the program proposed by the Crown, the parlements saw themselves as active participants in the government. They claimed to represent the nation in that they acted on its interests, relying not on direct knowledge of the grievances of particular constituencies but on the best practices determined by the republic of letters, what historians have called "public opinion."[17]

But what was this body, the Estates General, that lent some form of legitimacy to the parlements' pretended right to represent the nation to the king and the king to the nation? The premier consultative body under the French monarchy had been the meeting of the orders of the realm as

---

[14] Baker, *Inventing the French Revolution*, 233. See also Stone, *French Parlements*, 20–21.

[15] Baker, *Inventing the French Revolution*, 229, 231.

[16] Ibid., 234. At the end of the Old Regime, "nation" could mean anything from "bailliage" to "province" to "order," depending on the context. On the term "nation" in the eighteenth century, see D. A. Bell, *The Cult of the Nation of France: Inventing Nationalism* (Cambridge, MA, 2003).

[17] On the relationship between the Republic of Letters and public affairs, see Friedland, *Political Actors*, 52–90. On public opinion see H. Chisick, "Public Opinion and Political Culture in France during the Second Half of the Eighteenth Century," *English Historical Revue* CXVII 470 (February 2002), 48–77; Collins, *State in Early Modern France*, 279, 291, 324. See also R. Chartier, *The Cultural Origins of the French Revolution*, trans. L. Cochrane (Durham, NC, 1991), ch. 2; J. Habermas, *The Structural Transformation of the Public Sphere*, trans. Thomas Burger (Cambridge, MA, 1992); R. Koselleck, *Critique and Crisis* (Cambridge, MA, 1988). For different perspectives, see K. M. Baker, "Defining the Public Sphere in Eighteenth-Century France: Variations on a Theme by Habermas," in C. Calhoun, ed., *Habermas and the Public Sphere* (Cambridge, MA, 1992), 181–211; B. Nathans, "Habermas's 'Public Sphere' in the Era of the French Revolution," *FHS* 16:3 (Spring 1990), 620–44. See also D. Goodman, *The Republic of Letters* (Ithaca, 1994), and Gordon, *Citizens without Sovereignty*.

a formal body summoned by the king. Properly speaking, the Estates General was not a national representative body in any modern sense of the term. It had no legislative power, it did not meet regularly, and was not composed in any predictable way beyond having members drawn from all three orders of the realm.

Moreover, the body was long defunct. It had last met in 1614–15, under Louis XIII (r. 1610–43), when France faced a variety of fiscal and social challenges. Before then, the Estates General had been summoned on rare occasions to consult on the behalf of the dispersed subjects with their representative, the king, in order to aid the monarch in his duty of assuring the common good. The process was meant to be consultative only, with the deputies sent to represent specific constituencies and bring records of their grievances and requests, the *cahiers de doléances*, so that the king would have the best information possible when he made his decisions about how to solve the extraordinary problems that had made summoning the body necessary. The Estates General had been summoned infrequently at best, and over the centuries there had been no consistent way by which it had been summoned. Though it was always summoned according to the estates of the realm – the Clergy, the Nobles, and the Third Estate – deputies of each Estate were not always summoned in equal numbers, nor did they meet or vote in any consistent way.[18] Estates General had had no legislative function, nor had they served to represent the kingdom as a political unit to the monarch. Instead, they had served to express the needs and desires of the disparate corporate bodies to the king.[19] There had long been disagreement as to the optimal role of the Estates General in France. In the sixteenth and seventeenth centuries, the Estates asked for more regular consultation, if not a permanent representative body at the national level, and for the king to act more diligently on their suggestions. The Crown had refused to make the Estates General a more regular body, however, and it had remained a source of information and support for the monarchy to

---

[18] Baker, *Inventing the French Revolution*, 226; J. M. Hayden, *France and the Estates General of 1614* (Cambridge, 1974), 2–6. For the Estates General and its history, see Major, *From Renaissance Monarchy to Absolute Monarchy*; Major, *Representative Government in Early Modern France* (New Haven, 1980); Major, *The Estates General of 1560* (Princeton, 1951); J. B. Collins, "Noble Political Ideology and the Estates General of Orléans and Pontoise: French Republicanism," *Historical Reflections/Réflexions Historique* 27:2 (2001), 219–40. M. P. Holt, "Attitudes of the French Nobility at the Estates-General of 1576," *The Sixteenth Century Journal* 18:4 (Winter 1987), 489–504.

[19] Armand Brette defined the traditional Estates-General as "only having been a body of complainers, of which the function was to present grievances, and to submit without entering into any understanding of anything." A. Brette, *Recueil de documents relatifs à la convocation des États Généraux de 1789*, 4 vols. (Paris, 1894–915), 1: vi.

be summoned on a purely *ad hoc* basis as a way to rally support behind the Crown's plans to solve various crises.[20]

In this chapter, we discuss how the Estates General came to be seen as a legislative and even constituent body at the end of the eighteenth century, largely as a result of the shifts in representative practice engendered by the parlements as they struggled to limit changes demanded by the Crown. Historians have argued that the parlements, after 1753, claimed the right to represent the French people because they represented "public opinion," a term to which we will return.[21] Here we will focus on how the courts claimed a legislative role that came from their representative status and how this pretended legislative role came to engender new powers for the Estates General when Louis XVI summoned it in 1789. As we will see, it was only when the Crown and the parlements had shown themselves unable to solve the problems France faced that the Estates General was able to reappear as a political body. It was only because it became imbued with the pretended right to involve itself in ordinary legislative affairs that it had the potential to become a truly revolutionary body.

It is important to remember that an ongoing political crisis caused the major changes in how the Estates General was conceived. These changes came in a series of gradual steps rather than in a dramatic and sudden repudiation of traditional forms. The transformation of the Estates General into a representative and legislative body came in response to a crisis that originated with the Crown itself, not through the demands of the French for better political representation. It came out of a political crisis caused by the monarchy's dramatic missteps as it attempted to defuse and remediate problems in royal finance. We will briefly discuss the crisis as it unfolded in order to show how it facilitated the transformation of the Estates General from consultative to representative body.[22] The ability of the Estates General to become a representative body in a more modern sense came out of the Crown's adoption of one of the parlements' central claims, that it was necessary for the Crown to seek the approval of a representative body in order to legitimate the reforms the king wanted. The king and his ministers hoped to gain the support of public opinion

---

[20] Collins, *Tribes to Nation*, 266–70; Hayden, *Estates General*, 5–6.

[21] Friedland, *Political Actors*, 57–58.

[22] In this discussion, we rely on Doyle, *Oxford History*, 2nd ed.; J. Swann, "From Servant of the King to 'Idol of the Nation': The Breakdown of Personal Monarchy in Louis XVI's France," in J. Swann and J. Félix, eds., *The Crisis of the Absolute Monarchy: France from Old Regime to Revolution*, Proceedings of the British Academy no. 184 (Oxford, 2013), 63–89; Collins, *State in Early Modern France*, 2nd ed.; P. R. Campbell, "Paris parlement," and K. Margerison, "Pamphlet Debate over the Organization of the Estates General," both in Campbell, ed. *Origins of the French Revolution*.

without resorting to the parlements, but in doing so they opened up a contest between the ministers and the magistrates over who best represented the will of the nation. As this contest dragged on, it became apparent that only a resurrected Estates General had the necessary legitimacy to work with the king to solve the problems France faced. In the end, the Crown's plan to outfox the parlements when implementing major reforms unlikely to be popular with the judges backfired terribly.

By 1786, a fiscal crisis arising out of an antiquated and inefficient tax system required that the monarchy carry through deep reforms in how it taxed its subjects. It was apparent from the beginning that the parlements would resist changes that would impact the privileged orders, the clergy and the nobles.[23] Rather than enter into the predictable conflict between Crown and parlements, Louis XVI was convinced by his minister of finance, Charles-Alexandre de Calonne, to summon a body that could pretend to represent the nation and whose actions could generate the support of public opinion for proposed reforms. Calonne recommended summoning a handpicked Assembly of Notables rather than summoning the long-defunct Estates General, a body he feared would be much harder to control.[24] As a way to seek counsel, the Assembly of Notables was hardly an unprecedented body. The monarchy had convoked such a handpicked group of elites to discuss and accept reform programs in the sixteenth and seventeenth centuries as an alternative to summoning the Estates General.[25] In 1786, the point of calling the Assembly of Notables was to bypass the parlements and their claim to representative status by rallying public opinion behind the Crown.

The monarchy thus had to summon a body with a greater claim to represent public opinion than the parlements. The Crown did this by selecting 144 men from the parlements, the leaders of the French Catholic Church, and the aristocratic nobility to hear the Crown's proposals and to approve them, presumably with a minimum amount of discussion. This

---

[23] On the financial crisis, see G. Bossenga, "Financial Origins," in T. Kaiser and D. Van Kley, eds., *From Deficit to Deluge: The Origins of the French Revolution* (Stanford, 2011), 37–66, and J. Félix, "The Financial Origins of the French Revolution," in Campbell, ed., *Origins of the French Revolution*, 35–62; L. Hunt, "The Global Financial Origins of 1789," in Desan et al., eds. *The French Revolution in Global Perspective*, 32–41. J.-P. Jessenne, "The Social and Economic Crisis in France at the End of the Old Regime," in P. McPhee, ed., *Companion to the French Revolution*, 42–56. L. R. Clay, "The Bourgeoisie, Capitalism and the Origins of the French Revolution," in Andress, ed., *Oxford Handbook of the French Revolution*, 21–39. On Calonne's plan, see J. Félix, *Louis XVI et Marie Antoinette* (Paris, 2006), 359–75.

[24] Doyle, *Oxford History*, 2nd ed., 70.

[25] On the Assemblies of Notables, see Hardman, *Overture to Revolution*; V. R. Gruder, *The Notables and the Nation* (Cambridge, MA, 2007); Félix, *Louis XVI et Marie Antoinette*, 375–401.

strategy was hamstrung by the nature of the body summoned. The monarchy needed the notables to seem as though they spoke freely and adequately represented the opinions of the elites and, through them, public opinion. But the monarchy expected the deputies to the body to be nothing more than yes-men, adopting recommended reforms with little fuss.[26] Their decision to summon an assembly was a nod to the serious nature of the financial problems the monarchy faced, but also revealed that the Crown had accepted the argument made by the parlements during the constitutional struggles of the eighteenth century. From this point forward, public opinion operated as the legitimating factor of the monarchy.[27] The parlements had won the fight before it began. A major tenet of the absolute monarchy had been discarded. The king acknowledged that he could no longer rule without the assent of public opinion.

In the end, the Assembly of Notables was a disastrous failure for the monarchy. The decision to call it had not been supported by a majority of the king's ministers, and the king had had to deviate markedly from customary procedures to force its approval.[28] Opposition by some of the king's own ministers doomed the project from the start, as those who distrusted the king's motives coordinated at Court and in the Assembly of Notables to undermine Calonne. When the Assembly met in the winter of 1787, the notables refused to endorse the royal plan and then demanded reforms that would have ended the absolute monarchy, including a demand that the Estates General be summoned. The king refused to accept the notables' demands, dismissed Calonne and appointed archbishop Étienne-Charles Loménie de Brienne, leader of the opposition in the Assembly, to succeed him. Once Brienne came into office, he examined the accounts himself and saw that the financial crisis was real. He then accepted the necessity of the reforms Calonne had proposed. But Brienne also failed to convince the notables to rally behind the king's plans. In May 1787, the king dismissed the body on Brienne's recommendation. James Collins calls the period after the closing of the Assembly of Notables in May 1787 until the creation of a National Assembly in June 1789 an "interregnum," during which the monarchy abandoned its claims to absolute status. In his closing remarks, Brienne acknowledged that public opinion had become a key feature of the political system. Without its approval, no reforms could be made.[29] Having failed to convince the

---

[26] Hardman, "Decision-Making," 80–81. [27] Collins, *State in Early Modern France*, 2nd ed., 324.
[28] Hardman, "Decision-Making," 83. [29] Collins, *State in Early Modern France*, 2nd ed., 347.

notables, Brienne had to find a different way to rally public opinion behind the reforms.

Rather optimistically, Brienne hoped to reconcile the Crown with the parlements and get the legitimacy the reforms required from free registration by the great courts. In this, Brienne hoped to use the representative status the parlements had acquired in order to show that the Crown had the support of public opinion. Brienne's attempt to use the parlements failed as badly as had Calonne's attempt to use the Assembly of Notables. The parlements accepted minor reforms quickly enough but refused to accept any of the major reforms proposed by the Crown. Disputes between the Crown and the parlements over the proposed reforms led to two years of increasingly public conflict over what the traditional, unwritten constitution of France allowed the king and his government to do. During these two years, the old forms of political representation, those of the king as sole representative of the nation to itself and of the parlements as an intermediary body that represented the king to the nation and the nation to the king, came under sustained criticism. The parlements and the king each deployed pamphleteers to undermine the legitimacy of the other. Both emerged with tarnished reputations and with their constitutional roles brought into question.

Of tremendous importance was a failure of leadership at the highest level. Faced with the failure of the Assembly of Notables, Louis XVI withdrew from day-to-day affairs as early as the spring of 1787, depressed by the response given to Calonne's proposals. During the struggles between Brienne's ministry and the parlements, Louis's wife, Marie-Antoinette, found herself with unprecedented responsibilities for a queen of France, and "August 1788 saw the ship of state rudderless, with the king out of action and the key decisions in the hands of the queen and the Austrian ambassador."[30] With disarray at the very top of the monarchy, the king's ministers were even less likely to receive direction and support from above than before the crisis. Lack of consistent leadership and the parade of ministers in the period 1774–88 had hampered efforts to craft consistent policy.[31] The absence of royal leadership in the aftermath of the failed Assembly of Notables made matters immeasurably worse, leaving the ministers to interpret the king's silences the best they could and making opposition to their reform attempts much easier.

---

[30] Price, *Road from Versailles*, 29–30. See also Félix, *Louis XVI et Marie Antoinette*, 440.
[31] Collins, *State in Early Modern France*, 2nd ed., 315, 324.

This failure of leadership allowed the parlements to pose themselves as defenders of a traditional constitution against what they called "ministerial despotism." As Brienne took ever more dramatic steps to implement reforms without the approval of the parlements (including efforts in 1788 to completely reform the judicial system), public opinion rallied behind the magistrates, who became popular heroes. Attempts to push the Crown's reforms through the Parlement of Paris in 1787–88 led to predictable conflict between the Crown and its courts and the "political kabuki" by which the antagonists traditionally resolved their differences resumed, precisely the situation the Crown had hoped to avoid.[32] Brienne tried a variety of tactics to gather support for his reform plans, including making public for the first time the royal budget. But whatever he did, parlementary opposition increased. What had started as a defense of traditional parlementary privileges quickly turned into a cry for a meeting of the Estates General in response to the Crown's aggressive tactics.[33] The height of disarray for the monarchy came in the late spring and early summer of 1788, when it became clear that the ministers no longer had control of the country. Attempts to remodel the parlements and end opposition to the ministerial reform platform lead to unrest and disorder in many cities and triggered open defiance in the province of Dauphiné.

Brienne attempted to head off the unfolding crisis and regain initiative for the government by announcing, on 5 July 1788, that the Estates General would meet in 1792. He certainly hoped that by then the real crisis would be behind him and the Estates would be reduced to endorsing reforms the government had already imposed. Brienne also took steps to reconcile once again with the parlements, negotiating terms under which they could return to work without losing face or causing the monarchy to lose face. Brienne's 5 July 1788 decree asked for advice on how to summon the Estates General, showing that the government was not set on following the forms of 1614 and was open to increasing the influence of the Third Estate in the body. By August, the monarchy found itself unable to borrow money on any terms and was forced to start paying its creditors with interest-bearing government paper.

Historians disagree about why the conflict between the king and the parlements became so serious. Munro Price argues that the magistrates fought a principled campaign in 1787–88 against what they saw as

---

[32] Collins refers to the typical cycle of remonstrances, *lits de justice,* exile of magistrates, and reconciliation as "kabuki" to show how deeply formalized the process was. Ibid., 337.

[33] See Égret, *Prerevolution.* See also Jones, *Reform and Revolution,* 139–74, and 241.

a dramatic departure from constitutional norms on the part of the Crown. According to Price, the judges believed that the reforms the Crown envisioned were so extraordinary that only "a more representative body than an unelected judicial elite" could effectively "resist royal despotism." This claim that the parlements were aware that unelected judges might not have the legitimacy necessary to prevail in the ongoing struggle with the Crown indicates an awareness on Price's part, if not on that of the magistrates, that elected representatives had a more legitimate claim to political authority in the public eye than did men who held their position as property. Price gives the judges great credit for their foresight. He also blames the Estates General, not the Crown or the parlements, for sweeping aside the traditional representative systems of the Old Regime along with the absolute monarchy.[34]

Peter Campbell argues instead that the magistrates' actions came as the result of their own limited competence and insight combined with terrible mismanagement by the royal ministers. Campbell notes that the key to successful relations between the Parlement of Paris and the ministers during the eighteenth century had been good political management of the magistrates by the Crown. Crises that rivaled that of 1788 had been seen off again and again by competent ministers acting with the support of the king despite intense resistance by the parlements. Unfortunately, according to Campbell, skillful management was missing during the crisis of 1787–89. Intense rivalries within the Royal Court made the problems the Crown usually faced when dealing with parlementary opposition much worse, as both the ministers and the parlements were divided between Court factions. These divisions allowed some of the radical young judges who sat in the Parlement of Paris to insert what Campbell calls "patriotic ideology" into the crisis, with magistrates such as Jean-Jacques Duval d'Eprémesnil claiming that "the king was being misled by evil ministers and all would be well if the king could only be enlightened by the Nation." The parlements themselves had posed as the voice of this nation since mid century, but d'Eprémesnil and his allies claimed that only an Estates General would be able to speak for the nation during the current crisis. Calls for an Estates General initially came only from radical magistrates, but, as the crisis dragged on, this call became a way for the majority in the parlement to force the ministers to back down from proposed policies, with the unintended consequence that the claim that only an Estates

[34] Price, *Road from Versailles*, 27.

General could approve extraordinary reforms issued from both the Assembly of Notables and the parlements it had been meant to bypass.[35]

Whether the magistrates had acted on principle or were motivated by factional interests, the result was the same. By August 1788, the Crown had failed in its quest to push through major reforms and faced bankruptcy. Its efforts to rally public opinion had led to widespread unrest and even open rebellion in favor of the parlements. Brienne recognized that he had lost the fight and in August he took a series of actions meant to shore up support for the monarchy, allowing it to survive financially until it could enact the necessary reforms. He gave in to demands made by the parlements and announced that a meeting of the Estates General would take place in early 1789, rather than in 1792 as originally proposed. Then he facilitated the return to office of the only man anyone thought capable of keeping the monarchy financially afloat, the Swiss-born former minister Jacques Necker, darling of bankers and reformers alike. It would be up to Necker to find a way to preserve what he could of the king's authority while preparing for the return of the Estates General.

Before Necker could make his plans for reform known or announce the details about the convocation of the Estates General, the Parlement of Paris intervened. It had returned from exile on 23 September to the delight of the educated public and ordinary people alike, with the magistrates seen as heroic men who had endured much in order to defend the nation against ministerial despotism. The magistrates then unexpectedly committed collective political suicide. On 25 September, they issued a declaration that the Estates General must be summoned according to the forms used when it had last met in 1614–15. The forms of 1614 would have meant separately electing three bodies, the Clergy, the Nobles, and the Third Estate, each of which would have the same rough number of members and each of which would vote as an order. This ancient practice deviated sharply from the procedures the monarchy had established for the provincial assemblies created by Brienne in 1788 and the revived provincial estates of Dauphiné, where the Third Estate had double representation and the deputies voted by head, not by order.[36] It also meant that any decisions taken had to be made by consensus. Unless all three orders agreed, there would be no action. The forms of 1614 ensured that the privileged orders

---

[35] Campbell, "Paris parlement," 103–06.
[36] Collins calls the Parlement of Paris's decision to push for the forms of 1614 "collective suicide." Collins, *State in Early Modern France*, 2nd ed., 350. See also Doyle, *Oxford History*, 2nd ed., 88–89. Under the forms of 1614, the magistrates would have sat with the Third Estate. Collins, *State in Early Modern France*, 304–05.

could defend themselves against any attempts to erode their social and financial privileges by the Crown. Unfortunately, it was seen by the Third Estate as an attempt by the privileged to protect privilege for its own sake. The judges had misread public opinion and their power to issue such declarations became a problem to be solved rather than a resource to be used, either to reform France or to protect the nation.[37] Up until this point, the Third Estate had broadly supported the parlements in their resistance. After September, the paths of the privileged orders and the Third Estate increasingly diverged, beginning with the very important question of how the orders would meet and vote at the Estates General.

Necker found himself in an interesting bind. He needed the support of the Third Estate but could not risk further alienating the privileged orders. In considering how to convene the Estates General, Necker had to decide whether or not to organize them in the way he had organized experimental provincial assemblies in Berry and Haute-Guyenne in 1778–79, during his last term in office. This would have doubled the Third Estate's representation and required a vote by head in a unified assembly, giving the Third Estate and their allies in the Noble and Clerical orders great influence.[38] Otherwise, if the forms of 1614 were followed, the privileged orders would dominate proceedings and worse, disagreement between the privileged orders and the Third Estate might result in a stalemate and nothing being accomplished.[39] Rather than ignore the parlement's declaration or issue new regulations despite it, Necker asked the king to summon a new Assembly of Notables, hoping that it would endorse doubling of the Third Estate, if not a vote by head. Once again, an assembly dominated by traditional elites refused to endorse a minister's plans. The Assembly met in November and December and refused to support the doubling of the Third Estate or a vote by head. Facing a remarkable public backlash, on 5 December the Parlement of Paris walked back its earlier declaration, stating that it had only meant that elections should be by *bailliage* or *sénéchausée*, the traditional electoral districts for an Estates General. Nevertheless, it did not endorse the changes demanded by reformers. Even the majority of the princes of the blood, those relatives of the king closest in line of succession, opposed doubling of the Third Estate or a vote by head.[40] It appeared that if the privileged orders had their way, they would have veto power over any decisions made by the Estates General.

---

[37] Campbell, "Paris parlement," 109.
[38] On Necker's first term, see R. D. Harris, *Necker: Reform Statesman of the Ancien Régime* (Berkeley, 1979).
[39] Price, *Road from Versailles*, 32.   [40] Doyle, *Oxford History*, 2nd ed., 91–92.

Necker did not wish to allow the privileged elites to dominate the forthcoming assembly, especially given that their refusal to endorse necessary reforms had precipitated the crisis in the first place. On 27 December in the *Result of the King's Council of State*, Necker declared the principles that would govern the elections, though the actual regulations did not appear until 24 January 1789. The Third Estate would elect deputies equal to the number of the Noble and Clerical deputies combined. But Necker did not give the Third Estate the vote by head, instead stating his hopes that the deputies, once gathered, would agree to vote by head rather than order. In the *Report Made to the King* that accompanied the *Result,* Necker explained the reasons for doubling representation by the Third Estate, praising the Third Estate for its many contributions to the common good. Necker also stated that the ministry supported a vote by head in matters of common interest or whenever the vote by order generated a stalemate, without going so far as to require the vote by head.[41] As the historian William Doyle notes, "every elector casting his vote in the subsequent spring was aware that those he was helping to choose would need to confront [the question of whether to vote by head or by order] before they considered anything else."[42] Questions of financial reform and ministerial despotism were joined by those of how to organize the Estates General in a growing public discussion of the government's affairs.

Discussions about how to organize the Estates General took place in an atmosphere of remarkable political freedom. This allowed for the appearance of a new group that demanded even broader reforms than those proposed by the Crown. In the shadows cast by the epic struggle between parlements and ministers, a new conception of political representation began to cohere in the writings of those who felt that neither the ministers nor the parlements could be trusted to see through necessary reforms. After Brienne's call for information regarding procedures concerning the Estates General, the parlementary party and the supporters of the ministers published pamphlets that supported their ideas about how to organize the Estates General.[43] Given the practical collapse of censorship at the

---

[41] Margerison, "Pamphlet Debate," 228. There were precedents for discussion in common, such as the original meeting of the Estates General in 1484. In 1560, the Estates had discussed meeting in common but decided to meet separately, creating the precedent followed thereafter. The Clergy requested at the Estates General of 1614 that some debate be held in common. In a joint delegation to the king in 1614, the Third Estates was granted representation equal to that of the other two orders combined. Collins, *From Tribes to Nation*, 266–67; Hayden, *Estates General*, 112, 126.

[42] Doyle, *Oxford History*, 2nd ed., 93.

[43] Margerison, "Pamphlet Debate," 222. In addition to these pamphlets, massive amounts of information regarding previous meetings of the Estates General appeared, including reprints of the general

time, there was an opening for other players to make their opinions known. As the supporters of the ministers and parlements discredited each other in a tawdry spectacle, a new opposition group formed, one that hoped to move beyond ministerial despotism and parlementary privilege to solve the problems the monarchy faced. They would solve these problems by destroying the privileges of the parlements and restricting the powers of the king with a written constitution. The representative status of the parlements was completely rejected.[44] Only representatives elected by and accountable to the nation would henceforth represent the nation.

This new opposition group, which we can call the "Patriot Party," came to be informally led by the Society of Thirty, a group of aristocratic nobles, members of the Parlement of Paris, and some Third Estate supporters who gathered at the home of the magistrate Adrien Duport.[45] Another major shift in the debate over the constitution of the Estates General had come during the summer of 1788 when news of political developments in Dauphiné spread throughout France. The provincial estates there had long been defunct. Following the crisis of the remodeling of the parlements and uncertainty concerning how deputies would be chosen for the upcoming Estates General, a group of notables led by the lawyers Jean-Joseph Mounier and Antoine Barnave reestablished the provincial estates in defiance of royal orders. The reborn estates of Dauphiné sat like the provincial assemblies Necker had created, with the number of Third Estate deputies matching that of the privileged orders combined. Moreover, the deputies sat in a single body and voted by head. According to François-Henry, count of Virieu, a member of the new body, this composition was meant to curb the influence of the ministers in its discussions. The Dauphiné model provided a way for reforming elites to give the Third Estate influence without threatening the important distinctions between the traditional orders. It provided a way to bring the Third Estate over to the side of the Patriot Party without playing into the hands of the ministers. By making a doubling of the Third Estate and the union of orders the centerpiece of their model, the Society of Thirty created a new platform, one the historian Kenneth Margerison calls

---

cahiers de doléances. See, for example, Lalourcé and Duval, *Recueil des pièces originales concernant la tenue des États généraux*, 9 vols. (Paris, 1789).

[44] Collins, *State in Early Modern France*, 2nd ed., 355.

[45] On the Society of Thirty, see D. Wick, *A Conspiracy of Well-Intentioned Men: The Society of Thirty and the French Revolution* (New York, 1987); Wick, "The Court Nobility and the French Revolution: The Example of the Society of Thirty," *Eighteenth Century Studies*, 13 (Spring 1980), 263–84; Margerison, *Pamphlets and Public Opinion*.

"national constitutionalism."[46] No longer would the Estates General speak only for the disparate parts of the kingdom. It would speak to the king for the nation and to the nation for the king, taking over the role created by the parlements in the eighteenth century.

By the beginning of 1789, especially after the electoral regulations had been published, it was clear that the king had voluntarily ceded a tremendous amount of his authority and that there were many possibilities of how a new kind of representative body could be created out of the old Estates General. This newly reimagined Estates General would have a role quite different than that of the traditional body. First and foremost, it would be a regularly constituted body with some kind of legislative function. In contrast to the parlements or the Assemblies of Notables, the deputies to it would be freely elected according to uniform rules, rather than owning their offices or being appointed by the Crown. The Estates General would step into the void left behind by the collapse of the credibility of the king's ministers and the parlements as defenders of the common good. It remained to be seen what powers the new Estates General would have and who would actually get to wield them, a coalition of reforming Nobles and Clergy working with the Third Estate or Nobles and Clergy who sought to reform the monarchy without losing their privileged role in the state and in society at large.

The deputies were elected in a complex system of nationwide polls, with the Clergy and Nobles directly chosen by primary assemblies and the deputies to the Third Estate chosen indirectly in a series of three or four assemblies. The elections were an amazing enterprise, with unprecedented numbers of clergy and commoners involved in the process. Voting began in February and March for the May meeting, though there were many delays and the last deputies finally arrived in Versailles in July.[47] As tradition dictated, the electoral regulations commanded the deputies to bring with them a statement of the grievances, the *cahier de doléances*. The electoral assemblies were ordered to give the deputies a general mandate authorizing them to freely deliberate, "to propose, to suggest reforms, to advise, and to approve all that concerned the needs of the State, the reform of abuses, and the establishment of a fixed and durable order in all parts of the administration."[48] We will analyze the

---

[46] Margerison, "Pamphlet Debate," 225–27.

[47] On elections to the Estates General, see M. Crook, *Elections in the French Revolution* (Cambridge, 1996), 8–29; M. Edelstein, *The French Revolution and the Birth of Electoral Democracy* (Farnham, 2014), 11–42.

[48] From the electoral regulations decreed by Louis XVI on 24 January 1789. *Lettre du roi pour la convocation des États généraux à Versailles le 27 avril 1789*, AP 1: 543. Accompanying regulations

statements of demands and grievances the deputies carried in order to get a sense of what the general ideas concerning political representation were in the hundreds of different constituencies that elected deputies. We can look to the *cahiers* to see how the electoral bodies envisioned future Estates General and political reform in general. This is not because the deputies were expected to form a "corpus mysticum," as Paul Friedland claims, "re-presenting" the will of the nation, but because the deputies were expected to sort through the often-contradictory demands of their constituents and align them with those of other constituencies in order to craft a set of demands broadly acceptable to the majority.[49]

When the Estates General finally met in May 1789, it had become, in the popular imagination, the repository of all of the representative functions and pretensions developed by the sovereign courts in the preceding 150 years. In the absence of other comprehensive elected bodies, the Estates General came to stand in for the entire population of the kingdom in a new way, bypassing appointed officials, municipalities, and the newer provincial assemblies. Thus, in 1789 the deputies could claim to represent the interests of their electors to their king in a way that neither the parlements nor preceding Estates General ever had. Moreover, the elections to the Estates General took place without adequate leadership from the monarchy. The government had failed to define what the Estates General could and could not do, leaving it up to the electors and their deputies to decide what powers the new body would have. This remarkable situation, in which representatives elected under an absolute monarchy were implicitly given the freedom to determine the boundaries of their own powers, is one of the most stunning occasions of the early Revolution.

In order to show how the changes in conceptions of how the Estates General should function filtered through to the deputies, we will survey the lists of grievances they carried with them and see how they wished to change a system that was in the process of imploding. This requires a discussion of the legitimacy of the *cahiers* as representing public opinion. We also must ask whether the deputies felt bound to represent the opinions

emphasized that the deputies must be given "no instruction meant to stop or trouble the course of deliberations." *Règlement fait par le roi pour l'exécution des lettres de convocation du 24 Janvier 1789*, AP 1: 544, 549. Electoral assemblies from all three orders had artfully or boldly refused to comply with the king's instructions and mandates given the deputies often contained contradictory instructions. See A. Brette, "Les cahiers de 1789 considérés comme mandats impératifs," *Révolution française* 21 (1890), 123–39.

[49] Friedland, *Political Actors*, 29–51, 57–58. See also Y. Durand, "Les Etats généraux de 1614 et de 1789: vie et mort de la monarchie absolue," *XVIIe Siècle* 41 (1989), 131–44; P. Gueniffey, *Le nombre et la raison* (Paris, 1993); R. Robin, *La societé française en 1789: Semur-en-Auxois* (n.p., 1970).

of their constituents or if they thought that they could break with their local constituencies in order to represent the interests of the entire nation. The documents recommend major reforms, it is true, but are remarkably moderate given the depth of the crisis. This does not mean that radical documents did not appear, or that they had no influence on the overall path of events.[50] Nevertheless, a close study of the documents shows that instead of a dramatic transformation of concepts and practices of political representation in this early phase of the Revolution, we see a set of incremental steps meant to establish a kind of representation that would work, allowing for positive changes in the state and the government without permitting ministerial despotism to continue. Part of the challenge for the electoral bodies, though, was coming up with a definition for political representation that "worked." How exactly a political representative could be held accountable for his actions from below while being able to make the kinds of practical decisions required to make necessary reforms was not immediately apparent.

Claims about what the deputies intended when they arrived at the Estates General seem inherently difficult to make or to evaluate. After all, more than 1,100 deputies came to Versailles in the spring and summer of 1789 and most of them left no memoirs, letters, or traces of their opinions. But we do have a useful series of documents that can give us insight into what was expected of the deputies. The deputies came to Versailles as representatives of a specific order, the Clergy, the Nobles or the Third Estate, from an electoral district based on court jurisdictions. They were not representatives in the modern sense of the word, but bearers of instructions given to them by their electors meant to guide and regulate the political acts of their bearers. Each deputy (or delegation, as each electoral district sent two deputies to the Third Estate and some districts wrote joint documents for two or three orders) carried a "general" *cahier de doléances* drawn up by the assembly that sent him to the Estates General.[51] Upon receiving the *cahier*, each deputy swore an oath to faithfully present the grievances of his electors. (In Chapter 4, we will examine the matter of how faithfully the deputies followed the wishes of their electors and how

---

[50] For examples of more radical *cahiers*, see those of Burgundy collected and analyzed by Robin and those of the Third Estate and of the Nobles of the city of Paris. Robin, *La société française in 1789*; Ch.-L Chassin, *Les Élections et les Cahiers de Paris en 1789* (Paris, 1888), 1: 333–64, 321–29; AP 5: 281–90. We will return to the Paris *cahiers* in Chapter 2.

[51] In the Third Estate, there were a series of assemblies and elections to bodies which drafted *cahiers* for their regions. The general *cahiers* were those of the last electoral body, which had to evaluate the regional *cahiers* given to it and draft a formal document that would represent the best interests of the entire area it represented.

seriously they took the oaths they made, as this became a subject of dispute among the deputies and has generated a fair amount of scholarly argument.) The *cahiers* record the desires of a remarkable cross-section of French elite at the end of the Old Regime. Each *cahier* gives insight into the desires and complaints of the specific group that wrote it, including their thoughts on what kind of powers they felt the Estates General had and what reforms the elite electors throughout France sought.[52] Analysis of the *cahiers de doléances* shows that the elites involved in the electoral process wanted serious reforms to be enacted that had both local and national implications. Nevertheless, they had much more modest goals than a transformation of the Old Regime into a parliamentary republic as some historians have claimed.

In order to show that the *cahiers* pushed for substantial reforms without requiring a complete transformation of the monarchy, we here make a quantitative analysis of the demands made regarding political representation in the general *cahiers* of the Nobility and Third Estate. We used a sample of 129 Noble *cahiers* and 144 Third Estate *cahiers* to compile the data necessary to support our argument. Also included were two *cahiers* jointly drafted by the Noble and Third Estates, and six drafted by Noble, Clerical, and Third Estate deputies bringing the total number sampled to 281. (Overall, the *cahiers* from the Clergy showed less interest in matters of political representation.)[53] While historians have written many excellent

---

[52] Ran Halévi estimates that roughly 105,000 to 110,000 individuals took part in the highest level of the elections of 1789. Of the men involved in the elections, the Third Estate represented 42 percent, the clergy 34 percent, and the nobility 24 percent. Halévi, "Monarchy and the Elections of 1789," *JMH* 60, suppl. (September 1988), S87–S88. Tackett notes that the *cahiers* for the Third Estate generally reflect the opinions of a "relatively homogeneous group of urban, non-privileged notables," and "the non-peasant 'notables' within the Third Estate, and particularly those commoner elites living in urban settings." T. Tackett, "Use of the «Cahiers de doléances» of 1789 for the Analysis of Regional Attitudes," *Mélanges de l'École française de Rome* 103 (1991), 30, 33. See also Chisick, "Public Opinion and Political Culture," 58, 67–69; and G. Shapiro and J. Markoff, *Revolutionary Demands: A Content Analysis of the Cahiers de Doléances of 1789* (Stanford, 1998), 99–168. For claims the *cahiers* had little importance in determining the actions of the deputies, see Baker, *Inventing the French Revolution*, 244; Sutherland, *French Revolution and Empire*, 37.

[53] These *cahiers* are available in AP volumes 1–5 (used as corrected by Beatrice Hyslop), or appear in their entirety in B. Hyslop, *A Guide to the General Cahiers of 1789* (New York, 1968). There have been found to date only 167 Noble *cahiers* approved either singly or jointly by a Noble assembly, and 198 Third Estate *cahiers* likewise approved by Third Estate electors. The documents found in the AP and in Hyslop's *Guide* represent over three-fourths of the surviving *cahiers* and come from all over France, providing a more than adequate sample. For a discussion of the number of surviving *cahiers*, the flaws of the AP, and the considerable merit of Hyslop's corrections, see Shapiro and Markoff, *Revolutionary Demands*, 114–19. Also excluded were the *cahiers* from the order of the Clergy. Given the factional character of the Clergy during the early Revolution and the specifically clerical matters that concerned this order the most, we excluded them from the survey. There exist excellent content analyses of the clerical *cahiers*. See especially Tackett, *Religion, Revolution, and Regional Culture*. On

studies of the *cahiers*, none specifically address the relationship envisioned in them between the deputies, their monarch, and their electors or explores the forms proposed in them for future meetings of the Estates General.[54] Almost all of the *cahiers* surveyed here discussed the powers of the Estates General and sought to define its future role. However, one finds through a careful analysis of the *cahiers* that the electoral assemblies – and, by inference, the urban elite from which they were drawn – envisioned a reworking of political representation within the late-eighteenth century monarchy while preserving much of the power and authority of the monarch. The issues examined here – the role of the Estates General in legislative and financial matters, the need to increase the accountability of royal officials, and the periodicity of the Estates – form the outline of a plan for a reformed monarchy that reflects demands made by Estates General from time immemorial. Though these demands appear in a very different context, overall they fall far short of the revolutionary overthrow of the existing system in favor of parliamentary democracy or a republican monarchy.[55] The platform does show that a substantial group of electoral districts wished to replace the imperfect advice given by the ministers and the vague representative and legislative role of the parlements with a robust and regularly convoked body accountable to the nation.

A careful reading of the *cahiers* shows that there was no general consensus as to what kinds of political reforms would be necessary beyond demands that the Estates General be convened on a regular basis and be involved in the legislative process. Involving the Estates General in the

the factionalism of the Clergy, see M. G. Hutt, "The Curés and the Third Estate: The Ideas of Reform in the Pamphlets of the French Lower Clergy in the period 1787–1789," *Journal of Ecclesiastical History* VIII (1957), 74–92. Dale Van Kley pursues this theme in "The Debate over the Gallican Church on the Eve of the French Revolution," in *The Pre-Revolutionary Debate*, section 5 of the French Revolutionary Research Collection (Oxford, 1990), emphasizing the split within the Clergy between the Jansenists and the rest of the order and its lingering effect on French politics. See also Tackett, *Priest and Parish*. Twenty-five *cahiers* were excluded from the sample as they were either completed after the opening of the Estates General on 5 May 1789, show evidence of significant tampering by royal officials, or are of doubtful authenticity. See Hyslop, *Guide*, 85–88.

[54] On the political content of the *cahiers*, see Tackett, *Religion, Revolution, and Regional Culture*, 146–56, 251–75; C. Tilly, *The Vendée* (Cambridge, MA, 1964), 177–86; and Taylor, "Revolutionary and Nonrevolutionary Content in the *Cahiers* of 1789," 497–502. See also Shapiro and Markoff, *Revolutionary Demands*, and J. Markoff, *The Abolition of Feudalism* (University Park, PA, 1996); B. Hyslop, *French Nationalism in 1789 According to the General Cahiers* (New York, 1968); Tackett, "Use of the ≪Cahiers de doléances≫," 27–46; L. Pimenova, "Analyse des cahiers de doléances: l'exemple des cahiers de la Noblesse," *Mélanges de l'Ecole de Rome* 103 (1991), 85–101; Chaussinand-Nogaret, *French Nobility*, 130–165; Chisick, "Public Opinion," 117, 48–77.

[55] On republican monarchy, see F. Furet and R. Halévi, *La Monarchie républicaine* (Paris, 1996); R. Halévi, "La république monarchique," in F. Furet and M. Ozouf, eds., *Le siecle de l'avènement républicain* (Paris, 1993), 165–96.

legislative process marked a significant departure from the norms of the absolute monarchy and would require major changes to how political representation functioned in France. Nevertheless, only a minority of the deputies arrived in Versailles with instructions to change the way political representation functioned. The most coherent platform appears in a block of one-third of Noble and Third Estate *cahiers*. Around one-third of the electoral assemblies recommended replacing the hitherto appointed representatives of the monarchy – the ministers, the intendants, and even the sovereign courts – with bodies accountable to the Estates General, so as to better present counsel to the monarch and prevent ministerial despotism. Oversight of royal appointees would devolve to elected officials, presumably making them more responsive to those they represented. Nevertheless, the reforms did not attack the king's executive role, nor did they shift all legislative power to the Estates General. Instead, this model envisioned using some of the traditional powers of the Estates General to take over the representative and legislative functions pretended to by the parlements in the eighteenth century. Rather than stripping the king of his powers, the reforms seem intended to ensure that the king got good counsel, and the representative character of the Estates General meant that the king could expect that his decisions, as approved by his loyal deputies, would be obeyed without the predictable resistance of the sovereign courts.

The new representative character of the Estates General was also meant to translate into new powers for it. Given that the *cahiers* asked for a transformation in how the nation would be represented to its king and the king to the nation, we need to see just how far the demands found in the *cahiers* meant to shift power away from the king, his ministers, and the parlements toward the Estates General in the new order. Some historians have argued that the deputies arrived ready to seize the legislative power entirely for the Estates General, leaving the king with only a token role.[56] However, when one carefully examines demands related to legislative power in the *cahiers*, one can see no such clear demand on the part of the Nobles or the Third Estate. Instead, when the documents are not silent, the demands made are often ambiguous or even contradictory. The *cahiers* often demanded that the Estates General should be involved in the legislative power without specifying the extent or nature of its responsibilities. While this request marked a major change for the role of the Estates

---

[56] Chaussinand-Nogaret, *French Nobility*, 145–67. See also L. Hunt, "The 'National Assembly,'" in *The French Revolution and the Creation of Modern Political Culture: I. The Political Culture of the Old Régime*, ed. K. Baker (Oxford, 1987), 403–15; M. Fitzsimmons, "New Light on the Aristocratic Reaction in France," *FH* 10:4 (1996), 418–31.

General, the circumscribed nature of the demands regarding legislative power implies that many communities (especially in districts that lacked major cities) were prepared to leave the king as the primary legislator, seeking only to guarantee that the Estates General would be involved in the legislative process. These demands both endorsed and transformed claims by the parlements that the nation had a necessary role in the legislative power by writing such a role into the powers of the Estates General. In the new order, the king and the Estates General would together make the law, though there remained disagreement over who would hold the greater share of the legislative power.

Four different though not entirely exclusive models regarding the legislative role of the Estates General emerge on close reading of the *cahiers*. In the first, both the king and the Estates General would be able to create laws and the consent of both would be required for a decree to become law. The king and the Estates General would make the law together, though it is generally not made clear how this division would work in practice. The second model would give the Estates General no obvious role in creating laws, but would require the active consent of the Estates General before the king could promulgate a new law. In these two models, one can see the Estates General adopting the legislative powers claimed by the parlements in the eighteenth century, though in the first model this legislative role would be substantially expanded, as the Estates General would be able to propose laws, not merely react to laws proposed by the king. In the third, a very small number of *cahiers* claimed the legislative power exclusively for the Estates General, with no mention of any ability on the part of the king to influence them or refuse to sanction the laws they created. These radical demands were revolutionary indeed. Finally, in the fourth model the Estates General would be expected to discuss the proposed laws and make recommendations to the king, but the king would be under no obligation to accept this advice. This model falls more in line with the monarchy's interpretation of the Estates General: historically, the summoning of the Estates General had been the occasion of collecting information and gaining consent. The king had been expected to explain his policies and needs carefully before proposing solutions, but simple attendance at the assembly had implied the consent of the deputies. Nevertheless, the Crown had always summoned Estates General at moments of weakness and faced enormous pressure to draw legislation directly from the general *cahier* drafted by it. The practice of mandatory consultation combined with implied consent and the expectation that the king would take the Estates' advice into account when crafting legislation

Table 1.1 *Legislative role of the Estates General*

Grievance/Demand	Nobles #/%	Third Estate #/%
1. Estates General to be involved in Legislative matters in some way	97/75%	88/61%
2. Estates General may create laws	48/37%	34/24%
3. Estates General must deliberate over all new laws	10/8%	17/12%
4. Estates General must consent to all new laws proposed by the monarchy	75/58%	72/50%
5. Legislative power jointly held between Estates General and King or King must approve of all laws	74/57%	48/33%
6. King may make provisional laws, subject to eventual approval by Estates General	24/19%	20/14%
7. All laws created since 1614 void without approval of Estates General	2/2%	3/2%

Sources: *Archives Parlementaires*; Hyslop, *Guide to the General Cahiers*

may have been the mechanism represented by the verb "consentir" in many *cahiers*. This last model also implies that the Estates General would replace the parlements as the body that could advise and remonstrate when the king proposed decrees.

The *cahiers* of the Nobles and Third Estate show remarkable agreement that the Estates General should have a legislative role, with 75 percent of the Nobles and 61 percent of the Third Estate asking that the king and Estates share the legislative power. The king would retain a leading role in legislation, however. The vast majority of the *cahiers* from both orders implied that the king would propose most if not all legislation: Only 37 percent of Noble and 24 percent of Third Estate *cahiers* contained the demand that the Estates General have the ability to create new laws. Further, in one-half of the *cahiers* one finds the claim that the Estates General has the power of consent, with no mention of a role in actually initiating legislation, while only 8 percent of Noble and 12 percent of Third Estate *cahiers* demanded the right to deliberate over all proposed laws. If there was a plan on the part of the Nobles or Third Estate to seize the legislative power, it was not mentioned in the vast majority of the *cahiers*. For example, the deputies from the Third Estate of Bar-le-Duc, in Northeast France, asked that "the laws, which are the regulations made with the authority of the sovereign . . . must be accepted and consented to by the nation or by its representatives."[57] In this context, the "sovereign" is the king: the law is an expression of his will, not the will of the nation. Further, the king is seen as outside the nation, making the laws for it. Nevertheless, the nation *must* be consulted: the nation was to have a role in legitimizing the law, even if the law itself originated in the will of the monarch. The ability of the Estates General to originate laws was not discussed. The ability to freely accept laws proposed by the king was a power claimed by the parlements in the eighteenth century that was to be transformed into a right of the Estates General.[58]

Examining how often demands appear together in the same *cahier* helps us to see how ideas about legislative power are linked in the documents. The *cahiers* overwhelmingly demanded that the king and the Estates General would share legislative power in some way. First, we can see that if *cahiers* envisioned a legislative role for the Estates General but also rejected the idea that the Estates General would have to consent to laws proposed by the king, this combination implies that the Estates General would have the right to propose laws. But as we see in Table 1.2, only 3 percent of the Third Estate *cahiers* and 5 percent of the Noble ones in our sample sought to deny the king a role in creating laws, a result that is significantly lower than what we would expect to see given a random distribution of demands in the documents. Further, we see that more than half the Noble *cahiers* and one in three Third Estate *cahiers* explicitly required the participation of the monarch as well as the involvement of the Estates General for legislation to pass, a much higher number than we would expect from random distribution of demands. Finally, we see that a much higher than expected number of *cahiers* explicitly stated that the king and the Estates General had the power to propose laws. Overwhelmingly, the Noble and Third Estate *cahiers* that sought the ability to propose laws also sought to involve the king jointly in the legislative power, acknowledging his right to initiate legislation and to approve any legislation originating in the Estates General. While the Estates General was meant to have a legislative role, it was in no way meant to dominate legislative affairs.

The sharing of legislative power between king and Estates General would be a serious innovation, but it hardly meant the overthrow of the monarchy in France: it simply demanded for the Estates General something similar to the right of remonstrance long enjoyed by the parlements

---

[57] AP 2: 193.

[58] The notion that the Estates General had to approve of taxation was ancient. On occasion, orders had claimed the right to approve of all laws. The Crown had tacitly accepted the former but never the latter. Collins, *State in Early Modern France*, 2nd ed., xlii, 9–10.

Table 1.2 *Legislative power*

Clusters of Demands found in Cahiers	Noble		Third Estate	
	Expected	Observed	Expected	Observed
1. Estates General may create laws; Estates General must consent to all laws	28/22%	*42/33%*	17/12%	*30/21%*
2. Estates General may create laws; Ability to consent to laws not mentioned	20/16%	*6/5%*	17/12%	*4/3%*
3. Estates General to be involved in Legislative matters in some way; Legislative power jointly held between Estates General and King or King must approve of all laws	56/43%	*73/57%*	29/20%	*48/33%*

Sources: *Archives Parlementaires*; Hyslop, *Guide to the General Cahiers*
Note on tables. All italicized results in the Observed columns are statistically significant, as they deviate meaningfully from the expected number of *cahiers* that would contain the grievances listed if all demands were randomly distributed in the *cahiers*.[59]

on one hand, and a right to be involved in legislation as demanded by the parlements on the other. What is innovative is that the powers demanded would be given to an elected, representative body. These demands can be found in *cahiers* of all political stripes, from the most traditional Noble *cahiers* of Lorraine to the more radical and egalitarian Third Estate *cahiers* from Burgundy. The few that sought to deny the king a legislative role were as likely to come from the most intransigent of Nobles as from the radical outliers of the Patriot Party. For example, the Nobles of Longuyon, in Lorraine, carried a *cahier* dedicated to preserving their corporate privileges and extending them if possible. However, it declared that "all of the laws will be proposed, deliberated and sanctioned by the Estates General, then promulgated in the name of the Monarch."[60] This example cuts in two directions. First, this was a traditional demand, that the king put the

---

[59] For a result to be considered significant, we have used the chi-squared method of analysis with appropriate degrees of freedom, seeking a result in which the chance that a cluster of demands would appear randomly was less than 5 percent. If they appear or fail to appear at a rate significantly different from the expected rate, we interpret the result. For a broader and more detailed statistical interpretation of the *cahiers de doléances*, see Shapiro and Markoff, *Revolutionary Demands*.
[60] Hyslop, *Guide*, 317.

decisions made by the Estates General into law and that the sovereign courts not be able to modify them. However, in the context of 1789, when a periodic assembly was expected, this demand suggested that, in the future, the Estates General would legislate in the king's name. That this demand appears in an otherwise quite conservative document, brings into question claims that restricting the king's powers or giving precedence to the elected assembly originated in a revolutionary plan exclusive to liberal nobles or the Third Estate.

In discussing legislative matters, many *cahiers* used pseudo-Lockean terminology to describe how the government should function, arguing in favor of the separation of powers between the monarch and the Estates General. These arguments came out of Montesquieu's discussion of the separation and balance of powers, though the deputies identified the Estates General as the legislative branch, not the judiciary as Montesquieu had done.[61] The very concept of a separation of powers seems to imply an assault on the absolute power of the monarch. To some historians, the notion of a separation of powers implied a constitution that excluded the king from the legislative power and the Estates General from the executive power.[62] However, this modern version of the separation of powers was not the only one available to the deputies.[63] Many *cahiers* brought up the concept of executive power as well as that of legislative power, but in context, the implied separation of powers was incomplete and worked to preserve the monarch's legislative role. Fewer than 2 percent of the *cahiers* clearly demarcated the functions of the executive and of the legislative.[64] Instead, the king had both executive and legislative powers, though the legislative power was to be shared with the Estates General.

As we see in Table 1.3, 25 percent of Noble *cahiers* and 19 percent of Third Estate *cahiers* went further than a formulaic recognition of the king's authority, specifically reserving all executive powers to the king alone. Notably, all *cahiers* in this sample that specified the king was the sole

---

[61] For a discussion of the Lockean "English model" proposed by Montesquieu, see Baker, *Inventing the French Revolution*, 173–185. See also N. Hampson, *Will & Circumstance: Montesquieu, Rousseau and the French Revolution* (Norman, OK, 1983), esp. 59–64; and Collins, *From Tribes to Nation*, 458–59. R. R. Palmer argued that Montesquieu was "thinking of the balance between King, nobility, and Commons" and not the strict separation of judicial, executive, and legislative functions. R. R. Palmer, *The Age of Democratic Revolution, vol. 1: The Challenge* (Princeton, 1959), 58.

[62] Chaussinand-Nogaret, *French Nobility*, 157.

[63] See especially J. K. Wright, "National Sovereignty and the General Will: The Political Program of the Declaration of Rights," In *The French Idea of Freedom: The Old Regime and the Declaration of Rights of 1789*, D. Van Kley, ed. (Stanford, 1994), 216–24.

[64] For an example, see the *cahier* for the Third Estate of Etampes, AP 3: 283.

Table 1.3 *Balance of powers*

Grievances/Demands	Nobles #/%	Third Estate #/%
1. Monarchy retains monopoly on executive powers	32/25%	28/19%
2. Deputies are inviolable while in office	30/23%	25/17%
3. Estates General will be regularly summoned	122/95%	130/90%

Sources: *Archives Parlementaires*; Hyslop, *Guide to the General Cahiers*

executive power also demanded a role for the Estates General in legislation. As one can see in Table 1.4, most *cahiers* that specified an executive monopoly for the king and a legislative role for the Estates General mandated that the legislative power would be held jointly with the king. An illustrative example appears in the *cahier* of the Nobles of St. Mihiel, near Nancy. Despite claiming a legislative role for the Estates, the electors clearly sought to reinforce the authority of the king, declaring that "if the assembly of Estates General presumes to give to its decrees the force of law before having received the king's consent, it would [improperly] act as sovereign."[65] This was a truly new demand: to create the law without reference to the king was to be a crime, and an act of sovereignty here is the ability to autonomously make decrees. The authority of the king was explicitly recognized, even as an active role for the Estates General in government was demanded.

At first, when one sees that one in every six *cahiers* from either order gives a form of legislative power to the Estates General and guarantees the king his executive role, one might think that there was a push toward separation of powers in governing, even if only among a minority of the deputies who went to Versailles in May of 1789. However, the number of *cahiers* taking a position that would deny the king a legislative role is much smaller than one would expect assuming a random distribution of demands in the *cahiers*. Moreover, the *cahiers* reserving executive power for the monarch while also acknowledging his role in legislation appear far more frequently than a random distribution would lead us to expect. *Cahiers* that granted the Estates General a legislative role were more likely to recognize the king's right to legislate in their absence. When seen in context, demands

[65] AP 2: 235.

for a separation of powers actually seek to establish that the king and Estates General make the law together while recognizing the king's executive monopoly.

The *cahiers* show that the electoral assemblies had no uniform idea of what separation of powers meant, something that would become more evident once the Estates General met in May of 1789. In the *cahiers*, the practice of justice was sometimes portrayed as an extension of the executive power, and the legislative power was to be shared by different bodies in the government, as we have seen above. The analysis in Table 1.4 shows that the clusters of demands in the *cahiers* tended to undermine any effective separation of powers. This mixing of legislative and executive powers in the body of the king lends support to the claim that the Estates General was still figured at least in part as a traditional consultative body, not a modern independent and equal legislative body. The Estates General would provide counsel to the king by proposing and approving legislation, replacing the unaccountable ministers and parlements, a strong departure from Montesquieu's belief that the judiciary had a legislative function. The Estates General would not necessarily take a larger role than those other bodies had held, but it would institutionalize them in a way the monarch could not ignore. Moreover, the advisors would be selected by the nation, not the monarch.

Some electoral assemblies made this consultative role explicit, requesting that the Estates General formally advise the king even in executive matters. Roughly one tenth of Noble *cahiers,* but fewer than 5 percent of Third Estate *cahiers,* asked that the Estates General replace the ministers as the main source of counsel for the monarch. While this may seem truly revolutionary, it was a return to a demand made in sixteenth century *cahiers,* that there be some means by which members of the Royal Council be elected, rather than being chosen by the king. Whether taking on a new role or retaining the traditional one, the advice given by the Estates General would represent the interests of the king's subjects in a way that the ministers (or parlements) did not. The king, however, would retain the decision-making power, and thus the demand for the right to advise would not infringe on the king's executive authority. A demand much to the same point asked that the ministers and administrators have no representative function in the future.[66] Even though this specific demand appeared in fewer than 5 percent of the *cahiers* of either order,

---

[66] An additional 3 percent of the *cahiers* stated that the Estates General was the sole representative body. See the united *cahier* of Villers-la-Montagne in Nancy, AP 2: 245.

Table 1.4 *Separation of powers*

Clusters of Demands found in Cahiers	Noble		Third Estate	
	Expected	Observed	Expected	Observed
1. Estates General may create laws; Estates General must consent to all laws	28/22%	42/33%	17/12%	30/21%
2. Estates General may create laws; Monarch retains monopoly on executive powers	12/9%	17/13%	7/5%	17/12%
3. Monarch retains monopoly on executive powers; Legislative jointly held between Estates General and King or King must approve of all laws	18/14%	28/22%	9/6%	22/15%
4. Monarch retains monopoly on executive power; Estates General involved in legislative matters; Legislative jointly held between Estates General and King or King must approve of all laws	14/11%	28/22%	6/4%	22/15%
5. Estates General involved in legislative matters; King may make provisional laws while Estates General not in session, subject to eventual approval	18/14%	24/19%	12/8%	19/13%
6. King may make provisional laws while Estates General not in session, subject to eventual approval; Estates General may create laws; and Estates General must consent to all laws	5/4%	11/9%	2/1%	7/5%

Sources: Archives Parlementaires; Hyslop, *Guide to the General Cahiers*

the fact that it appears at all merits notice, as such a change would have overturned a central function of the Old Regime bureaucracy, as appointed officials would lose their power to present the grievances and protect the interests of their charges. It would also indicate that the king would no longer be able to take counsel only from those he chose to consult, undermining a major principle of the absolute monarchy.

The desire to replace appointed or venal administrative officials with elected representatives was central to the change in representation demanded in the *cahiers*. Under the absolute monarchy, if one wished to present one's opinions or grievances to the king, one had to use intermediaries appointed by the government or beholden to the monarchy. These officials, including the regional administrators known as "Intendants" and the ministers themselves, were vital in presenting the needs of the nation to the king, and vice versa. However, they were in no way popularly elected, and only widespread and violent public disorder could meaningfully influence public policy decisions made by these officials in the monarch's name. This problem was apparently well understood, as the *cahier* of the Third Estate of Bailleul, in Lille, pointed out "the deplorable state of the commonwealth, which only allows citizens to express their opinions through public disorder."[67] Even if the *cahiers* did not explicitly demand that the king take his counsel from the Estates General, there were other ways to ensure that the opinions of the Estates General would be consulted. Brienne had attempted to redress this particular grievance through the creation of elected provincial assemblies in 1788, but these assemblies were a failure. Appointed by the Crown, the deputies to these bodies were more likely to perpetuate abuses than rectify them.[68] The *cahiers* show evidence of a plan to fix this failure of local accountability by making the Estates General into a body that could oversee state officials, making certain that officials acted in the public interest.

As we see in Table 1.5, 45 percent of Noble *cahiers* and 38 percent of Third Estate *cahiers* favored making ministers responsible to the Estates General for their conduct in all executive matters, not just those limited to finance, where other studies of the *cahiers* have found that 85 percent of Noble *cahiers* demanded the responsibility of ministers. An additional handful of *cahiers* asked that the ministers be made answerable to the

---

[67] AP 2: 174. This point is also made by François Ménard de la Groye, deputy to the Third Estate from Maine, in a letter to his wife dated 23 June 1789. Ménard de la Groye, *Correspondance (1789–1791)*. F. Mirouse, ed. (Le Mans, 1989), 49–50. The Nobles of Tartas, in Bordeaux, argued instead that disorder in government caused the disorder of the countryside, not that the disorder was an attempt to influence the government. AP 1: 700. On the idea that a disorderly group of people can be representative, see Colin Lucas, "The Crowd and Politics between the Ancien Regime and Revolution in France," *JMH* 61 (1989), 421–57.

[68] See Collins, *State in Early Modern France*, 2nd ed., 353. The *pays d'état* had through their provincial estates and parlements retained more direct ways to communicate with the king, though their personnel could hardly be called elected representatives. Jones, *Reform and Revolution in France*, 35–38.

Table 1.5 *Government accountability*

Grievances/Demands	Nobles #/%	Third Estate #/%
1. King will prefer the advice of the Estates General to that of his ministers	12/9%	3/2%
2. Ministers and administrators will have no representative or legislative role	4/3%	5/3%
3. Estates General is sole representative body	4/3%	2/1%
4. Ministers accountable to Estates General for non-financial matters	58/45%	55/38%
5. Ministers accountable to nation for non-financial matters	9/7%	15/10%

Sources: *Archives Parlementaires*; Hyslop, *Guide to the General Cahiers*

nation, presumably through its representatives, leading us to conclude that close to one-half of the *cahiers* favored making the ministers accountable to the Estates General. Making ministers responsible to elected officials would recognize the *de facto* representative function of the ministers without infringing on the right of the king to compose his own government. Royal ministers would be subject to the same laws as the governed – a safeguard against ministerial despotism as well as paralleling the attempt to replace ministers with the Estates General as the primary source of counsel to the king. This was in many ways an unprecedented demand on the part of the Estates General, who had previously asked for oversight of ministers when the king was a minor.[69] It was also an extension of policy originating from the monarchy in which elected provincial officials would oversee the appointed or venal officials who administered the state.

The move to make royal officials accountable to the electorate did not stop with those subject to appointment and dismissal by the king. The *cahiers* show that a significant number of Third Estate and Noble electoral assemblies wished to take from the sovereign courts both the legislative powers they had claimed during the eighteenth century and the representative role the courts had acquired in the absence of the Estates General. In part, these demands were traditional. The Parlement of Paris had long claimed the right to modify decrees requested by the Estates General, and

---

[69] See, for example, the Estates General of 1484 and 1560–1. Major, *Representative Government in Early Modern France*, 183–84. J. R. Major, "The Third Estate in the Estates General of Pontoise, 1561," *Speculum* 29:2 (April 1954), 471–72.

Table 1.6 *Parlementary reforms*

Grievances/Demands	Nobles #/%	Third Estate #/%
1. Parlements to lose rights of remonstrance and must register laws without modification or delay	44/34%	41/28%
2. Provincial Estates to register laws in future	11/9%	13/9%
3. Parlements to remain a secondary bulwark against tyranny, beneath Estates General	42/32%	20/14%
4. Parlements to be responsible to Estates General for their actions	6/5%	4/3%
5. All courts to be reorganized to have 1/2 their members come from Third Estate	2/2%	27/19%
6. Judges inviolable while in office	20/16%	14/10%
7. Judges appointed according to their knowledge and merit	9/7%	26/18%

Sources: Archives Parlementaires; Hyslop, *Guide to the General Cahiers*

the Estates General had long denounced this practice.[70] When compared to deputies to the Estates General as political representatives, the magistrates left much to be desired. They were not elected and by definition did not come from a background similar to those whom they claimed to represent. Worse, since they held their offices as a form of property, it was nearly impossible for those whom the sovereign courts claimed to represent – king and nation – to remove them from office. Finally, while capable of limited dissent, the sovereign courts were part of the apparatus by which the monarch ruled, not a body independent of the monarchy.[71]

As one can see in Table 1.6, 34 percent of Noble *cahiers* and 28 percent of Third *cahiers* asked that the king remove from the parlements their right of remonstrance and subordinate the courts to the Estates General. This is best shown in the *cahier* of the Third Estate of Toulon, which states,

> neither the superior courts nor any authority that represents the sovereign [i.e., the king] may modify, interpret, halt or limit a law, still less promulgate one on their own authority under the title of decree, regulation or other

[70] See, for example, the Estates General of 1560. Major, "The Third Estate in the Estates General of Pontoise, 1561," 468–69.

[71] In the eighteenth century, the king could usually get what he wanted despite the resistance of the parlements, with the important exception of reforms involving the courts themselves. See W. Doyle, "The Parlements of France and the Breakdown of the Old Regime, 1771–1788," *FHS* 6:4 (Fall 1970), 415–58; Doyle, *Origins*, 2nd ed., 66–77.

Table 1.7 *Parlements*

Clusters of Demands found in Cahiers	Noble		Third Estate	
	Expected	Observed	Expected	Observed
1. Parlements stripped of right of remonstrance and parlements as secondary bulwark against tyranny	14/11%	19/15%	6/4%	8/6%
2. Parlements stripped of right of remonstrance and Courts must be reorganized to have 1/2 of members from Third Estate	1/1%	1/1%	8/6%	11/8%

Sources: *Archives Parlementaires*; Hyslop, *Guide to the General Cahiers*

imperative tendency, all law deriving essentially from the nation and its Head [*Chef*].[72]

This unambiguous separation of the courts (and other administrative officials) from any representative or legislative function challenged judicial elites who acted in the monarch's name and claimed to represent the nation to the king. And yet, it defended the role of the king himself in creating the law, stating that all laws come from the nation and its head. It is worth emphasizing here that the law did not come from the nation, but from the nation *and its leader*. In context, this is a blending of a traditional notion of a body politic, in which the king represents the head, and a new politics in which a nation exists and has rights. In a few cases (less than 10 percent of the *cahiers* of either order), the function of registering new laws was to be transferred to the provincial assemblies, taking all legislative power away from the courts. One tenth of the Noble or Third Estate *cahiers* demanded that the courts be interested only in the administration of justice, a different way of stripping the courts of their pretended legislative and representative powers.

As we see in Table 1.7, nineteen of the forty-four Noble *cahiers* that would strip the parlements of their right of remonstrance did so in

[72] Hyslop, *Guide*, 421. Corrections by Hyslop. See also the *cahier* of the Third Estate of Brest, AP 2: 470.

a limited way, retaining the parlements as a safeguard when the Estates General was not in session. The parlements would not be able to block a law duly passed by the Estates General, but they would be required to stop any law promulgated without their approval. The Nobles of Etain, in Lorraine, expressed this well, beginning with the traditional claim that the parlements could not modify a decree once approved by the Estates General. Having established the subordination of the parlements to the Estates General when that body was in session, the *cahier* stated that when the Estates General was in recess, the courts would retain the right of remonstrance, thus remaining a secondary bulwark to protect the constitution and the nation's laws.[73] The Estates General would be the legislative body, but it would rely on the sovereign courts to protect its prerogatives when it was not in session. For deputies of the Third Estate this also meant establishing the superiority of the Estates General, in which they had a role, over the parlements, bodies entirely dominated by noblemen.

A different tactic to change the role of the sovereign courts was to alter their composition rather than limit their powers. As we see in Table 1.6, one-fifth of Third Estate *cahiers* demanded a reorganization of the courts to include qualified men from the Third Estate, in most cases filling one-half of the seats of each court. For example, the Third Estate of Aval, in Franche-Comté, asked that the sovereign courts be formally suppressed and replaced with courts having at least half of their members drawn from the Third Estate.[74] Notably, very few Noble *cahiers* endorsed this idea. The issue of juridical competence as a prerequisite for entering the parlements aroused more interest from the Nobles (though still only 7 percent of the *cahiers* demanded it), and it was also important to the Third Estate (with 18 percent of the *cahiers* seeking it). The Nobles of Charolles, in Burgundy, gave a typical formulation of this demand, asking that "the powers of magistrates and judges be conferred only after a public and rigorous examination," and that the candidates meet certain standards for experience in the legal profession and demanding that the office no longer be venal.[75] Removing the venal character of judicial offices and requiring that candidates have experience at the bar and pass examinations would have opened up the closed parlementary caste, providing new opportunities to provincial nobles and elite commoners alike.[76]

---

[73] AP 2: 215. For another example, see the combined *cahier* of the Clergy and Nobles of Lixheim, in Nancy, AP 5: 715.

[74] Hyslop, *Guide*, 209.   [75] AP 2: 616.

[76] Declamations against venality of office were nothing new. In the closing speech by the Noble order at the Estates General of 1614, the speaker asked for venality to be abolished and replaced with merit,

Changing the composition of the sovereign courts to include commoners or limiting judicial careers to men experienced in the law would open judicial careers to talented men from the Third Estate and change the court system so that elite commoners would be judged by their own peers. These changes would also allow the Third Estate to participate in bodies that had claimed a position as representatives of the nation to the king, and of the king to the nation. Including more commoners in the courts or replacing venal officials with those considered to have special merit would have altered the balance of power on the courts, allowing the Third Estate to better represent its own interests to the monarch. Demands to alter the composition of the sovereign courts shows that changes in how the courts viewed their role in society led to changes in perceptions of how the courts should be composed. More representative courts were necessary if the courts were to continue to have a political role.

One of the distinguishing features of the traditional Estates General was that each deputy had to be elected in a formal and free process. In 1789, an unprecedented number of men had been involved in the elections, especially in the order of the Clergy, in which parish priests had been given much more representation than had been usual. In order for the Estates General to adequately represent the nation, the deputies would have to be held accountable for their actions to prevent them from acting in their own interests rather than those of their constituents. The main method proposed in the *cahiers* for keeping deputies faithful to their electors' wishes was the practice of regular and free elections. The *cahiers* evinced widespread concern with the elective nature of local, provincial, and national representative bodies. As Table 1.8 shows, over one-half of the *cahiers* of either order mention free elections of one kind or another, with the Third Estate showing more interest than the Nobles.

The demands focused on restoring the elective status of municipal officials and replacing appointed members of the provincial assemblies with elected ones. Further, the *cahiers* overwhelmingly supported the creation or reestablishment of provincial assemblies, with over 80 percent of either Noble or Third *cahiers* making this demand, though the Third Estate seemed more concerned with making them elective.[77] The demands were by no means uniform, with different *bailliages* asking for everything from the restoration of defunct provincial estates to the creation of new

---

giving preferment to nobles of the sword over those who held nobility only from their office. Hayden, *Estates General*, 159.

[77] This represented 33 percent of the Third Estate *cahiers*, compared to 19 percent of the Noble *cahiers*.

Table 1.8 *Free elections*

Grievances/Demands	Nobles #/%	Third Estate #/%
1. Free Elections mentioned	72/56%	94/65%
2. Free Elections to municipal bodies	39/30%	68/47%
3. Free Elections to provincial estates or assemblies	25/19%	48/33%
4. Free Elections to Estates General	28/22%	29/20%
5. Establish/restore provincial estates or assemblies	108/84%	118/82%
6. Replace Intendants with provincial estates or assemblies	21/16%	23/16%

Sources: Archives Parlementaires; Hyslop, *Guide to the General Cahiers*

assemblies on the model of Dauphiné to the simple request that the assemblies created by Brienne in 1788 be made elective ahead of schedule. One-sixth of the Noble and Third Estate *cahiers* went so far as to demand that provincial bodies replace the Intendants.[78] This would place provincial administration in a body responsible to the local electors, guaranteeing adequate representation at the provincial level, much as the Estates General would provide at the national level.

But requesting that local offices or provincial bodies be elective did not mean an unprecedented assault on the authority of the monarchy. After all, deputies to the Estates General had long been freely elected and requests for free elections of deputies to local and general estates had been made at the Estates General of 1614.[79] The monarchy itself had provided the model for making local bodies elective in order to facilitate obedience to the law and faithfulness in payment of taxes.[80] Requesting that locally elected authorities have a supervising role over royal appointees may seem radical. However, it is best understood as a demand originating out of an offer made by the Crown. Brienne had proposed that provincial assemblies would have a kind of superintending role over royal appointees. The *cahiers* demanded that this system be put into effect and made permanent. Additional powers sought for the assemblies were seldom more than those held by the Intendants and

---

[78] For example, see the *cahier* of the Third Estate of La Rochelle. AP 3: 479.

[79] Major, *Representative Government in Early Modern France*, 407–08.

[80] Attempts to create elected officials at the local level had been made in the 1760s. Collins argues that these reforms created the foundation for the municipal revolts of 1789–90. Collins, *State in Early Modern France*, 2nd ed., 292.

Table 1.9 *Accountability of deputies*

Grievances/Demands	Nobles #/%	Third Estate #/%
1. Deputies accountable to electoral body	9/7%	2/1%
2. Deputies must correspond with electoral body	4/3%	8/6%
3. Deputies prohibited from taking bribes	6/5%	5/3%
4. Deputies represent nation, not any particular interest or area	6/5%	7/5%

Sources: *Archives Parlementaires*; Hyslop, *Guide to the General Cahiers*

never more than those of the Intendant's office combined with the right of remonstrance. In replacing the Intendants, the elected bodies would have had a function in the administration of the king's will and in transmitting local opinions to the Crown. But local representation by no means meant a direct role in the creation of laws or policies. Presumably, the deputies to the provincial bodies would have been more qualified to understand and act on the needs and desires of local constituencies than had been Intendants appointed by the monarchy. As their function would have been to transmit more efficiently the king's will to his subjects, and the needs of his subjects to the king, the system of provincial estates and assemblies would ensure that the king received adequate counsel and could rule well.[81]

In the general system of the Estates General, the bearer of a mandate only represented his constituents insofar as he expressed their wishes as found in the *cahier* he carried. The electors showed some concern that their deputies might be pressured by the Crown or tempted by bribes to approve royal proposals that would not benefit their constituents. Thus, many communities included specific instructions in their mandates that ordered their deputies to ask for certain things. A small number of these demands were expressed as binding or imperative demands. If a deputy strayed from a binding condition he had been given, his constituents declared their intention to disown him as their representative. A community might request that a deputy not agree to raise taxes or approve loans, for example, until other matters had been handled. Or, a group might demand that all

---

[81] The idea that provincial and general estates made it possible for the king to rule France well was ancient. Jean Bodin had argued as much in his *Six Books of the Republic* in 1583, and both the Noble and Clerical orders had demanded restoration of provincial estates at the Estates General of 1588. Major, *Representative Government in Early Modern France*, 163, 257.

voting be done by order, not by head. In the context of the *cahiers* and their multiple demands, these requests were meant to protect constituencies from royal pressure on or the corruption of their deputies, rather than as a bulwark against the decisions of the Estates General itself. (We return to the matter of the mandates deputies received in Chapter 4.) A similar but less common tactic forbade deputies to accept titles and rewards from the monarch while sitting in the Estates General. Five percent of Noble *cahiers* so constrained their deputies, and 3 percent of Third Estate *cahiers* did likewise.[82] Other electoral bodies declared that their deputies would be directly accountable to them for their actions in Versailles, or established a formal correspondence committee to oversee their behavior. Though relatively few *cahiers* included additional demands of this sort, they show that the electors were worried that the deputies they sent might end up acting as the king's representatives, not theirs. One other demand is of particular interest. The deputies carried *cahiers* filled with concerns specific to their region and order. Only 5 percent of the Noble or Third Estate *cahiers* departed from the generally local character of the *cahiers* and declared that the deputies to the Estates General represented, and were accountable to, the nation as a whole, even when requests in the documents revealed a national scope for their requested reforms.

The *cahiers* proposed another mechanism by which the king and deputies would receive counsel: the debates of the educated public conducted in a free press. Historians have long known that demands in the *cahiers* were only indirectly linked to Enlightenment rhetoric and reveal more influence by French legal culture than by the *philosophes*.[83] Freedom of speech was not really an issue for the Estates General itself, as the deputies had long been assured that they could speak freely. Unambiguous evidence of liberal politics appeared only in the demand for a free press, and even here caution outweighed any absolute defense of abstract rights. Though Chaussinand-Nogaret claims that the Nobles sent to Versailles were "preoccupied with safeguarding total freedom of expression," we see in Table 1.10 that almost all *cahiers* that demanded freedom of the press asked that this freedom be limited either by the king or the Estates General to preserve decency.[84] Outside the Clerical *cahiers*, not one electoral assembly asked for more censorship, however.[85]

---

[82] See, for example, the *cahier* of the Third Estate of Ploërmel, in Brittany. AP 5: 385.
[83] See Chartier, *Cultural Origins*, 172–77.   [84] Chaussinand-Nogaret, *French Nobility*, 164.
[85] The Clergy were much more interested in censorship. Of the 147 clerical *cahiers* Tackett studied, 52 percent demanded more censorship and only 7 percent wanted a free press. Tackett, *Religion, Revolution, and Reform*, 150.

Table 1.10 *Free press and publicity*

Grievances/Demands	Nobles #/%	Third Estate #/%
1. Free Press to be established with various limitations	99/77%	105/73%
2. More censorship needed to protect morals	0/0%	0/0%
3. Deliberations of Estates General to be made public	5/4%	9/6%
4. State Finances to be made public	44/34%	59/41%

Sources: *Archives Parlementaires*; Hyslop, *Guide to the General Cahiers*

Calls for freedom of the press rested on the belief that the best ideas were forged in the broad arena of public opinion rather than within the secret councils of the monarchy. This implied that the knowledge of the monarch was finite, and that there were French subjects who knew more than their monarch. A free press, in opening up the market of ideas, was part of the attempt to broaden the base of the king's advisors to theoretically (and very indirectly) include all literate citizens. This very stance had been treated as *lèse-majesté* in the recent past, when the division between the Republic of Letters and the advisors of the king had been in theory an absolute one.[86] In practice, while only the Estates General would directly advise the king, demands for a free press show that local electors intended to institutionalize the political role public opinion had assumed during the recent struggles between the parlements and the ministers. With the institution of a free press, public opinion would be recognized as a valid source of influence on government affairs. Nevertheless, calls for a free press did not necessarily mean that all government affairs would be made public. We see in Table 1.10 that only around one in three *cahiers* formally demanded that royal finances be made public. Similarly, there was a lack of enthusiasm for publishing the debates of the Estates General. In previous Estates General, deputies had sworn an oath not to discuss the proceedings with non-deputies and the reluctance to publish their debates seems to endorse this practice. However, with state finances made public and a free press to discuss them, the deputies would have access to much more information

---

[86] Certainly as recently as the reign of Louis XV. Farge, *Subversive Words*, 138. Collins argues that the role of legitimating government action had shifted from the sacral authority of the king to that of public opinion during Louis XV's reign. Collins, *State in Early Modern Europe*, 2nd ed., 324.

Table 1.11 *Finances*

Grievances/Demands	Nobles #/%	Third Estate #/%
1. Estates General to decide all spending, including the king's household budget	8/6%	8/6%
2. All taxes passed since 1614 declared invalid and to be renewed on a provisional basis only	13/10%	9/6%

Sources: *Archives Parlementaires*; Hyslop, *Guide to the General Cahiers*

and many more ideas than ever before. The monarchy would benefit from the counsel of the Estates General and both would benefit from vigorous debates in a free press, but the affairs of state and the deputies' words would not necessarily be made public.

An obvious use for a free press would have been to provide commentary on financial matters, so that a well-informed Estates General could advise the king. Electoral assemblies throughout France recognized that the serious and continuing fiscal problems had led to the summoning of the Estates General; as we see in Table 1.10 over one-third of the Noble *cahiers* and two-fifths of the Third Estate *cahiers* asked that the financial affairs of the monarchy be made public. Given the depth of the financial crisis, this number seems surprisingly low, especially given the contradictory publications on royal finances by Necker in 1781 and Calonne in 1787. It makes more sense, however, once we realize that despite demands that the Estates General gain access to and influence over the king and establish the responsibility of the king's ministers to the Estates General, the *cahiers* evinced surprisingly little desire in financial matters beyond the right to approve of new taxes and the responsibility for ministers in fiscal matters. Fiscal oversight was to be established – as had been promised to the Assembly of Notables in 1787[87] – but this seems to have been aimed toward preventing fraud and mismanagement rather than establishing control over policy. Taxes were to be approved by the Estates General, but the king was implicitly or explicitly left discretion over how to spend whatever money he received. The deputies continued to recognize the king as the executive power and showed little desire to discuss the issue.

As we can see in Table 1.11, fewer than 10 percent of the *cahiers* sought control over the budget by the Estates General. The rest of the *cahiers*

[87] Égret, *Prerevolution*, 62.

sought to regulate the finances of the monarchy indirectly by assuring that there was a periodic Estates General to advise the king. Elites who sat in the electoral assemblies of early 1789 as a rule sought to ensure fiscal prudence by the monarchy based on counsel rather than control. Day-to-day control of royal finances was to be left to the king.

Nevertheless, 6 percent of Noble or Third Estate *cahiers* sought complete control over royal spending, including the king's household expenses. This degree of control over the budget would have meant the end of the monarch's autonomy, as the king would have to seek the approval of the Estates General for all matters that required expenditure. Moreover, some communities sought to make the rule that no taxes could be raised without the approval of the Estates General fully retroactive. Ten percent of Noble *cahiers* denied the validity of all taxes enacted since 1614 based on the argument that if taxes had not been consented to, they were not legal.[88] Six percent of Third Estate *cahiers* contained similar claims. Demands for the repeal of taxes not consented to by the Estates General were actually quite traditional, appearing in 1614 and before. It is no surprise that such traditional demands appeared in some of the Noble *cahiers* most dedicated to preserving privilege, while demands for the verification and nationalization of the debt appear in a cross-section of *cahiers* from both orders. Overall, however, consent figured more prominently in demands found in the *cahiers* related to taxation than demands for outright control of the budget.

Given that demands for fiscal responsibility had been made first by the Assembly of Notables, it seems odd that demands for making royal finances public or for control of the budget were not more common. Given the depth of the crisis, it also seems odd that demands for the repeal of existing taxes or demands that they be subject to consent by the Estates General were not present in more *cahiers*. Moreover, both the traditional character of such demands and their appearance in conservative Noble *cahiers* should make us more cautious about locating the origins of major Revolutionary reforms within a narrowly defined "radical" group centered on a small number of Third Estate deputies. Nobles who sought to protect their privileges, who had no interest in founding a liberal, participatory monarchy, were also interested in protecting the moral and fiscal rights of the "nation." They made demands for fiscal control and responsibility that have in the past been taken as proof of the Revolutionary intentions of the

---

[88] For examples, see the *cahiers* of the Nobles of Alençon in Alençon (AP 1: 715) and of Dourdan in Orléans (AP 3: 249). Two percent of the *cahiers* deny the validity of *all* laws passed since 1614.

Third Estate.[89] The demands from the *cahiers* seeking financial oversight or the repeal of taxes almost certainly show that the elites who elected the deputies to the Estates General were more concerned with ensuring honesty and responsibility in government than with taking direct control over policy.

The main way in which the Estates General would influence royal policy would be through its advice and consent. For this method to be effective, the Estates General would have to convene on a regular basis. Regular convocation of the Estates General had been a recurring and traditional demand in previous meetings of the body, and the overwhelming majority of *cahiers* foresaw a regularly convened Estates General, with an interval of at least two years and as much as ten years between meetings. (The traditional demand had been that it meet every three or five years.)[90] Only a small number of *cahiers* demanded that the Estates General meet yearly or sit permanently. The proposed duration and the length of the period between meetings shows that the electors expected the king to handle routine matters, with the Estates General playing a recurring role in order to approve legislation and approve taxes. After all, the Estates General could only act as a consultative or legislative body if it were in session, and the length of the period between meetings changes the way in which we must view its anticipated role in governing.

As we see in Table 1.12, the Nobles and Third Estate *cahiers* overwhelmingly included the traditional demand of a periodic return for the assembly. But the *cahiers* also demanded that the Estates General meet at an interval of two or more years, with demands of five- or ten-year intervals common.

Demands that the Estates General meet yearly or remain sitting indefinitely implied a much different role for the body and posed a challenge to the sovereignty of the monarch. A permanent Estates General would have meant the transformation of an *ad hoc* consultative body into a something like a modern legislative body. This would have dramatically altered the way in which the French government functioned, ending the absolute monarchy and dramatically limiting the king's power. However, as we see in Table 1.12, only 6 percent of the Noble *cahiers* and only 2 percent of

---

[89] Furet claimed that the decision to guarantee the monarchy's debt and repeal of existing taxes by the National Assembly on 17 June 1789 represented the "birth of the Revolution." Furet, *Revolutionary France 1770–1880*, 63; see also Doyle, *Oxford History* 2nd ed., 105.

[90] In 1614, the general *cahier* of the Third Estate had asked that the Estates General be summoned at least once every ten years, a perennial desire on the part of all three orders. Hayden, *Estates General*, 188, 212.

Table 1.12 *Periodicity of Estates General*

Grievances/Demands	Nobles #/%	Third Estate #/%
1. Estates General to be regularly convened at an interval of two or more years	122/95%	130/90%
2. Estates General to be convened yearly or sit permanently	8/6%	3/2%

Sources: *Archives Parlementaires*; Hyslop, *Guide to the General Cahiers*. The percentages of Noble demands add up to more than 100% due to rounding.

those of the Third Estate favored a permanent assembly or yearly meetings. (This should not surprise us, as even state legislatures in the new United States did not uniformly choose to sit yearly.)[91] The rest of the *cahiers* that mentioned a specific frequency for meetings opted for a longer, often much longer, interval between them. A longer interval left the king's authority more intact, as he was required only to seek the advice of the Estates General when they were in session, and to bear in mind their interests when they were not. All of the demands for publicity, accountability, participation, and consultation in the *cahiers* add up to fairly moderate claims if there were to be ten years between meetings of the Estates General. Such infrequent oversight by the Estates General would have ended the king's absolute political authority, but it would not have instituted a parliamentary democracy. The more frequent the meetings, the more likely the Estates General would be to replace the ministers and the parlements as the primary advisors and representatives to the king. Setting the interval at two or more years seems intended to insure that the Estates General could adequately participate in the legislative power, provide the king with moral guidance ensuring that the monarch would be more responsive to his subjects' needs, all while not unduly usurping his authority. This conclusion reinforces what we saw above in our discussion of the legislative role of the Estates General in the future. It was to share authority with the king, but the king was to rule.

As we have seen, in these documents there is a remarkable blend of new and traditional demands. The traditional demands appear in a new

---

[91] See, for example, the Constitution of State of South Carolina, adopted 26 March 1776, http://avalon .law.yale.edu/18th_century/sc01.asp [accessed 20 May 2018]; or that of New Hampshire from 1784, www.nh.gov/glance/house.htm [accessed 20 May 2018].

context, that of the creation of an Estates General that would have a mandatory legislative role. There were remarkable similarities between Noble and Third Estate demands concerning the future role of the Estates General and reforms in political representation. While the Noble and Third Estate *cahiers* disagreed sharply on questions of how the Estates General would meet or vote, they generally agreed on the relationship of the Estates General with the king, the ministers, and the sovereign courts.[92] There was also broad agreement on the need for a free press, free elections, and financial reforms. A substantial minority of the *cahiers* of the Nobility and the Third Estate agreed that there needed to be changes in the way the nation was represented to its government. Over one-third of the *cahiers*, Noble or Third Estate, placed the Estates General in a position of authority over either the sovereign courts or the king's ministers. One-fifth of the Noble and one-tenth of the Third Estate *cahiers* asked for both, reserving representative roles in government to the Estates General and the monarch alone. The *cahiers* also show that many electoral assemblies intended to replace the parlements with the Estates General as the primary line of defense against ministerial despotism.

The deputies to the Estates General of 1789 did not see themselves as simple servants of the king come to passively consent to government-sponsored reform. The king had summoned a body to garner support for his policies and provide him with information about his kingdom. What arrived was a body dedicated to serving those who had sent them and to creating a regularly constituted representative body. They intended to take back from appointed or venal officials the right to represent the dispersed peoples of France to their monarch. While there was no single program of reform, there was a widespread desire to reorganize the representative practices of the late eighteenth-century monarchy toward the ends of greater efficiency and justice. Many *cahiers* from both orders asked that the appointed municipal, provincial, and judicial officials of the bureaucratic monarchy be replaced by elected officials, who were clearly presumed to be more beholden to their electors than to the central government and thus more likely to present accurately the grievances of the governed and to administer fairly – and legally – the orders of the king. Moreover, these

---

[92] The *cahiers* of the Nobles overwhelmingly demanded a vote by order, though a fair number were willing to make exceptions in specific cases. Third Estate *cahiers* almost universally demanded a vote by head. Hyslop, *Nationalism*, 67–69; Tackett, *Becoming a Revolutionary*, 99; Shapiro, "What Were the Grievances of France in 1789?" in *Revolutionary Demands*, 277–78. Many thanks to James Stinchcomb for helping me clarify my views on this subject.

demands were not limited to Third Estate *cahiers*, appearing in those of the Noble order as well.

The *cahiers* also indicated that the king would retain considerable authority in the new system. The *cahiers* do not support claims that the deputies arrived in Versailles ready to install a parliamentary democracy or a constitutional monarchy that sharply constrained royal authority. Most *cahiers* demanded that the king share legislative power with the Estates General, a clear departure from the traditional role that body held in France. As a rule, the *cahiers* reserved the executive power for the king, and often allowed the king to legislate in the absence of the Estates General, subject to their eventual verification. That the majority of *cahiers* asked for the right to consent to new laws, rather than for the power to unilaterally create them, indicates that these demands sought to combine the traditional role of the Estates General with the legislative role claimed by the parlements during the eighteenth century. The legislative role of the king was preserved, as the Estates General sought only the guarantee that they would be consulted in legislation, not that they be its sole source. The goal was to ensure that the Estates General could advise the king prior to the implementation of new laws. This indicates that the elites who elected men to the Estates General followed the traditional narrative of the "good king badly advised" and sought an end to ministerial despotism and the abuse of privilege rather than to seriously weaken the king's authority. Even with the powers of government theoretically divided into executive, judicial, and legislative fields, the responsibility for the first two were to mix in the body of the king, and he would either dominate or share (often retaining the lion's share) in the function of the third. With veto power over legislation, the right to initiate legislation, the right to legislate in the Estates General's absence, and control of the central administration, the king would have retained much more power in office than his English counterpart or the American President.

In May of 1789, a significant minority of the Noble and Third Estate deputies arrived in Versailles prepared to replace the rule of ministers and the influence of the Court by the rule of a king advised by the Estates General and influenced by public opinion. Let there be no doubt that such a demand was a call for serious change, but it was not the revolution envisioned by the abbé Sieyès in his epic and radical *What Is the Third Estate?* Given that the Estates General had long requested regular meetings in order to gain the ear of the king, it is difficult to place demands that the king be advised by the Estates as "revolutionary" in the modern sense of that word. More than demanding an overthrow of the centralized monarchy created by Louis XIV, the *cahiers* showed recognition that government under Louis XVI meant, for the most part, rule by ministers, subject to the approval of the king. Through the *cahiers*, the electoral assemblies sought to restrict the role of these ministers while preserving the rights of the king, leaving him as the ultimate political authority: the primary legislator, sole executive, and final source of justice.

Nevertheless, there were radical demands in the *cahiers*, especially those of the Parisian deputies. If the Revolution had followed the demands found in a plurality or majority of the *cahiers*, there would have been significant change. But when the deputies from the three orders met in Versailles in May 1789, they embarked on a program of reform that appeared to contemporaries as breathtaking in its scope. In a period of just six months, between 5 May and 2 November 1789, the deputies of the Third Estate (with a handful of allies from the Clergy) would declare themselves a National Assembly capable of writing a constitution for France. Acting with their allies from the Nobles and the Clergy, the deputies of the Third Estate would end the division of the Estates General by order and institute a vote by head. Braving royal attempts to hem them in, the deputies would vote through major structural and social changes, culminating in the decision to have a one-chamber legislative body that would sit permanently and be elected every two years. The king would be denied the right to initiate legislation and would be given only a suspensive veto. By November, it would be clear that the new legislative body was a co-ruler of France, rather than a faithful advisor. Our task in the next five chapters is to see how the deputies came to move from the moderate reformist positions found in many of the *cahiers* toward the more radical solutions found in a minority of the Noble and Third Estate *cahiers*. We will see that the deputies did not ignore, abandon, or repudiate the will of their constituents as found in the *cahiers*. Nevertheless, the changing circumstances around them called for a much more ambitious and thorough constitutional reform than had been possible at the beginning of 1789. Great problems require grand solutions, and as the monarchy imploded during the summer of 1789, the deputies had to build a new structure to preserve what they could of it and to build new institutions to prevent such a collapse in the future.

CHAPTER 2

The Estates General Sitting as a National Assembly

In early May, as the deputies from all three Estates came to Versailles for the scheduled opening of the Estates General they carried with them *cahiers* enjoining them to reform the constitution in broadly similar ways. One major matter that divided them was the question of how the deputies would meet and vote. Deputies from the Third Estate came determined to pursue common meetings of the three orders with matters decided by a vote by head. Noble and Clerical deputies were split on the issue, but a majority in both orders carried *cahiers* encouraging or requiring them to seek separate meetings and a vote by order. The electoral regulations sent out by the king in January had not settled which form would prevail. From the very first meeting of the Estates General, the orders entered into a prolonged stalemate as the Third Estate refused to conduct business without first verifying all deputy credentials in common in the main meeting hall and the Nobles insisted that credentials be verified separately by each order. Failure of the Estates General to do anything between 6 May and 15 June but squabble over how to verify credentials led to a hardening of the divisions between conservative deputies from the Nobles and the Clergy and their liberal colleagues. Leadership from the Crown was conspicuously absent during the entire period, and this absence allowed hostility to develop between the Nobles and the Third Estate. Leaders arose in the Third Estate and the Nobles who pursued mutually exclusive plans for organizing the Estates General.

These mutually exclusive positions did not arise initially out of radical or conservative opinions of deputies as much as they did out of their decision to be faithful to the instructions they had received in their *cahiers*. But the stalemate over how to verify credentials prevented action in areas on which the three orders agreed. It prevented the Estates General from fulfilling its mandate to provide advice and assistance to the king as he sought solutions to the great problems France faced. Much more important, though, was the way in which this stalemate pushed the deputies of the Third Estate to adopt tactics and pursue an outcome that few of them had envisioned when they first sat in the common hall in Versailles, listening to the king welcome them to the Estates General. As the stalemate dragged on into its second month and belated attempts by the Crown to mediate between the orders failed, the deputies of the Third Estate took matters into their own hands and on 17 June declared themselves, along with perhaps a score of deputies from the Clergy, a "National Assembly" acting with the powers of the Estates General. They did this to end the stalemate, to allow for the Estates General to begin meeting and deliberating as a union of the orders with a vote taken by head, and to allow the Estates General to fulfill its mandate to advise and assist the king. As we shall see, the deputies did not do this to exclude the privileged orders or to seize power from the king. Nevertheless, they insisted that this National Assembly meeting in the common hall was the voice of the Estates General and it would brook no rivals, declaring that there would be no veto between the Assembly and the king. The traditional principle that the Estates General functioned on the consensus of the three orders was to be replaced by majority rule within a common assembly.

The Third Estate deputies struggled to find a name for the acting body of the Estates General that best indicated who they were, what their powers were, and what they intended to do in the future. There was one obvious title, that of "National Assembly" found in a minority of *cahiers*, most importantly that of the Parisian deputies. But at first, no one proposed it. Instead, many awkward and confusing names were suggested, debated, and in the end, rejected. When the deputies settled on the pithy and evocative title "National Assembly," their decision was more about the politics of the moment than about staking out a constitutional role that went beyond what the *cahiers* of the Third Estate (or indeed of the Nobles) had requested. The Third Estate deputies held an open and vigorous debate over the title on 15–16 June and came to a compromise title and a compromise decree. The compromise involved taking a name that most of them could agree on and an explanation of it that would satisfy most critics within the Third Estate. Once they had chosen a new name, the deputies rallied around it and prepared to move on to the important matters ahead: deciding how to finance the monarchy and finding a way to make the Estates General a regularly convoked body with the powers necessary to remedy the abuses of the past.

The deputies arrived in Versailles in late April and early May of 1789 aware that France was in difficulty, and they understood that it was up to the Estates General to make the changes necessary for the king to move

France past its crisis. The official decree laying out the rules for elections to the Estates General had appeared on 24 January and elections took place nationwide during February, March, and April (with a few exceptions). Most of the deputies travelled to Paris and Versailles in mid-April so they would be ready for opening ceremonies slated to begin on 2 May in Versailles. The deputies had high hopes for what they would accomplish, but they travelled through a disturbed landscape. By spring 1789, the troubles that France faced went beyond the fiscal and political crisis at the top. In late 1788 and early 1789, an economic crisis developed that had little to do with the Crown's weakness. First, there was a general depression related to increased competition in manufacturing from the kingdom of Great Britain, the result of a free trade pact negotiated by Calonne that came into effect in 1787.[1] Second, there was an unrelated problem with grain supplies, especially in the north of France and the region around Paris. The harvest of 1788 had been poor, especially in the north of France, where severe weather had hurt the wheat crop. The winter of 1788–89 had been unusually cold, freezing rivers and making it difficult to transport grain and to grind what grain could be found. Bread prices began their yearly rise awaiting the new harvest much earlier than usual. This would have been a problem under any circumstances, but with its finances in terrible disarray the state had trouble purchasing grain to be sold at a loss to keep prices down. Neither the Crown nor municipal governments throughout France could react to the necessary degree to the crisis. Grain prices rose, and rose, and rose. High grain prices aggravated the manufacturing slump as domestic demand fell. High grain prices combined with increasing urban unemployment to make for protests and disorder almost everywhere in France.[2]

When the deputies traveled to Versailles they saw evidence of public disorder all around them. As they arrived in Paris, they saw just how bad matters could get. Paris was by far the largest city in France. With a population of around 600,000, it was close to six times the size of its largest rival. It was also a city in ferment, with unemployment high and bread prices rising. A local jurisdictional dispute had delayed Parisian elections to the Estates General and the necessary electoral regulations had not been published until mid-April. In most of France the franchise for

[1] See J. Horn, *The Path Not Taken: French Industrialization in the Age of Revolution, 1750–1830* (Cambridge, MA, 2006), 66–77.
[2] On the economic problems and crowd disturbances leading up to the summer of 1789, see Jones, *Reform and Revolution*, 166–74; D. Andress, *The French Revolution and the People* (London and New York, 2006), 89–103; Andress, *1789*, 276–79.

electing Third Estate deputies was quite broad among men, but in Paris it had been deliberately restricted, excluding most of the working people from the electoral assemblies. Crowd pressure was the only means by which common people could influence the proceedings. As the Parisian electors got ready to draft their *cahiers* and choose their deputies in late April, they also discussed what to do about the worsening economic conditions. Remarks by Third Estate electors in two different districts caused popular demonstrations when garbled versions of their pleas to keep the price of bread affordable reached the streets. After days of protests, matters came to a head on 27 April in the so-called "Réveillon Riots," when angry Parisians sacked the homes and businesses of the men thought responsible for the remarks. The royal authorities in Paris were quick to respond, dispatching units of the French Guards, an army group headquartered in Paris and meant to maintain order there, to stop the rioting. When the crowd refused to disperse, the French Guards fired on them, killing and wounding many.[3] Hearing about this terrible event, the deputies gathering in Versailles knew that Paris was a powder keg primed to explode. They knew that conditions in their home cities and the countryside through which they had passed were hardly better. Something had to be done to relieve the distress of the French people. It had to be done quickly, and it had to be accomplished by the Estates General. It was with a sense of urgency that the deputies gathered for opening events of the first Estates General called in 175 years.

It turned out that the Estates General would not resolve matters of any kind quickly. The first few days of May were consumed by protocol as the king welcomed each deputy individually at the royal chateau on 2 May and the deputies participated in a religious procession through Versailles before mass at the church of Saint-Louis on 4 May.[4] Finally, on 5 May the deputies marched by order in a grand parade to the common meeting hall, a large room in the *Hôtel des Menus Plaisirs du Roi,* a grand complex just outside the royal chateau's grounds. The people of Paris and Versailles were present en masse for the event: contemporaries claimed that hundreds of thousands turned out to see the deputies march. The Noble deputy Charles-Elie Ferrières-Marçay, among others, found the event tremendously moving.[5] Though the meetings and processions had been designed to emphasize the king's majesty and the dignity of the Estates General, the

---

[3] Alpaugh, *Non-Violence,* 49–55; Andress, *French Revolution and the People,* 98–101; Doyle, *Oxford History,* 2nd ed., 98–99.

[4] Tackett, *Becoming a Revolutionary,* 121.

[5] See Friedland, *Political Actors,* 132–35, where he discusses Ferrières's response to the events of 4–5 May 1789. C.-E. Ferrières-Marcay, *Mémoires,* 2 vols., 2nd. ed. (Paris, 1822–25), I: 17–25. On

events revealed tensions among the deputies and showed that the Crown and the deputies were not in agreement as to how events should proceed. Some Third Estates deputies refused to go along with the protocol established for the event, marching out of order or refusing to wear the sober black attire prescribed for the commoner deputies, refusing to do things clearly meant to reinforce the distinctions between the orders and by implication the inferiority of the Third Estate.[6]

Once inside the large meeting hall refurbished for the occasion, the *Salle des Menus Plaisirs*, separation between the privileged orders and the Third Estate was continued, with the deputies of the Third Estate set apart from the privileged orders and the king by a low barricade.[7] This ceremonial separation was ham-handed to say the least, almost guaranteed to cause offense to Third Estate deputies whose cooperation would be necessary to save the state. But much worse, the Crown failed to provide a sense of what the Estates General was meant to do. It was a tremendous opportunity for the king to set the terms for the coming debates, and the deputies were eager to hear what the Crown proposed.[8] At the very least, when Necker spoke he needed to give the deputies a plan to follow or at least direct their debates toward plans acceptable to the king. Instead, Necker spoke only briefly before handing his speech to an aide who continued for more than two hours.[9] When the deputies were finally dismissed after almost four hours of mostly inaudible speeches, they had been given no instructions as to how they should set their priorities or even what matters in particular they should discuss. The deputies would have to make their own way forward without knowing precisely what it was that the king wished for them to do.[10]

On May 6th, prospects for a quick resolution of France's problems got immeasurably worse. Without notifying the deputies of the Third Estate,

---

Ferrières and other deputies to the Estates General, see E. H. Lemay, *Dictionnaire des Constituants*, 2 vols. (Oxford, 1991).

[6] Tackett, *Becoming a Revolutionary*, 121–22. Lefebvre, *Coming of the French Revolution*, 73–74. Many Third Estate deputies carried *cahiers* that demanded the deputies be treated with respect at the Estates General. Differential treatment had been the norm in the past, but it appeared the Third Estate electors had had enough of it in 1789. Collins, *From Tribes to Nation*, 530–31.

[7] Tackett, *Becoming a Revolutionary*, 3.   [8] Sutherland, *French Revolution and Empire*, 37.

[9] A. Young, *Travels in France during the Years, 1787, 1788, and 1789* (London, 1792), 161. G. Morris, *A Diary of the French Revolution*, ed. B. C. Davenport (Boston, 1939), vol. 1: 69–70. M. Fitzsimmons, "From the Estates General to the National Assembly, May 5–August 4, 1789," in Campbell, ed., *Origins of the French Revolution*, 273. Lefebvre, *Coming of the French Revolution*, 74. On Morris, see M. M. Mintz, *Gouverneur Morris and the French Revolution* (Norman, OK, 1970).

[10] For a contrasting view, see Félix, *Louis XVI et Marie Antoinette*, 453–54.

Necker had arranged for the orders to meet in separate halls where they could verify their credentials and organize themselves as functioning bodies. The Clergy and Nobles met in their assigned rooms and immediately took up the task of organizing themselves and verifying their credentials. But Necker had kept the Third Estate in the hall where the opening ceremonies had been held. The Third Estate deputies found themselves alone in what they quickly dubbed the "national chamber."[11] Conditions in the hall were hardly suitable for debate. It was too large for the number of deputies who appeared on 6 May, leaving half of the deputies' seats open for the audience, who quickly took them. The hall had been arranged for an audience with the king and the benches still faced the front. There was no podium and it was almost impossible to tell who was speaking or to hear what they were saying, let alone to know whether or not the speaker was a deputy. It took extraordinary presence to be heard at all and only the most talented of orators were able to make their proposals heard.[12] Confused and astonished, the Third Estate deputies found themselves in the main hall without the privileged deputies. The first step the deputies took, to refuse to organize as an order, was to have tremendous impact.

Working around the difficulties presented by the chamber itself, the deputies starting discussing what to do about the absence of the privileged orders. In informal debate it became apparent that the vast majority of the deputies carried *cahiers* that demanded or desired the vote by head. Likewise, a large majority of the deputies feared that separate verification of deputy credentials would lead to separate meetings and a vote by order. Two deputies, the Breton lawyer Isaac-René Guy Le Chapelier and Honoré Gabriel Riquetti, count of Mirabeau, a controversial nobleman elected to represent the Third Estate of Aix, made their voices heard over

---

[11] On 6–7 May, Laurent de Visme variously referred to the common meeting hall as the "national chamber, "the "chamber of the Third Estate," the "national hall," and the "hall of the Estates." Visme, Manuscript Journal, BNF, Nouv. acq. fr. 12938, 3r, 4v. On the physical layout of the chambers in which the deputies met, see Brasart, *Paroles de la Révolution*, 17–21. Mirabeau had referred to the body meeting in the main hall as the "national assembly" on 5 May as the deputies entered the chamber. H. Perrin de Boussac, *Un témoin de la Révolution et de l'Empire: Charles-Jean-Marie Alquier* (Paris, 1983), 34. On Mirabeau, see G. Chaussinand-Nogaret, *Mirabeau* (Paris, 1982); B. Luttrell, *Mirabeau* (Carbondale, IL, 1990).

[12] Lefebvre, *Coming of the French Revolution*, 75. Tackett, *Becoming a Revolutionary*, 122. The meeting was tumultuous, given that there were no rules of order and that there were some 600 deputies. Visme, "Journal," 3v. Only in late May did the deputies vote to move the audience from the empty deputy benches to the galleries that surrounded the floor. J.-B. Poncet-Delpech, "Documents sur les premiers mois de la Révolution," ed. D. Ligou, *AHRF* 38 (1966), 430; Visme, "Journal," 22r–22v. Young was present at the much later debate of 15 June and remarked that "the room is too large; none but stentorian lungs, or the finest clearest voices can be heard." Conditions on 6 May were much worse. Young, *Travels in France*, 163.

the din. They argued for total inaction by the deputies and a refusal of all contact with the upper orders unless they first agreed to a verification of their credentials in common. The deputies decided not to organize themselves as a body or to move on to verifying their credentials. On the next day, Mounier, leader of the deputies who had reestablished the provincial estates in Dauphiné and Pierre-Victor Malouet, a deputy from Riom known to have close connections at Court, pushed back against the radical stance that the deputies should refuse all contact with the privileged orders. They urged the deputies to remain unconstituted, a strategy meant to prevent the appearance that they approved of the privileged orders moving on to verify their powers. But they also urged the deputies to contact the Nobles and Clergy in order to convince them to verify all credentials in common in the main hall. Mounier suggested that an unofficial group of deputies go to the other orders in their chambers to discuss compromise. Malouet urged the deputies to exercise caution and moderation, fearing that a confrontational stance vis-à-vis the privileged orders could alienate the public. The more radical Breton deputies, led by Le Chapelier, agitated for a less cautious approach, repeatedly denouncing the privileged orders. Discussion of the two competing paths led to the first real vote held by the body, which accepted Mounier's plan to send delegates to the other orders in order to pursue union. Nevertheless, the deputies refused to set up rules of order or elect officers.[13]

Despite the overtures of the Third Estate, the Noble deputies quickly verified their credentials and on 11 May constituted themselves as an order. The Clergy also began to verify their credentials, but responded to requests from the Third Estate by taking on the role of peacemaker, delaying a vote to constitute their order separately. As befitted their traditional role as mediators, the Clergy suggested that the three orders form a conciliation commission to discuss the matter.[14] The Nobles agreed to participate on 12 May, but tipped their hand on 13 May when a representative came to the Third Estate and declared that while they wished to form a "fraternal union" with the Third Estate, the Nobles would continue to meet and vote separately.[15] This left the Third Estate to decide whether or not they would participate in a commission that seemed likely to fail from the outset.

This question of whether or not to participate in discussions with the other orders led to the first major debate undertaken in the Third Estate. Two

---

[13] AP 8: 29; Tackett, *Becoming a Revolutionary*, 127.
[14] The king and the queen mother had asked the Clergy to establish harmony between the orders at the Estates General of 1614. Hayden, *Estates General*, 122.
[15] Margerison, *Pamphlets and Public Opinion*, 130.

platforms were put forth. The first, proposed by the Protestant clergyman Jean-Paul Rabaut de Saint-Étienne and seconded by Mounier, declared the Third Estate ready to participate in the commission proposed by the Clergy in order to seek union of the orders and a vote by head.[16] The second, proposed by Le Chapelier, asked that the deputies refuse to participate in discussions, instead "inviting and summoning" the other deputies to meet in the "national assembly" to verify their credentials in common. If the privileged deputies refused, then the Third Estate would have to go on ahead as if the deputies were the Estates General itself. These platforms reflected the different pre-revolutionary experiences of the deputies from Dauphiné, who sought to gain victory through negotiation, and those from Brittany, who sought victory through conflict. In Brittany, there had been ferocious clashes between the Third Estate and the privileged orders in the run-up to the Estates General. The Nobles had demanded that the Estates of Brittany meet according to its traditional forms and choose the deputies for all three orders. Men of Third Estate throughout the province wanted broader electoral rights and a vote by head in the provincial estates. In November and December of 1788 there were revolts in the major cities of Brittany in support of the Third Estate. When the Estates met at the end of December, the Nobles refused to allow business to be conducted in protest of Necker's decision to double the representation of the Third Estate. Eventually Necker intervened, declaring that the Nobles and Clergy could meet according to their traditional forms, but that the Third Estate would elect its deputies according to the electoral regulations sent out in the winter of 1778–79. The Third Estate duly elected deputies, but the Nobles and Clergy refused to send deputies to Versailles, claiming their traditional rights had been violated. This experience left the Breton Third Estate deputies tremendously embittered and convinced that the privileged deputies could not be trusted. In Dauphiné, the Nobles and Third Estate had worked together to craft a common platform. The deputies from Dauphiné and their allies, Mounier at their head, knew that they had friends in the privileged orders who would demand a vote by head in a unified assembly and sought to use this knowledge to the advantage of the Third Estate in negotiations. The deputies from Brittany and their allies in the Breton Club simply refused to believe that Noble deputies could be relied on to do anything but defend their privileges to the detriment of the greater good.[17] The Third Estate debated the issue over five days, with the deputies called by *bailliage* to give their opinions

---

[16] Rabaut de Saint-Etienne was working in coordination with the Viroflay Society, an offshoot of the Society of Thirty. Margerison, *Pamphlets and Public Opinion*, 130.

[17] Jones, *Reform and Revolution*, 149–55; Fitzsimmons, "From the Estates General to the National Assembly," 268–75.

and make suggestions. After this extensive process, Rabaut's proposal convincingly won, with a vote of 320–66 in favor of participation in the conciliation commission. The deputies chosen the next day to participate in the commission included fourteen moderates and only two radicals.[18]

The two privileged orders were more divided on the matter of voting by head or by order than was the Third Estate. In the Noble chamber, partisans of a vote by order had a strong majority from the very beginning, with the liberal deputies never managing to get more than 25 percent of the votes. As the stalemate dragged on in May and June, the conservatives actually gained strength, building an *esprit de corps* around the honor of their order, so much so that deputies who had been tasked by their constituents to seek a vote by head refused to do so. By the time the conciliation commission met at the end of May, only two liberal Nobles were chosen to join the eight-man delegation, ensuring that the vote by order would be protected.[19] The order of the Clergy was sharply and bitterly divided between aristocratic bishops and abbots on the one hand and "citizen priests," men from the lower levels of the church hierarchy, on the other. The aristocratic leaders were able to muster a small majority behind a vote to constitute the order in early May, and as the stalemate dragged on, the elite leaders were able to peel more and more deputies away from the minority, making it harder and harder for those who favored union to believe they could succeed.[20] Still, the Clergy had a traditional role as mediators and they worked hard to bring the Nobles and Third Estate to the table to discuss possible compromises.

The historian Timothy Tackett identifies the period during which the conciliation commissions met, between 23 May and 9 June, as pivotal in the transformation of the way Third Estate deputies saw themselves as political actors. Tackett notes that it was out of the ongoing debates during this period that deputies began to appreciate the stakes of the contest for power between the Third Estate and the conservative deputies from the privileged orders. As the deputies discussed how to resolve the stalemate between the orders, they found common purpose and a dawning consciousness of the real worth and power of their estate. During this time, neither the deputies from Dauphiné nor the Breton deputies could

[18] Tackett, *Becoming a Revolutionary*, 123–28. Margerison, *Pamphlets and Public Opinion*, 126–29. For Friedland, it was two visions of the constitution that clashed, not two estates. Friedland, *Political Actors*, 136–37.
[19] Tackett, *Becoming a Revolutionary*, 134–37. P.-M.-G., duc de Lévis, "Lettres du duc de Lévis, 1784–1795," ed. duc de Lévis-Mirepoix, *La Revue de France* 4 (1929), 441.
[20] Tackett, *Becoming a Revolutionary*, 129–32.

command a majority. They had to convince uncommitted deputies to support their plans. The debates between the moderate and radical deputies educated the less committed deputies about their possible role in a new political order, in effect allowing the deputies to craft a coherent political platform out of the demands found in Third Estate *cahiers*. This transformation was reinforced by the approval of the audience watching the deputies' debates and by the actions of people in Paris and Versailles, who showed enthusiasm for the reforms the deputies pursued.[21]

If the conciliation commissions allowed for stronger *esprit de corps* in both the Noble and Third Estates as each rallied around its own ideas about meeting and voting, the sessions failed entirely to encourage compromise over how to verify deputy credentials. Far from bringing the deputies together on center ground, the meetings allowed direct confrontation between Noble deputies who refused to cede an inch toward a vote in common and Third Estate men who matched them in determination.[22] In some ways, this clash arose out of a misperception. As we have seen from our analysis of the *cahiers* in the previous Chapter, the two orders sought many of the same reforms. Aside from a minority of hotheads, deputies of the Third Estate did not have any plan to eliminate the distinctions between the orders in the assembly or in society at large at this point. Noble deputies clearly supported major reforms, and had already voted to sacrifice their fiscal privileges. Nevertheless, the Nobles were convinced that a vote by head meant the end of the distinctions between the orders in society, and they refused to compromise. The meetings of the commission opened on the 23rd but were already on the point of collapse by the 28th. At the end of May, the king sent letters to the presidents of the three orders asking that they continue the work of the commission. The deputies listened to the king and continued participating, the last time that a royal initiative met with such success in all of 1789. Nevertheless, there were signs that deputies in the Third Estate were losing patience, especially after the Nobles voted never to deliberate or vote in common on 26 May, making future meetings seem pointless.[23]

---

[21] Ibid., 139–42.   [22] Lévis, "Lettres," 441.

[23] On 27 May, the Third Estate deputies learned of the decision by the Nobles to never meet or vote in common. They saw this as a real rupture and thought that their only hope for a vote by head remained convincing the Clergy to participate. Visme, "Journal," 20r. This hope was borne out when the bishops in the Clergy appealed to the king to set up a conciliation commission led by the Crown. Ibid., 21v. Margerison, *Pamphlets and Public Opinion*, 131–32; Fitzsimmons, "From the Estates General to the National Assembly," 275–77.

Two things, very different in kind, pushed events forward. First, on 25 May the Paris delegation arrived in Versailles, their delay a consequence of difficulties organizing elections in the city. The Parisian Third Estate deputies brought with them a *cahier* somewhat to the left of the majority but very consonant with the one-third of the *cahiers* that proposed a serious, coherent set of reforms that would transform the absolute monarchy into a constitutional one. The *cahier* insisted on a vote by head and in common. It also contained a clear demand that the Estates General (the document frequently uses this term) was called to write a constitution with a declaration of rights. It insisted that no new taxes or loans could be approved until the constitution was achieved. In addition, it requested that the Estates General share the legislative power with the king and be periodic, meeting by right every three years. Ministers were to be accountable to this body, and it would determine the conditions of any regency. The *cahier* also demanded that all taxes be repealed and then replaced with taxes only valid during the sitting of the Estates General, and that the king's debt be consolidated, verified and then brought under the guarantee of the Nation.[24] Paris had always held the right to speak first in the Third Estate, and Parisian deputies quickly took on leadership roles in the body. (Jean-Sylvain Bailly was elected doyen of the order on 3 June; Guy-Jean-Baptiste Target became a frequent speaker.) The demands of their *cahier* came to the front again and again, making them the anchor point around which debates formed themselves. Sieyès immediately joined with the Breton deputies in seeking to establish the Third Estate as the legitimate body of the Estates General without the participation of the privileged orders.[25] This position had had garnered little support in the debates of early May, but the arrival of the Paris deputies gave it important new support, as their arrival coincided with the failure of the conciliation commission and a growing sense of frustration on the part of the Third Estate deputies.[26] While the deputies as a group continued to seek come kind of conciliation, the number of those willing to risk confrontation grew as the stalemate dragged on.

---

[24] Chassin, *Les Élections et les Cahiers*, I: 333–41. The *cahier* of the Noble order from Paris made similar demands, with one major exception. The Noble deputies were instructed to deliberate by order, though they were not to take actions that would block the adoption of necessary laws. The Parisian delegation brought with it Clermont-Tonnerre and Lally-Tollendal, who quickly established themselves as leaders among the center-right reformers later called "Monarchiens," and d'Epremesnil, who became a lion of the far right. Ibid., I: 321–23.

[25] M. Forsythe, *Reason and Revolution: The Political Thought of the Abbé Sieyès* (Leicester, 1987), 101.

[26] Margerison, *Pamphlets and Public Opinion*, 129.

Second, during this critical period came the death of the king's son and heir, the *dauphin*, causing Louis XVI once again to withdraw almost entirely from public affairs. Historians often understate the effect of the dauphin's death on 4 June. Third Estate deputies had already begun to believe that the Noble deputies would never change their minds (and they were probably right). But around the time of the dauphin's death, deputies began to worry that reactionary nobles at Court were keeping the king from hearing the pleas of the Third Estate. This seemed confirmed when after the dauphin's death, the Third Estate deputies had to communicate with the king via his ministers, but the Noble and Clerical deputies had direct access to his person.[27] Cut off from the king and mistrustful of those who surrounded him, the deputies to the Third Estate increasingly believed that they would have to act on their own to end the stalemate.

Soon after the dauphin's death, Necker suggested the creation of a committee including all three orders meant to examine disputed credentials. He also stated that if the three orders could come to no decision, the king himself would decide how to proceed. The Clergy had invited the royal initiative and welcomed it; the Nobles did not, as they did not want any credentials to be decided by all three orders working together. The majority of the deputies of the Third Estate did not like Necker's plan either. In the end, the Third Estate was spared the embarrassment of rejecting the king's proposal because the Nobles did so first.[28] What to do instead was far from clear. There was a sentiment among the Third Estate deputies that a moment of crisis was approaching, and some thought that they would have to compromise on their insistence on voting by head in order to move forward.[29] Nevertheless, the deputies did not wish to act in violation of their promise to the king that they would await the outcome of the conciliation commission.[30] While the radicals in the Third Estate were gaining support, they lacked the numbers necessary to force a final confrontation with the privileged orders.[31]

While the Third Estate deputies waited for news from the conciliation commission, the important debates had shifted from their daily meetings

---

[27] Tackett, *Becoming a Revolutionary*, 143–44. See also R. Reuss, ed., *L'Alsace pendant la Révolution française*, vol . 1, *Correspondance des députés à l'Assemblée nationale (Année 1789)* (Paris, 1880), 100.
[28] Lefebvre, *Coming of the French Revolution*, 77.
[29] Reuss, ed., *L'Alsace pendant la Révolution française*, 1: 101–02.
[30] J.-M. Pellerin, *Correspondance inédite de J.-M. Pellerin . . . (5 mai 1789—29 mai 1790)*, ed. G. Bord (Paris, 1883), 46.
[31] On 7 June, Visme noted in his diary that the Breton deputies were gaining influence in the Third Estate as a result of the ongoing stalemate. Visme, "Journal," 29v–30r. Margerison, *Pamphlets and Public Opinion*, 132. See also Young, *Travels in France*, 152–53.

to evening meetings in the *bureaux*, where smaller groups of deputies met to discuss proposals raised during the day. On 8 June, Sieyès read a motion at the Breton Club that proposed summoning the privileged orders to meet in common and threatening to go it alone if they refused. On 9 June, the Nobles stated that they could not accept the king's proposal without changes, and the conciliation commission broke up without result.[32] This refusal gave Sieyès and the Breton deputies an opening. In meetings in the bureaus and in provincial groups on 9 June, the deputies vented their frustrations and the Breton deputies sought to rally support for Sieyès's coming motion. The Breton deputies declared that noble intransigence was the sole cause of the stalemate and said that reconciliation was a dead issue.[33] The deputies were certainly aware of the deteriorating economic conditions in Paris and the provinces.[34] Something had to be done. Thus, it was to a group of well-prepared men that Sieyès proposed on 10 June that the deputies should issue one final summons (*sommation*) to the deputies from the upper orders to come to the common hall and verify their credentials. Sieyès shifted the onus of obstructionism onto the Nobles and put the Third Estate on the road to declaring itself the legitimate body representing the nation and acting as the Estates General.[35] This first step toward declaring a National Assembly was incredibly important, as the debate over Sieyès notably radical proposal set the terms for the later debate over what to name the new body.

When the session started on 10 June, Bailly stated that the conciliation commission had finished its work, and that it was time to discuss the king's plan. Mirabeau then asked that Sieyès be allowed to make a proposal first.[36] When he spoke, Sieyès rehearsed many of the themes introduced by Le Chapelier and his allies in May. He blamed the privileged orders for the ongoing stalemate. He claimed that the Nobles and Clergy had repaid the frank and honest behavior of the Third Estate with "hypocrisy and

---

[32] Visme, "Journal," 32r.

[33] Tackett, *Becoming a Revolutionary*, 145. Visme, "Journal," 32v; Ménard de la Groye, *Correspondance*, 40. Bouchotte noted that the deputies planned to go ahead and verify their credentials and ask the other deputies to join them. On their refusal, they would ask the king if he would approve of them going on alone to constitute themselves as the nation. F.-J. Bouchette, *Lettres de François-Joseph Bouchette (1735–1810)*, ed. C. Looten (Lille, 1909), 227.

[34] Young wrote on 10 June in his diary, "Every thing conspires to render the present period in France critical: the want of bread is terrible: accounts arrive every moment from the provinces of riots and disturbances, and calling in the military to preserve the peace at the markets." The deputies were hardly less well informed than he was. Young, *Travels in France*, 154.

[35] Margerison, *Pamphlets and Public Opinion*, 131–34, Fitzsimmons, "From the Estates General to the National Assembly," 275–77.

[36] AP 8, 84.

subterfuge." Appealing to the loyalty of the deputies to their constituents, Sieyès argued that, "The assembly cannot sit inactive any longer without betraying its obligations and the interests of its constituents." He noted that the verification of deputy credentials could not take place other than in front of "the collection of the representatives of the nation."[37] Sieyès moved that the Third Estate constitute itself as the acting Estates General after summoning the missing deputies to present their credentials. While he did not go so far as to proposing to exclude the other orders from participating if they did not immediately appear, Sieyès's proposal was quite radical. As historians have noted, he proposed to *summon* the other orders, implying that the Third Estate had a superior position in the Estates General.[38]

Sieyès's motion was tactically brilliant. He put the onus of the stalemate squarely on the privileged orders, despite the Third Estate's own refusal to compromise. Seeking broader support for his motion, he dropped a point he had pursued in his published work by allowing the privileged deputies to take part if they were willing to accept a "summons" from the Third Estate.[39] But many deputies thought that use of the word "summon" went too far. Target spoke immediately after Sieyès. He argued that although the Nobles had rejected the king's plan and thus were at fault, the Third Estate must not act to exclude them from the assembly. The upper orders had to be brought to the common hall without prejudice, Target argued, though they also had to be warned that should they fail to appear the majority would be willing to act in their absence. He then asked that "summon" be replaced with "invite" in Sieyès's motion. His speech in favor of a union of the orders and a less confrontational approach hit the right note. A deputy present later wrote that Target had been applauded where Sieyès had not.[40] While few deputies opposed Sieyès's motion outright, many deputies wished to modify it, mostly along the lines Target had suggested.[41] Several deputies followed Target in opposing "summoning" the privileged orders to verify their powers and threatening them with "default" if they refused to come. Changing "summon" to "invite" avoided implying that

---

[37] Ibid.

[38] W. Sewell, *A Rhetoric of Bourgeois Revolution* (Durham, NC, 1994), 17. AP 8: 85.

[39] Margerison, *Pamphlets and Public Opinion*, 135. Lally-Tollendal had made a similar argument in the Noble chamber on 5 June, seeking to shift blame for the stalemate onto the Third Estate. Lally-Tollendal, "Sur le plan de conciliation proposé par le Roi," in *Pièces justificatives, contenant différentes motions de M. le comte de Lally-Tollendal* (n.p., n.d.), 42–43.

[40] AP 8: 85–86; A. Duquesnoy, *Journal d'Adrien Duquesnoy*, ed. R. de Crèvecouer, 2 vols. (Paris, 1894), vol. 1: 84.

[41] Ibid.

the Third Estate had jurisdiction over the other orders, making the new body seem more like a union of the orders and less like the Third Estate acting alone.[42] In addition, some pointed out that the Clergy had been quite reasonable and asked that only the Nobles be blamed for the stalemate.[43]

It was only after many deputies protested that the proposal was amended, with Sieyès's approval, to *invite* the other orders to join the Third Estate rather than *summoning* them.[44] Then the matter passed to an indecisive vote: 246 deputies voted to amend the proposal by sending an explanation of their actions to the king; 247 voted in favor of the motion without amendment; 51 for delay, to send the matter back for discussion, or against it entirely. After the votes were tallied, someone pointed out that with over 500 deputies present, a motion would need more than 250 votes to pass and neither version had crossed this threshold. This led to vigorous discussion of what to do next and the session became stormy. With opinion evenly divided over whether or not to send an explanation to the king, the president pushed the decision off until the evening session. When the matter was taken up then, a Breton deputy appealed to his compatriots to support the more moderate amended version of the motion in order to present a commanding majority, and that motion passed with only three dissenting votes. The deputies of the Third Estate would issue one last invitation to the other deputies to verify their powers in common before moving forward, and they would inform the king of their actions and their reasoning.[45] Their decision showed the continuation of a pattern begun in early May. Radical proposals were often made in the Third Estate, but they could not garner the support of the majority. Over time, as the stalemate persisted, the radical deputies gained more support, but as of 10 June they could still not muster a majority within the Third Estate. Only when the Breton deputies toned down their rhetoric and adopted motions more favorable to the unionist deputies could they pass a motion to begin a roll call. The unnamed Breton deputy was correct to seek a motion that could carry a massive majority. With 490 deputies voting to invite the other deputies to attend the final roll call, the Third Estate showed a unity of purpose that the other orders and the king had to notice.[46] In their address

---

[42] Visme, "Journal," 33r.

[43] AP 8: 85. There were precedents for both beginning the process of verifying powers without all deputies being present and with inviting those absent to come to the agreed meeting place. What was new was the request that they all sit in the same room as one body, something that had not happened since 1484. See Major, "The Third Estate in the Estates General of Pontoise," 461–62.

[44] AP 8: 86; Visme, "Journal," 33r.   [45] Ibid. Aulard, ed., *Récit des séances*, 108–10.   [46] AP 8: 86.

to the king, the deputies blamed the Nobles for their intransigence and explained the motives of the Third Estate while reaffirming their devotion to the king. Even as the Third Estate moved toward rupture with the Noble order, the commoner deputies sought the approval of the king for their actions and they refused to use unnecessarily confrontational language.[47]

Not all historians have appreciated the changes that were made to Sieyès's proposal and how this showed the influence of deputies who favored a union of orders. In his discussion of the events of 10 June, Friedland refers to the invitation as "an unequivocal summons," that threatened the deputies of the upper orders that should they not appear, "they would forfeit the right to be present within the common assembly of the nation's representatives." Friedland further argues that by passing Sieyès's motion the deputies set themselves up as "authorities," with "sovereign authority ... vested entirely in them."[48] Friedland ignores the way in which Target and other center-left deputies forced changes on Sieyès's motion to tone down his rhetoric and make it clear that the privileged orders were welcome and expected to participate. As we have seen, the moderates successfully defeated the most radical parts of Sieyès's proposal, the summoning of the other deputies and threatening them with default. Neither of those features appeared in the declaration the deputies voted on 10 June. The move to constitute the present deputies did not threaten an end to the Estates General or contain an assertion of the sovereignty of the Third Estate. It betokened an end to the stalemate through a union of the orders, with deputies meeting and voting by head.

While initially uncertain as to how bold they had to be in confronting the upper orders, on 10 June the deputies of the Third Estate overwhelmingly agreed that it was necessary to act. Speakers had emphasized the circumstances that pushed them to take unprecedented action. The move to send one last invitation to the other orders was, as Mirabeau claimed during the debate, "an extraordinary action that circumstances demanded," rather than a right held by the Third Estate.[49] The deputies recognized that the Third Estate was taking a step that in the end required the king's approval, tacit or overt. Some deputies feared that the king would not approve of their acts, but believed that by taking a firm

---

[47] Many deputies felt that the Nobles were entirely at fault, since they had chosen to ignore the king's advice. Ménard de la Groye, *Correspondance*, 41–42.

[48] Friedland, *Political Actors*, 137–38.

[49] AP 8: 85. Jean-Baptiste Treilhard had likewise emphasized the extraordinary – and not structural – reasons that the Third Estate had to act, appealing to the "salut public" as the reason that the three orders needed immediately to combine to verify their powers. AP 8: 86.

principled stand they would at least avoid dishonoring themselves. Writing to a friend the next day, the conservative Third Estate deputy Adrien-Cyprien Duquesnoy predicted that after constituting itself, the Third Estate would most likely be dissolved and sent home, but with its honor intact and "without having compromised the rights of our constituents."[50] Duquesnoy posed confronting the Nobles over the matter of voting by head or by order as a question of doing one's duty as a representative of the Third Estate, as following the instructions the deputies had received in their *cahiers*, rather than as a move to seize control of the government. Breaking the stalemate by moving to a roll call in order to verify deputy powers did not mean that the Third Estate had a right in and of itself to represent the nation. Instead, many deputies argued that, given the recalcitrance of the upper orders, the needs of the nation justified the decision override traditional forms.[51] Surely, they thought (or hoped), the king would agree.

The Third Estate began calling roll on 12 June and through the day deputies presented their credentials. No one from the upper orders appeared until 13 June, when three deputies of the Clergy arrived and were greeted with great applause. Not a single deputy from the Nobles came, and over the next few days only sixteen more clerics appeared.[52] The privileged orders had held firm. Having failed to attract deputies from the privileged orders, the Third Estate would have to carry out its threat and constitute the deputies present as the acting Estates General. But what name could they use? They had to find a name that showed they were the active part of the Estates General without acting so boldly that they offended the king or ended any chance of reconciliation with the privileged orders. The name "National Assembly" had appeared in many Third Estate *cahiers,* notably that of Paris. But as one deputy wrote in his journal on 14 June, the deputies had to come up with a title that fit between those of "National Assembly," meaning the Estates General meeting together and voting by head, and "Third Estate," the body of men currently in the room.[53]

---

[50] Duquesnoy, *Journal,* 1: 85.

[51] This means of settling a stalemate was hardly unforeseen. Necker had written in December of 1788 that a major reason for doubling the number of Third Estate deputies was that the larger numbers of Third Estate deputies would allow them to break any stalemate between the orders with a vote by head. In the event that the Estates General fell into crisis, Necker thought, it was up to the deputies of the Third Estate, representing the most numerous portion of the population, to use their expertise to find a way forward. *Rapport fait au roi,* AP 1: 493.

[52] Tackett, *Becoming a Revolutionary,* 145. Doyle, *Oxford History,* 2nd ed., 104.

[53] Visme, "Journal," 40v–41r.

During the stalemate between the orders, the men of the Third Estate had begun to re-evaluate their role in the Estates General. The debate on the naming of the new body accelerated the process. Without ministers to guide them or colleagues from the privileged orders to oppose them, the deputies were free to explore and define the relationships they held with their constituents, their peers in the other estates, and the monarchy itself. The crux of this process of self-definition occurred on 15–16 June during the debate over the transformation of the Third Estate into an active version of the Estates General. As we will see, on 17 June the deputies settled on a compromise title, voting 491–90 to call themselves the "National Assembly." But what did this title mean to the deputies? Given that the name had been used both as a synonym for "Estates General," as a rallying point for patriot deputies who wanted a vote by head, and as a way to describe a periodic Estates General with new constitutional powers, it remains for us to discover what the deputies meant by choosing it.[54]

Historians have long agreed that the declaration of the National Assembly is one of the major turning points of the French Revolution. Nevertheless, there is no consensus on the meaning of the name "National Assembly" and its importance in the earliest stages of the French Revolution. On the one hand, historians claim that the declaration of the National Assembly on 17 June was the necessary outcome of a long process, one that determined the actions of the Third Estate and led to a serious break from past political practices. As Lynn Hunt argues, the declaration of the National Assembly "did not come about as a result of struggles that occurred within the Estates General itself." Rather, it was the result of the constitutional debates of late-July 1788 to January 1789, when "all past 'constitutions' turned to dust" and the possibility of "breaking

---

[54] Before the debate of 15–16 June, deputies had referred to the larger body gathered in the *Salle des Menus Plaisirs* as the "National Assembly" or the "Estates General." The terms had been more or less interchangeable. On this, see P. Bastid, *Sieyès et sa pensée* (Paris, 1939), 67–68; and P. Lamarque, "La naissance de l''Assemblée nationale,'" *Dix-Huitième Siècle*, 20 (1988), 111–18. According to Armand Brette, the confusion of "National Assembly" and "Estates General" started as early as 21 January 1789. A. Brette, *Recueil de documents relatifs à la convocation des Etats généraux de 1789*, 4 vols. (1894–1915), vol. I: xxxii. Tackett locates the confusion between the terms in the letter of convocation issued by Loménie de Brienne in Louis XVI's name on 5 July 1788. Tackett, *Becoming a Revolutionary*, 83–84, and also n. 111, p. 147. It was not solely radicals who used the term: Malouet used the title "National Assembly" on 6 May to describe the body sitting in the *Salle des Menus Plaisirs*. See Lamarque, "La naissance de 'l'Assemblée nationale,'" 112. The term appears as a synonym for "Estates General" in the proclamation of the National Assembly on 17 June. AP 8: 127. Moreover, the declaration of a National Assembly did not end the use of the term "Estates General," even by the Third Estate deputies.

entirely with the past" came into being. This possibility allowed the deputies of the Third Estate to read the "unraveling of events in very similar ways," despite their broad regional differences.[55] This made it "virtually inevitable from the very moment that the Estates General first met" that the deputies would form a national assembly, though "the naming of the assembly did not seem very obvious to those concerned."[56]

On the other hand, historians argue that the majority of the Third Estate deputies arrived at the Estates General without fixed ideas about how to proceed and that the eventual declaration of a National Assembly was the result of both the struggle for power between the Noble and Third Estate deputies and the lack of leadership from the Crown. According to this argument, the weeks of stalemate provided a period during which deputies entered into a kind of school, educating themselves as to the opportunities and obstacles they faced in helping the king reform France. During the debates on 15–16 June over what to call the new assembly, this "'school' of the Revolution entered into full session. All of the greatest orators came forward to offer wide-ranging reflections on how the Assembly should be conceived, what its immediate goals ought to be, how it should handle taxation and the debt and what should be its relations with the people and the king."[57] Frustrated by inaction, many Third Estate deputies were "prepared for a break with the past, but they were far from certain where and how far they should go, and to what extent the past should be reformed or replaced."[58] This line of argument also has the merit of leaving room for

[55] Hunt, "The 'National Assembly,'" 413. See also K. M. Baker, "Introduction," in Baker, ed., *The French Revolution and the Creation of Modern Political Culture*, xi–xxiv. For opinions that give more weight to the name eventually chosen, see J. Guilhaumou, *L'avènement des porte-parole*, 71–75; M. Fitzsimmons, "The Invention of Citizenship," in R. Waldinger et al., ed., *The French Revolution and the Meaning of Citizenship* (Westport, CT, 1993), 30–31. Sewell and Forsyth have separately argued that the declaration of the National Assembly was an outcome predicted (and perhaps caused) by Sieyès's own arguments in *What Is the Third Estate?* Sewell, *A Rhetoric of Bourgeois Revolution*; Forsyth, *Reason and Revolution*.

[56] Hunt, "The 'National Assembly,'" 410. Likewise, Ran Halévi portrayed the moderate electoral assemblies and the *cahiers de doléances* they drafted as vehicles that brought men who were already revolutionaries to Versailles, though the *cahiers* were not revolutionary themselves: R. Halévi, "Estates General," in F. Furet and M. Ozouf, eds., *A Critical Dictionary of the French Revolution* (Cambridge, MA, 1989), 46–47.

[57] Tackett, *Becoming a Revolutionary*, 146. Charles de Paule de Barentin, Louis XVI's Keeper of the Seals, called the oratory during the run-up to 16 June "cette École démocratique" in a letter sent to the king denouncing the actions of the Third Estate. Barentin, Letter to Louis XVI, in G. Lefebvre and A. Terroine, eds, *Recueil de documents relatifs à séances des États Généraux de 1789*, vol. 1, 1st part, *Les préliminaires: La séance du 5 May* (Paris, 1953), 12–13.

[58] Tackett, *Becoming a Revolutionary*, 148. See Applewhite, *Political Alignment*, 69–74. See also David Bell, "Afterword," in K. M. Baker and D. Edelstein, eds., *Scripting Revolution* (Stanford, 2015), 345–53.

the influence of the deputies of Paris, who arrived in late May ready to lead the Third Estate and to fulfill the more radical demands found in their *cahier,* and for the influence of the Patriot movement in general, despite their lack of influence in the drafting of the *cahiers.*

Despite the great weight historians have given to the declaration of a National Assembly, there has been no systematic attempt to describe the number, order, or content of the many speeches delivered on 15–16 June 1789 in the Third Estate. In part this is because the debates of the early Estates General were poorly recorded. As part of their decision to avoid appearing to be an active body, the deputies had opted not to record their debates.[59] From the available sources, contemporary newspapers and the letters and diaries of witnesses, we know that the principal speakers spoke frequently and repeated their ideas with variations as they responded to criticism. Nevertheless, it can be difficult to understand exactly what was being proposed. Contemporary accounts of the major speeches given on 15–16 June often leave out or misidentify speakers, abbreviate or paraphrase speeches, and mix the opinions of the author in with his record of the speeches.[60] Moreover, the process of taking votes on 17 June was almost comically cumbersome. The final vote was as an *appel nominal*: each deputy voted individually and was invited to explain his vote. There must have been 600 or more speeches (most very brief) given between 15 and 17 June on the topic.[61] The vast majority of these speeches is lost, and historians who discuss the debate have typically relied on the very few speeches recounted in the incomplete account of the debates found in the *Archives Parlementaires.*

Here we consult a much more comprehensive body of sources in order to reconstruct the debate, using the surviving diaries, letters, and retrospective accounts of several deputies as well as contemporary newspaper accounts and the *Archives Parlementaires,* focusing on accounts left to us by deputy

---

[59] The Third Estate had debated keeping public records on 21–22 May. The order had chosen to avoid keeping notes in order to avoid being mistaken as a constituted body. AP 8: 44–45. See also Duquesnoy, *Journal*, 1: 28. Furet and Halévi have identified many of the problems with reconstructing any of the early debates of the Estates General and early National Assembly. See F. Furet and R. Halévi, "Note sur la présente édition," in Furet and Halévi, eds., *Orateurs de la Révolution française*, vol. 1 *Les constituants* (Paris, 1989), cxxiii–cxxv.

[60] For example, Maximilien Robespierre was identified as 'Robert Pierre' by Creuzé-Latouche. Jacques Antoine Creuzé-Latouche, *Journal des Etats Généraux de début de l'Assemblé nationale, 18 mai–29 juillet 1789*, ed. Jean Marchand (Paris, 1946), 117.

[61] Deputies complained at the time that the process took too long, and that the right to speak should not be abused in such a way as to endlessly lengthen the process. See Creuzé-Latouche, *Journal*, 118. On the *appel nominal* as a voting procedure, see A. Simonin and C. Lechevanton-Gomez, "L'appel nominal, une technique pour la démocratie extrême (1789–1795)?" *AHRF* 357 (2009) 67–101.

participants. Combing these documents, we find evidence of fifty-seven speeches by thirty-seven different deputies. Though the men who recorded these speeches did so under conditions less than conducive to accurate transcription, their accounts may be taken as indicative of the spectrum of ideas present among the deputies. The sources reveal that a great deal of compromise and constructive debate occurred on the issue of how to proceed, contradicting the common notion that the deputies had, even at this early stage, adopted a *modus operandi* of confrontation or had failed to develop a concept of majoritarian politics.[62] Moreover, we will see that, in the process of reaching a compromise, the deputies reached a legalistic conclusion that allowed them to break the stalemate with the Noble order over how to verify deputy credentials in the Estates General without having to break with the king. We will consider here the main speakers – Sieyès, Mirabeau, and Mounier – and the speeches given that supported their positions serially, and in an order that suggests the way in which they responded to one another's criticism. This will help us to see how the deputies came to agreement on the title "National Assembly" on 17 June and, in particular, we will see both how contingent this decision was and how it arose out of a compromise between radical and center-left deputies and was not the unqualified victory of a radical idea of revolution over the more moderate idea of a union of the orders.

It was in a defiant and somewhat fatalistic frame of mind that the deputies moved on to naming the new body. The debate itself can only be described as chaotic. A witness noted that the president struggled to maintain order among the deputies, with up to a hundred demanding the right to speak at any time. Moreover, the deputies made complex motions and responded to each other by supporting some parts of motions and disagreeing with others. On top of the lack of order in the assembly, a large audience was present and applauded when it approved of what the deputies said.[63] Nevertheless, there were areas of almost complete agreement. The deputies present for the debates agreed that representatives could neither deliberate nor vote outside the common meeting hall. They also agreed that the ability of the Third Estate to push forward with only minimal cooperation from the other orders came in part from their relationship to their constituents, who formed the largest part of the French population.

---

[62] For a contrasting opinion, see Hampson, *Prelude to Terror*, 187–88. Likewise, Applewhite notes the inability of the deputies to develop "concepts of loyal opposition and of majority rule and minority rights that could stabilize a liberal regime," and locates the origins of this flaw in the earliest debates of the Estates General. Applewhite, *Political Alignment*, 2–3, 208, 214.

[63] Young, *Travels in France*, 166.

Serious disagreements divided the speakers into three groups, however. The debate of 15–16 June revolved around three concepts of why the Third Estate could take an exceptional and unprecedented step. Initially, none of these groups could rally anything like a majority of the deputies behind their proposed titles. The smallest group of deputies used the "people" of France as a legitimating concept. Deputies like Malouet, Rabaut de Saint-Etienne, and Mirabeau sought to identify the assembly as the representatives of the "Commons" or of the "French People." The deputies of the Third Estate had initially referred to themselves as the "Commons" (*les communes*) in early May to avoid giving the impression that they had organized themselves as an order. When they adopted the name, few of them had any real idea what the medieval communes had been. According to Lefebvre, "the word evoked a vague memory of popular resistance to feudal lords, an idea strengthened by what knowledge they had of English history. To the Third Estate, the name meant refusal to recognize a social hierarchy that relegated it to third rank."[64] Deputies like Mirabeau and Malouet saw the ability of the Third Estate to move forward without the other orders as a temporary expedient. They were at pains to make it clear that the deputies did not wish to efface the distinctions between the orders, and their reliance on the "French People" as the body represented allowed them to support a unilateral move by the Third Estate without denying the privileged orders their own status as representatives. Their efforts suffered from the perception that they were acting on Necker's behalf to create a two-chamber legislative body.

The proposals made by Sieyès and Mounier both agreed that the object being represented at Versailles was the French nation, and that the individual deputies represented parts of it through their election at the level of the *bailliage* or *sénéchaussée*. Their proposals attracted far more supporters than had that of Mirabeau. Those deputies who rallied around Mounier used the concept of quorum to support their claim to act in the absence of the other orders. Since the deputies were both a majority of the sitting deputies and represented a majority of the population of France, they could move on to conduct business, as a minority never had the right to prevent the majority from acting. They also relied on the idea of France as a nation divided into geographic constituencies, each of which was adequately represented by the deputies that location had sent. The third and largest group of speakers, those supporting Sieyès, agreed with claims that the French nation was represented

---

[64] G. Lefebvre, *The French Revolution*, trans. E. M. Evanson, 2 vols. (New York, 1962), vol. 1: 111; Lefebvre, *Coming of the French Revolution*, 78.

by its elected deputies, and argued that due diligence and due process gave the present deputies specific legal standing to represent their constituents. According to this line of thinking, because the deputies from the Third Estate were the only ones who had followed the proper procedures, they were the only legitimate representatives of their individual constituencies and thus of the French nation. It did not matter whether or not they formed a majority of the elected deputies, because the other deputies had failed to appear and could be ignored.[65] From the floor, all three proposals sounded quite similar, with their differences expressed by various sub clauses in the title each deputy proposed. It was from overlapping and complementary claims that the eventual declaration would be constructed, and it would be made up of features from each.

Sieyès opened the debate on 15 June, making due process and due diligence the central push of his argument. Fresh off his limited victory of 10 June and well regarded as a thinker, he was at the high point of his influence over the Third Estate. His speech, though read without eloquence or grace, set the tone for the entire debate as deputies either spoke in support of Sieyès's formulation or provided alternatives.[66] He began by reiterating the main points of his speech of 10 June, arguing that the men in the room represented 96 percent of the French, and that there could be no veto between the assembly and the king, and attacking the forms of 1614 which guaranteed each order a veto over matters it considered vital to its own interests.[67] Nevertheless, Sieyès aimed for middle ground in the debate by suggesting that the deputies present formally constitute themselves with the title "Assembly of the recognized and verified representatives of the French nation." This title represented a tactical choice designed to end the stalemate by making the nation, not electoral bodies from each order, the source of political legitimacy.[68] Sieyès focused on the technical claim that only through a common verification of powers could the deputies together represent the nation.[69] Cleverly, by shifting the focus

---

[65] Friedland instead portrays the debates as clashes between a modern "quantitative" idea of representation and an older, "qualitative" notion. See Friedland, *Political Actors*, 136–37.

[66] Young, *Travels in France*, 163–64.

[67] Left unsaid was the fact that in 1614, the Third Estate had only represented town dwellers in large regions of France, as had been true in Brittany until the winter of 1788–89. It was only with Louis's electoral regulations of 1788–89 that the Third Estate came to represent the people of the countryside for all of France.

[68] AP 8: 109. Forsyth notes that Sieyès chose this particular formulation as "proof of the spirit of conciliation," despite his own desire to call the new body the National Assembly. Forsyth, *Reason and Revolution*, 101.

[69] Creuzé-Latouche, *Journal*, 114.

from the Estates General to the French nation, his title made it possible for the representatives of any order to represent an entire electoral district in the absence of its other deputies. While he did not propose barring the privileged orders from serving in the assembly, he did make their privileged status irrelevant when it came to representing the French nation. It was enough that some deputies had been properly verified for them to act on behalf of the nation.

Sieyès's vocal supporters tended to come from the radicals in the assembly. They proposed variants of his motion rather than simply state their support for it. For example, Le Chapelier asked that Sieyès's motion be modified to read "the representatives of the French nation, legally recognized and verified."[70] The Dauphinois deputy Alexis-François Pison du Galand proposed that the body call itself "the active and legitimate assembly of the representatives of the French nation."[71] Nicolas Bergasse, deputy from Dauphiné and later an enemy of the Revolution, made a stirringly radical speech. Bergasse argued that taking a title that was less than all-encompassing would give his fellow deputies "the appearance of consenting to a division that distresses you." He departed from Sieyès by openly condemning the privileged orders, identified a government based on privilege with the abuse of power, and argued that only the elimination of the orders would guarantee the legitimate authority of the king. Nevertheless, he still favored the union of the orders rather than the exclusion of the Nobles and Clergy. He avoided the legalisms of "recognized" or "verified," proposing "the assembly of the representatives of the nation." He claimed that the deputies of the other orders would have to accept this name, as they would otherwise have to declare *themselves* representatives of the entire nation in order to have a right to make universally binding legislation.[72] He thus brought out into the open the reasoning behind using "representatives of the nation" as part of a title. Only the deputies verified in common and sitting in the common hall were representatives of the nation: only they could act as the Estates General.

---

[70] Ibid., 114–15. AP 8: 118. The speech itself is not recorded.
[71] AP 8: 122. See also J. Pellerin, ms. "Journal de la Tenue des Etats Généraux de 1789," B.M. Versailles, ms. 823F, 29v. Creuzé-Latouche recorded Pison du Galand as proposing that the body be called the "National Assembly." Creuzé-Latouche, *Journal*, 120. Remarkably, despite the similarity of Pison du Galland's title to that of Sieyès's original, when the proposals came to a full reading on 16 June, Pison du Galand's was read, in addition to those of Mounier, Mirabeau, and Sieyès. His motion must have been considered different enough from the revised one Sieyès proposed to deserve separate consideration, implying that some of Sieyès's earlier supporters wished to avoid the name "national assembly" if possible. Pellerin, "Journal," 28v.
[72] AP 8: 114–17.

In striking contrast to Sieyès's lackluster delivery, Mirabeau spoke freely, with warmth and eloquence, easily and effortlessly keeping the attention of deputies and audience alike.[73] He emphasized the political constraints under which the deputies worked. Mirabeau reminded the deputies that they had been called to Versailles by the king, and were there according to the forms he had proposed. He worried about whether or not the king would approve of the actions of the Third Estate, and whether he would agree to be bound by something that he had not proposed.[74] Far from coming out of the actions of the assembly, the new constitution would result from both the people's desires and the king's generosity.[75] While they could and indeed had to change the organization of the Estates General, Mirabeau argued, they needed to be careful how and when they did it. He was certain that the king would not accept a name like "national assembly," and worried that his refusal to accept what the deputies proposed would lead to an unnecessary and unjustifiable civil war. There was already quite a bit of disorder in the kingdom, Mirabeau argued, and the Third Estate had to be careful not to cause more. He then brought up the state of the monarchy's finances as an object of concern, and implicitly proposed to trade the willingness of the Third Estate to solve the financial crisis for the king's support in their struggle with the privileged orders. Mirabeau proposed that all existing taxes be suspended and provisionally upheld, despite their illegal nature, and that the debt be verified and guaranteed by the assembly. Then the deputies should immediately pass a new loan, obviously meant to ensure the acceptance of the new assembly by the Crown.[76]

Responding specifically to the name Sieyès had proposed, Mirabeau asked if Sieyès's motion "would give you deep roots," or if it was just a first step. They had to choose a name that reflected who they were, a name that was beyond dispute by the privileged orders, and a name that they would not have to change once the privileged orders joined them in the common

---

[73] Young, *Travels in France*, 164.

[74] AP 8: 110–11. Malouet made the same point. AP 8: 119–20.

[75] Creuzé-Latouche claimed that Mirabeau's main goal was to make a resolution that would lead to the king's acceptance of the constitution. Creuzé-Latouche, *Journal*, 107–08.

[76] AP 8: 107–09. Visme noted that the point of provisionally accepting the existing taxes was to make the king less likely to dismiss the deputies if he disapproved of their actions. Visme, "Journal," 41v. Young had heard on 14 June that the popular leaders decided to declare existing taxes illegal and then provisionally grant them for two years or the duration of the current Estates General. Young, *Travels in France*, 163. The idea of securing the debt and provisionally accepting existing taxes was in the air long before Mirabeau proposed it: it can be found in the *cahiers* of both the Nobles and Third Estate of Paris. Chassin, *Les Élections et les cahiers*, 1: 323, 338.

hall. Mirabeau claimed that the people were not interested in the metaphysics of representation, despite the very real need for the deputies to debate matters of national representation, the "basis of all constitutions." The role of a man involved in governing was not to seek "truth in its energetic purity," but to be prepared to accomplish what was possible, taking into account any problem that might be encountered along the way. It was not the time to create a new name, one that would give the assembly's detractors a reason to denounce it. The name they chose had to be one immediately comprehensible to the people and beyond dispute by the enemies of the Third Estate. It had to be one that reflected both who the deputies present were and who they would be once all three orders came together. Mirabeau proposed the title "assembly of the representatives of the French people" as the least confusing title and the one least likely to be disputed.[77]

Though Mirabeau tried to avoid the metaphysics of representation and propose a clear name for the assembly, the main objections to Mirabeau's speech had to do with the meaning of a word he chose to emphasize, "people." Sieyès had interrupted Mirabeau to argue that using the word "people" in a title would imply the very separation of orders that the deputies sought to end. Other deputies argued that naming the assembly after the "people" would be a mistake, because the French the word *peuple* meant more than the current assembly, but less than the nation.[78] Mirabeau responded to his critics, stating that by "people" he meant the largest part of the nation, as in the English usage. He then went on to say that he used the word "people" precisely because it was considered a vile word by the privileged. Mirabeau wished to adopt the word "people" in order to remind the privileged orders (and implicitly the members of the Third Estate) of whom the government was meant to serve.[79]

Despite his oratorical powers and penetrating insights, Mirabeau did not receive much support from his fellow deputies. His stance in favor of

---

[77] AP 8: 110, 111–13. Delandine reported Malouet had attempted to have the order named "Assembly of the Deputies of the Commons, representing the people of France." *Mémorial historique*, 2: 118. Both names perpetuated the choice made in early May by the deputies of the Third Estate to refer to themselves as the "Commons," marking them off from the other orders while refusing to accept that the "people" were in some way beneath the other orders.

[78] Creuzé-Latouche, *Journal*, 108; Duquesnoy, *Journal*, 1: 96.

[79] AP 8: 118. The verbatim speech is not recorded. Alexandre de Lameth later wrote that Mirabeau's motion had "raised murmurs because the expression 'people' had been so reviled in all times by the superior classes and that the deputies who were at the highest rank of the Third Estate were repulsed [by the idea of] constituting national representation under a name so reviled." A. de Lameth, *Histoire de l'Assemblée constituante*, 2 vols. (Paris, 1828–29), 1: 18, 20. See also Delandine, *Mémorial historique*, 2: 133–34.

an immediate grant of funds led to the suspicion that Mirabeau and his supporters had sold themselves to the ministers.[80] Mirabeau was also suspect by association: Pierre-Samuel Dupont de Nemours and Malouet made motions similar to his, and being supported by either of these known creatures of the government, the deputy-witness Duquesnoy wrote, was reason enough to distrust anyone.[81] Mirabeau did have one well-regarded supporter, however: Rabaut de Saint-Étienne. He followed Mirabeau's lead, identifying just whom the deputies represented and on what basis their authority rested. He proposed a longer variant of Mirabeau's title, that of "the assembly of the representatives of the French people, verified by their fellow deputies, authorized by their constituents to occupy them-selves with their interests and able to execute the mandates with which they have been charged." Like Mirabeau, he proposed a new loan "in order to calm the people" as well as to aid the government. Like Mirabeau, Rabaut suggested asking for the king's approval of their actions. One witness noted that the assembled deputies warmly received Rabaut's suggestion that the debt be consolidated and existing taxes provisionally accepted, but his request for new loans received no support and led to a brief debate over whether or not it was appropriate to discuss measures to relieve the financial crisis before the new constitution for France had been written.[82] Rabaut's formulation restricted the representative status of the assembly to their own electors. Like Mirabeau, and unlike Sieyès, Rabaut made no pretense that the deputies of the Third Estate could ever represent the constituencies of the privileged orders.

Mounier spoke after Mirabeau and had much more success rallying supporters to his proposed title. His proposal was not, on the surface, that different from Sieyès's. He focused, as had Sieyès, on the notions that the present deputies represented the vast majority of the French and that the unit to be represented was the nation itself, not any specific order. But according to Mounier it mattered less that the deputies were the only

---

[80] Many deputies feared that there was a plot among the king's ministers to thwart the Estates General and that any moderate deputy was a part of it. Creuzé-Latouche, *Journal*, III; Duquesnoy, *Journal*, I: 103.

[81] Duquesnoy, *Journal*, I: 96. See also Creuzé-Latouche, *Journal*, 109.

[82] AP 8: 113–14. Rabaut de Saint-Étienne's proposal stirred up the assembly, as many deputies protested against the idea of passing a new loan before the current financial problems were solved and the constitution was set. Creuzé-Latouche noted that "a general murmur seemed to reject this system." Creuzé-Latouche, *Journal*, 110. See also Young, *Travels in France*, 165. Many *cahiers* enjoined their deputies to reject such requests for funds prior to settling the new constitutional order. See, for example, that of the Third Estate of Paris. Chassin, *Les Élections et les cahiers*, I: 334. Félix argues that Rabaut was working to support Necker's plan for a bicameral legislature. Félix, *Louis XVI et Marie Antoinette*, 460.

properly verified deputies than that they formed the majority of all deputies. He argued from what we might call the principle of quorum:
a majority of the deputies in a representative body can always act, regardless
of the will of the minority. Mounier asked that the body name itself "the
legitimate assembly of the representatives of the largest portion of the
nation acting in the absence of the smaller portion." The body to be
activated was "the assembly formed by the representatives of the largest
portion of the nation, and by the majority of all the deputies sent to the
Estates General." Seeking a balance between confrontation and reconciliation, Mounier said that the assembly "would never recognize the pretended
right of the Nobles and Clergy to deliberate separately or oppose the
actions of the assembly," but "nevertheless did not renounce the hope for
a reunion of all deputies."[83] Mounier denied the right of a minority to act
separately from the main body at the same time that he reinforced the
notion that the majority of deputies present in the common hall formed
a quorum and could proceed unimpeded by those missing. An absent or
recalcitrant minority could never prevent the majority from acting.

At first Mounier's motion seemed likely to win the day.[84] However,
because of conditions in the hall, some confusion arose over exactly what
Mounier had proposed. In the surviving records, Mounier's motion
appears in several variants, all of which suggest that the deputies were
acting as the majority in the absence of the minority. In some sources, the
deputies have the authority to move forward because the deputies represented the vast majority of the population, and in others because they
represented a majority of the elected deputies. These two notions, both
present in Mounier's original proposal, were only on occasion reported
together. This division reveals that the deputies remained unclear about
their relationship to an ill-defined concept of "nation."[85] The deputy

---

[83] AP 8: 113. Mounier later claimed that he had proposed declaring that, "The majority of the deputies,
deliberating in the absence of the minority of the deputies, duly invited, has decreed that deliberations will be taken by head and not by order, and that we will never recognize the right of the Clergy
or Nobles to meet separately." J.-J. Mounier, *Exposé de la conduit de M. Mounier dans l'Assemblée
nationale et des moties de son retour en Dauphiné* (Paris, 1789), 6. For other variants, see Duquesnoy,
Journal, 1: 96; Lameth, *Histoire*, 1: 17; S. Bailly, *Mémoires d'un témoin de la Révolution*, Berville and
Barrière, eds, 3 vols. (Paris, 1821–22), vol. 1: 147.

[84] AP 8: 113. Jean Egret, citing Mirabeau's *Onzième lettre de Mirabeau* (n.p., 1789), 24–25, noted that
Mounier had the open support of Barnave and Thouret and seemed likely to sway the majority to
his side. J. Egret, *La révolution des notables*, 71. See also *Journal des États généraux convoqués par Louis
XVI . . .* (Paris, 1789), 1: 92. Mounier could not explain the later collapse of support for his title. See
Mounier, *Exposé*, 7.

[85] On difficulties defining the term "nation" in June of 1789, see Bell, *Cult of the Nation*; M. Cranston,
"The Sovereignty of the Nation," in Lucas, ed., *French Revolution and the Creation of Modern
Political Culture*, 97–104.

Joseph-Michel Pellerin recorded Mounier as proposing on 15 June that the assembly be called "the Representatives of the largest portion of the nation."[86] Jean-François Gaultier de Biauzat noted that Mounier's motion tended "to declare us representatives of the nation," but he did not state how. Duquesnoy recorded Mounier as proposing that the Commons "constitute itself as representatives of the largest portion of the nation, deliberating in this quality in the public interest in the absence of the representatives of the smaller portion."[87] Dupont de Nemours claimed that Mounier's title was "representatives of the citizens forming the majority of the Nation," which makes the same case.[88] Others, like the Norman lawyer Jacques-Guillaume Thouret, argued that the "nation" resided in the current assembly hall.[89] Julien-François Palasne de Champeaux noted that Mounier had proposed a name that "reduced our title to that of the largest portion of the nation exercising the rights of the minority in its absence."[90] One wonders whether the representatives present thought that they formed the largest portion of the nation, or if they represented those who formed it. They certainly did not feel that the Third Estate alone was the nation.

Supporters of Mounier's motion requested minor changes that similarly illustrate confusion over the role of the deputies in forming or representing the nation. Louis-Pierre-Joseph Prugnon, from Nancy, supported Mounier but wished to substitute "waiting for the minority" in place of "in the absence of the minority," thus emphasizing the indivisible nature of the assembly, as well as encouraging reconciliation between the orders.[91] Like Mirabeau and Rabaut, he demanded that the deputies quickly grant "subsidies to save the state," which was, he thought, the most pressing item facing them. He also urged the deputies not to declare themselves to be the "nation" prematurely.[92] For Prugnon, the "nation" included the privileged orders, though he recognized that in exceptional circumstances, the representatives of the larger portion of the population could act alone. The speech given by Claude-Ambroise Regnier supported this notion, as he feared the danger that the assembly would claim for itself "the authority of

[86] Pellerin, "Journal," 27r.   [87] Duquesnoy, *Journal,* 1: 96.
[88] Creuzé-Latouche, *Journal,* 1: 113.
[89] J.-F. Gaultier de Biauzat, *Gaultier de Biauzat, député du Tiers état aux Etats généraux de 1789: Sa vie et correspondance,* F. Mège, ed. 2 vols. (Clermont-Ferrand, 1890), 1: 117; Thouret in Creuzé-Latouche, *Journal,* 115.
[90] J.-F. Palasne de Champeaux and J.-F.-P. Poulain de Corbion, "Correspondance des députés des Côtes-du-Nord aux Etats Généraux et à l'Assemblée nationale constituante," *Bulletin et Mémoires de la Société d'Emulation des Côtes-du-Nord,* 26 (1888), 234.
[91] Duquesnoy, *Journal,* 1: 99.   [92] Creuzé-Latouche, *Journal,* 1: 116.

the king if we constitute ourselves as the nation or something approaching it."[93] This implied that whatever the nation was, it included the privileged orders and the king himself. In reporting their speeches, the deputy Antoine-François Delandine linked them, claiming that both had supported the title, "The largest portion deliberating, while awaiting reunion with the minority," with both deputies resting claims on the legitimacy of the body on the number of deputies present, not the numbers of constituents they represented.[94]

Mounier's proposal was also recorded by witnesses as specifying a number of people represented by the Third Estate deputies in order to shore up the legitimacy of their actions within the Estates General. In recorded variants, the deputies were presented as the representatives of twenty-four, twenty-five, or twenty-six million Frenchmen, shifting the meaning of "majority" from the number of deputies to the number of constituents represented and overlapping with Sieyès's claim that the deputies represented 96 percent of the population. Jacques-Antoine Creuzé-Latouche, deputy from Poitiers, recorded Mounier as proposing to call the new body the "representatives of 25 million citizens forming the majority of the Nation."[95] Bailly recorded the proposals of two unnamed speakers, both of whom suggested titles similar to that of Mounier. One proposed naming the assembly "the representatives of almost the entirety of the French people" and the other "the representatives of twenty-four million men."[96] These formulations shade away from the notion of quorum toward one of popular sovereignty. Pellerin noted that an unnamed deputy proposed the name "the legitimate representatives of twenty-five million French or of the largest portion of the French and [the largest portion] of the national assembly," between whom and the king no veto existed.[97] This proposal, very similar to that of Mounier, linked the authority of the assembly to act to its association with the vast majority of the citizens and with a quorum of deputies sitting in the Estates General. As with Sieyès's proposal, these variants on Mounier's proposed name relied on a two-pronged argument to defend their action. For Sieyès, the first prong focused on procedural matters, and that of Mounier relied on quorum. For both, the second prong was that Third Estate represented the largest number of constituents.[98]

[93] Duquesnoy, *Journal*, 1: 98, 99.   [94] Delandine, *Mémorial historique*, 1: 113.

[95] Creuzé-Latouche, *Journal*, 1: 110.

[96] Bailly, *Mémoires d'un témoin*, 1: 147. The former is likely the proposal of Target, as reported in Creuzé-Latouche, *Journal*, 113.

[97] Pellerin, "Journal," 26r.

[98] In this, both echoed Necker's explanation of why the Third Estate had been doubled in the first place. Margerison, "Pamphlet Debate," 228.

Mounier himself argued that the moral authority of the Third Estate came from its attachment to the majority of the population, and that this moral authority, coupled with its physical presence as the majority of the sitting deputies in the Estates General, allowed it to act in the absence of the minority. He argued that such authority could not rest solely on the claim to represent the vast majority, nor could it rest on a technical claim about verification of credentials that the other orders might dispute, an obvious attack on the proposals of Mirabeau and Sieyès. On 16 June Mounier argued against Sieyès' proposal that only the "verified" deputies had a right to act, noting that if the deputies constituted themselves as "the Assembly composed of the majority [acting] in the absence of the minority ... [the recalcitrant Nobles and Clergy] must agree to obey the majority despite the opposition of a minority. By this title, [the deputies currently in the common hall] incontestably have the right to do all, to decide all, because [they] are the majority," something that he claimed Sieyès's title did not guarantee.[99] Sieyès had earlier attacked the principle of quorum, claiming that the Third Estate did not have a reliable majority of deputies. Instead, Sieyès had argued, only through the common verification of powers had the deputies become representatives of the nation in the absence of the other orders.[100] Mounier countered that the deputies would be forced to abandon the title Sieyès proposed, because it left the other chambers the right to constitute themselves and claim that they too were "verified," leaving "national" representation an empty claim for the Third Estate.[101] Thouret noted that if Sieyès's motion passed, nothing would prevent the deputies of the Clergy and Nobles from coming to verify their powers in common with the Third Estate, and then returning to their own chambers in order to deliberate.[102] Only the principle of majority rule could prevent such an outcome.

Sieyès and Mounier had both proposed convoluted titles that proved confusing to the deputies and vulnerable to attacks based on the many implications arising from their complex formulations. Mirabeau had attacked the complexity of the proposed titles from the very beginning of the debate, arguing that such titles would only confuse the people they represented. He had attempted to avoid metaphysical complications by proposing a simple title: representatives of the people. But Mirabeau was not the only deputy to propose a simple name. On 15 June, Jérôme Pétion de Villeneuve, member of the Breton Club and ally of Le Chapelier and

[99] AP 8: 123.   [100] Creuzé-Latouche, *Journal*, 114.   [101] AP 8: 123.
[102] Mirabeau cited Thouret in his speech of the evening of 16 June. AP 8: 125.

Sieyès, proposed that the deputies use the most obvious name possible: "National Assembly." Like Mounier, Pétion sought to emphasize the imprescriptible unity of the legislative body, denying the privileged orders the right to meet separately. Like Mirabeau, he wanted to give the assembly a simple name, one that could be easily said and easily understood. He argued that the name "national assembly" had "the advantage of leaving no place around which our enemies could equivocate or engage in chicanery regarding the sense of words." Against Mirabeau's similar push for a simple, easily understood name, Pétion deployed the criticism that "the people of France" could mean two things: either the Third Estate, or the nation at large, including the privileged orders. If the former were true, it played into the hands of the Nobles by perpetuating the separation of the orders; if the latter, the term "National Assembly" was a better term in that it left no room for confusion.[103] Though vigorously argued, his proposal gathered no support from the floor. The debate for the day ended without any decision being made.

During the next day's session, the three main speakers defended their motions. Sieyès carefully took into account arguments for a simple title that avoided despoiling the privileged orders of their representative status. Early in the day, he proposed a new title, "assembly of the recognized and verified representatives of the French nation, exercising the powers of the national assembly."[104] This version clarified that the deputies in the common hall were not by themselves the nation assembled, avoided any mention of separate orders so as to deny them a right to meet separately, and implied that other, unverified and unrecognized deputies existed. Creuzé-Latouche noted that Sieyès argued in favor of his title on the 16th by claiming that it was only name appropriate to the current circumstances, in which the upper orders were welcome to join the Third Estate, but the deputies who had gone ahead and verified their credentials in common would move to end the stalemate by constituting themselves as an active body, without recognizing any divisions within the Estates General.[105]

We have seen how Mounier defended his proposal and attacked that of Sieyès. Also on the 16th, Jérôme Le Grand sought to clearly define the meaning of the name "national assembly," proposed by Pétion on the 15th.[106] Le Grand expanded on the reasoning behind calling the body

---

[103] Creuzé-Latouche, *Journal*, 109.   [104] Pellerin, "Journal," 28r.
[105] Creuzé-Latouche, *Journal*, 108.
[106] Pellerin, "Journal," 28r. Bastid noted that Le Grand was reputed to have made the speech at Sieyès's urging on the one hand but, on the other hand, it was claimed that Le Grand's motion had only

a "national assembly" instead of the Estates General, while urging the deputies to drop all of the confusing verbiage so far proposed. He argued that,

> The name "Estates General of the kingdom" correlates in the three orders of citizens who were called to represent the nation; this name is not applicable to the current circumstance, as the largest portion of the members who represent the Clergy and the Nobles has not united with the other deputies.

The phrase "Estates General" could describe the united orders, but no such unity existed. Le Grand accepted that the two upper orders were a part of the nation, but went on to claim that,

> The nation in [allowing] distinct classes of citizens never agreed that the absence of these classes would keep it from constituting itself in its representatives. If that were so, it follows that a people composed of twenty-four million individuals ceases to be a political and national body, cannot constitute itself, because the deputies of three or four hundred thousand men of the nation oppose themselves to its constitution and its legal representation.[107]

Le Grand recognized the representative status of the privileged deputies and acknowledged that they would be recognized and admitted to the assembly as soon as they presented their powers. Nevertheless, he proposed that the present deputies constitute themselves as the "National Assembly" to show that having duly called the other deputies and representing the majority of the citizens, they could act on behalf of the entire nation, not just the Third Estate.[108] His motion combined elements of both Sieyès's and Mounier's proposals, making the deputies from the upper orders representatives as individuals within a national body, with the attractive simplicity of a name that even the most humble Frenchman would comprehend. The name "National Assembly" served the dual purpose of addressing the concerns of many deputies over the complexity of the names proposed while claiming for the deputies sitting in the common hall the standing necessary to break the stalemate between the orders. Nevertheless, the name did not gather the support necessary to end the debate.[109] When

---

caught the imagination of the deputies in private conversations during the evening recess of 16 June. Bastid, *Sieyès et sa pensée*, 64. See also Lefebvre, *Coming of the French Revolution*, 79.

[107] AP 8: 122.   [108] Ibid. See also Creuzé-Latouche, *Journal*, 118.

[109] Different sources disagree as to whether or not Le Grand's motion received support during the day, but it was only with difficulty that he was able to re-read his proposal in the evening session, revealing limited support for his proposal at that time. See Lameth, *Histoire*, 1: 22–23; *Journal des Etats généraux*, 1: 113, 119; *Le Point du jour*, unnumbered volume, 395, 406.

the assembly recessed in the late afternoon to discuss the proposals in smaller groups it was not clear that any title could gather a majority behind it.

When the session resumed at 5:00 pm, Mounier, Mirabeau, and Sieyès once again defended their proposed titles. Mirabeau defended the distinctions between the orders, even as he praised the people of France, rather transparently playing to the audience viewing the proceedings. He spoke, he claimed, "the language of liberty" and followed the example of the English and the Americans, "who have always honored the name 'the people.'" He then stated that they dared not call themselves the Estates General, as the Third Estate had to avoid the appearance of despoiling the other orders of their rights. Mirabeau argued that "a common fault with the names" proposed by Sieyès and Mounier "was that they were long, they were unintelligible to the immense portion of the French which has honored us with its confidence." Worse, the names proposed by Mounier and Sieyès failed to distinguish between the deputies of the different orders, allowing the Clergy or the Nobles to simply adopt the name of "verified." "Let us suppose," he said, "that you address yourselves to the king. Would you dare to tell him that you are the only representatives of the nation that are recognized by His Majesty?" Mirabeau pointed out that the king might not agree that the Clergy and Nobles were "unrecognized," as implied by Sieyès's title. It would be better to use "representatives of the people," he claimed, as it would allow the deputies to act regardless of the reaction of the other orders, and would avoid appearing to infringe on their rights.[110] Mirabeau implied that the only reason that the current assembly could act was that there was a special power gained by representing the people of France. His speech, with its apparent appeal both to the rights of the other orders and the sentiments of the masses led to great tumult in the assembly, with deputies shouting out that his claim that the deputies insulted the people by refusing to call themselves their representatives was false, demanding that Mirabeau stand down from the podium and even leave the hall.[111]

The tumult Mirabeau's speech caused continued for the rest of the session. The assembly was deeply divided over the meaning of its actions. Otherwise moderate deputies were becoming more willing to take dramatic steps simply to end the internal stalemate. Le Grand reread his

---

[110] AP 8: 124–25.
[111] Gaultier de Biauzat, *Correspondance*, 1: 120; Duquesnoy, *Journal*, 1: 100; Creuzé-Latouche, *Journal*, 120; *Le Point du jour*, unnumbered volume, 396–406.

motion, and Pison du Galand argued (with difficulty due to continuing noise) that the Clergy and Nobles were merely subsets of the nation. Then, Sieyès suddenly proposed that the new body be called the "National Assembly."[112] Far from controlling events, Sieyès responded to the changing mood of the Third Estate when he shifted away from his awkward title. Julien-François Palasne de Champeaux and Jean-François Poulain de Corbion show this in their report from late in the session of 16 June: "The abbé Sieyès made an amendment to his motion. As he had seen in the debate that the opinion prevailed to constitute into the National Assembly, he had adopted this title." They thought that this clever move would guarantee that his proposal would "pass by a large majority."[113] By adopting the title "National Assembly" without explanation or qualification, Sieyès clearly intended to coopt the supporters of Le Grand and Pétion and push through the self-activation of the order without further debate. According to the Third Estate deputy Laurent de Visme, Sieyès took over Le Grand's motion "without scruple," using the reasoning that "if the motion is a good one, it doesn't matter who made it." Sieyès's apparent opportunism led to an increasingly disordered debate over whether or not the new version of his motion had been adequately discussed.[114] Finally four motions were selected to be read, a preliminary to a vote on the constitution of the order. The motions were those of the Sieyès, Mirabeau, Mounier, and Pison du Galand.[115] As Sieyès had stolen his thunder, Le Grand's motion was not read.

The debate over these motions ran from 8:00pm to midnight. Bailly recorded in his memoirs that when it came time for a vote, "several members claimed that it was too late and that it was necessary to recess until the next day." For Bailly it was a question of voting the measure under the most auspicious circumstances. Like the unnamed Breton deputy who had proposed that the deputies rally behind the less confrontational decree on 10 June, Bailly understood that no matter how important it was for the body to formally constitute itself, it was equally necessary to do so in such a way that the two upper orders could not attack it by claiming that the vote had been somehow illegal. There were fewer deputies in the hall to approve of the motion than Bailly would have liked, both because fewer deputies generally attended the evening sessions and because of the late hour. He was hesitant to move forward, believing that it would be

---

[112] AP 8: 126; Pellerin, "Journal," fol. 28r.
[113] Palasne de Champeaux and Poulain de Corbion, "Lettres," 234.   [114] Visme, "Journal," 43r.
[115] Pellerin, "Journal," 29r–29v.

a good idea to delay such an important measure to the next morning.[116] But some deputies feared that the government would dissolve the Estates General in order to prevent the Third Estate taking action, and they pushed for an immediate vote.[117]

Despite Bailly's misgivings, when the motion to move to a vote carried, he began an *appel nominal*. However, as the voting began there was such an outcry that it was impossible to hear what the deputies were saying. Bailly later estimated that three or four hundred deputies wished to speak in favor of the motion, and about one hundred against it, but no one would be quiet long enough for the vote to take place.[118] Tremendous disorder ensued, as those who wished further discussion to clarify the particulars of the naming of the body worked hard to disrupt the vote, shouting down any speaker who rose.[119] One deputy protested that the vote could not be free in the face of a hostile audience.[120] Menaced by spectators and suspected by their own colleagues of complicity with the government, the deputies who sought further discussion felt threatened and intimidated.[121] The environment became so toxic that at least one witness felt that the meeting would have fallen to blows between the opposing sides, if not for a large table between the groups. Rational discussion of the available options had clearly ceased. Bailly knew that, in such a situation, it was the president's duty to adjourn the meeting, but he feared that only the minority would follow him out, and that the majority would then elect a new doyen and proceed with the constitution of the order.[122]

After an hour-long standoff, most of the disruptive deputies left and Bailly was able to regain control of the meeting.[123] A group of approximately eighty deputies had walked out rather than vote on any of the motions. Creuzé-Latouche noted that many in the assembly were shocked and saddened that some "bad citizens" among them would resist the will of the majority and "the judgment of the public." He named among the

---

[116] Bailly, *Mémoires d'un témoin*, 1: 150–53.

[117] Creuzé-Latouche noted that the fear of a ministerial coup had pushed the Commons to vote to end the discussion in the first place. Creuzé-Latouche, *Journal*, 1: 121–22. J.-P. Boullé agreed. Boullé, "Correspondance de Boullé," in "Ouverture des Etats généraux de 1789," A. Macé, ed., *Revue de la Révolution* 6:13 (1888), 12–13.

[118] Bailly, *Mémoires d'un témoin*, 1: 152–53.   [119] Creuzé-Latouche, *Journal*, 122–23.

[120] Duquesnoy, *Journal*, 101–02.

[121] Creuzé-Latouche, *Journal*, 121–22; Mounier, *Exposé*, 7. Duquesnoy reported that spectators acted to silence and marginalize those who wished to continue the debate over constituting the order. He further noted that it was dangerous to oppose the majority opinion, as the opinions of the deputies were all noted and circulated by the spectators. Duquesnoy, *Journal*, 1: 101–02, 104. See also Visme, "Journal," 43v–44r.

[122] Duquesnoy, *Journal*, 1: 154.   [123] Ibid., 1: 155.

dissidents "all the deputies of Paris," Malouet, Thouret, the deputies of Rouen, Prugnon and Régnier, Lebrun, Dupont du Nemours, and the Garat brothers from Bordeaux.[124] These men were hardly ultra-conservatives, and, in fact, they included the most vocal and staunch supporters of Mounier and his motion, and included deputies linked to Necker. Surprisingly, the group also included Target, a leader among the Paris deputies.[125] Rather than proceed under such inauspicious circumstances, Gaultier de Biauzat proposed that the vote be put off to the next day. The deputies who remained in the hall passed a motion requiring that each deputy sign a record of his vote when it was taken at the next session.[126] After that, the motion to delay the vote passed unanimously.[127]

When the Third Estate reconvened on 17 June, the main hall was again filled with spectators, but they watched in silence.[128] Bailly sought to reassure the deputies and calm any tempers still hot from the night before. He argued against having the deputies sign the resolution constituting the assembly according to their vote, as decided the evening before, out of fear that it would expose the lack of unanimity and sow discord in Paris and the countryside. The deputies voted to rescind their decision.[129] The motions of Sieyès, Mounier, Mirabeau, Pison du Galand, and Le Grand were read out, and someone suggested that rather than voting on all five motions, the deputies ought to consider that of Sieyès first and only move on to the others should it fail to gain a majority. The deputies agreed, and in an unremarkable vote Sieyès's motion passed by a vote of 491–90, followed by cries of "Long live the king!" and "Long live the king and the nation!"[130] According to a deputy witness, the title "National Assembly" won because it brought together the most important points made by the different speakers. The deputies present in the common hall became the National Assembly because it held the only verified deputies, they represented most of the French, and the nation, one and indivisible, could not be broken into three autonomous parts. The decree they passed also reminded individuals of their duty to the Estates General and to the nation, and

---

[124] Creuzé-Latouche, *Journal*, 124.

[125] Gaultier de Biauzat minimized the conflict in his report to his constituents, stating only that "it was decided to proceed to a vote," and that after hours of discussion, "there had been conflict on this subject." Gaultier de Biauzat, *Correspondance*, 122.

[126] Duquesnoy, *Journal*, 1: 101–02; *Le Point du jour*, unnumbered volume, 407.

[127] Bailly, *Mémoires d'un témoin*, 1: 155.   [128] Creuzé-Latouche, *Journal*, 125.   [129] AP 8: 127.

[130] Ibid.; Creuzé-Latouche, *Journal*, 126. Creuzé-Latouche noted that the ninety voting against the motion more or less included the eighty protesters from the night before. But Visme noted that some who had spoken most openly against the motion changed their minds and voted for it on the next day. Among these, he numbered Target. Visme, "Journal," 44v.

made it clear that this was an attempt to move the Estates General out of its stalemate. But it also implicitly recognized the right of the privileged orders to send deputies, as long as those deputies sat in the common hall.[131]

We can now attempt to understand what the deputies meant, more or less, when they chose the name "National Assembly." Choosing the name "National Assembly" resulted from a struggle between the need for accuracy and for simplicity. Simplicity won, but left the assembly with a name that meant different things to different members and did not clarify the relationship of the elected to their electors, or of the assembly to its king. Nevertheless, the deputies had declared that they could act in the name of the nation, and that no other body of deputies could prevent them from so acting. The name "National Assembly" was adopted to keep the momentum generated during the verification of credentials going, to put pressure on the Nobles and Clergy to join the Third Estate in the "national hall" and to accomplish both without alienating the king. If successful, this would have allowed the Third Estate, with their allies among the liberal Nobles and progressive Clergy, to hold the balance of power within the assembly and commit the National Assembly to a progressive agenda.

The key to understanding the declaration of the National Assembly is the final paragraph of the proclamation voted on that day:

> The assembly will never lose hope of bringing together within its midst all the deputies absent today; it will not cease to call [*appeler*] them to fulfill the obligation imposed upon them, that of contributing to the meeting of the Estates General. It declares in advance that, whenever in the course of the session now beginning the absent deputies present themselves, it will hasten to receive them and to share with them, after their powers have been verified, the continuation of the great work that must effect the regeneration of France.[132]

All of the deputies with the correct credentials would be allowed to participate, *all* of the deputies elected were obligated by their constituents to participate in the current meeting of the Estates General. And this phrase, "contributing to the meeting of the Estates General" indicates that the deputies still, in choosing the name "National Assembly," interpreted it, as seen in many Third Estate *cahiers*, as the name for the orders

---

[131] Ménard de la Groye, *Correspondance*, 45.

[132] AP 8: 127. K. M. Baker, ed. and trans. *University of Chicago Readings in Western Civilization*, vol. 7, *The Old Regime and the French Revolution* (Chicago, 1987), 200. We have chosen to modify Baker's translation in one small way. We translate "appeler" as "call," where Baker used "summon." We do this to emphasize that the final proposal did not replicate Sieyès's initial motion of 10 June in which he had used the word "sommation," before the deputies modified it to "invitation."

united in the common hall.[133] The transformation of the body into something truly new, beyond an Estates General meeting and voting in common, would await another day.

Bailly left us an explanation of the title that supports this analysis. In his
memoirs, he refuted any challenge to the right of the Third Estate to the
title "National Assembly," noting that they were the largest portion of the
Estates General, that they sat in the common chamber of the Estates
General, and that they had formally invited the other deputies to attend.
"With these forms," he wrote, "the assembly composed of the deputies
present, and despite those absent, is the National Assembly, formed of the
legitimate and verified representatives of the nation." Bailly accepted that
the deputies from the privileged orders were legitimate representatives of
the nation, but denied that they had the right to meet separately.

Bailly noted that the term "National Assembly," like that of "Estates
General," was technically inappropriate for the body but that the incon-
venience of a misleading title was justified by the indispensable unity of the
orders that it implied.[134] While the deputies of the Nobles and Clergy,
strictly speaking, had the right to meet separately, the representatives of the
great mass of the French overrode this right when confronted by the refusal
of the other orders to join them in the common hall to verify their
credentials. Bailly then moved on to the names used by Mounier and
Sieyès and how they related to numbers of constituents, noting that
"almost the entirety of the people, the representatives of 24 million men;
[these] were vague and numerical expressions that were not appropriate for
the name of an august senate. The *National Assembly* was the appropriate
name in all respects."[135] Mirabeau had been entirely correct in one important respect: one could not choose an equivocal, vague or confusing title for
the assembly and expect to garner the support of one's fellow deputies or
one's constituents. The only term on which the deputies and their constituents alike could finally agree was that of "National Assembly," a title
found in the *cahiers de doléances* the deputies carried with them, their
correspondence with their constituents and in political pamphlets of the
time, a title synonymous with a vision of the Estates General as a novel
union of the powers of the traditional body with the representative and
legislative powers associated with the parlements.[136]

---

[133] Fitzsimmons has similarly argued that the goal of the deputies in constituting themselves as the
National Assembly remained a union of the orders and a vote by head, rather than the end of the
orders as such. Fitzsimmons, *Remaking of France*, 42.
[134] Bailly, *Mémoires d'un témoin*, I: 147–48.   [135] Ibid. Emphasis in original.
[136] Lamarque, "La naissance de 'l'Assemblée nationale'," 111–18.

Friedland has forcefully argued that the decision to call the newly active body the "National Assembly" resulted in a complete transformation of the system of political representation:

> Traditionally, the legitimacy of the deputies to the Estates General had rested upon the *cahiers* to whose will they were bound by their mandates. But had the deputies consulted their *cahiers* before severing themselves from France's traditional political body? They had not. For no one's *cahier* would have empowered him to make such a move. The deputies had constituted a new political body solely on their own authority, consulting no one's will but their own. In many quarters it was no doubt a popular move. But it was also a move that effectively severed the representatives from the foundation of their legitimacy. . . . In the new political order, one no longer needed the sort of tangible, material artifacts of legitimacy that had been so important to the old regime. The National Assembly's legitimacy would come not from its *cahiers* or its mandates but from the willingness of the people to regard it as legitimate.[137]

Friedland goes too far here. First, the deputies were only deputies in that they had been verified as such by an examination of their mandates, proving their election was valid and that they did in fact represent the constituency they claimed to. This use paper mandates shows the clear reliance of the assembly on a material artifact of legitimacy. The point of declaring a national assembly was to deny the other orders the right to declare their powers verified without having done so in the common hall, again reliance on a material artifact, not on a vague presupposition of popular approval. Similarly, the deputies of the Third Estate were doing their best to enact the demands found in their *cahiers*, demands that the assembly deliberate and vote in common. It would be absurd to give a deputy a list of grievances and then prohibit him from acting on them, and the mandates given to the deputies of the Third Estate left plenty of room for the men to behave as political actors, resolving problems on behalf of their constituents. Moreover, it was not the responsibility of the men of the Third Estate to act according to the mandates given to *other* deputies. That a nobleman had been prohibited by his mandate from participating was a problem for that deputy and his constituents, but according to the declaration of 17 July, such an individual mandate could not stop the Estates General from meeting. We see this most clearly in the accompanying proclamation: "So weighty a delegation should not remain inactive because of the absence of a few *bailliages*, or of some classes of

---

[137] Friedland, *Political Actors*, 140, 141.

citizens, for those who have been called but remain absent cannot prevent those present from exercising the plenitude of their rights, especially when the exercise of those rights is an imperious and pressing duty."[138] It was the refusal to follow the protocol established in the common hall that denied the deputies their status, not their "quality" as a member of a privileged order. Moreover, in a break from the traditional practices of the Estates General, no individual order would be able to block the actions of the majority of the deputies elected.[139] The three factors that entitled the deputies present in the common hall to act in the absence of their fellows combined the claims of Mounier and Sieyès. They were the presence of a quorum of deputies in the common hall, the fact that they had followed the proper procedure to verify their status as deputies, and the weight of the number of constituents they represented.

But if the deputies thought that a victory over the conservative deputies was ensured, the declaration also set up a conflict with the Crown.[140] The deputies saw the potential for conflict, and they hoped to avoid it. They sought to strengthen their position by acting on demands found in their *cahiers* to consolidate and guarantee the royal debt and by claiming a power to oversee and approve of all taxation. Immediately following activation of the present deputies as the National Assembly, Target and Le Chapelier separately proposed what was contained in only 6 percent of the Third Estate *cahiers* (and 10 percent of Noble ones as well), the verification and guarantee of the "national" debt and the repeal and temporary approval of all existing taxes.[141] Their proposals were combined and the National Assembly adopted them unanimously as its first act.[142] The deputies then voted to print the decrees constituting the National Assembly and

---

[138] AP 8: 127. It is important to note here that the declaration uses the word "appelé," not "sommé" as one would expect if the other deputies were "summoned" to join the other deputies by their superiors. Trans. by Baker, *Old Regime and the French Revolution*, 200.

[139] The deputies declared that "there can exist no veto, no negative power . . . between the throne and this assembly." AP 8, 127. Trans. by Baker, *Old Regime and the French Revolution*, 200. This impacted the Third Estate as well. When the deputies from Brittany had introduced the idea on 14 May that the rights of their province would allow them a veto power over the actions of the assembly, this was immediately dismissed as absurd. See Visme, "Journal," 40v–40r.

[140] Guilhaumou, *L'avènement des porte-parole*, 74.

[141] Target was a deputy from Paris, and Paris' Third Estate included such demands in its *cahier*. Chassin, *Les Élections et les cahiers*, 1: 338. As we have seen, the principle that only the Estates General could approve taxation was ancient and mostly accepted by the Crown.

[142] AP 8: 128–29. On the demands in the *cahiers* to repeal taxes created without authorization by the Estates General and to verify and consolidate the royal debt, see Chapter 1. Mirabeau and Rabaut had urged such a declaration on 15 June as a means to create stability and, as Rabaut put it, "to calm the people." AP 8: 113; Creuzé-Latouche, *Journal*, 110.

concerning the royal debt and taxation and ordered them distributed throughout France.[143]

Target had been a critic of the title "National Assembly." He was a supporter of Mounier who had walked out in protest on 16 June. Now, he collaborated with the leader of the Breton faction that had consistently attempted to exclude the upper orders. They proposed an action found in Paris's more radical *cahier*, but which had been first made in the debate by Mirabeau, a man seen to be a supporter of Necker. The reasoning Mirabeau had given during the debate for the motion was to offer something to the king, to make it more likely to accept their decision to move forward. The deputies saw the move to provisionally approve taxes and nationalize the debt as a challenge to those around the king who opposed Necker and his reforms, not to the king himself. In discussing the actions of the Third Estate on 17 June, the Clerical deputy from Poitou Jacques Jallet wrote that the decree voiding and provisionally renewing taxes "provided new material to the cries of the cabal [of great nobles and bishops]," but the decree "concerning public debt disconcerted them; there was no longer a way to dissolve the Assembly without causing bankruptcy and alarming the whole nation."[144] Rather than seeing these two decrees as moves to seize sovereign power from the king, we should view them and the order to publicize the decrees as the means to guarantee the existence of the Estates General against dissolution by the "cabal" formed by the queen, Artois, and their supporters at Court. Above all else, the deputies wished to fulfill the demands of their constituents as found in their *cahiers*. They sought to end the stalemate between the orders and establish the vote by head in a unified assembly. Declaring themselves to be a National Assembly that could guarantee the national debt and approve of taxation would, without question, achieve both goals, but only with the support of the king.

The declaration of the National Assembly and subsequent decrees led to great and immediate success in putting pressure on the privileged orders and on the Crown, which took rapid action to come up with its own solution to the stalemate. In fact, the king's efforts to end the clash between the conservative deputies and the new National Assembly led to a rapid escalation of the claims for independence made by the deputies themselves, as we shall see in the next Chapter. In an attempt to regain control of the

---

[143] AP 8: 129; Ménard de la Groye, *Correspondance*, 45.

[144] J. Jallet, *Journal inédit de Jallet, Curé de Chérigné, député du clergé du Poitou, aux États-Généraux de 1789*, ed. J. J. Brethé (Fontenay-le-Comte, 1871), 94–95.

situation, the government denied the deputies use of the *Salle des Menus Plaisirs* on 20 June and denied them use of the name "National Assembly" on 23 June. The government's heavy-handed tactics backfired. Having declared that the Estates General could only meet as a National Assembly and that the privileged orders could not meet separately on 17 June, the same deputies declared on 20 June that they would not allow the king to choose when, where or whether they could meet. When on 23 June Louis held a Royal Session to impose a plan for reconciliation that allowed the upper orders to meet separately, the deputies from the National Assembly refused to accept it, arguing in line with the traditions of the Estates General that the king's own wishes were irrelevant concerning the constitution of the body and its internal policies. Faced with continuing opposition from recalcitrant deputies and tactical mistakes by the government, the deputies became progressively radicalized in the "school of the Revolution," accepting more and more of the demands for action found in *cahiers* like that of Paris that had proposed a more radical line of action.[145]

---

[145] Tackett, *Becoming a Revolutionary,* 146.

CHAPTER 3

The King Responds

One of the most remarkable features of the early Revolution was the absence of direct communication between the Third Estate and Louis XVI. The king had given no instructions about how to regulate communication between himself and the orders. The matter devolved to the Keeper of the Seals, Charles Louis François de Paule de Barentin, who took it upon himself to act as the supervisor for everything related to the Estates General. He became the conduit through which communication between the orders and Louis passed. But Barentin was deeply hostile to the pretensions of the Third Estate, going back at least as far as the time of the *Result of the King's Council of State* of 1788. Until mid July, Barentin managed communications to the benefit of the Noble order, generally refusing to find times for members of the Third Estate to meet with the king. During the stalemate, the deputies of the Third Estate had only been given one meeting with Louis and it was at the worst time possible, coming two days after the death of the king's oldest son. Even when the king would have benefitted greatly from knowing what the Third Estate was doing, the deputies were prevented from making their case to him in person.[1] Throughout May and June, the Third Estate and the king acted without any direct knowledge of each other's intentions.

This lack of communication helped cause the greatest failure of Louis XVI's reign: his inability to capitalize on the rise of the Third Estate as a political force, even though the Crown had worked hard to bolster it as a political actor. What had been framed in 1787–88 as a struggle between virtuous nobles and despotic ministers had been successfully channeled into a struggle between the privileged elites and the Third Estate. Nevertheless, neither Calonne, nor Brienne, nor Necker had any real plan to manage the rise of this body even as the Crown hoped it would act as a counterweight to the ambitions of the privileged elite. Necker's plan to double the number of Third Estate deputies while leaving matters

[1] Hardman, *Louis XVI* (1993), 147–49; Joël Félix, *Louis XVI et Marie Antoinette*, 457.

of organization to the Estates General had satisfied no one. Able political management could have made a major difference, but Louis had made no effort to influence events during the run-up to the Estates General. He seemed, in fact, to take it for granted that he should not interfere. When he did act, he seemed to oppose the privileged elites who had caused him so much grief in 1787–88. After the deputies had met in Versailles, Louis continued his habitual silence, and deputies of the Third Estate were given no reason to think that he did not support their efforts.[2]

As the stalemate between the orders persisted, the Crown had slowly become more involved in the affairs of the Estates General, pushing the orders to continue with conciliation commissions and finally proposing a means of reconciliation on 5 June, as we have seen above. The declaration of the National Assembly pushed the Crown to act with vigor and in particular pushed the queen and the king, who had originally sympathized with the Third Estate, toward a more conservative position.[3] Even before the Third Estate's dramatic action, Necker thought that the best way to resolve the stalemate would be a Royal Session (*Séance Royale*), a meeting at which the king and his Court would appear before all three Estates and at which the king could make his opinions known. Necker expected the deputies to accept a compromise if personally suggested by the king. He had suggested such a meeting to the king in mid-June, but it only came up for serious discussion on 17 June at a meeting between the two in Versailles. Necker sought some kind of compromise in which general matters would be settled with a vote by head (including the incredibly important matter of how future Estates General would meet) but in which matters specific to the Nobles or Clergy would be voted by order. His nascent plan foundered on the decision of the Third Estate to declare itself the National Assembly, annoying Necker to no end and setting off new discussions of what to do. Despite the apparent urgency of the situation, Louis put off discussing the possibility of a Royal Session with the Royal Council until 19 June, at the king's hunting chateau at Marly.[4]

It was not clear what would be decided at the meeting. The marquis of Ferrières was convinced the Court was set on the dissolution of the Estates General and that the king planned to impose the major demands

[2] Hardman, *Louis XVI* (1993), 145–46. This scruple was new. The queen regent had done much to ensure favorable election results in 1614. Hayden, *Estates General*, 77–78.

[3] Price, *Road from Versailles*, 57–61. Morris was convinced that the crisis resulted from the decision on 19 June of the Clergy to join with the Third Estate for a common verification of powers. Morris, *Diary*, 1: 116.

[4] Hardman, *Louis XVI* (1993), 149–51.

from the *cahiers* by fiat. The well-informed American Gouverneur Morris thought that the conservatives on the Royal Council would be overawed by the Clergy's decision to join with the Third Estate.[5] Necker certainly seemed convinced he would prevail. Despite the changes in circumstance, he stuck to his original plan. He practiced his proposal on his ministerial allies during the ride from Versailles to Marly on the 19th and appeared confident that he would convince the king. He was probably not aware that Marie-Antoinette had decided to take a stand against the actions of the Third Estate. When Necker arrived at the chateau, Marie-Antoinette summoned him to meet with her. With the support of the king's younger brothers, the counts of Provence and Artois, she tried to talk Necker out of reading his proposal to the king. Necker persisted and in the council meeting Louis agreed that it was necessary to hold a meeting with all three Estates. Necker seemed on the verge of winning over the king to his entire plan when one of the king's attendants brought Louis a message, presumably from the queen. The king then left the room, and when he came back he put off a final decision on what would be announced.[6] He had agreed to have a Royal Session on 22 June and had ordered that the meetings of the Estates General be suspended. But no platform had been agreed on to announce.

Artois and the queen had outmaneuvered Necker on 19 June and would press their advantage the following day. Duty called Necker back to Versailles on the morning of 20 June, but Louis remained at Marly. The queen, Artois, and the queen's favorite, Gabrielle, the duchess of Polignac, went to great lengths to convince the king to side with the privileged orders in their struggle with the Third Estate. Representatives of the Parlement of Paris came promising to approve loans if Louis would dissolve the Estates General. The archbishop of Paris and the president of the Clergy begged Louis to defend religion and the rights of their Estate. With tremendous emotional pressure, these defenders of the privileged orders convinced Louis to summon another council meeting for that night at Marly, one at which Necker would be absent and at which Artois and Provence would be present. This meeting would mark a spectacular deviation from the regular procedures by which decisions were made on the Royal Council. As Price argues, Louis had lost control of his family and faced not only an

---

[5] Ferrières, *Mémoires*, 1:37–38; Morris, *Diary*, 1: 118.
[6] Hardman, *Louis XVI* (1993), 151–52. Félix, *Louis XVI et Marie Antoinette*, 463–64. F.-E. Guignard, comte de Saint-Priest, *Mémoires: Régnes de Louis XV et de Louis XVI*, ed. baron de Barante, 2 vols. (Paris, 1929), 1: 222–23.

unruly Estates General, but a family "fronde" as well.[7] Then, before a meeting of the expanded Royal Council could be held, the political situation was transformed. The king's decision to suspend the meetings of the Estates General pushed the deputies of the National Assembly to act to defend their right to meet.

The decision to suspend the meetings of the Estates General until after the Royal Session had a tremendous impact on the course of the Revolution. Until 20 June, the deputies of all three orders had acted in accordance with the king's will, even though the Nobles had refused to accept his proposals. The decision of the Third Estate, with a handful of Clergy, to call itself the National Assembly had finally pushed the king to act, even though it was not clear what he would do. But Louis's decision to close the meeting halls pushed the National Assembly to act in response. Thus began a profound shift in the dialectic of the Revolution. Up until 17 June, the primary cause of changing attitudes in the Third Estate had been the struggle with the recalcitrant Nobles and Clergy. After the declaration of the National Assembly, though, the dialectic was no longer one in which the upper orders directly participated. The deputies henceforth reacted more to what the king and his Council ordered, and less to what the Nobles and Clergy did or did not do.

In Versailles, the morning of 20 June had begun like any other for the deputies of the three orders, but when they arrived at their halls they found the doors barred and guarded by soldiers. Beginning at 8:00am, heralds had proclaimed in the streets that there would be a Royal Session on the 22nd and that the meetings of the Estates General were suspended until after that date. The deputies of the National Assembly had not heard (or did not obey) this royal command. When Bailly arrived at the *Hôtel des menus plaisirs* he found the deputies milling about outside their accustomed hall, the doors closed and guarded. He demanded to see the officer in charge, who informed him that the hall was closed on the king's orders while it was refurbished for the upcoming Royal Session. This appears to have been the first news Bailly had of the suspension of the Estates General.[8] He was furious. The officer on duty told Bailly that he and the Third Estate's secretaries could enter the hall to retrieve their most

[7] Price, *Road from Versailles*, 61, 63–64; Hardman, *Louis XVI* (1993), 152–53; Hardman, "Decision-Making," 86. The other princes of the blood (save Orléans) soon requested seats at the council table. Lefebvre, *Recueil de Documents*, t.1, II: 202–4.

[8] Louis had not notified the presidents of the orders of the suspension. Saint-Priest, *Mémoires*, I: 223–24; *Correspondance de MM. les députés des Communes de la province d'Anjou, avec leur commettans*, 2 vols. (Angers, 1789), I: 191.

important papers. After calming the angry deputies, Bailly and the secretaries entered the hall. They found soldiers and workers inside and preparations being made for the upcoming meeting. When he came back out, Bailly led a brief discussion about what the deputies should do next. On the Parisian deputy Joseph-Ignace Guillotin's motion they decided to move to another space that could accommodate their numbers. The one they found was an old indoor tennis court, the *Jeu de paume* three blocks away.[9] As the deputies gathered in their new hall, the galleries filled with spectators and a huge crowd formed just outside the doors and in the streets. Bailly later recalled that their presence "announced that it was the nation that honored the Tennis Court with its presence."[10]

By the time the deputies were ready to come to order, Bailly had received two letters from Henri Evrard, the marquis of Dreux-Brézé, the king's Master of Ceremonies. Bailly read them aloud to the deputies. Responding to Bailly's anger at being shut out of the hall, Brézé noted that he had, on the king's orders, sent heralds through the streets announcing the suspension of meetings of the Estates General leading up to a Royal Session to be held on 22 June. He also urged Bailly to give him the names of the secretaries of his order so that they would be allowed to retrieve their papers. Bailly had written Brézé that he had received no orders from the king for the suspension of the Assembly or regarding a Royal Session. Since the Assembly had planned to meet on 20 June, it was his duty to open the meeting as agreed. Brézé had sent a response stating that it was the king's express order that sessions of the Estates General be suspended during preparations for the coming Royal Session.[11] Conflict between the king and the Third Estate had begun.

Their every move watched by a huge and supportive audience, the deputies debated what to do next. Sieyès suggested the Assembly move as a body to Paris where their supporters would be all around them, ensuring that their meetings would continue. Mounier spoke up immediately, cutting off discussion of this idea by proposing what we know as the Tennis Court Oath.[12] Mounier preempted Sieyès by asking that the deputies take a major step, swearing a solemn oath never to part until they had written a constitution for France. He said that he thought it

[9] AP 8: 137; Bailly, *Mémoires d'un témoin*, 1: 182. Duquesnoy noted that the deputies had gone to the tennis court with a "sudden and almost involuntary" movement. Duquesnoy, *Journal*, 1: 111.

[10] Bailly, *Mémoires d'un témoin*, 1: 188.

[11] AP 8: 137–38. See also Visme, "Journal," 47r. Some nobles also protested the closing of their hall on the same day. Ibid., 48r.

[12] Lefebvre, *Coming of the French Revolution*, 81. Bailly, *Mémoires d'un témoin*, 1:189.

strange that when they came to meet their hall was occupied by soldiers, that no alternative meeting place had been offered to them, that their president had been notified by a letter from the Master of Ceremonies and the deputies themselves only by a poster on the door of their hall. He argued that they had been injured both in their rights and in their dignity by this treatment, but he did not blame the king for the disaster. Instead, he blamed those who surrounded the king, saying that as the deputies were "aware of the liveliness of the intrigue and the eagerness with which [plotters] seek to push the king to disastrous acts," and that "the nation's representatives should bind themselves to the common good and the interests of the *patrie* with a solemn oath." Mounier assured the deputies that the king himself had nothing but good intentions in briefly suspending the National Assembly, but that the means by which it was announced were clearly the acts of the "enemies of the state and of the people" meant to force its dissolution. Target, Le Chapelier and Barnave, representatives of three different groups in the Assembly, then spoke in support of Mounier's motion. Once debate ended, the motion passed by general approbation, and the deputies formally swore that they would not allow the Assembly to be dissolved, and that they would meet wherever and whenever circumstances allowed, until "the constitution of the kingdom is established and strengthened on solid foundations."[13]

The oath took the entire day to finalize. The deputies came forward by *bailliage, sénéchausée*, province and city to sign it. It took until 6:00 pm for process to finish.[14] After this solemn act, Le Chapelier quickly reviewed the document and announced that amongst the hundreds of signatures, one deputy had written "opposed" beside his. Le Chapelier asked the Assembly what to do. Bailly asked the deputy, Joseph Martin d'Auch, for his reasons and Martin said that he refused to take an action that was not subject to the king's sanction. The Assembly puzzled over what to do, but then voted to leave his signature in place as proof that they had deliberated and voted freely.[15] The substitute deputies and those who had yet to verify their credentials came forward and were allowed to sign the oath. Finally, Le Chapelier proposed sending a letter to the king denouncing as enemies of

---

[13] Malouet and Joseph Martin d'Auch raised a point reminiscent of the push against Sieyès's radical proposal of 10 June. They sponsored an amendment making the Tennis Court Oath subject to the sanction of the king, but their motion failed. Bailly, *Mémoires d'un témoin*, 1:189; AP 8: 138; Creuzé-Latouche, *Journal*, 132, 134. On Barnave, see E. D. Bradby, *The Life of Barnave*, 2 vols. (Oxford, 1915).

[14] Duquesnoy, *Journal*, 1: 111–12. The Tennis Court Oath was signed by deputies called according to delegation, not by name. The deputies still saw themselves as representatives of specific regional constituencies. AP 8: 138.

[15] AP 8: 139–40; Bailly, *Mémoires d'un témoin*, 1:192–93.

the state those who had kept them out of their hall. Mounier responded that it would be better to use milder language. The deputies needed to keep their stronger weapons for a more opportune time, and above all they needed to find out whether the king intended to come out in favor of the Third Estate or against it. Barnave and Louis-Marthe de Gouy-d'Arcy, a Noble deputy from Saint-Domingue, then spoke against Le Chapelier's motion and the Assembly decided not to pursue the matter further.[16]

Swearing the oath had served to unite the deputies in the face of ministerial opposition.[17] The deputies followed Mounier, leader of the moderates, in refusing to push further against the authority of the king until they knew for certain what was happening. They had reconfirmed their acts of 17 June, and they had added to them a defiant oath signaling that the king had no right to dismiss them or interrupt their meetings. Taking this oath was a tremendous innovation, a revolutionary step. But strangely enough this radical step was also a victory of the moderate deputies over their more radical rivals. Crucially, two radical proposals had been defeated. The deputies would not move to Paris as Sieyès had suggested, and they would not denounce the king's advisers, as Le Chapelier had demanded. Most deputies continued to believe that the king's advisors had misled him. Some deputies even thought that the Royal Session would break in their favor, with the king coming out in support of the Third Estate.[18] After a long and emotionally draining session, the deputies dispersed.

After the session, Third Estate deputy François-René-Pierre Ménard de la Groye wrote home to his wife, "We think that the object of the Royal Session will be to unite, if possible, the three orders and restore among them a joyous harmony."[19] He did not suspect that the Royal Session would be used as a kind of *lit de justice,* the traditional meeting at which the king could enforce his will on a parlement, with the king taking the side of the privileged orders. On 20 June, most of the Third Estate deputies remained convinced that the king was on their side. They thought (or rather hoped) that the closing of the main hall had only been contrived to spare the privileged orders from the dishonor of appearing to submit to the wishes of the Third Estate.[20] Still, they were dissatisfied by how it had all come to pass. Ménard de la Groye claimed that the deputies took the order to suspend their meetings until the Royal Session as an unjust act.

[16] AP 8: 140; Duquesnoy, *Journal,* 1: 112; Mounier, *Exposé,* 9.   [17] Creuzé-Latouche, *Journal,* 132.
[18] Creuzé-Latouche, *Journal,* 130–31. Tackett, *Becoming a Revolutionary,* 152–53; Shapiro, *Traumatic Politics,* 63.
[19] Ménard de la Groye, *Correspondance,* 46.   [20] Creuzé-Latouche, *Journal,* 130–31.

Nevertheless, all would go well because the deputies had the support of that powerful voice of the nation, public opinion.[21] The only plausible explanation the deputies found for the way the session had been announced was that the king's advisors had misled him. This revealed a profound ambiguity in the way deputies related to royal authority. While they looked to the king for protection and for guidance, they also worried that he was firmly in the grip of an aristocratic cabal.[22] On 20 June, Mounier had said as much.[23]

When Bailly later reflected on the events of 20 June, he compared how the king had acted to the way Louis had treated the parlements before the Revolution. As we saw in the previous Chapter, this sense that the Estates General had acquired the representative powers of the parlements was a main theme in the *cahiers,* and it became an important trope for the deputies to help them comprehend the king's actions. Bailly wrote in his memoirs that when the king communicated with the Parlement of Paris, the king himself wrote a letter to its first president instead of delegating the task to his Master of Ceremonies. Given the importance of the Estates General relative to the parlements, Bailly thought that the Assembly ought to be treated at least as well as they were. He further noted that the form of the Royal Session that had preempted their meeting looked to be a *lit de justice.* But Bailly asserted the importance of the National Assembly, writing that it "was not the parlement emanating from the king and subject to his authority as its creator." It was by implication a separate and equal part of the government. In any event, according to Bailly, with the calling of the Estates General the time of *lits de justice* had passed. Thus, according to Bailly, on 20 June the National Assembly adopted the role of the Estates General as being something like a parlement in that it had representative status and a legislative function, but also maintained the traditional position that the Estates General outranked the parlements.[24] After 20 June, the National Assembly had become a new kind of Estates General, one that confidently asserted its own importance and presumed to act in its own defense.

Still, the matter of how the National Assembly and the king related to each other had not been settled. The deputies had not openly discussed the question of whether or not the king had the right to suspend the Assembly, but Bailly thought the sense of the meeting was that it would be dangerous for

[21] Ménard de la Groye, *Correspondance,* 46–47.   [22] Tackett, *Becoming a Revolutionary,* 152.
[23] Creuzé-Latouche, *Journal,* 132.
[24] Bailly, *Mémoires d'un témoin,* 1: 183, 189. On the pretensions of the Parlement of Paris, see Stone, *French Parlements,* 118.

the king to have that right. Though they refused to be dissolved, they carefully kept from discussing the extent of the king's powers, and they refused to personally challenge him. We have seen this refusal to directly confront royal authority in the failure of Sieyès's attempt to move the National Assembly to Paris and of Le Chapelier's motion denouncing the authors of the scheme for a Royal Session. Despite the shock of being locked out of their meeting hall, the deputies were not yet ready to follow the lead of their radical colleagues and dramatically step up the level of confrontation. Even Bailly followed the trope of a good king badly advised, writing that in taking the oath, the Assembly had armed itself against despotism, but not against the king. He was certain that the oath of 20 June would prevent dissolution of the Estates General or even major changes on the Royal Council. After all, he reasoned, if its enemies could not prevent a meeting of the National Assembly in Versailles, then how could they prevent a meeting in Paris or elsewhere? One could arrest a few deputies, but where would one imprison 600?[25]

The deputies did not have plans to meet until after the Royal Session to be held on 22 June, but when the Crown announced that it would be delayed by a day, the National Assembly chose to meet. In some ways, the decision to meet on 22 June was more radical than the decision to meet on 20 June. While the deputies could plausibly claim that they had promised to meet on the 20th and had to keep that promise, their decision to gather on 22 June came after the king had suspended the meetings of the Estates General. The session of 22 June thus reinforced the declaration of 20 June, showing that it was up to the National Assembly to decide when and where it met. Having stated the principle, the deputies lived up to it in practice. Moreover, the deputies of the Clergy met as well on 22 June, showing that they too were willing to disobey the king's order.

In the middle of the night on 21 June, a royal herald had awakened Bailly and given him a note telling him that the Royal Session was postponed until the 23rd. Bailly had been surprised to see that the note said nothing about the Tennis Court Oath, and did not specifically prohibit the National Assembly from meeting again.[26] But when the deputies arrived at the common hall on 22 June, they found it still closed. On 19 June the Clergy had voted to verify their powers in common by a slight majority, and Bailly knew that they intended to meet with the Third Estate deputies for verification of their powers. The tennis court seemed both too small and lacking in dignity for such an important moment, so the National Assembly chose to meet in a larger space, the church of Saint-Louis, where

---

[25] Bailly, *Mémoires d'un témoin*, I: 189–91.   [26] Ibid., 197.

they had met for the *Te Deum* of 4 May. To make the meeting space in the church more welcoming to the Clergy, chairs were set out so the deputies would sit according to their orders and the meeting was opened. With tremendous joy the deputies of the National Assembly greeted the majority of the Clergy. The clergymen whose powers had already been verified led the way in welcoming their colleagues, and the credentials of the new deputies were sent to committee. Bailly welcomed the arriving deputies, noting that now those meeting in common not only had the majority of the deputies who had come to Versailles (Mounier's argument of quorum again) and the deputies who represented the vast majority of the French population (Sieyès's and Target's argument of "almost the totality"), but also now had the majority of the orders as well, with the First and Third Estates in attendance.[27] The triumph of the united orders seemed assured.

But before the National Assembly could declare victory, the deputies had to find out where the king stood. As day turned to night on 22 June, rumors multiplied. What came out of the king's mouth on 23 June would show who had won at Court and on the Royal Council. The Council had met two times to settle the details of the Royal Session after they had heard news of the Tennis Court Oath. Necker and other ministers worked to quash rumors that the Estates General was going to be dissolved, giving hope to those who wished for a triumph of the Third Estate.[28] There was hope that the king would impose a settlement, as Morris put it, arranging the Estates General in "such a Way as that they may act instead of being as present an useless Herd."[29] Nevertheless, Necker had been surprised on 21 June to see Artois and Provence at the Council meeting. Still, despite adding conservative voices to the Council, Louis did not make up his mind about what to do until late on the 22nd.[30] The rumors coming out of the royal chateau reflected Louis's indecision. On the morning of the 22nd it still seemed possible that the king's proposals would favor the Third Estate, but by that night it was understood that Artois and the queen had won.[31]

[27] Doyle, *Oxford History*, 2nd ed., 105. Bailly, *Mémoires d'un témoin*, 1: 191, 199–202; AP 8, 140–42; Mirabeau, *Douzieme lettre du comte de Mirabeau à ses commettans* (np, nd), 8–9.

[28] J.-B. Poncet-Delpech, "Documents sur les premiers mois de la Révolution," ed. Daniel Ligou, AHRF 38 (1966), 433; Morris, *Diary*, 1: 119; Lefebvre, *Recueil de Documents*, t.1, II: 181–85.

[29] Morris, *Diary*, 1: 118.

[30] Félix, *Louis XVI et Marie Antoinette*, 464–65. Ménard de la Groye reported seeing Necker leaving the council meeting of 21 June looking defeated, and thought that this meant Necker's advice had not been taken. Ménard worried that Necker's dismissal would soon follow. Ménard de la Groye, *Correspondance*, 48.

[31] Armand-Marc, count of Montmorin, and Saint-Priest had both been asked to submit memos to the king on 22 June, so Louis had probably not yet made up his mind. Lefebvre, *Recueil de Documents*,

Necker had been defeated, and with him the hopes of the Third Estate. The final proposal was too conservative by half.[32] Defeated in the Council and asked to support a plan he did not think could succeed, Necker decided to show his displeasure and not to attend the meeting of 23 June.

The deputies worried and hoped as they waited for the morning of 23 June. Though it seems unlikely that the deputies of the Third Estate slept well the night before, only Bailly left us a detailed record of his disrupted sleep. He went to bed early, exhausted by the events of the previous few days. He was awakened twice. First, Brézé sent a request asking Bailly to come see him at the royal chateau. When Bailly arrived, Brézé informed him that the king requested that he make no speech at the session, and said that the doyens of the other orders had already agreed not to speak. Bailly told Brézé that he had no intention of making a speech. At first glance this seems a puzzling exchange, and Bailly gives us no guidance in his memoirs on how to interpret it. In previous Estates General, it had been normal for the presidents of the orders to speak in joint sessions held before the king. But this was something different. To understand, we need only remember that Bailly had feared that the Royal Session would simply be a *lit de justice*. In the last Royal Session held by the king, that of 19 November 1787 before the Parlement of Paris, Louis had explained via his ministers what needed to be done in order to move France past the growing crisis in royal finance. Then the magistrates had been allowed to debate the king's proposals freely until it appeared that the platform satisfied the majority. But the meeting had unraveled when the king flatly stated that the platform had become law because he willed it.[33] By obliquely referring to this previous Royal Session and stating that the king did not wish for deputies to give any speeches, Brézé seemed to signal that in the presence of the king, the approval of the Estates General would not be necessary for the king's platform to become law. Given demands found in the vast majority of the *cahiers* that the king should share legislative power with the Estates General, this pretense was a non-starter. Bailly returned home to sleep, but a few hours later men shouted his name from the street outside. Bailly received them and found that they were deputies from the Noble order. They brought news that Necker had failed to rally the Royal Council behind his plans. They told Bailly that all indications were that the

t.i, II: 197–202. Morris heard from a noble acquaintance on 22 June that the Nobles would be the winners of the Royal Session. Morris, *Diary*, I: 120.

[32] Hardman, *Louis XVI* (1993), 150–53; and *Louis XVI: The Silent King* (2000), 103–04.

[33] Stone, *French Parlements*, 8–9; Doyle, *Oxford History*, 2nd ed., 79–82; Campbell, "Paris Parlement," 106–08.

king would dismiss Necker the next day.[34] Even the English traveler Arthur Young heard that Necker had been defeated, and he could hardly be better informed than the deputies themselves.[35] When the deputies arrived at the common hall the next day, most knew that the session would break against the National Assembly.

The weather on 23 June was perfect for the occasion. It was cool and rainy, weather to match the gloomy mood that had settled over the Third Estate. Nevertheless, the Third Estate had not expected the cold reception that awaited them. The deputies of the different orders were to enter the building through different doors and that of the Third Estate had only a modest antechamber. Most of the deputies found themselves left outside for hours in the rain while waiting to take their seats. This led to murmuring among the deputies and calls to leave given the poor treatment they were experiencing. Bailly struggled to keep a mutiny from breaking out. He repeatedly pounded on the door to the hall, asking the officer in charge to bring Brézé, but the officer reported that Brézé was nowhere to be found. Only when Bailly threatened that the Third Estate would leave if not seated did Brézé appear, stating that the delay had been caused by the unexpected death of one of the Secretaries of the King. He then invited the Third Estate to enter and take its seats. The death had not prevented the other orders from being seated. Bailly fumed, and wondered if the delay had been caused simply to prevent the men of the Third Estate from taking their seats before the upper orders had had a chance to sit.[36] Observers noted that when the deputies of the Third Estate entered the hall on 23 June they seemed to despair, entering silently and looking as if they were marching to the scaffold.[37] It was hardly an auspicious start.

Before the king opened the meeting it became apparent that Necker would not attend. Third Estate deputies worried that Necker had been dismissed.[38] After a few preliminaries, the king spoke. Louis briefly scolded the deputies for being unable to take the most preliminary actions during the two months since they had met. He stated that it was his duty as king to move them past this problem. His orders were then read out. They were

---

[34] Bailly, *Mémoires d'un témoin*, 1: 205–6.   [35] Young, *Travels in France*, 174.

[36] AP 8: 142; Bailly, *Mémoires d'un témoin*, 1: 207–08; Creuzé-Latouche, *Journal*, 137.

[37] Tackett, *Becoming a Revolutionary*, 153–54. See also Mirabeau, *Treizième lettre du comte de Mirabeau à ses commettans* (np, nd), 8.

[38] Bouchette, *Lettres*, 230–31; N.-J. Camusat de Belombre, "Le journal de Camusat de Belombre, député du Tiers de la ville de Troyes," ed. H. Diné, *AHRF* 37 (1965), 265. Rumor had it that Necker had been replaced by the prince of Conti, and the prince of Condé had been given control of the army. Both men were princes of the blood and notoriously opposed to the Third Estate. *Correspondance d'Anjou*, 1: 212.

almost everything the deputies of the National Assembly had feared. The king came out in favor of verification of credentials and voting by order. He quashed the actions of the Third Estate taken on 17 June as "illegal and unconstitutional." But Louis did not come down unequivocally in favor of a vote by order. He urged the deputies in the strongest terms to meet and vote in common on matters "of general utility" but not those "regarding ancient and constitutional rights of the three orders." The orders would keep their traditional vetoes, and Louis emphasized that the order of the Clergy would have to approve anything that had a bearing on religion or on the organization of the Catholic Church in France. Nevertheless, the use of the word "constitution" in the speech amounted to a major concession to changed circumstances. Louis also addressed the issue of binding mandates, which some deputies of the privileged orders claimed prohibited them from meeting or voting in common. He declared them, like the acts of the National Assembly, "illegal and unconstitutional." But the king recognized the sanctity of the oaths deputies had sworn and left it to them to ask their constituents to be released from these restrictions. Instead of ordering them to participate, he asked them to remain present and "to assist in all deliberations on the pressing affairs of state and to give consultative opinions."[39] These rules for the organization of the Estates General amounted to a near total victory for the conservative Noble and Clerical deputies. Articles 11 and 12 were particularly galling to the Third Estate: In these articles the king offered to recognize a necessary vote of 2/3 for matters deliberated in common, and the principle that any 100 deputies could demand that a matter once voted be opened for new deliberation on the following day. These rules gave a veto to the most recalcitrant deputies on any issue. Article 15 excluded the public from sessions.[40] The king had come down squarely against the National Assembly.

Having produced the stick, the king then brought out the carrot. He offered most of what the deputies had wanted and what the *cahiers* demanded, with the internal organization of the Estates General excepted. The king accepted that no new tax would be established without the consent of the nation's representatives and that all taxes would only be valid for the interval between meetings of the Estates General. The king

[39] AP 8: 143. In his account of the session, the Noble deputy Boniface-Louis-André, count of Castellane, focused on two portions of the speech: the quashing of the acts of the National Assembly and the quashing of all binding mandates. Castellane, Manuscript notes, BNF, Nouv. acq. fr. 4121, 45. Henceforth called "Journal." On the sanctity of the oaths the deputies had sworn, see Tackett, *Religion, Revolution and Regional Culture*, 17.

[40] AP 8: 144.

would not seek new loans without the approval of the Estates General. Emergency loans could be had given the need for the executive to act quickly, but only to the total of 100 million *livres*. The Estates General would be given all the information they required to make their decisions regarding finances. The king also promised to sanction the end of financial privilege if freely voted by the upper orders. But he insisted that all property would be protected, even that coming from privilege or from rights associated with titles or with noble land. He agreed to eliminate *lettres de cachet*, the arbitrary warrants used to detain people in France without trial or judicial hearing. He looked forward to freedom of the press, subject to limitations. In a nod to the pretensions of the Third Estate, he proposed to ensure that half of all deputies to provincial assemblies would be from the Third Estate, that their deliberations would be in common, and that they would be able to police their own affairs. He was even willing to do away with unpopular taxes as long as the changes were made with an eye to keeping revenue equal to expenditure. Importantly, in Article 29, the king stated that laws made during the sitting of the Estates General would be not be subject to parlementary remonstrances, meeting a goal found in the *cahiers* of the Nobles and Third Estate deputies alike that the Estates General would function as the guardian of the nation, not the parlements.[41] In short, leaving aside the important issues of internal organization and privilege, the offer the king made was an outstanding one, meeting with or exceeding the demands found in *cahiers* of the Nobles and the Third Estate and going far beyond the demands made by the Assembly of Notables in 1787.[42] But the king's new platform enshrined the dominance of the privileged orders. It did not satisfy the demands of the Third Estate that they have a meaningful role.

After his ministers had presented the platform on the king's behalf, Louis spoke again. By tone and phrasing he made it clear that adoption of the platform he announced was not optional. The deputies were expected to turn his declarations into positive laws. Noting that what had been read for him represented his real intentions, he said that,

> if, by a destiny far from my thoughts, you abandon me in such a beautiful enterprise, alone, I will do good for my people. Alone, I will consider myself their true representative; and knowing your *cahiers*, knowing the perfect accord that exists between the most general will of the nation and my

---

[41] Ibid., 144–45.
[42] Young thought that the plan was "a good one," giving to the people much of what they had wanted. He was surprised that the popular party rejected the king's offer. Young, *Travels in France*, 175–76.

beneficent intentions, I will have all the confidence that such rare harmony must inspire; and I will march toward the goal that I wish to attain with all the courage and firmness that it inspires.

The king made no bones about declaring that he could represent the nation without the assistance of the Estates General. To disobey him was to court disaster, as the king would simply dismiss them and carry out his plans. Moreover, they should have no thought of outflanking him. "Be sure to consider, my dear sirs, " the king said gravely, "that none of your projects, none of your arrangements can have the force of law without my special approval."[43] Though the king had made many concessions to the demands found in the *cahiers* of all three orders, he had refused to admit to one of the most important, the request that the Estates General become a necessary part of the legislative process and that by this the absolute monarchy become a constitutional one. Morris had written in February 1789 that the key question the French faced was whether they would have a proper constitution and the rule of law, or if the system would remain one of the king's will. The king had made it clear that he retained the final say. Even the constitution would be an act of his will.[44] The king ordered the deputies to leave immediately and go the next morning to their separate chambers to resume meeting. The king and his entourage then departed. The Nobles and most of the Clergy followed them out of the hall, but the members of the Third Estate and many curés stayed put.[45]

Left alone once again in the common hall, the deputies of the National Assembly began discussing what they should do. Mirabeau angrily asked what emergency justified the presence of so many soldiers in the streets of Versailles and around the meeting hall of the nation's representatives. Invoking a moment of existential crisis the ancient Roman Republic had faced in 68 BCE, certain to be familiar to the classically educated deputies, Mirabeau demanded to know if Catalina himself were at the gates, leading an army to overthrow the republic.[46] He then moved that the deputies renew their oath of 20 June never to separate until the constitution was

---

[43] AP 8: 146; Creuzé-Latouche, *Journal*, 140. This was no idle threat. Kings had implemented reforms on their own after the dismissal of Estates General and Assemblies of Notables in the sixteenth and seventeenth centuries. Collins, *State in Early Modern France*, 2nd ed., 56–57.

[44] Collins, *Tribes to Nation*, 543–44. Morris, *Diary*, xlii–iii.

[45] AP 8: 146. Many Noble deputies then went to the royal chateau where they thanked Artois for helping them retain their right to meet as an order. He received them graciously, as did the queen. Ferrières, *Mémoires*, 1: 59–60.

[46] On Mirabeau's use of classical references in general and use of the Catiline Conspiracy in particular, see R. H. Blackman, "Did Cicero Swear the Tennis Court Oath?" *FH* 28: 4 (December 2014), 471–97.

written and to meet wherever and whenever necessary. While Mirabeau spoke, Brézé walked up to Bailly and reminded him that the king had specifically ordered the deputies to leave the hall.[47] Bailly informed Brézé that Bailly could not dismiss the Assembly without allowing them to deliberate. Though truer to his sentiments, he did not wish to say to Brézé that the king could not order the Assembly to leave, because the "assembled nation cannot take orders." He later wrote that he had given a less than forthright response to Brézé out of respect for the king, knowing it would do no good to insult the king by stating such things too obviously.[48] But as Bailly tried to sort out Brézé, Mirabeau turned and reminded Brézé that he had no role in the National Assembly, telling him that if he intended to make the deputies leave, he would have to use force, that they would not leave until driven out by bayonets. The deputies cried out their assent, and Brézé retired. But after this brief confrontation with royal authority, a mournful silence hung over the Assembly, as if the deputies had suddenly become aware of the gravity of their actions.[49]

Though no soldiers entered the hall, bayonets fixed to drive the deputies out, workers did arrive to put the hall back into order so the Third Estate could meet on the following day. The workers made more than enough noise to disrupt the session.[50] Pison du Galand proposed that the deputies adjourn and return the next day to discuss the king's plan.[51] The Parisian deputy Armand-Gaston Camus proposed instead that the deputies declare that they persisted in all of the Assembly's previous decrees before leaving the hall. Someone yelled out that the deputies were in essence a national convention, sent to "renew, reform and complete the French constitution."[52] Sieyès and Barnave spoke in support of Camus's proposal, noting that the deputies were "sent by the nation," and were the "organs of its will to make a constitution," and that they needed to remain assembled "as long as . . . necessary in the interest of [their] constituents."[53]

[47] AP 8: 146.

[48] J.-B. Colaud de La Salcette, "Lettres de Colaud de la Salcette," *Bulletin de la Société départmentale d'archéologie et de statisque de la Drôme* 69 (1944), 143. Bailly, *Mémoires d'un témoin*, 1: 215.

[49] AP 8: 146. Bailly was upset that Mirabeau had spoken brusquely to Brézé. Mirabeau had no right to speak for the body as he was not its president, and in any case, Brézé had not mentioned bayonets. Bailly, *Mémoires d'un témoin*, 1: 215.

[50] Ferrières later claimed that the disruption was intentional, meant to force the Third Estate to end their meeting. Ferrières, *Mémoires*, 1: 58.

[51] Bailly, *Mémoires d'un témoin*, 1: 215–16. Duquesnoy, *Journal*, 1: 120. *Correspondance d'Anjou*, 1: 209. Pellerin reported that many other deputies made motions. Pellerin, "Journal," 37r.

[52] *Correspondance d'Anjou*, 1: 210.   [53] AP 8: 146.

Jacques-Marie Glezen, a deputy from Rennes, said what many must have been thinking when he compared the treatment the deputies had received to the way in which the king had treated his great law courts, calling the Royal Session a "*lit de justice* held in a National Assembly." Where the king had needed to consult with the deputies regarding the will of the nation, he had instead spoken as if he were their master. Glezen then emphasized that the king himself was not to blame and that the struggle against those who had misled the king had only just begun. The costs of the struggle would be high, he said: "Let the aristocrats triumph; they have only the one day: the prince will soon be enlightened. The grandeur of our courage will equal the grandeur of the circumstances . . . . You have taken, my dear sirs, wise deliberations; an act of authority must not frighten you." Returning to the motif Mirabeau had invoked of the enemy at the gates, Glezen reminded the deputies that they had to be ready to die for their country.[54]

Finally, Sieyès spoke, reminding the deputies whom they served:

> My dear sirs, however stormy the circumstances appear, we always have a light to guide us. Let us ask ourselves whose powers we exercise and what mission has brought us together from all parts of France. Do we hold our mandates only from the king? Are we officers of the king? Then we must obey and leave. But we are men sent by the people. Let us fulfill our mission freely, courageously.

His next words must have had additional impact given the clerical habit Sieyès wore. "We have sworn it, my dear fellows," he said, referring both to the oaths they had sworn to their constituents on becoming deputies and to the Tennis Court Oath, "and our oath will not be in vain. We have sworn to reestablish the French people in its rights . . . . Is there a power on earth who can prevent you from the right to represent your constituents?"[55] The deputies had sworn to be faithful to their mandates, and they had sworn the Tennis Court Oath. No ministerial platform could change those things. Their obligation was to represent the interests of their constituents, regardless of the consequences they faced. With a "majestic silence" and before forty or fifty witnesses, the deputies then voted unanimously to persist in their previous decrees. Mirabeau proposed that they vote the inviolability of the deputies to the National Assembly, a motion that carried 493–34. Bailly thought that there had never been a moment so

---

[54] Ibid. Jallet also characterized the king's effort as a *lit de justice*. Jallet, *Journal*, 97.

[55] AP 8: 146–47. Creuzé-Latouche reported a different version of the speech. Creuzé-Latouche, *Journal*, 143.

grand for the Assembly, in which it made a declaration "so simple, so precise, and at the same time so firm."[56] The National Assembly would not be cowed by the ministers.

In their accounts of the event, the deputies overwhelmingly interpreted the Royal Session as an attempt to establish ministerial despotism once and for all. Witnesses focused less on the proposals themselves, some of which were very much what the deputies wanted, and more on the language the king used. The king had said "I will," "I ordain," "it is my will" and "I forbid," when stating how the Estates General would meet and what the Estates General would consider. The king's words showed no commitment to the rule of law, only commitment to rule by the king's will, the very foundation of ministerial despotism. Mirabeau noted that the use of this language indicated a seizure of power by the throne without precedent. He wondered how it was that a king who had so recently "solemnly abjured despotism" could revert to such despotic usages and rituals.[57] Ferrières wrote that he found the repeated use of "I will" by the king distasteful.[58] Mounier wrote that many good things had been proposed, but "in forms which were not appropriate to freedom." Writing months later, he claimed the Royal Session "was certainly one of the principle causes that had led to anarchy" in France by lessening the respect the people had for the armed forces. What else could happen when the king used his soldiers to surround the hall and keep his people from seeing what happened inside?[59]

Creuzé-Latouche had been shocked by the event, writing in his diary that the king's plan to reform the Estates General was "the most bizarre and despotic and most contradictory of which history can furnish an example."[60] Duquesnoy, hardly one of the most radical men in the Assembly, wrote in his journal "that never had despotism expressed itself in more audacious terms, that never had slaves heard orders more imperious." He felt that the ministers who had written the royal proposal had failed to take into account "the men or the times." Whoever wrote it had no idea that "the moment of a great revolution had come, that one might slow it down or . . . give it another course, but that it would be impossible

---

[56] AP 8: 147. Bailly, *Mémoires d'un témoin*, 1: 216. Visme, "Journal," 52r. Jallet claimed that 100 curés had stayed behind when the king dismissed the orders, and so we may assume that most of the witnesses were men like these, deputies from the Clergy who had not yet had their powers verified and so could not vote. Jallet, *Journal*, 100.
[57] Mirabeau, *Treizième lettre*, 8, 2.   [58] Ferrières, *Mémoires*, 1: 58.
[59] Mounier, *Exposé*, 10–11. Young agreed. Young, *Travels in France*, 175.
[60] Creuzé-Latouche, *Journal*, 139.

to halt it."[61] They had certainly failed to take into account the clause in the mandates carried by so many deputies encouraging them to reject treatment meant to intimidate or degrade them. Far from scaring the deputies into obeying the king, the event had strengthened their courage and made them less likely to submit to any plan that dissolved the National Assembly.

The Royal Session had backfired. The meeting had pushed the deputies to make a "new act of sovereignty," as Bailly later put it. When they found that there was a clash between the king and the National Assembly regarding its powers, they decided the matter in their own favor.[62] Ferrières, no friend to the pretensions of the Third Estate, aptly described the consequences of the proceedings. The session "offered the odious appearance of a *lit de justice*," with the king "speaking above all as a despot who commands rather than as a monarch who discusses with representatives of the people the interests of a great nation." Far from establishing their control of the situation, the conservatives at Court had been far too timid and uncertain and "proved, by the lack of use that they made of force, that force, when one does not know how to use it, is a useless and even dangerous weapon, because it is a measure of weakness of character of those who deploy it without effect."[63] As the deputy Visme put it, "We were sent to treat with the monarch, to propose laws to him, and not for us to submit in slavery to the will of an arbitrary authority."[64] To "treat" with the king is very different from "pleading" with the king or "persuading" the king. This new Estates General, sitting as a National Assembly, was not the traditional body that had met under quasi-judicial circumstances in the sixteenth century, one in which the king sat on his "bed of justice," listened to the petitions of his subjects and dispensed justice.[65] The two representative bodies, the National Assembly and the king, were to meet as equals. This great revolution of 23 June involved the birth of an assembly coequal to the king, one that had adopted all of the constitutional pretensions of the parlements and more.

In their memoirs and letters, the deputies raged at the way in which they were treated. They declared that the National Assembly would not back down. The deputies referred again and again to the parallel between the Royal Session and attempts to discipline the parlements before the Estates General met. For us, it can be difficult to understand why they focused so

[61] Duquesnoy, *Journal*, 1: 120.   [62] Bailly, *Mémoires d'un témoin*, 1: 216.
[63] Ferrières, *Mémoires*, 1: 57–58.   [64] Visme, "Journal," 51r–51v.
[65] Major, *The Estates General of 1560*, 115–16.

much on this parallel. The most obvious contemporary point of comparison was with the Royal Session the king held with the Parlement of Paris on 19 November 1787, as we have mentioned.[66] In both sessions, the king sat before a body that in royal eyes had failed to function as circumstances required. In both, ministers had hammered out a platform that satisfied no one but seemed acceptable to those who mattered, the essence of a compromise. And the king enraged the members of both bodies with the language he used in his personal remarks. In 1787, Brienne's careful maneuvers had been undone when Louis plainly stated that the platform had passed into law because the king willed it. In 1789, the king's insistence on the efficacy of his will in creating a new system was intentional. A principle pertaining to the royal courts, that in the king's presence the body had no will other than that of the king, had been overlaid onto the workings of the Estates General. But the National Assembly was not about to accept this innovation given the insistence in *cahiers* that they establish some kind of constitutional monarchy.

In 1787, the Parlement of Paris had refused to adjourn after the king and his party left and proceeded to nullify the king's orders. They then moved on to issue a series of proclamations outlining their interpretation of the constitution of France in the winter and spring of 1788. Likewise, on 23 June, the deputies of the National Assembly refused to leave the hall and acted to nullify the king's order that they strike their own acts from the metaphorical books. In January of 1788, the Parlement of Paris had declared *lettres de cachet* illegal, making it clear that the king could not take arbitrary action against the magistrates without violating the constitution. Similarly, on 23 June, the deputies decreed their own inviolability, making it impossible for the government to legally imprison them for their defiance. They even created a crime of "lèse-majesté national" to describe acts that violated the rights of the nation as represented by its assembly.[67] But in neither case were these directed against the king himself or against monarchy *per se*. They were meant to break the grip of despotic ministers over the king.[68] That the ministers thought a tactic that had failed so spectacularly could succeed under even more trying circumstances reveals

---

[66] Doyle notes the similarity between the two events and uses it to highlight Louis's incompetence. Doyle, *Oxford History*, 2nd ed., 107. On the session of 19 November 1787 and subsequent attempts to outline the constitution, see Stone, *French Parlements*, 8–9; Doyle, *Oxford History*, 2nd ed., 79–82; Campbell, "Paris Parlement," 106–08; Félix, *Louis XVI et Marie Antoinette*, 424–28.

[67] Ménard de la Groye, *Correspondance*, 49.

[68] Creuzé-Latouche wrote that the vote on inviolability was a way to inspire "terror in the satellites of the agents of despotism." Creuzé-Latouche, *Journal*, 143.

just how desperate they were. In both cases, a Royal Session meant to shore up royal authority and end a crisis led only to further escalation of the conflict and a lessening of royal power.

Moreover, because the king had spoken in his own voice on the terms of the new settlement, the deputies had started reevaluating their relationship to the king. It was one thing to defy privileged deputies or royal ministers, but it was another to defy the king himself. They decided that the king had been fooled by his advisors rather than accepting that the king himself might be against them. During the debate after the meeting, several deputies had spoken, ruing that Louis had been deceived by the Court into making a tyrannical set of statements.[69] Mirabeau wrote in his newspaper that the king would never have supported such terrible ideas "if he had not been surrounded by aristocrats and ministers sworn to despotism." He could tell because there were ideas expressed that were "truly paternal" which were "constrained by formulas of tyranny." Since the king was known to have the good of the people in mind, the very terms the king used and demands he made were proof that Louis had not written the speech. It had been written by aristocrats in the name of the king.[70] But the deputies seemed to think everything would end well. All that remained was for the National Assembly to wait out its foes, to wait until the king became more enlightened and accepted them as fellow representatives of the nation. Without such a strange pageant of ministerial despotism, there would have been no need to starkly defy the king. They had shown that when the king and the deputies did not agree, it was not for the king to exercise his authority via a *lit de justice*. There would have to be some kind of discussion, some kind of compromise.

Given the refusal of the National Assembly to back down or modify its decrees, the Royal Session turned into an unmitigated disaster for the conservatives at Court. Necker had ostentatiously avoided the meeting, making it clear that the Council was split and giving hope to his supporters. The deputies of the National Assembly had refused to leave the hall, and the king had proved unwilling to use force. The attempt to cow the National Assembly and sideline Necker had failed. When Necker reappeared on 23 June, it was obvious that he had the support of public opinion. As Necker went to meet with the king a crowd of thousands escorted him. Marie-Antoinette saw that her party had lost, at least for the

[69] Ibid., 142.
[70] Mirabeau, *Treizième lettre*, 3. See also Creuzé-Latouche, *Journal*, 142. Though the deputies remained publicly committed to the king, some more privately criticized the king in terms they had never used before. Tackett, *Becoming a Revolutionary*, 154–55.

moment. She realized that without Necker's support, the king's platform was doomed. Worse, if Necker were to leave the Royal Council, public unhappiness could quickly turn into rebellion. When Necker reached the royal chateau, the queen intercepted him and urged him not to resign. Seeing that the political situation had changed, a confident Necker went in to see the king. We have no record of what was said during the meeting between Louis and Necker on that day. We do know that ministers in a nearby room heard the king lose his temper at one point, shouting that Necker wanted all of the credit for the sacrifices the king was making. Louis needed Necker to stay on and refused to accept Necker's offer to resign. Meant to reassert the king's authority, the Royal Session turned out to be a humiliating failure for the king and a triumph for Necker.[71]

One particularly negative consequence was the realization on the part of the king and queen that they were dangerously dependent on Necker. The king and his advisors recognized the danger and started taking measures to strengthen the king's position. On the 22nd, Louis had signed orders bringing more troops into the region, and at a meeting of the Royal Council following the Royal Session the decision was made to bring in even more. Steps had to be taken to defend Paris and Versailles from public disorder, not least to ensure the king's safety should he need to break with Necker. Though perhaps necessary to protect the king's freedom of action, the presence of ever more troops in and around Versailles escalated tensions between the Crown and the National Assembly.[72] The deputies had been offended by the presence of troops in the streets and around their meeting hall. How could increasing the number of troops do anything but further antagonize them? Moreover, the arrival of more troops only seemed to make public disorder worse.

There was no sign on 24 June that the king intended to give in. The deputies returned to the *Hôtel des menus plaisirs* on 24 June to find their halls ready but guarded by soldiers who had orders to keep the public out and separate the deputies by order. Certainly the presence of troops was meant to remind the deputies of the king's authority and enforce his commands. This angered the deputies of the Third Estate. Once their meeting began, Mounier declared that the Assembly was responsible for its own security and argued that there was no free deliberation in the presence of armed men.[73] Before the deputies could discuss Mounier's vigorous

[71] Hardman, *Louis XVI* (1993), 153–55; Price, *Road from Versailles*, 68–69. Bailly, *Mémoires d'un témoin*, I: 223; Ferrières, *Mémoires*, I: 61–62; Morris, *Diary*, 121.
[72] Price, *Road from Versailles*, 70–71.
[73] *Correspondance d'Anjou*, I: 229–33. Bailly, *Mémoires d'un témoin*, I: 227; Duquesnoy, *Journal*, I: 124; Visme, "Journal," 53r; AP 8: 148.

challenge to royal authority, a large group of Clergy arrived. Far from barring the Clergy from entering the hall, the soldiers had led them to an unguarded passage so the men could enter unseen. The deputies of the Third Estate were heartened by the appearance of the majority of the Clergy and immediately arranged for their colleagues to take part.[74] Elation in the National Assembly redoubled on 25 June with the arrival of forty-seven deputies defecting from the Noble chamber, including a prince of the blood, Louis-Philippe, the duke of Orléans. Though Trophime-Gérard Lally-Tollendal announced that his mandate prevented him from participating in a formal union of the orders, he, like the rest, had come to verify his credentials in common.[75] A strong majority of deputies to the Estates General was now present in the common hall. Duquesnoy wrote in his journal that at this point full union of the orders was inevitable. As he noted, it was no longer a matter of finely balancing the constitution or calculating what each person's rights were. It was a matter of saving the state, preventing a looming disaster and "reaffirming royal authority" after the "infernal" meeting of 23 June.[76] For the moment, the remaining minority of the Clergy and the majority of the Nobles continued to meet separately, but there was no question that the National Assembly had established the common hall as the place in which the active body of the Estates General met. As if to confirm this development, on 25 and 26 June more deputies from the upper orders arrived singly or in small groups.

The meetings of the Assembly happened with a background rumble of popular unrest, a kind of *basso continuo* for their deliberations. On 24 June, a large crowd gathered outside of the *Hôtel des menus plaisirs*, even though no one was allowed to enter the main hall. After the meeting of the rump Clergy broke up, the crowd harassed several of the deputies as they left, booing and mobbing the archbishop of Paris. The French Guards moved quickly to protect him, but it was clear that the common soldiers sympathized with the crowd. The incident caused considerable distress to the privileged deputies. Ferrières worried that the mob planned to target the recalcitrant Nobles and Clergy, and reported to his wife the rumor that marks were being put on the doors of the men to be killed, an action reminiscent of the Saint Bartholomew's Day Massacre.[77] On 25 June, the crowd had again gathered outside the main hall. After word reached them

---

[74] Tackett, *Becoming a Revolutionary*, 156. Bailly, *Mémoires d'un témoin*, 1: 223–24.

[75] Lally-Tollendal, "Déclaration à l'Assemblée," 60–61.   [76] Duquesnoy, *Journal*, 1: 131.

[77] Bailly, *Mémoires d'un témoin*, 1: 229–30. Ferrières, *Mémoires*, 1: 44. See also Poncet-Delpech, "Documents sur les premiers mois de la Révolution," 435; Colaud de la Salcette, "Lettres," 143;

that some Noble deputies had entered the hall, a group forced the door and attempted to come in. Alerted by the guard, Bailly and the leaders of the Clergy and Nobles went to the entryway and dissuaded the crowd from entering the hall against the king's orders. After a few tense moments, the intruders agreed to step back outside.[78] Though the National Assembly believed it had the right to determine its own rules of order, its leaders encouraged the crowd to obey the king's command and remain outside the hall. Bailly later noted the wisdom of the Assembly in believing that when there was a dispute between the king and the Assembly over how the Assembly was being treated, it was not up to the people to adjudicate it. The Assembly did not want the people to lose their respect for the forces of order.[79] Far from riling up the crowd to force a victory upon the king, the deputies did what they could to maintain public order and deference to royal authority.

Then, on 27 June, the king seemed to come over to the side of the Third Estate. Undoubtedly persuaded by the public support the deputies had in Versailles and Paris and by concern with rising levels of public disorder, Marie-Antoinette convinced the king of the futility of resisting the union of the orders. Louis invited by letter the conservative Noble and Clerical deputies to join with the Third Estate in the common hall. Even then a hard core of recalcitrants resisted. Ferrières described the tumultuous meeting of the Nobles and the rump Clergy in his memoirs. Several deputies had spoken forcefully in favor of joining the Third Estate and others disagreed "with more vehemence than judgment." It was only with a second letter, written by Artois, stating that the lives of the king and his family were in danger that the mood of the room shifted. Anne-Charles Sigismond, the duke of Montmorency-Luxembourg and president of the Noble order, rose and said, "It is not a question of debate, it is a question of saving the king and the *patrie*. The person of the king is in danger. Which of us would dare to hesitate even one instant?" The deputies rose quickly as a body and followed their president out of the hall.[80] The enemies of the National Assembly were in full retreat. Though Louis continued to address them as the

---

and the letter of G. Romme to Dubreuil and to Boirat, 23 June and following days), in A. Galante Garonne, *Gilbert Romme* (Paris, 1971), 420.

[78] AP 8: 155; Visme, "Journal," 55v; Colaud de La Salcette, "Lettres," 144.

[79] Bailly, *Mémoires d'un témoin*, 1: 233–34.

[80] Ferrières, *Mémoires*, 1: 47–48; C.-E. Ferrières-Marçay, *Correspondance inédite (1789, 1790, 1791)*, ed. H. Carré (Paris, 1932), 76–77; Duquesnoy, *Journal*, 1: 139–40; R.-A. de Banyuls de Monferré, in J. Capeille, *Histoire de la maison des chaveliers de Banyuls de Montferré* (Céret, 1923), 455. Hardman, *Louis XVI* (1993), 153–55; Price, *The Road from Versailles*, 68–69.

"Third Estate" in his correspondence, the deputies reasonably assumed that Louis had accepted the existence of the National Assembly.

When news reached the Assembly that Louis had asked the privileged deputies to join them, the deputies decided to keep their session open as long as necessary for the hold-outs to arrive. When the last of the recalcitrants finally arrived, late in the day, they appeared defiant, sorrowful and angry. Ferrières remembered that they had entered the hall in silence. The triumph of the Third Estate and their liberal allies from the upper orders had come at last. But the deputies of the National Assembly were resolved to make the newcomers feel welcome.[81] It was not yet clear how the newly united deputies would organize themselves. When a member of the Clergy urged the leader of his order to end the session so that they could go and dine, Bailly interrupted, noting that the cardinal of La Rochefoucauld was not the president of the Assembly and could not end the session. He stated that deputies were free to come and go individually as they pleased, but he stuck to the point of protocol in order to emphasize that the National Assembly was a body with its own rules. Nevertheless, Bailly realized that pushing too hard on this point would be counterproductive. He worried that the deputies were indeed hungry and that sticking too strictly to a point of order might undo the joy that the arrival of the privileged deputies had triggered. He decided it would be wise to declare it a festival day and end the session, giving the deputies two days off to celebrate the union of the orders in the national hall. He set the next meeting for 30 June and adjourned the session. Before the next session, Bailly would meet with the doyens of the other orders and establish his own authority as president.[82] As Duquesnoy put it in his journal, no order or body had ever made sacrifices as "grand and magnanimous" as had the Nobles that day by coming to the common hall. By yielding, they had covered their order in "immortal glory" and had saved the king and the state.[83] It was a spectacular victory for the Third Estate.

Arthur Young realized that this was a spectacular defeat for the king. He wrote in his diary that "The whole business now seems over, and the revolution complete. The king has been frightened by the mobs into overturning his own act of the *seance royale* [sic]." Young claimed that the decision was taken from fear of popular disorder spreading throughout France, "that all sorts of misery and confusion would follow his adherence

---

[81] Ferrières, *Mémoires*, I: 48. Tackett, *Becoming a Revolutionary*, 158.
[82] AP 8: 168–69; Bailly, *Mémoires d'un témoin*, I: 252–53.   [83] Duquesnoy, *Journal* I: 139.

to the system announced in the *seance royale* [sic]."[84] After the deputies left the hall, a huge crowd gathered in the courtyard of the royal chateau. People of all kinds – deputies, priests, nobles, officers, soldiers, women and men – called out for the king and queen. When Louis and Marie-Antoinette appeared (with the queen in a simple white dress), they were greeted with tremendous cheers and cries of "Long live the king!" and "Long live the queen!" The crowd asked to see the dauphin and cheered him as well. The crowd then visited Necker's house, and next visited Bailly at home.[85] The symbolism of this movement by the crowd was hard to miss. The king's approval was most important of all, but Necker and Bailly were visited as well. The people gathered in Versailles, coming from every class and position, recognized that their representatives were the king, his chosen minister, and the National Assembly. The king remained the most important figure, but he no longer ruled alone. The victory of the National Assembly over its conservative opponents appeared complete.

Looking back on what the deputies had accomplished during the period 10–27 June, Bailly claimed that they had established the sovereignty of the nation. It had taken a series of steps, though, first establishing that the deputies in the common hall could invite those absent to attend, then constituting the National Assembly, then securing the national debt and provisionally accepting existing taxes. Faced with opposition from the Crown, they had to take further steps. When the king attempted to suspend the Estates General on 20 June, the deputies declared that they would meet as and where necessary to establish a constitution. On 23 June they had defied the king's order to disperse and declared the inviolability of the deputies. They had done this, Bailly wrote, to secure their role in national governance against the vetoes of the privileged orders and the plots of despotic ministers. But more important was the fact that this transformation had occurred without an uprising and without shedding blood. Theirs had been a peaceful revolution.[86] Rather conspicuously, Bailly did not state that they had established national power against the authority of the king. While they were not to be lectured to or commanded by the king, they were not his masters, either. The king and the elected deputies together represented the sovereign nation. While this was

---

[84] Young, *Travels in France*, 182–83.
[85] Alquier, *Un témoin de la Révolution*, 35; Jallet, *Journal*, 108; *Correspondance d'Anjou*, 1: 255; Bailly, *Mémoires d'un témoin*, 1: 253.
[86] Bailly, *Mémoires d'un témoin*, 1: 254. Félix refers to the events of 27 June as the end of a French version of the English Glorious Revolution. Félix, *Louis XVI et Marie Antoinette*, 470.

a revolutionary transformation of the locus of sovereignty in France, the ability to act on this sovereign power had not been placed entirely in the National Assembly.

The great historian Georges Lefebvre long ago recognized the limitations of the demands the National Assembly had made in June. He argued that the Third Estate had tended more toward the thought of Mirabeau, an ardent monarchist, than to that of the more radical Sieyès, thinking that sovereignty was to be shared in equal measure by the king and the Assembly. As the deputies assumed a major role in the new system, they did not yet question the need of the king's approval of the constitution or laws, nor did they see themselves as somehow superior to the monarch. Moreover, the system of orders was not attacked, only the notion that the different estates could sit and vote separately. Democracy was not pursued: the tiniest slice of the French people continued to hold half the votes in the new Assembly.[87] Lefebvre here overstates the case somewhat. As we saw in Chapter 1, the elections to the Third Estate had involved men (and some women) from the level of the local parish on up.[88] The Clergy had elected curés from a Third Estate background in unprecedented numbers as deputies. Still, the deputies of noble if not aristocratic background had retained their right to sit as Noble and Clerical deputies and still held more than a third of the seats. Most important, though, was the continuing faith the deputies had in their king. Though their belief in the king's good will had been shaken by the Royal Session of 23 June, it would take further events to push the deputies to limit the king's role in approving the constitution to a simple yes or no decision and to deny him initiative in making the laws.

Though the actions of the deputies in defying the king's order to disperse were certainly dramatic, we ought to hesitate before declaring them unprecedented acts of revolutionary defiance. In declaring their right to sit and to meet and their legislative powers, the deputies were following down the path established in the eighteenth century by the sovereign courts. The difference in June 1789 was that the deputies appeared to have won. The king had regularly quashed the rebellions of his great law courts, exiling the magistrates,

---

[87] Lefebvre, *Coming of the French Revolution*, 86.

[88] Inclusion of the peasantry in the Third Estate meant that millions more men participated in the elections to the Estates General than ever before. Collins, *From Tribes to Nation*, 537. Edelstein argues that despite the large numbers involved, the elections were done on a corporate basis and were not very democratic. Nevertheless, women were not excluded by law from the lowest level of the Third Estate franchise. Edelstein, *Birth of Electoral Democracy*, 16–17. Robin notes the participation of women at the parish level in the Third Estate in Burgundy. Robin, *La societé française en 1789*, 349. Patrice Gueniffey emphasizes the lack of democratic practices in the elections of 1789. Gueniffey, *Le nombre et la raison*, 34–36.

arresting the ringleaders and even on occasion remodeling the courts themselves. In the eighteenth century, the parlements had gradually ratcheted up their constitutional pretensions but they never triumphed over the king. But the actions Louis took in the days after 23 June implied that the king recognized the power and pretensions of the Third Estate, so much so that the historian François Furet called the king's decision to order the estates to meet in common the end of the absolute monarchy.[89] As we have seen, though, the Old Regime had passed as a practical administrative body when Brienne recognized the necessity of courting public opinion in May 1787. Nonetheless, after 23 June the absolute monarchy ceased to exist as a legal entity. Having lain in state for two years, the corpse was finally buried. It remained to be seen how the newly constituted National Assembly and the traditional monarch would work together and divide power in a constitutional monarchy.

The recalcitrant elites had decisively lost their fight to establish themselves as a major political force in a new constitutional order. Since 1787, it had looked possible for the men of the parlements and of the great families to have a kind of influence that the nobles had never enjoyed in France. At first, their defiance made them into heroes, but it also triggered Calonne's attempt to increase the political power the Third Estate. Though Calonne's attempt to use the Third Estate as a counterweight to noble ambitions had been a complete failure in 1787, by early 1789 the leaders of the Third Estate had become determined to keep the privileged elites from dominating politics. Two months of stalemate simply made the Third Estate and their allies more determined to carve out a meaningful political. By 27 June, the privileged elites had lost some of their prestige and had agreed to the loss of their fiscal privileges, though the details remained to be worked out. They had also lost their bid to dominate the Estates General. Given rising levels of social resentment, the elites risked much more if they tried to obstruct the work of a body that had shown it could function without their full participation.[90]

The deputies of the Third Estate and their liberal allies had established the union of the orders and were ready to begin work. As Morris wrote in his diary, after 27 June "It only remains to form a Constitution," since the king was likely to agree to whatever the National Assembly proposed.[91] While the deputies enjoyed their two-day break, they knew that the Assembly faced serious, immediate problems. There was continuing public

[89] Furet, *Revolutionary France*, 65.   [90] Doyle, *Aristocracy and Its Enemies*, 202–03.
[91] Morris, *Diary*, 1: 125.

unrest in Paris and Versailles and deterioration in the morale of the French Guards. The king's response to the unrest had been to order more troops into the region and ask the privileged deputies to meet in common with the Third Estate. In their response to the unrest, the deputies of the National Assembly pushed forward with a plan that became their main strategy, setting to work on a constitution that would create an orderly and reliable system of government. A new structure of government would allow the National Assembly and the king to address France's many problems. As a first step, they would tamp down unrest by emphasizing the competence of the new system, by creating a patriotic union of the deputies, by working with the king and with Necker. Then they would ensure that the new system persisted by writing a constitution outlining the powers of the government. But for any of this to happen, there had to be public order. Mirabeau had argued in the aftermath of 27 June that the best way to prevent or stop the convulsions of the people was the have their representatives make it as clear as possible that they cared for the rights of the people and their interests. As he put it, "bayonets only ever establish the peace of terror and the silence that pleases despotism." In order to establish real peace, the deputies had to apply the "balm" of hope and the "power of persuasion and reason." The "tranquility" of the National Assembly would provide the foundation for a peaceful France.[92]

Faced with the ongoing financial crisis and continuing popular disorder, it seemed more important than ever that the Assembly get to work. Then, to the surprise of the reforming deputies, a new roadblock appeared. On 30 June, at the first full meeting of the National Assembly with all deputies present, over 100 deputies protested against the acts of the Assembly and declared that they would not be able to participate until new orders from their constituents arrived, releasing them from their binding mandates not to sit in common or vote by head. A hard core of Nobles and Clergy continued to have separate meetings by order and showed no sign of accepting the existence of the National Assembly.[93] At the very least, it appeared that a new delay was at hand. Something had to be done to encourage the recalcitrant deputies to participate. Something had to be done to keep them from delaying the actions of the Assembly and from inflaming public opinion. If their mandates prohibited them from participating fully in the National Assembly, then perhaps the ancient system of mandates had to be reconsidered.

---

[92] Mirabeau, *Quatorzième lettre*, 16–17. See also Bailly, *Mémoires d'un témoine*, 1: 244–45.

[93] Tackett, *Becoming a Revolutionary*, 158–62. In this, they obeyed the desires of their own constituents much as the Third Estate deputies had by demanding meetings in common and the vote by head.

CHAPTER 4

The King Resists

27 June had marked a triumph for those who supported a union of the orders. The stalemate finally broken, it was time to write a constitution and help the king repair his finances. Then, on 30 June, at the first full meeting of the united orders, scores of deputies protested against the activities of the National Assembly. To a man these deputies, all from the privileged orders, claimed that instructions from their constituents prohibited them meeting in common with the other orders or accepting a vote by head. They based their protests on the mandates they had received from their electors. Almost all of the deputies of 1789 had sworn an oath upon receiving the *cahier* of his electoral district to faithfully present the grievances contained within. In most cases, they had sworn an oath to obey certain commands their electors made on pain of being, at least in theory, disowned as a representative. This was the "binding" or "imperative" mandate. The deputies who claimed a binding mandate against meeting as a union of orders would not easily surrender their supposed right to meet separately and the ability of their order to veto any action that involved its privileges. Their vehement protests derailed the session and seemed to have, as one deputy put it, "no other object than to suspend the activities of the Estates General."[1] The protests led immediately to discussion of how the National Assembly should handle deputy attacks on its legitimacy and the legitimacy of its decrees. The deputies had to decide to what extent the binding mandates held by individual deputies would affect the workings of the Assembly as a whole.

The electoral regulations of 24 January 1789 had specified that each deputy be given a mandate "general and sufficient to propose, discuss, advise and consent to all that may concern the needs of the State, the reform of abuses, the establishment of a fixed and durable order in all parts of the administration."[2] Accompanying regulations emphasized that the

---

[1] Ménard de la Groye, *Correspondance*, 55.
[2] *Lettre du roi pour la convocation des États généraux*, AP 1: 543.

deputies must be given "no specific instructions to halt or disturb the course of deliberations."[3] Electoral assemblies from all three orders artfully or boldly refused to comply with the king's instructions.[4] In addition to the "general" mandate required of each deputy by the Crown, electoral assemblies often gave more direct instructions to their deputies in the form of a "special" mandate, which put emphasis on a specific task, but stopped short of disowning a deputy who found that circumstances prevented carrying out the electors' wishes. Many electoral bodies also gave their deputy a binding mandate.[5] The electoral assemblies did not see the three kinds of mandates as mutually exclusive: two or three kinds generally appeared in the same document. Technically speaking, any mandate that deviated from the electoral regulations was invalid. But the Crown at first did nothing to stop improperly restrictive mandates from interfering with the workings of the Estates General.

The trouble binding mandates caused was clear to all concerned. As we have seen, stubborn adherence to the wishes of their constituents about how the Estates General would meet had led deputies from the Third and Second Estates into a long stalemate in May and June. Imperative demands in their *cahiers* had pushed the deputies of the Third Estate, with a handful of Clerical allies, to form the National Assembly on 17 June. At the Royal Session of 23 June, Louis XVI had declared binding mandates invalid and ordered the deputies to seek new powers from their electors that conformed to the electoral regulations of 24 January.[6] After the meeting, many deputies from the privileged orders set about getting their powers revised to conform to the king's wishes. Deputies from the Third Estate did not. During their debate over how to react to the king's declaration, Sieyès had focused in on the mandates the deputies had received as a reason to disobey the king's order that they leave the hall immediately and resume meetings separated by order the following day. Sieyès had made entirely traditional arguments about the function of the mandates the deputies had received. He claimed that the deputies derived their legitimacy as representatives from the mandates given to them by their constituents. Since they had received those mandates from their electors, they were duty-bound to execute their will as expressed in the

---

[3] *Réglement fait par le roi,* AP 1: 544, 549.   [4] Brette, "Les cahiers de 1789," 123–39.

[5] On the nature of the mandates, see Hyslop, *Guide,* 99–100.

[6] AP 8: 143–44. The king's demand that the deputies seek new powers had ample precedent in previous meetings of the Estates General. For an example of deputies seeking new powers, see the letter of Banyuls de Montferré and Coma Serra to their constituents. In Capeille, *Histoire de la maison des chaveliers de Banyuls de Montferré,* 453.

cahiers, not the will of the king as expressed in his declaration. Sieyès had denied that the king could interfere in the relationship the deputies had with their electors. Following his speech, the deputies had voted to affirm their declaration of a National Assembly and their oath of 20 June not to disperse until a constitution had been established on a firm foundation.[7] They did not, however, further define what rights and responsibilities their status as mandate holders granted them.

Disputes over the meaning of deputy mandates were almost as old as the institution itself. In the earliest meetings of the Estates General, the deputies had been required by their mandates to refer back to their constituents for permission to take any action not approved in their *cahiers*. In the sixteenth century, this had changed. At the Estates General of 1560, deputies begged off approving new taxes on the grounds that their constituents had not explicitly authorized them to do so. In the end, they did grant a tax meant to end in a short period of time. Disappointed with the outcome, the queen mother then summoned a second meeting, requesting in the order of convocation that the deputies be given powers sufficient to debate and approve proposals made by the king. This meeting, held in 1561, had been quite unusual, with one deputy summoned from each order in thirteen broad governing districts, the *gouvernements*. After that meeting, royal letters convoking the Estates General always specified a general mandate to debate and approve the king's platform. Nevertheless, the electors continued to give the deputies specific orders requiring them to support some actions and refuse others. These special mandates were never meant to stop the Estates General from functioning, and they were always subject to the will of the majority within each order. Time immemorial had hallowed the practices of negotiation and of voting to determine what measures would be included in the final *cahier* or *cahiers* presented to the king. In fact, deputies had long made formal protests when the will of the majority did not match the demands found in an individual deputy's *cahier*. But these protests had never been meant to impugn the legitimacy of the Estates General and they never led to the exemption of that minority from the binding will of the majority.[8]

---

[7] AP 8: 146–47. On the question of whether "fixing" a constitution meant framing a new one or restoring an old one, see Baker, "Fixing the French Constitution," in Baker, *Inventing the French Revolution*, 252–305.

[8] In this paragraph, we rely on R. Carré de Malberg, *Contribution à la Théorie générale de l'État*, 2 vols. (Paris, 1920–22), vol. 2: 247–52; Brette, "Les cahiers de 1789"; Major, *Estates General of 1560*, 57, 105; Major, *Representative Government in Early Modern France*; J. R. Major, *Representative Institutions in Renaissance France, 1421–1559* (Madison, 1960); Collins, "Noble Political Ideology and the Estates

The deputies sorted out what impact binding mandates would have on the activities of the National Assembly in debates held on 3, 7, and 8 July. To prevent another stalemate from developing in the Assembly as recalcitrant deputies made protests, issued reservations, demanded the perpetuation of meetings by order, and proclaimed the right of their order to veto actions of the assembly, Charles Maurice de Talleyrand-Périgord, bishop of Autun and deputy to the Clergy, proposed on 3 July that the Assembly declare some mandates void and decree that no mandate could halt the activities of the Assembly. The matter was taken up again on 7 July in a much broader and sustained debate and finally resolved on 8 July, when the Assembly adopted Sieyès's motion declaring that deputies who refused to participate because of their mandates would be considered as absent. His motion also declared that since the Assembly had no interest in the relationship between individual deputies and their electors, they would do nothing to regulate or repeal existing mandates. In effect, this was a compromise action that allowed the National Assembly to remain active while admitting that individual deputy mandates existed and that the deputies were bound to obey them.

Historians have incorrectly claimed that the debates of early July 1789 led to the nullification of the binding mandates and a declaration that the deputies were no longer bound to consider the wishes of their constituents or the content of their *cahiers* when legislating or writing the constitution. Interpretations of the debates have differed over what the effect of this supposed nullification was, rather than whether or not it actually happened. The main division has been between those who see the nullification of the mandates as evidence that the deputies had adopted a radical and exclusive definition of political representation and those who see the move as one more sign that moderates had taken up the leadership of the National Assembly and were working toward a system that would function despite pressures put on it from the right and the left alike.[9] But as we shall see, the deputies never voted to sever their traditional ties to their electors. Instead, they decided that the bonds between an individual deputy and his electors were not the business of the National Assembly, and that no

General of Orléans and Pontoise," 219–40; Collins, *From Tribes to Nation*, 266–70; Hayden, *Estates General*; Friedland, *Political Actors*, 32–38.

[9] On this historiographical question, see Kates, *The French Revolution*, 1–14; Hanson, *Contesting the French Revolution*; Campbell, "The Origins of the French Revolution in Focus," and Linton, "The Intellectual Origins of the French Revolution," in Campbell, ed., *Origins of the French Revolution*, 1–34, 139–59. See also C. Jones, "Bourgeois Revolution Revivified: 1789 and Social Change," in C. Lucas, ed., *The French Revolution and Social Change* (Oxford, 1990), 69–118.

individual deputy or minority faction of the Assembly could halt its workings through their protests, reservations, or absence. This decision amounted to a victory for the more moderate deputies who had pursued the union of the orders. It represented a defeat both for conservative deputies who sought a return to a vote by order and radical deputies who demanded that deputies bound by mandates ignore those mandates and participate as if they had never received them.[10]

When interpreting the larger meaning of the debate over mandates, historians have long relied on the speeches of Talleyrand, Sieyès, and others as found in the *Archives Parlementaires*. However, as we have seen, this source is incomplete and gives a misleading view of what was said during the early debates of the French Revolution. Placing deputy speeches into a context derived from the larger give-and-take of debate is crucial to seeing that the early Revolution was dominated by a moderate, not radical, conception of how the National Assembly would function. Broadening our sources to include the letters and memoirs of many deputies, as well as contemporary newspaper accounts, allows us to see how the deputies continued to value the links they had to their individual constituencies and how moderate and even radical deputies saw their mandates as a long hallowed and traditional way of defending the interests of their constituencies from interference by the Crown.[11]

Things did not start well on 30 June, the date set for the first meeting of the union of orders sitting as a National Assembly. Many deputies from the privileged orders failed to appear for the 10:00am opening of the session. Bailly opted to wait for them and did not call the meeting to order for more than an hour. Even then, Bailly avoided moving on to serious business and instead read letters from various cities declaring their support for the actions of the Assembly. At 11:30am the missing deputies appeared, led by the former doyens of their orders. After they took their places, Bailly invited them to deposit their credentials at the secretaries' desk. This request was met with declarations on the part of many deputies that they could not deliberate in a body of the three orders united until they had received new powers from their constituents. More than 100 deputies deposited written protests and statements of their reservations along with

---

[10] For a discussion of the mandates in context of longer term constitutional development, see Carré de Malberg, *Contribution*, 2: 247–64.

[11] Our survey of the debates on 3, 7 and 8 July shows that at least 31 deputies contributed to a greater or lesser extent, of whom 27 can be identified by name. For a list, see R. H. Blackman, "What Does a Deputy to the National Assembly Owe His Constituents? Coming to an Agreement on the Meaning of Electoral Mandates in 1789." *FHS* 34:2 (Spring 2011), Appendix I.

their credentials, and more than forty spoke out as they did so.[12] Their statements broadly fell into one of two types, the first recognizing the National Assembly but stating that they could not currently vote, and the second rejecting its legitimacy and demanding adherence to the king's platform of 23 June.[13] In the first group, deputies stated that they were subject to the terms of binding mandates not to meet in common or vote by head and that they had to wait until they had received new powers in order to participate fully. These deputies acted in grudging obedience to the king's order from 23 June that deputies bound not to vote by head or in common seek new powers.[14] Some of these men stated that they would participate with a consultative voice as the king had requested.[15] Others from this group, like the count of Sérent, deputy to the Nobles from Nivernais, said that they would have to leave the Assembly in order to seek new powers but that they would trust the Assembly to act wisely while they were gone.[16] In the second group, deputies sought to halt the activity of the National Assembly, probably in the hopes of engineering a return to separate meetings by order.[17] They refused to accept the legitimacy of the Assembly at all, protesting in advance against any actions it took while the deputies awaited new powers and promising to issue reservations against these actions.[18] Some of these deputies went further and claimed that the constitution required that the orders meet separately and vote by order. These deputies recognized that the Estates General would have to meet in common for items of common interest, making it clear that they would adhere to the king's platform of 23 June. But they demanded the right to meet by order for things that related to the privileges of their order or to

[12] Charles-Alexis Brulart de Sillery counted forty-four protests read out from the podium before a motion was made to stop them. The protests and discussion of them took up the whole session from 11:30am until 3:00pm, when they broke up to meet in bureaus. Brulart de Sillery, Ms. "Journal des Etats généraux," AN KK 641–43: 267. The AP lists protests and reservations from 135 deputies left at the bureau on the day. AP 8: 173–75.

[13] Duquesnoy, *Journal*, 1: 142. Visme, "Journal," 61r.

[14] On 27 June, "there was an order in council . . . declaring that imperative mandates were null and void and that new mandates must be sought." New assemblies were convoked to grant these powers. Hyslop, *Guide*, 101–02. Friedland claims the order in council was not made public until 30 June. Friedland, *Political Actors*, n 24 p. 146 (note appears on page 322).

[15] See the statement of Le Peletier de Saint-Fargeau, Noble deputy from Paris, and that of the deputies from Amiens, AP 8: 172–73.

[16] AP 8: 172; Creuzé-Latouche, *Journal*, 168.

[17] Ménard de la Groye feared that this was the point of all the protests. Ménard de la Groye, *Correspondance*, 55. See also Creuzé-Latouche, *Journal*, 168–72.

[18] See the protest of the deputation from Poitou or the statement of the baron of Montagu, AP 8: 172; protest of the deputies of the Nobles from Roussillon, in Capeille, *Histoire de la maison des chaveliers de Banyuls de Montferré*, 457. For the Poitou protest, see Jallet, *Journal*, 109. Creuzé-Latouche, *Journal*, 167.

constitutional matters. They announced that since their powers prohibited them from meeting or voting in common, they would not participate until their powers had been renewed.[19]

Moderate and radical Third Estate deputies met the protests with incredulity and anger, but liberal Nobles tried to defend their colleagues. Pétion and Rabaut de Saint-Etienne both argued that men who had not had their credentials verified were not yet deputies and should not have their protests heard. François-Emmanuel, vicomte of Toulongeon and Noble deputy from Aval, replied that there had been no law prohibiting the swearing of binding mandates and that the protests were simply acts by which the deputies showed their adherence to the wishes of their constituents. In this, he showed a clear understanding of how the Estates General had traditionally functioned. Deputies had always been able to protest against decisions made that broke with their individual mandates. After prolonged debate, the Assembly compromised between these two positions, decreeing that protests and reservations would not be heard in the open session but that deputies were free to deposit them with the secretaries along with their credentials. The Assembly further declared that once the powers of all the deputies had been verified, the Assembly would take up the matter again.[20] Over the next few days, deputies continued to bring their credentials to the secretaries, and they continued to file protests and reservations. But they did not disrupt the session.

They did act to undermine of the rules of order the National Assembly had adopted by trying to force the Assembly to recognize the king's platform of 23 June. On 2 July, cardinal Dominique de La Rochefoucauld read out an act prepared by the members of the Clergy who had continued to meet separately by order. He declared that the Clergy had reservations about participating in the National Assembly. In obedience to the king's declarations of 23 June and the king's letter of 27 June, they had agreed to come to the common chamber in order to discuss those things that were of common interest to the three Estates. But by their presence they did not yield their right to meet and vote separately and declared that their right to do so was expressly given to them by the king on 23 June. They thereby defended the right of the Clergy to veto any act that would impact its privileges.[21] They demanded that the Assembly

[19] See the protest of the deputations from Brest and from Périgord, AP 8: 173.
[20] AP 8: 173. Castellane, "Journal," 51. Jallet noted with satisfaction that none of the protests actually denounced the name "National Assembly" or contested its constitution on 17 June. Jallet, *Journal*, 110. See also Delandine, *Mémorial historique*, 2: 216–17.
[21] Bailly, *Mémoires d'un témoin*, 1: 271–72; AP 8: 182; Creuzé-Latouche, *Journal*, 176; Visme, "Journal," 63r–63v. The rump of the Order of the Nobles issued a similar proclamation on 4 July, but deposited it with the secretaries rather than having it read aloud. Bailly, *Mémoires d'un témoin*, 1: 282–85.

respect the old principle that all decisions had to be made by a consensus of the orders, not a vote by head.

The cardinal's declaration caused "an explosion of disapproval" in the Assembly, Bailly later recalled.[22] The first challenge to the cardinal's announcement came from a more liberal bishop and hinged on the notion of quorum. Le Franc de Pompignan, the archbishop of Vienne, implicitly accepted the notion that the Clergy represented a separate order, but pointed out that the decision to protest had been made by a minority of the Clergy. It thus had no standing and could not be considered the view of the Clergy as a whole.[23] Mirabeau took a much more confrontational line, saying that it was absurd to think that one could protest from within the Assembly against the existence of the National Assembly. He argued that no one could remain in what he called "the Assembly of the Estates General" who refused to recognize its sovereignty.[24] The conservative cleric Jean de Dieu-Raymond Boisgelin de Cucé, archbishop of Aix, ignored Mirabeau and replied to Le Franc de Pompignan's objection. He said it was not a question of the majority of individuals, but of the law. La Rochefoucauld had simply stated that the Clergy wished to maintain the rights that belonged to them. The Clerical deputies had to remain faithful to their mandates.[25] Mounier then returned to Le Franc de Pompignan's argument and its focus on majority rule, noting that the declarations of individuals could not be taken as the will of the entire order as a matter of principle. Pétion followed up with an attack on the rump Clergy's reliance on the king's declarations of 23 June as justification for their continued resistance to fully joining the National Assembly. He noted that the king's declarations had no standing as law and could not be accepted by the National Assembly, as they clashed with decrees the Assembly had decided to persist in.[26] He then said that he found it astonishing that anyone would base their reservations on "declarations that one had read in some kind of *lit de justice*, held by the king in the very bosom of the Estates General; declarations that without a doubt no member had approved, because when the nation is assembled, there is no power that can force it to submit to laws that have not been deliberated, discussed, and consented to." The protests of the Clergy could not be admitted because they were based on acts that the Assembly did not recognize.[27] He could have continued: the protests could not be admitted because the orders no longer had standing.

[22] Bailly, *Mémoires d'un témoin*, 1: 272–73.
[23] AP 8; 182; Bailly, *Mémoires d'un témoin*, 1: 273; Creuzé-Latouche, *Journal*, 176–77.
[24] Bailly, *Mémoires d'un témoin*, 1: 273.   [25] AP 8: 182; Creuzé-Latouche, *Journal*, 177.
[26] Bailly, *Mémoires d'un témoin*, 1: 273–74; Creuzé-Latouche, *Journal*, 177–78.   [27] AP 8: 182.

Stanislas-Marie-Adélaïde, the count of Clermont-Tonnerre, tried to shift the mood of the debate away from Pétion's anger. He agreed with Pétion that the deputies were united in the "national bosom" and that they were all integral parts of the legislative power. But while no one could command the body, no one had the right to bring up the "unhappy times of discord" that had led up to the union of the orders. As Toulongeon had urged the Assembly to receive deputy protests on 30 June, Clermont-Tonnerre now urged the Assembly to let individuals speak freely, secure in the knowledge that in time they would change their minds. He said that the Assembly should receive the protest of the rump Clergy, but not act on it. Mirabeau was not satisfied. He remained outraged by the thought that deputies could denounce the workings of the National Assembly from within it. He stated that allowing deputies to pretend that the orders could still meet separately meant undermining all that the Assembly did. Deputies could not invoke the king's declarations of 23 June. They could not state that they refused to obey the will of the majority. They could not pretend they had a veto power. As Mirabeau so memorably said, "No power under the heavens, not even the executive power, has the right to say *I will* to the representatives of the nation." The Assembly then moved to the order of the day and declared that it did not recognize the protest read by the cardinal as anything other than the opinion of an individual deputy.[28]

Later that day, a group of moderate deputies decided that something had to be done to counter the conservative deputies' attempts to undermine the legitimacy of the National Assembly and thwart attempts to maintain a veto power for the privileged orders. They appear to have met the night of 2 July in order to hammer out a plan and late in the day on 3 July, Talleyrand and Target made proposals declaring that binding mandates requiring deputies to leave the Assembly were void and could not halt its work.[29] With this began a major debate over the boundaries of the powers of the National Assembly. Unfortunately, neither of these speeches has survived. We have only brief accounts by witnesses of the

---

[28] Ibid., 183; Bailly, *Mémoires d'un témoin*, 1: 274. The emphasis appears in the originals. Duquesnoy noted that Mirabeau went on to say that it was beneath the dignity of the Assembly to accept acts like that of the rump Clergy. Duquesnoy, *Journal*, 1: 155. See also Creuzé-Latouche, *Journal*, 179.

[29] Visme, "Journal," 64v–65r; Duquesnoy, *Journal*, 1: 160–61; Castellane, "Journal," 56–58. Jallet thought Talleyrand's motion was meant to prevent the king's order from delaying the activity of the Assembly. To prevent this delay, it was necessary to show that the Assembly had the ability to "declare null all limiting powers." Jallet, *Journal*, 116. Historians who rely on the heavily on the *Archives Parlementaires*, such as Carré de Malberg, Baker, and Friedland fail to mention this early debate as it does not appear in that source.

speeches and the responses of opponents to let us know what was proposed. As this debate does not appear in the *Archives Parlementaires*, historians have long left the events of 3 July out of their discussions of how deputies dealt with the imperative mandates. Nevertheless, as we shall see, it is impossible to understand the speeches deputies made on 7 and 8 July without reconstructing the proposals Talleyrand and Target made on 3 July, the speeches of their supporters, and the resistance they encountered from conservative deputies.

The Noble deputy Boniface-Louis-André, count of Castellane, reported that Talleyrand sought a declaration that those mandates ordering deputies to abandon the Assembly if their constituents' demands as expressed in their *cahiers* were not followed were "radically voided," and could not impede the activity of the Assembly. Talleyrand said that deputies who carried such mandates needed to seek new powers from their constituents. He did not state that deputies subject to binding mandates must immediately participate in the deliberations and decisions of the Assembly.[30] Clermont-Tonnerre and the Clerical deputy Jean-Baptiste-Joseph Lubersac, bishop of Chartres, both spoke in support of Talleyrand's proposal, with Lubersac making an appeal to the "principle of reciprocity, or interest and of obligation that must reign between all of the deputies of one nation."[31] Only the Third Estate deputy Visme left an account of Target's proposal, claiming that Target's and Talleyrand's proposals amounted to much the same thing: both recognized that mandates could bind an individual deputy, but could not impede the functioning of the entire Assembly. Both also noted that those who were bound ought to return to their constituents to receive updated powers.[32]

Deputies who refused to accept the legitimacy of the National Assembly responded with appeals to the sanctity of the oaths they had sworn to their constituents and to the precedent of previous meetings of the Estates General. They either opposed or sought to modify Talleyrand's motion. On 3 July, the Noble deputy Victorien-Jean-Baptiste-Marie, duke of Mortemart,

> attacked the motion saying that imperative powers remained in full force, that they were supported by the religious nature of the oaths taken, that this type of power [i.e., the imperative mandate] was authorized by former use,

---

[30] Castellane, "Journal," 58.
[31] *Le Point du jour*, 1: 101. The Clerical deputy G.-L. Du Tillet, the bishop of Orange, spoke in support of Talleyrand. Duquesnoy, *Journal*, 1: 161.
[32] Visme, "Journal," 64v–65r; Duquesnoy, *Journal*, 1: 161–62.

and that it must be maintained for this session of the Estates General, unless the assembly abrogates [the French verb is "abroger"] all binding limitations of powers by an article of the constitution that it is going to create.

He focused on the sanctity of oaths in just the way Sieyès had on 23 June, and even admitted that the purpose of the current assembly was to write a constitution. But he objected nonetheless to the idea that the constitution should be written by a unified body voting by head. The Clerical deputy César-Guillaume de La Luzerne, the bishop of Langres, objected in the same way, arguing that he had to respect "the power of his constituents." Such commitment to the link between deputy and electors seemed to have widespread support: the Third Estate deputy-journalist Bertrand Barère opined in his newspaper that La Luzerne's appeal would resurface among opponents to Talleyrand's proposal.[33] No decision was made on Talleyrand's proposal. As the matter of the mandates had arisen late in the session and no clear consensus was evident, the matter was sent to the bureaus to be discussed by the deputies.[34]

The discussions held in the bureaus brought out a variety of issues implicit in Talleyrand's motion and these issues led to divisions among those who supported it and to sharpened opposition to the motion. Proposals that would modify Talleyrand's motion developed in both more radical and more conservative directions. One was a more extreme version of Talleyrand's proposal that claimed the Assembly could free the deputies from their oaths to their constituents. This was posed as an amendment to his motion. Noble and Clerical deputies who intended to work within the united orders sought to amend Talleyrand's proposal in order to allow for a delay in the activity of the Assembly until the end of July at the earliest, so that bound deputies could return to their districts and get new mandates that allowed them to participate fully. The only full-blooded opposition to Talleyrand's motion came from a small number of Noble and Clerical speakers who denied that the National Assembly had any right to exist at all.

While it is not entirely clear from the surviving sources what Talleyrand changed between his proposals of 3 and 7 July, eye-witness accounts indicate that he modified his proposal to moderate its tone, if not its content. Barère and Delandine both provided accounts of Talleyrand's 3 July speech that appear more confrontational than his 7 July proposal.

---

[33] *Le Point du jour*, 1: 101. On Barère, see L. Gershoy, *Bertrand Barère: A Reluctant Terrorist* (Princeton, 1962).
[34] See Bailly, *Mémoires d'un témoin*, 1: 277; Duquesnoy, *Journal*, 1: 161.

Delandine reported that Talleyrand, Target, Clermont-Tonnerre, and Lubersac had supported the radical proposal that all deputies required unlimited mandates for them to come together and form one nation, something other sources do not support.[35] Duquesnoy instead reported that the speeches given by Talleyrand, Target, and their followers all came down to the same basic two points: that no *bailliage* could halt the workings of the Assembly and that everything decided in the Assembly would be binding on all of France. But Duquesnoy also thought that Target (whom he identified as making much the same speech as Talleyrand) had argued that the Assembly could relieve the deputies of the burdens of a binding oath, which Duquesnoy refused to accept. He argued much on the lines Sieyès had on 23 June that no one could rupture the bond the deputies had to their constituents. "No power," Duquesnoy wrote, "not even God, can relieve a man from an oath that he had sworn."[36] As we will see, when the Assembly returned to the topic on 7 July, Talleyrand went to some trouble to make clear that he did not believe the Assembly could relieve the deputies of their oaths, nor did he wish to declare that all instructions given to the deputies by their constituents were invalid.

We examine Talleyrand's speech of 7 July here at some length, as his careful discussion of how deputies related to their constituents and to the National Assembly was a critical step in the education of the deputies about their role in the new Assembly. Furthermore, it was to his proposal that other speakers responded, opposing it or proposing amendments rather than producing new motions, and it is through examining criticism of his motion that we can see what the deputies themselves thought their proper role was. Seeking a means for the Assembly to continue its activity without further antagonizing its Noble and Clerical critics, Talleyrand returned frequently to the principle of majority rule, even as he recognized that constituents could legitimately bind their deputies to act in specific ways and the importance of the oaths deputies had sworn.[37] Talleyrand began by asking and answering the major questions that surrounded the mandate, seeking to clearly define the role of the deputies as elected representatives to a national body. He asked what a deputy was, and answered that "it is a man that the *bailliage* charged to will in its name, but to will as it would itself, if it could be transported to the general meeting." He then defined the mandate as "the act that transmits to [the deputy] the powers of the *bailliage*, which makes him representative of his *bailliage*, and through this

[35] *Le Point du jour*, 1: 100; Delandine, *Mémorial historique*, 3: 31.   [36] Duquesnoy, *Journal*, 1: 161.
[37] For a different take on Talleyrand's speech, see Friedland, *Political Actors*, 148–49.

representative of the whole nation."[38] In Talleyrand's opinion, the National Assembly consisted of men trusted to act as their constituents would if they were present, and who represented not just their particular districts but, through this, the entire nation.

Talleyrand sought to resolve the contested matter of the mandates by recognizing the validity and importance of the *cahiers* and the general and even the special mandates contained in them. Nevertheless, he denied that the limits given to individual deputies by their electors applied in any way to the Assembly itself. In order to distinguish between valid and invalid limitations, he gave three examples that electors could freely impose on their deputies:

> relating to duration;
>
> relating to goals;
>
> relating to the order in which the demands in the *cahiers* could be implemented.

He went on to explain each of the just limitations in varying amounts of detail. For the first type, he noted that it was acceptable that some communities had declared that after a year the powers of their deputy would expire and require renewal. Implicitly, this recognized that the *bailliages* could hold their deputies to account through the electoral process.

For the second, he explained that deputies could be required to pursue certain goals, always subject to the principle of majority rule. Electors were well within their rights to send their deputies "to compose (*régler*) the constitution, legislation, taxes and reform all of the abuses of the administration. Following this, once the constitution has been made stronger, and that a declaration of rights exists which will serve as a guide for the *bailliages*, mandates will necessarily be much more restricted as to their content."[39] That is, until constitutional reforms had taken place, the *bailliages* needed mandates to direct the deputies to achieve certain goals rather than deciding freely what matters to pursue.

For the third type of limitation, Talleyrand argued that the electors could require the deputies achieve particular goals before moving on to other matters. The electors were free to say that some issues in the *cahier* should take precedence over others. If enough deputies had received similar instructions, then they would be able to set the agenda for the Assembly.

---

[38] AP 8: 201. For a clear summary of Talleyrand's speech from an eyewitness, see Creuzé-Latouche, *Journal*, 195–96.

[39] AP 8: 201.

For example, he noted, during "this sitting of the Estates General, it would appear that the larger number of *bailliages* do not permit their deputies to handle matters concerning taxes before they deal with the constitution."[40]

In making these claims, Talleyrand recognized the importance of the special mandate for the success of the National Assembly. Though Talleyrand did not make this explicit in his speech, these three limitations had a common theme. All were ways in which a community could restrict its representative and his actions, but these limitations only had a meaningful effect at the national level if the majority of communities so restricted their deputies. Accepting the validity of these limitations on deputy powers entailed recognizing the principle of majority rule and accepting the existence and legitimacy of the National Assembly. If a mandate limited the behavior of a deputy, it was a matter of an agreement between a deputy and a community. None of these limitations meant that an individual deputy or a minority could stop the Assembly from its work.

Talleyrand refused to accept the validity of binding mandates, those that constrained a deputy in a way that harmed the ability of the National Assembly to represent the nation and violated the terms by which the deputies were elected. In defining such mandates, he gave three examples:

> requiring that a deputy vote "yes" or "no" when a particular subject arose;
> prohibiting entering into deliberation in some specific circumstance;
> ordering a deputy leave the Assembly if it adopted a particular opinion.

Talleyrand claimed that these were the only truly imperative clauses to be found in deputy mandates, and he denied that the various demands made in the *cahiers* exhorting deputies to support certain policies were properly imperative. To accept that all of the articles found in the *cahiers* were imperative, he argued, would imply that the Assembly existed only to count up the opinions of the different *bailliages* in order to reach a decision and that the deputies themselves were superfluous.[41] As Talleyrand noted, why would one send deputies, if not to discuss, to debate, and to agree? In supporting this position – that each deputy was

---

[40] Ibid. On 4 July an unnamed deputy had noted that the mandates the deputies carried ordered them to take no vote on taxation before fixing the constitution. See also, 194.

[41] AP 8: 201. Jérôme-Marie Champion de Cicé, the archbishop of Bordeaux, argued that previous meetings of the Estates General had never authorized imperative mandates and that they were therefore void. Creuzé-Latouche, *Journal*, 199. Carré de Malberg noted that the institution of the binding mandate was never meant to impede the resolutions of the majority of deputies sitting in the Estates General. The decisions of the body had always been taken within the orders on the basis of majority rule, and individual mandates had never been able to prevent this from happening. Carré de Malberg, *Contributions*, 2: 250.

sent "in order to deliberate, in order to contribute to deliberations" –
Talleyrand adopted the essence of the general mandate as demanded by the
Crown in the electoral regulations issued on 24 January. Adopting this
general mandate had been a condition of participation in the Estates
General, and adopting binding mandates went against its provisions.
Talleyrand cleverly played on the king's own declaration that mandates
prohibiting meeting and voting in common were void, made at the Royal
Session of 23 June and in the king's order in council of 27 June. Talleyrand
then moved on to a proposal that recognized traditional practices the
Estates General had followed and applied them to the National Assembly.

Given that some kinds of mandates were illegitimate, the National
Assembly had to act

> as if they did not exist; that they authorize no protest against [the National
> Assembly], that they can neither halt the operations of the Assembly nor
> give even the least pretext for misconstruing its decisions; that all votes given
> in the Assembly are presumed to be free; that all members not participating
> are presumed absent and that no failure to attend can weaken the force of its
> decrees.[42]

Talleyrand carefully kept the legitimacy of the National Assembly rooted
in the instructions the deputies had received from their electors, even as he
distinguished between legitimate and illegitimate instructions. A deputy
might be legitimately bound to return home after a certain period, to bring
up certain grievances, or to seek the discussion of goals in a certain order.
A deputy could not be required to refuse discussion in certain ways or of
certain things, nor could he be bound to leave if a certain opinion were to
win the day, implicitly declaring that his electors would refuse to obey the
decisions of the National Assembly. No individual deputy or minority
group could prevent the Assembly from acting by protesting or refusing to
participate. Moreover, Talleyrand argued that no deputy could be constrained to vote in a certain way once he had entered into the Assembly.
Cleverly here, Talleyrand used the practices of previous Estates General to
justify the move to a National Assembly. *Cahiers* had often contained
contradictory elements meant to satisfy local groups, meaning that strict
adherence had always been impossible. Voting in the Estates General had
always been free. Importantly, though, Talleyrand broke with the long
tradition of allowing deputies to file protests to show that they had
followed the orders of their constituents.

[42] AP 8: 202.

Having firmly rooted the legitimacy of the Assembly in the relationship between the deputies and their electors, Talleyrand moved on to the real problem, the sanctity of the oaths deputies had sworn to follow the instructions found in their *cahiers*. Responding to points his critics had raised on 3 July, Talleyrand acknowledged that some deputies had sworn oaths that prohibited them from freely participating in the National Assembly. He recognized that "there was no law that prohibited them [from voluntarily taking restrictive oaths]," and that the oaths taken were binding on the individual deputies. Deputies were bound to obey all the terms of the mandates they held, even if the terms violated the general mandate and made them unable to participate fully in the National Assembly. Once a deputy had sworn to uphold the wishes of his constituents, only his constituents could lift the obligation. While Talleyrand denied that the electors had the inherent right to bind their deputies in ways that prevented them from participating, he acknowledged that, "the deputy has had the right to submit to them, and this voluntary submission that he has shown, in receiving his powers, is the true title of his engagement."[43] A deputy could voluntarily enter into bad agreements, and such ill-advised engagements were the very proof that a man was a legitimate representative!

To resolve the problem generated by improperly binding mandates, Talleyrand urged the Assembly to make a clear statement that it was not bound by the dictates of any individual deputy's mandate, while recognizing that some individual deputies were themselves so bound and needed to seek new powers from their constituents before they could honorably participate. Talleyrand moved that the Assembly make the following decree:

> The National Assembly, considering that a *bailliage* or portion of a *bailliage* has the right to form only the general will, and not to evade it, or to suspend the activity of the Estates General by imperative mandates, which contain only a particular will, declares that all imperative mandates are radically void, that the kind of engagement which resulted from them must be promptly lifted by the *bailliages*, as such a clause could not be imposed, all protestations to the contrary being inadmissible, and that by a necessary consequence, all decrees of the National Assembly will be rendered obligatory on every *bailliage*, when it has been made by all without exception.[44]

Here again we see the old rules used to justify the new system. But Talleyrand's most important words came after he had made his motion:

---

[43] Ibid.   [44] Ibid., 203.

"I would add these words, *radically null in relation to the Assembly,* because this nullity is truly only relative: it exists for the mandate holders, it does not exist for the Assembly."[45] Deputies could be and were bound to obey the oaths they had sworn to their electors. However, the actions of the Assembly would be determined the same way they always had been in the Estates General, by a majority vote. In this way, the imperative mandates were recognized as truly binding on individuals even as the Assembly declared that no individual deputy could halt the functioning of the Assembly. This clever formulation ensured that the National Assembly recognized the traditional links between the electors and their deputies, that all votes would be taken by head a united body, and that the veto by order would not be recognized.

Some moderate and conservative deputies supported Talleyrand's motion overall while asking for a delay in the activity of the National Assembly while deputies bound by imperative mandates sought new powers. Second Estate deputy Alexandre de Lameth wrote that the deputies who opposed Talleyrand were those "who pretended that the Assembly did not have the right to invalidate the mandates, but that it had to send the bearers of the *cahiers* which restricted the free expression of votes back to their constituents." Visme dismissed them as being neither numerous nor persuasive.[46] Most prominent among them was Lally-Tollendal. Lally-Tollendal was one of the Noble deputies who had entered into the common hall on 25 June and he acknowledged both the existence of the National Assembly and the principle of majority rule. He rejected the idea that the Assembly could interfere in the relationship between a deputy and his electors, recognizing that the oaths deputies had taken were binding even as he rejected the ability of a minority to overrule the majority.[47] Referring to Talleyrand's motion, Lally-Tollendal said that "it calms the conscience, it pardons scruples, it does not tell us, 'You have not sworn such and such an oath'; it makes us see that we have been wrong to swear it, but it does not release us."[48] But he did not wish for the Assembly to move forward without the participation of the improperly bound deputies. He proposed an amendment to Talleyrand's motion: "The Assembly, by a voluntary and patriotic condescension, will accord a very short delay

[45] Ibid. Emphasis in the original.   [46] Lameth, *Histoire,* 1: 38–39; Visme, "Journal," 68v.
[47] *Le Courrier des départements,* 1: 55–56. Lally-Tollendal refers here to the protests recalcitrant deputies had deposited at the bureau on 30 June and in early July.
[48] AP 8: 204; *Le Courrier,* 1: 55–56. Lally-Tollendal had stated on 26 June that he could not fully participate in the Assembly until he had received new powers from his constituents. He did not file a protest on 30 June. Bailly, *Mémoires d'un témoin,* 1: 238; AP 8: 158.

which is for no other purpose than to give those who are bearers of imperative mandates the time to receive new powers." The purpose of this delay was to remove the ground for complaint and protest against the formation of the Assembly, and it is worth emphasizing that the bound deputies could not demand a delay by right – it was a "voluntary and patriotic" courtesy given the bound deputies by the Assembly. His appeals to conscience, to courtesy and to patriotism struck a chord: his speech was followed with a long round of applause.[49] Here we see a reference to the medieval practice of seeking approval from constituents for any changes to be made, without any claim that the Assembly could be halted.

Deputies who had protested against the very existence of the National Assembly spoke more and at greater length than previous histories of the event would lead one to believe. If the sanctity of oaths had predominated in the speeches of those deputies who proposed a delay until deputies could receive new powers, personal honor and the need to adhere to an already-existing constitution dominated the comments of those who opposed the existence of the Assembly. The first resistance to Talleyrand's motion came from cardinal La Rochefoucauld. He pointed out that he had received a mandate that Talleyrand described as improper. "Can I," he asked, "overstep my mandate without weakening the sentiments of probity that animate me?" In this simple question he reminded the Assembly that the deputies were honor bound not to betray their mandates and that they could not be coerced into participating.[50] He also indirectly reminded the deputies of his 2 July speech on behalf of the rump order of Clergy, in which he protested against the formation of the National Assembly and stated that the order would adhere to the king's instructions of 23 June.[51] Count Toustain de Viray, Noble deputy from Lorraine, asked how "it can be that, in the sanctuary of honor and virtue, one can wish to weaken our obligations: 'We come here to defend your liberty, and you, you attack ours.'"[52] The Estates General was meant to defend honor, not undermine

---

[49] AP 8: 204–5. See also *Le Point du jour*, I: 131–32; Creuzé-Latouche, *Journal*, 196–97. Castellane and Bousmard made similar proposals. *Le Point du jour*, I: 132; Castellane, "Journal," 62–64; Creuzé-Latouche, *Journal*, 197–98. Friedland argues that Lally-Tollendal's speech attacked the notion that the National Assembly adequately represented the nation in the absence of a minority of the deputies. Friedland, *Political Actors*, 150–51. Lally-Tollendal's speech does not support this conclusion, as Lally-Tollendal asked only for a voluntary delay and never claimed that one should be accorded by right to the privileged deputies. Creuzé-Latouche recounts Lally-Tollendal arguing that it would be impossible for the protests of a single deputy to impede the workings of the National Assembly. Creuzé-Latouche, *Journal*, 196–97.

[50] AP 8: 203.   [51] La Rochefoucauld's 2 July speech appears on AP 8: 182.

[52] Duquesnoy, *Journal*, I: 168.

it. The Nobles had come to discuss and defend the liberty of the Third Estate, and yet the Third Estate attacked the rights of the Nobles to adhere to the wishes of their constituents.

Charles-François, marquis of Guilhem-Clermont-Lodève, Noble deputy from Arles, made the clearest statement of the recalcitrant position concerning the constitution. He denied that the deputies were there to write one, saying, "We already have a constitution that requires us to vote by order, and we do not have the right to change it."[53] He claimed that, "the Assembly did not have the right to act, in that it was not complete, since the two premier orders were without the power to vote by head."[54] Moreover, the united orders could not exist, as the constitution prohibited a vote by head. Without a division of the body into separate orders, there could be no active Estates General. The Assembly lacked the quorum necessary to pursue business: its acts were automatically void. In making this claim, Clermont-Lodève simply ignored the history of the Estates General, which had long met and voted in a variety of ways, including sitting and voting as a single assembly in 1484. René des Montiers de Mérinville, bishop of Dijon and a deputy of the Clergy, claimed that the Assembly could not constitute itself in the first place, implying that Talleyrand had no right to discuss limiting or canceling the mandates of others.[55] After all, if the Third Estate did not have the right to constitute itself as the National Assembly without the cooperation or approval of the other two orders, it could hardly judge the oaths other deputies had taken.[56]

At the other end of the developing political spectrum, a small number of deputies wished to completely eliminate binding mandates and insisted that all deputies present participate fully. Some historians have found in their radical proposals the real meaning of the debate, arguing that the abrogation of all mandates was the point and the final outcome.[57] While it is important for us to hear the radical arguments, it is also important for us to keep in mind that these opinions did not win the day and in fact gained little support. Gaultier de Biauzat refused to recognize the need for the

---

[53] Ibid., 169 . Duquesnoy remarked that "he could scarcely be heard" even though he was a formidable speaker. One may presume that he could hardly be heard over a hostile audience.

[54] Jallet, *Journal*, 119. Clermont-Lodève's speech was greeted with a disapproving murmur from the Assembly. *Le Courrier*, 1: 61.

[55] AP 8: 205.

[56] Lameth gave only one example of such a conservative deputy, the duc of Mortemart, a deputy from Sens. But from other deputy reports, it appears that his speech took place on 3 July, not 7 July. Lameth, *Histoire*, 1: 38–39.

[57] See, for example, Friedland, *Political Actors*, 151–52.

bound deputies to correspond with their constituents, and wished for the Assembly to simply "authorize all its members and command (*enjoint*) them to vote their soul and conscience." The Assembly had the right to relieve deputies of improper oaths and must use its power to do so. He proposed an amendment to Talleyrand's motion to this effect:

> The Assembly quashes, annuls and declares void all imperative and prohibitive clauses in the powers of all deputies; it authorizes all of its members in general and each of them in particular and commands them to propose and to vote according to their soul and conscience on all subjects, common and general. In consequence and to this end, the Assembly relieves its deputies of all oaths that had been made to assure the execution of imperative and prohibitive clauses of their mandates [and] the remaining oaths regarding the extra general and particular obligations of each deputy, to faithfully fulfill, with zeal and his soul and conscience, the office with which he is charged."[58]

Barère chose a different tack. He carefully distinguished between two kinds of representatives, those who represented electoral assemblies and those who represented individual concerns. The first kind of representation was properly political, in which primary assemblies gave to their deputies "the power to be members of a legislative assembly and to vote there in the place of their constituents." The second case was not, when a representative had been sent to represent a personal concern. Only in the second case could a representative be bound by a mandate and repudiated if he deviated from it. To confuse the two kinds of representative would lead to endless deadlock. "If one admits the system of limited and imperative mandates," he said, "one evidently impeaches the resolutions of the Assembly in recognizing a dreadful *veto* in each of the ... *bailliages* of the kingdom." He believed that only the general mandate was valid and wished for all limits on the ability of the deputies to debate and decide be lifted. Therefore, while he supported Talleyrand's motion, he rejected the part that required the bound deputies to seek a revision of their mandates by their constituents.[59] According to Barère, there were no electoral bodies to return to. After the *bailliages* had elected their representatives, their powers had expired.[60] These two proposals have in common a disregard for the personal obligations of deputies or the differences

[58] Gaultier de Biauzat, *Correspondance*, 2: 150.
[59] AP 8: 205. Barère had no grounds to claim that the deputies envisioned each *bailliage* as having a veto over the workings of the Assembly. Mandates had never worked in this way. Carré de Malberg, *Contribution*, 2: 250–53.
[60] *Le Point du jour*, 1: 129–31.

in mandates granted by particular communities. They also both go beyond freeing deputies to work within the Assembly by forcing them to disregard their constituents' wishes. Both espouse the radical claim that the deputies were free to act as they thought best.

At some point during the debate Sieyès also spoke, though it is not clear from the evidence we have when he did. He claimed that Talleyrand's motion was largely pointless and that no action needed to be taken regarding deputy mandates. Instead, the Assembly should decree that the electors who had given their deputies binding mandates ought to relieve them of those burdens. His speech does not appear to have made much impact at the time. Creuzé-Latouche recorded Sieyès as claiming that "The National Assembly has no interest in changing imperative mandates, it must ignore whether or not there are particular arrangements between the deputies and their deputizers." Since the Assembly had no interest in the private oaths of the deputies, there was no place for a decree regulating them.[61] In another account, Sieyès agreed with Talleyrand that binding mandates meant to limit the activities of the National Assembly were invalid, but he believed that this meant that there was no reason to deliberate on them. Instead, Sieyès "judged that nothing prevented that the Assembly, tempering its principles by a spirit of condescension, decree only that it is up to the *bailliages*, authors of the imperative mandates, to revoke them, and that this revocation is, for them, very important."[62] Sieyès supported the essence of Talleyrand's motion, but separated out the competence of the Assembly to act from the admittedly useful plan to allow deputies to seek new powers. They needed to encourage *bailliages* to give their deputies new powers, as Castellane had suggested, but they would not interfere in the private arrangements deputies had made. He also used Lally-Tollendal's language, suggesting that it was only out of the Assembly's generosity that it would suggest that the *bailliages* act.

The day had ended without a vote being taken, but witnesses thought it likely that Talleyrand's motion would pass the next day. The Noble deputy Charles-Alexis, marquis of Brulart de Sillery, himself a descendent of a chancellor of France, wrote in his diary after the session that,

> the general opinion is that the *bailliages* were not able to give imperative mandates tending to impede the movement of the united Estates General; and that the *bailliages* can only be considered as a portion of the nation, and

---

[61] Creuzé-Latouche, *Journal*, 199.

[62] *Le Point du jour*, 1: 133–34. What one can take from the *Archives Parlementaires* is insufficient. AP 8: 205.

not being able to, in any case, halt the operation of the National Assembly; that the *bailliages*, in giving imperative mandates to their deputies, run the risk of not being represented and that they will nonetheless be subject to the laws promulgated; that the National Assembly will not admit any protests; that the deputies are no less committed to their constituents, and that it is up to each of them to decide to what the mandates they have received obligate them.[63]

The opinion of the Third Estate deputy Jean-Pierre Boullé supports Brulart de Sillery's conclusions, but also introduces the point that Sieyès had made that no action was necessary. Boullé wrote on 7 July that:

It appears that the general opinion is that although the binding mandates are not void in regard to the relationship of the constituents and their mandate holder, that a *bailliage* or a portion of a *bailliage* cannot oppose itself to the general will of the nation, and that their deputation would even be virtual and implied if it were not to submit itself to the majority. But in this case, one could say that there is no reason to deliberate, because this principle, which may be posited, has already been decreed in the constitution of the Assembly of 17 June.[64]

Both deputies came to the same conclusion. The sense of the Assembly was that they did not wish to free the deputies from their mandates and declare that they must participate and vote in the National Assembly. Instead, it was a matter of recognizing two points: that no individual deputy or minority group of deputies could halt the activity of the Assembly, and that each constituency would be better off if its representatives could participate in the assembly.

Duquesnoy agreed in his diary that the whole debate was pointless because the question of whether or not recalcitrant deputies could somehow delay or halt the work of the Assembly was moot:

It is astonishing that no one has dared to say that this question had been sovereignly judged on 17 June, by the constitutional decree in which one finds the relevant words, "One such a group of deputations will not be rendered inactive by the absence of deputies from some *bailliages* or of some classes of citizens: because the absent who have been called cannot prevent the present from exercising the plenitude of their rights, which is a duty both imperative and pressing."[65]

He attacked the notion that the National Assembly ought to suspend its activities until the bound deputies received new powers, noting that if they

---

[63] Brulart de Sillery, "Journal," 288. [64] Boullé, "Correspondance," 51.
[65] Duquesnoy, *Journal*, 1: 169–70.

recognized that principle, they ought to have waited for them before declaring themselves constituted. He also made a vital point about the way in which voting was taken in the Assembly. In the history of the Estates General, being in the minority was never the same as not having a voice. As he wrote:

> When the mandates force those who carry them to have an opinion different than that of the majority, the voice given is not nullified, but does not count. So, when we constituted ourselves on 17 June, 90 people did not hold the opinion that prevailed: can one say that the votes of 90 people were void? No, without a doubt, they were not void, but they were without effect.[66]

In this he upheld an entirely traditional understanding of the Estates General. Deputies were free to express the opinions contained in their *cahiers*, but they could not expect those opinions to have effect unless a majority agreed with them. Hence the practice in past Estates General of deputies making an *acte* in which they registered their objections and showed that they had followed the wishes of their constituents.

Duquesnoy must have been gratified the next day when Sieyès spoke again. Sieyès called for an end to the debate because the question had already been decided, saying, "The principles on which my opinion is based have already been consecrated by the decree of 17 June." As declared on that day, the Assembly contained the only duly verified deputies and this was sufficient justification for its activity. The Assembly had declared, "that the French nation [was] always entirely legitimately represented by the plurality of its deputies." The communities that gave improper mandates had deprived themselves of their fair representation, and he invited these communities to give their deputies liberty to discuss any matter freely. Sieyès reminded the deputies of what the National Assembly had decided on 17 June:

> Neither imperative mandates nor the voluntary absence of some members, nor the protests of a minority will ever be able to halt its activity, nor alter its liberty, nor attenuate the force of its statutes, nor finally put limits on the area submitted to its legislative power.[67]

Here we see Sieyès adopting the point of Talleyrand's motion, even as he proposed no action be taken on the question of the binding mandates. He reminded the recalcitrant deputies that the National Assembly would continue without them, should they decide to retire, and that the laws promulgated therein would bind all of France equally. Thus it was in their

[66] Ibid.   [67] AP 8: 207.

interest and that of their constituents to seek the powers necessary to participate in the united assembly. Sieyès remained true to the principle he had announced on 23 June. The Assembly had no more business interfering in the oaths deputies had sworn to their electors than did the king. Sieyès attacked the ability of a deputy to halt the activities of the National Assembly, not the ability of a community to give its deputy detailed instructions. Sieyès agreed with the most recalcitrant deputies that the Assembly could not relieve them of their oaths.[68]

But despite Sieyès's efforts to stop it, the debate continued and more proposals were made. Finally, the proposals of Talleyrand and several others were read out. Then Mirabeau took the podium. After he appeared to mock a conservative deputy, he was interrupted by murmurs from the Nobles and their cry, "to the order of the day!" The Clergy and the Third Estate replied, "let's vote!" and chaos ensued. An unnamed deputy cried out above the clamor, asking that Sieyès's motion be read once more. It was, and there followed a long debate on how to pose the question. What the Assembly declared, by an overwhelming majority of 700 to 28,[69] was that

> The National Assembly, regarding its principles fixed in this regard, and considering that its activities cannot be suspended nor the force of its decrees be weakened by the protests or absence of some representatives, declares that there is no reason to continue deliberations on this matter.[70]

As Alexandre de Lameth later wrote,

> The Assembly resumed the day's business, on the reasoning that the question had been resolved by the decree of 17 June, which had posited in principle that those who refused to have their credentials verified in the general Assembly would be considered as absent; deciding, thus, that it would be the same for those who believed themselves bound by their mandates.[71]

This settled the central question of the whole debate: whether or not the National Assembly could be delayed or its actions disobeyed by the constituents of recalcitrant deputies. But the matter of the mandates so central

---

[68] In contrast, Friedland finds that Sieyès's proposal differed from Talleyrand's in that it allowed the electors no influence whatsoever on the decisions made by their deputies. Friedland, *Political Actors*, 149, 151–52.

[69] The sources give similar vote totals, all agreeing that at least 700 voted in favor and only 28 against. AP 8: 208; Creuzé-Latouche, *Journal*, 203; Delandine, *Journal*, 80; *Le Point du jour*, 1: 139; Bailly, *Mémoires d'un témoin*, 1: 293. It appears that the majority of the Nobles and Clergy did not vote and may not have been present. Tackett, *Becoming a Revolutionary*, 159 n. 36.

[70] AP 8: 208.   [71] Lameth, *Histoire*, 1: 40–41.

to Talleyrand's proposal had been dropped. No action was taken to void the mandates or to relieve deputies of the oaths they had sworn. We must now try to understand why the Assembly rejected attempts to do away with limited and binding mandates. As we shall see, there were traditional uses for mandates beyond preventing or ensuring a vote by order, and it was over these traditional uses that Talleyrand's motion had failed.

Historians have often assumed that only conservative Nobles and Clergy wished to retain strong links to their constituents and saw mandates as a crucial guarantee of this link. This was not the case at all. Creuzé-Latouche, for one, understood that imperative mandates had been used since the beginnings of the Estates General and had perfectly legitimate uses. Binding mandates were for protecting the Assembly from royal pressure, not for preventing deliberation in the Assembly. On the night before the final vote, he had worried that the public might mistake Talleyrand's motion as prohibiting both legitimate and illegitimate kinds, when only the latter was targeted.[72] The historian Beatrice Hyslop reminds us that the binding mandate was not solely used to seek or prevent a vote by head or a vote by order. The deputies were also bound by their constituents in order to prevent corruption through "court influence, the grant of pensions, offices, or other rewards, [that] would make the deputies disregard the wishes of their constituents." Binding mandates were used to ensure that significant reforms would be made before new taxes would be granted.[73] Given that after the union of the orders the latter problems – fixing a constitution before granting new taxes and preventing deputies from becoming corrupt – were still relevant, one can understand that deputies might not wish to have the special or binding mandates eliminated too soon.[74]

Like Creuzé-Latouche, Jallet thought that the proper use of the mandates was to protect constituencies from the government. He thought that deputies from the Third Estate had rallied around keeping their mandates out of fear that without them, the Polignac faction (those courtiers associated with the queen) and the count of Artois might manipulate the Crown into pushing through bad legislation. He wrote that support for Talleyrand's proposal had diminished because, on 8 July:

---

[72] Creuzé-Latouche, *Journal*, 198.   [73] Hyslop, *Guide*, 100.
[74] Tackett, *Becoming a Revolutionary*, 237. Deputies sought guidance from their constituents and took it upon themselves to explain to their electors that binding mandates would not halt the activities of the Assembly. See for example F.-A. Boissy d'Anglas, "Lettres inédites sur la Révolution française," *Bulletin de la Société de l'Histoire du Protestantisme français*, 75 (1926), 284–85. Pellerin, *Correspondance*, 101–04.

We were informed that its author often went to meetings of the Polignac committee. That was enough to render the motion suspect. One examined it closely, and it appeared that it was dangerous. It would declare void all imperative mandates; one saw that this was a trap placed by the cabal around Artois. In effect, in declaring void all imperative mandates, one also condemns those that require the framing of the constitution before consenting to taxes; this gives freedom to the voters and new hope to the cabal.[75]

Talleyrand was aware of these sentiments and tried to modify his motion on 8 July to lessen the threat it had implied to the relationship deputies had to their electors. As Boullé recorded, on 8 July, Talleyrand,

> knowing the apparent result of diverse opinions, proposed a few changes to his motion. It was no longer on the mandates themselves that he would have fall the pronouncement of nullity, but on the reservations and protestations to which they had led, and which could not stop the operations of a legitimately constituted and necessarily active Assembly, and he asked only that the *bailliages* change the clauses of their mandates that were contrary to the majority. This project so modified would have been adopted without controversy, but [the Assembly] was already determined to reject a motion that appeared to weaken the rights of constituents and rendered useless the imperative mandates that been our safeguard and our strength.[76]

On 8 July Talleyrand found that deputies from the Third Estate and the Clergy were more interested in preserving their mandates than he had expected. This explains why the Assembly would adopt Sieyès's motion over that of Talleyrand. Once it became clear that the deputies would not vote to void their own mandates, it was just a question of stating that the Assembly could not be halted by absence or unwillingness to participate. That question had indeed already been decided on 17 June.

Baker thus goes too far when he claims that the essential outcome of the debate over the binding mandate was "a revolution of the deputies against the conditions of their election" and a "dramatic repudiation" of the traditional imperative mandate.[77] As we have seen, the resolution of the debate over the binding mandate recognized the importance of mandates: it did not repudiate them. A substantial majority of the deputies present confirmed both the

---

[75] Jallet, *Journal,* 119–20.

[76] Boullé, "Correspondance," 83–84. See also A.-L. de Gontaud, duke of Biron, *Lettres sur les Etats généraux,* ed. R. de la Lande (Paris, 1865), 14.

[77] Baker, *Inventing the French Revolution,* 244–45. Friedland concludes that the deputies had "conferred an almost absolute power on themselves, and yet because they had cast the mandate as a tool of the aristocracy, they could portray themselves as defenders of the people." This does not jibe with the arguments made by deputies present at the debate as to the meaning of their actions. Friedland, *Political Actors,* 152.

validity of their oaths to their constituents and that the National Assembly
would remain active. Those who refused to vote were a sizeable minority, but
could not have altered the outcome. A coalition of moderates had, as of 8 July,
finally cemented the status of the National Assembly as the body in which all
three orders sat, debated, and voted. As such, it was a victory for the Society of
Thirty and the Patriot Party, not the radical Breton deputies or the Sieyès of
What Is the Third Estate? who had argued for the exclusion of the privileged
orders from the National Assembly. Deputies still carried mandates and were
still honor-bound to obey the wishes of their constituents. But no individual
deputy, regardless of his mandate or the constituency he represented, could
impeach the legitimacy of the National Assembly or halt its proceedings. The
decision to accept the validity of binding mandates while simultaneously
declaring that the National Assembly would not suspend its actions took the
wind from the sails of the recalcitrant deputies. An attempt to draft a formal
statement of defiance fizzled when most of the recalcitrants refused to sign it.
Instead, they sought new powers from their constituents and began participating as they could. Over the next few days, the number of deputies
attending separate meetings by order plummeted.[78] It had taken more than
nine weeks of inactivity and delay, but on 8 July 1789 the Estates General,
sitting as a union of orders and calling itself the "National Assembly," was
ready for business. The Third Estate and its allies were full of the confidence
born from their struggles with the conservative deputies and with the king
himself. They held a commanding majority in the Assembly and were ready
to set the agenda for reform.

What looked like a final victory for the Third Estate was complicated by
the ongoing and intensifying unrest in Paris and by the king's own political
maneuvering. As the deputies had debated the legitimacy of the National
Assembly, public order in Paris had deteriorated. The French Guards there
became less and less reliable. On 24 June, soldiers had refused to obey
orders to patrol Paris, and on 28 June, their colonel jailed several men he
identified as troublemakers. On 30 June, some 400 Parisians left the Palais
Royal and marched through the city, gathering supporters as they went. By
the time they reached the Abbaye prison on the left bank, the crowd had
reached some 10,000 men and women. They broke the soldiers out and
took them back to the Palais Royal. Soldiers sent to stop them fraternized
instead. The next morning, a delegation from the marchers went to see

---

[78] C.-G. Rousselot, *Correspondance de l'Abbé Rousselot, Constituant, 1789–1795*, A.-M. Malingrey, ed.
(Besançon, 1992), 36–37. Tackett, *Becoming a Revolutionary*, 160–62.

Bailly in Versailles. They asked that the Assembly do something to protect the rioters and the freed soldiers.[79]

Bailly knew that the National Assembly had no right to interfere in matters of military discipline. Nevertheless he recognized that unrest in Paris was growing and that the problem of the freed mutineers would make matters worse if left unresolved. Bailly assured the men who had come to see him that he would do what he could and he sent them to wait for him at the Assembly hall. He then went across town to speak with Necker. Necker already knew about the events of the previous day. He confessed that the king could no longer enforce order in Paris. But Necker knew it would be dangerous to let the people of the Palais Royal and mutinous soldiers act with impunity. That risked spreading unrest throughout the kingdom by demonstrating the king's inability to maintain order. Necker and Bailly had to hide the king's inability to keep order in Paris. They came up with a plan. Bailly would encourage the Assembly to plead with the king to show mercy to the rioters and the freed soldiers. Necker would encourage the king to accept their suggestion. The king would forgive those he could not punish. Louis would appear generous, not weak.[80]

Later that morning, Bailly brought the matter before the Assembly, asking them to consider what actions it might take. The deputies were divided over what to do. Some Noble and Clerical deputies protested against discussing the matter at all out of respect for the king's prerogatives. Others reminded the Assembly that it had no right to interfere in military affairs.[81] Two Third Estate deputies from Paris, the lawyers Target and Camus, asked that the Assembly write to the electors of Paris urging them to restore order. Camus suggested sending a delegation of bishops to the king, asking him to show mercy to those involved.[82] Only a few deputies wanted to go further. Le Chapelier wanted the assembly to send a commission of six deputies to work with the royal ministers to restore order in Paris. This flagrantly violated the boundaries between the legislative and executive powers, but Le Chapelier argued that the circumstances

---

[79] On the uprising and the Assembly's debate, see M. Rouff, "Le peuple ouvrier de Paris aux journées du 30 juin et du 30 août 1789," *La Révolution française* 63 (1912), 430–54, 481–505; and E. L. Howie, "The Counter-Revolution of June-July 1789: Rôle of the Assembly from June 30 to July 11," *University Studies of the University of Nebraska* 15 (1915), 283–419, especially 387–97. See also Alpaugh, *Non-Violence*, 56–58; Andress, *French Revolution and the People*, 104; J. Godechot, *The Taking of the Bastille* trans. J. Stewart (New York, 1970), 175–77.

[80] Duquesnoy, *Journal*, 1: 149; Bailly, *Mémoires d'un témoin*, 1: 264–67; Ferrières, *Correspondance*, 79.

[81] Bailly, *Mémoires d'un témoin*, 1: 268; Duquesnoy, *Journal*, 1: 149–50; AP 8: 175; *Correspondance d'Anjou*, 1: 263.

[82] AP 8: 176; *Correspondance d'Anjou*, 1: 263.

required such bold action, especially since, as he claimed, the king's attempts to interfere with the Assembly's powers on 23 June had caused the problem in the first place.[83] After a long debate, the Assembly blended Target's proposal with that of Stanislas Jean, chevalier de Boufflers, a moderate Noble deputy.[84] The Assembly would declare that it did not approve of the rioting and remind the citizens of Paris to stay calm. The deputies would send a delegation to Louis asking him to show mercy.[85] It was the outcome Necker and Bailly had hoped for.[86] The king saw the wisdom in their request and assured the Assembly that he would act on it. Working with Parisian officials, the king arranged a token punishment for the soldiers, who were then allowed their liberty. The Assembly and the king had cooperated to restore order while hiding the king's weakness.[87]

But Louis had his own ideas about how to restore order in Paris. On 22 June, he had signed orders to bring troops to Paris. After the Royal Session, he summoned more. The deputies could hardly miss the build up of troops near Paris, nor fail to see that the troops were largely German speaking, though of long service to the king.[88] On 8 July, the Assembly debated what to do about the growing number of troops in the Paris basin. Immediately after the end of the debate over mandates, Mirabeau went to the podium. The problem was, he said, that the newly arrived troops were causing the very unrest in Paris they were meant to prevent. Only by moving them away from Paris could the unrest be calmed. Moreover, Mirabeau argued, the troops were in danger of being caught up in the effervescence of Paris, the same effervescence that had made the French Guards unreliable. Though he did not broach the idea, the unspoken fear hung over the Assembly that that the troops might be used against them. Mirabeau proposed sending a delegation to politely ask the king to remove the new troops, arguing that the king's response to their previous petition revealed his good will and merciful nature.[89] After a brief debate, the Assembly voted to send a delegation to the king and ask him to withdraw the troops.[90]

[83] AP 8: 176; *Correspondance d'Anjou*, 1: 265–66; Delandine, *Mémorial historique*, 3: 8.
[84] AP 8: 177; Duquesnoy, *Journal*, 1: 150.   [85] AP 8: 177–78.
[86] Bailly, *Mémoires d'un témoin*, 1: 269; Duquesnoy, *Journal*, 1: 150.
[87] Duquesnoy, *Journal*, 1: 152; Bailly, *Mémoires d'un témoin*, 1: 270–71, 275–76.
[88] On troop movements, see Godechot, *Taking of the Bastille*, 179–80. Félix argues that the troops were being brought to protect the king and his family. Félix, *Louis XVI et Marie Antoinette*, 479–82.
[89] AP 8: 208–10.
[90] Bailly, *Mémoires d'un témoin*, 1: 293–96; Duquesnoy, *Journal*, 1: 174–76; AP 8: 208–11. Shapiro, *Traumatic Politics*, 85–86.

Louis received a delegation from the Assembly, just as he had on 1 July, but this time he rejected its humble request. On 11 July, Louis sent his formal reply. The troops gathered near the capital were necessary for the maintenance of order, Louis wrote. The king offered to relocate meetings of the Estates General away from Paris and Versailles if the deputies felt threatened. The deputies were stunned by his response. But after a brief discussion, they dropped the matter and moved on to other business.[91] The deputies did not know that the king's response was disingenuous. Louis knew that he would need more troops in and around Paris because he had already decided to change the composition of the Royal Council, dismissing Necker and his allies and replacing them with much more conservative men. The king, working closely with Marie-Antoinette, Artois and the Polignacs, had chosen a former minister close to the queen, Louis-Charles Auguste le Tonnelier, baron of Breteuil, to lead the council. What Louis really hoped to do is lost to us and historians remain divided on the issue of whether or not he intended to dissolve the Estates General and arrest its leaders.[92] What is certain is that he expected there to be trouble. Louis's new Secretary of War, the very conservative Victor-François de Broglie, knew that rebellion in Paris was likely to happen and the orders he gave, with the approval of the king, were meant to defend the king's interests there without provoking unnecessary unrest.

Necker and his allies were dismissed on the night of Saturday 11 July, apparently timed so that the deputies would find out on a Sunday, when the National Assembly was not in session. But word of Necker's departure caused great tumult in Paris the next morning. A procession protesting Necker's dismissal started at the Palais Royal, seized busts of Necker and the king's cousin, the duke of Orléans, from a wax museum and paraded them through Paris, forcing theatres to shut as they went. German-speaking cavalry led by Charles-Eugène, the prince of Lambesc, entered Paris from the west and attempted to disperse a large body of protestors gathered at the Place Vendôme and in the Tuileries gardens. When a rumor that troops were massacring civilians reached units of the French Guards, they mutinied and rushed to the defense of the people. Faced with military opposition, Lambesc withdrew to the Place Louis XV (now the Place de la Concorde) and requested reinforcements. They were dispatched far too slowly and Lambesc had to withdraw. After his cavalry left the city,

---

[91] AP 8: 219–20; Bailly, *Mémoires d'un témoin*, 1: 312–13.
[92] Ferrières believed that the king intended to impose his plan of 23 June and was willing to use force to do so. Ferrières, *Mémoires*, 1: 131.

Paris slipped entirely out of royal control. Faced with the possibility of a descent into chaos, the electors of Paris, who had continued to meet after electing deputies to the Estates General, entered Paris's city hall, the Hôtel de Ville, and demanded to be made part of the city government. A new body, the Commune of Paris, was created on the spot and without royal approval. The king's man in Paris, the *Prévôt des Marchands* (a kind of mayor appointed by the king) Jacques de Flesselles, was made head of the new city council, but he was only nominally in charge. The first order of business for the new city council was to raise a bourgeois militia to maintain order and protect property.[93]

As word of Necker's dismissal and the growing disorder in Paris reached Versailles, the deputies decided to meet immediately and sit in permanent session so they would avoid being locked out of their hall if the king decided to suspend or dismiss the Estates General. On 13 July, hearing dire news from all quarters and fearing for their own safety, the deputies debated what to do. The sense of the room was that Necker would have to be recalled, but the deputies tangled themselves in knots trying to decide whether or not they could ask the king to recall him without overstepping the boundaries of the legislative power. Mounier spoke first, noting that the Assembly had no right to request Necker's return. But he justified an incursion into the king's prerogatives by the unique circumstances the deputies found themselves in.[94] The count of Virieu supported Mounier and added a motion that the deputies should reswear the Tennis Court Oath in order to show that the Assembly would not be intimidated. The liberal Noble deputy Emmanuel Marie Fréteau de Saint-Just suggested a return to the tactic of 1 July. He suggested that the president of the Assembly come up with some beautiful words to convince the king to recall Necker as a favor to the Assembly.[95] After hours of debate, the Assembly sent a delegation to beseech the king to send away the new troops, to allow a militia to form in Paris, and to recall Necker. When approached, the king flatly refused to grant their requests.[96] The delegation returned to the

---

[93] In the previous two paragraphs, we rely on Hardman, *Louis XVI* (1993), 155–58; Godechot, *Taking of the Bastille*, 178–97; Price, *Road from Versailles*, 75–87, 91–92; Sutherland, *French Revolution and Empire*, 56–58; Andress, *French Revolution and the People*, 106–08; Shapiro, *Traumatic Politics*, 87–93.

[94] He was supported by Target, Clermont-Tonnerre, and Lally-Tollendal. Mirabeau, *Dix-neuvième lettre de comte de Mirabeau à ses commettans* (n.p., n.d.), 13; AP 8: 223–27; Bailly, *Mémoires d'un témoin*, 1: 334. In fact, the Estates General had long sought to influence the composition of the Royal Council or force the dismissal of ministers. Hayden, *Estates General*, 130.

[95] Bailly, *Mémoires d'un témoin*, 1: 335; Duquesnoy, *Journal*, 1: 196–97; AP 8: 226–27.

[96] Duquesnoy, *Journal*, 1: 197; AP 8, 229; Bailly, *Mémoires d'un témoin*, 1: 339–40. Bailly noted that the deputies were "frozen" by the king's response. Bailly, *Mémoires d'un témoin*, 1: 340.

Assembly hall, and after more discussion, the deputies declared that they persisted in their decrees of 17, 20 and 23 June. This declaration marks a critical turning point, as Noble and Clerical deputies who had previously refused to participate voted in favor of the act.[97] Facing the possible dissolution of the Assembly and the arrest of its leaders, an enlarged and passionate majority declared its determination to persist as a National Assembly. Far from intimidating the deputies, the king's dismissal of Necker had encouraged even more deputies to rally to the Assembly.[98]

The events of 14 July culminated in the destruction of royal power in Paris. This changed the king's mind where the Assembly's humble pleas could not. In the aftermath of that epic day, the king once again had to accept the Assembly's suggestions because he was not strong enough to enforce his will. While the deputies had tried to convince Louis to recall Necker, the new city government in Paris had begun putting together a bourgeois militia to maintain order. To be effective, the new militia needed arms and munitions. So did less organized groups of people throughout Paris, if they intended to defend themselves against an all-too-plausible assault by troops loyal to the king. Gun shops were raided throughout the city. On the morning of 14 July, a crowd demanding arms mobbed Les Invalides, a military hospital at the western edge of Paris where retired soldiers lived under military discipline. More than 30,000 muskets were taken, but powder was nowhere to be had. It turned out that all of the gunpowder in Paris had been sent to the Bastille, a medieval fortress in the eastern part of Paris. The fortress had long used as a prison, especially for political prisoners, and was defended by retired soldiers from Les Invalides and a contingent of the Swiss Guards. By the time the crowd had moved from Les Invalides to the Bastille, the new city government had already entered into negotiations with the governor of the fortress for its surrender and the delivery of gunpowder and arms to the city. Seeing the Bastille surrounded by a large and growing crowd, the governor prepared to defend the fortress. Negotiations stalled, and after a series of misunderstandings between the crowd, the city, and the governor, the fortress was taken by force. The violence largely abated with the taking of the prison, with only seven of the defenders killed, as opposed to over a hundred of the attackers.

[97] Duquesnoy, *Journal*, 1: 197–98. Duquesnoy noted that some of the most recalcitrant bishops snuck out before the vote. For the decree, see Bailly, *Mémoires d'un témoin,* 1: 340–42.

[98] AP 8: 230. During the debate, Noble deputies had risen up stating that it was necessary to forget the divisions in the body that had passed by, and that all of the deputies had to rally to save their "patrie," even at the cost of their lives. AP 8: 227. The recalcitrant Noble deputy Bousmard swore once Lally-Tollendal assured them that swearing to stay assembled did not require them to approve of the Third Estate's actions on 17 and 23 June. Duquesnoy, *Journal,* 1: 198. On 16 July, the remaining recalcitrants formally agreed to participate in the activities of the Assembly. AP 8: 238.

Nevertheless, the governor of the fortress and his lieutenant were brutally killed while being taken to the Hôtel de Ville, as it was widely believed that the governor had given a command to his soldiers to fire on the crowd under a flag of truce. At the Hôtel de Ville, Flesselles was killed when he attempted to leave, similarly suspected of treachery by the crowd. The rest of the royal officials in Paris quickly went to ground fearing the same fate. Paris had been lost to the king.[99]

Unable to impose his will in Paris or on the deputies in Versailles, Louis made the very practical decision to declare his willingness to work with the National Assembly. On the morning of 15 July, as the deputies debated again how to ensure Necker's recall, the Assembly received word that the king was on his way. Louis arrived with minimal pomp, accompanied only by his brothers and a small honor guard. He took the podium and announced that he had ordered the troops around Paris to be withdrawn, that he recognized the Paris militia, and that he looked forward to working with the National Assembly to restore order in Paris. It was the first time the king had used the term "National Assembly" in a formal setting, and to the deputies it marked his acceptance of the body.[100] In an instant Louis granted two of the three things asked for by the delegation he had met the previous day. When the president of the Assembly brought up the third request, politely mentioning that Necker's dismissal had triggered the unrest in Paris, Louis did not respond. Nevertheless, Louis's concessions on the other two matters were met with wild applause and the deputies as a body escorted the king back to the royal chateau.[101] When the Assembly resumed its meeting later that day, Barnave suggested the Assembly seek the dismissal of the current ministers. But Clermont-Tonnerre opposed any attempt to send a delegation to Louis, saying that the king fully understood the will of the Assembly. It was better to give Louis time to act and avoid spoiling the appearance of unity. The Assembly sided with Clermont-Tonnerre. They would give the king the time to make the right decision.[102] Still, the deputies worried about the future. After the king's

---

[99] In this paragraph, we rely on Godechot, *Taking of the Bastille*, 185–97; Sutherland, *French Revolution and Empire*, 58–60; Andress, *1789*, 282–96; Andress, *French Revolution and the People*, 108–10; Collins, *From Tribes to Nation*, 547–49.

[100] On the king's visit to the National Assembly, see Bailly, *Mémoires d'un témoin*, 2: 1–10; Mirabeau, *Dix-neuvième lettre*, 28–31; AP 8: 236–37; Ferrières, *Mémoires*, 1: 135–42; *Correspondance d'Anjou*, 1: 373–74; Creuzé-Latouche, *Journal*, 232–35.

[101] Mirabeau, *Dix-neuvième lettre*, 29–31; Bailly, *Mémoires d'un témoin*, 2: 4, 6–10; AP 8: 236–37; Ferrières, *Correspondance*, 89–90; *Correspondance d'Anjou*, 1: 374. Tackett, *Becoming a Revolutionary*, 163–64.

[102] AP 8: 237.

visit, two Third Estate deputies from Anjou, Urbain-René Pilastre and Jean-Baptiste Le Clerc, noted in a letter to their constituents that "the Assembly is nevertheless on guard against the ministers. It is not the heart of the king that we doubt, it is those of the men who counsel him."[103]

The deputies were right to worry about the intentions of the king's new ministers. Breteuil had made efforts to get new loans to allow the monarchy to survive the fall of Necker, but the collapse of order in Paris threatened his attempt to stabilize royal finance.[104] That night, in a meeting of the Royal Council, Breteuil nevertheless recommended that Louis retreat to Metz, a fortress-town near the border of the Holy Roman Empire. Louis at first agreed to go, though how he planned to finance his government was unclear. But then Broglie informed him that the army was no longer reliable and that he could not assure safety of the royal family on the road to the frontier. Fearing for the safety of his family, Louis decided to stay in Versailles. He realized that he had no choice but to accept the National Assembly, to recall Necker, and see what the Assembly could do to salvage the awful situation in Paris. The decision made, his conservative ministers fled, as did Artois and the Polignacs.[105]

Word of the collapse of the conservative ministry overnight did not reach the Assembly.[106] On the morning of the 16th the matter for discussion was once again how to ensure Necker's return. Barnave began the debate by proposing a way in which the Assembly could *force* the king to recall Necker. He declared that the Assembly always had the right to refuse to work with a given minister. They could refuse to work with the current ministers until the king dismissed them and recalled Necker. Mounier found this line of reasoning absurd. He defended a strong separation between the powers of the legislature and the executive. The king had specifically asked them to advise him on how to restore order in Paris, Mounier said, and that was the reason they could ask him to recall Necker. In the future, he claimed, the legislature would not be able to interfere at all with the king's choice of ministers. It was only the unusual circumstances they faced that allowed them to infringe on the king's prerogatives.[107]

---

[103] *Correspondance d'Anjou*, 1: 374. On the subject of the deputies' anxiety, see Shapiro, *Traumatic Politics*, 100–10.

[104] J. Hardman, *The Life of Louis XVI* (New Haven, 2016), 325–26.

[105] Price, *Road from Versailles*, 92–93; Sutherland, *French Revolution and Empire*, 61; Félix, *Louis XVI et Marie Antoinette*, 490–91. Félix argues instead that Louis ordered them to leave France following his decision to recall Necker. Félix, *Louis XVI et Marie Antoinette*, 491–92. Hardman, *Life of Louis XVI*, 329–30.

[106] Godechot, *Taking of the Bastille*, 257–58.

[107] AP 8: 241–43; Mirabeau, *Dix-neuvième lettre*, 40–46; Jean-Joseph Mounier, *Exposé*, 15, 18–19; Bailly, *Mémoires d'un témoin*, 2: 36–38. Barnave's demand that the Assembly have some role in

Clermont-Tonnerre again said that the king knew the will of the Assembly and would come around in time.[108] He wanted to guard the king's dignity: the king had to be allowed to make his decisions without appearing to be forced into them by the Assembly. Then Lally-Tollendal made a critical intervention. He stated that the people had made it clear what they wanted. The deputies had to ask the king to dismiss his current ministers and recall Necker. Lally-Tollendal avoided the matter of the Assembly's rights entirely, and his speech worked like a tonic. The deputies voted to send a new delegation to ask for Necker's recall. But before it could send the delegation, the king sent word that he had recalled Necker.[109] Louis had given in on all three demands made by the Assembly on 13 July. With the king's decision to recall Necker and his acceptance of the revolution in Paris, the last recalcitrant finally signaled his acceptance of the existence of the National Assembly.

The uprising in Paris and the inability of the army to control the city demonstrated to everyone, the king included, that the royal government was impotent. It would be up to the Assembly to craft a constitution that would enable the government to be more effective in the future. The clear lesson for all to see was that disorder at the very top of the government, whether a struggle between the king and his parlements or between the king and his National Assembly, guaranteed disorder in the cities. But the king's assurances that he would work with the National Assembly and his recognition of the new Paris government and its militia did little to restore order. On 22 July, unruly crowds killed two former royal officials in front of the Hôtel de Ville, the former intendant of Paris and the man who had replaced Necker briefly on the Royal Council. Their bodies were mutilated and their heads paraded through Paris. Deputies who had cheered the fall of the Bastille were appalled by the massacre of two royal officials who had done little more than faithfully serve their king. That the murder of these men came after the king's concessions and his visit to Paris made the city seem ungovernable. Worse, disorder had spread into the provinces along with word of Necker's dismissal. Having seen off the threat of ministerial despotism, the deputies now had to find a way to prevent a descent into anarchy.[110]

As the deputies embarked on writing a constitution for France, they took the problem of public order very seriously. If they wanted to prevent

naming royal ministers echoed efforts by the Estates General since time immemorial to have a say in composing the Royal Council.
[108] AP 8: 244.   [109] Ibid.; Ferrières, *Correspondance*, 91; Duquesnoy, *Journal*, 1: 40–47.
[110] Tackett, *Becoming a Revolutionary*, 165–69. Lucas, "The Crowd and Politics," 444–45.

anarchy, they had to boost the faith the French had in their government. The deputies did this by taking steps in August and September to craft a constitution that would prevent a return to ministerial despotism. They had to ensure that the rights of the people were protected and that the legislative and executive powers were firmly established. They had to minimize clashes between the executive and legislative powers that might stir up public disorder. As we will see in the next Chapter, they hoped that a clear demonstration of their determination to establish a new constitution would help restore public order. In August and September of 1789, the deputies faced their greatest task to date. They had to write a constitution that would ensure that the government ruled in the interests of the common good, rather than the particular interests of the deputies or of the king. Only such a constitution, they believed, could ensure public order. With unrest smoldering in Paris and disorder spreading through the kingdom, the stakes could not have been higher.

CHAPTER 5

Toward a Defensive Constitution

The next major question the deputies faced was that of how to balance the powers of the legislative and executive offices in the new constitution. There were no self-evident answers to the questions of how powerful the legislature ought to be in relation to the king, or what role the broader public would have in legislative affairs. When Clermont-Tonnerre presented a report summarizing the content of the *cahiers* on 27 July, speaking on behalf of the Constitutional Committee, he noted that all of the *cahiers* demanded the "regeneration of the French Empire [*l'Empire français*]," but that they disagreed as to whether this regeneration required a new constitution or a simple reform of a few abuses.[1] This lack of uniformity meant that the deputies could not simply derive the constitution directly from the *cahiers*. They would have to decide what the new constitution would be like. In addition, they faced widespread popular violence, both in Paris and in the provinces. Settling constitutional issues would be intrinsically linked to the issue of calming public disorder. Of necessity, discussions over how to frame the constitution took place at the same time as debates over how to restore civil peace.

While the deputies accepted that the violence of 12–14 July had saved the Revolution, they were reluctant to create a role for the popular classes or for popular violence in the new political order. The events of 22 July, culminating in the brutal murder of two former government ministers by a Parisian crowd, had appalled most of the deputies and they looked for a way to prevent violence in the capital.[2] As disorder spread through the kingdom, the deputies sought ways to calm the people of France. The problem of popular unrest filled their discussions in the last days of July,

---

[1] AP 8: 283. Fitzsimmons, *Remaking of France*, 51.

[2] Tackett, *Becoming a Revolutionary*, 167–69; Fitzsimmons, *Remaking of France*, 50. Morris was impressed by the actions of the people when they took the Bastille and horrified at their behavior when they paraded the heads of the two royal officials killed on 22 July past him at the Palais Royal. Morris, *Diary*, 148, 150, 158–59.

and in early August a small group of deputies came to the conclusion that strong action to resolve grievances against the feudal system would help spread peace through the nation. The night of 4 August began with a reading of the latest proposal for a decree to reestablish law and order in the kingdom, but two great nobles, Louis-Marc Antoine, vicomte of Noailles, and Armand, duke of Aiguillon, came forward one after the other to propose an end to many practices deemed oppressive in the *cahiers*. They were followed to the podium by a parade of deputies renouncing every privilege from the old order.[3] It took the better part of a week to translate the many renunciations into decrees, and the final version was completed on 11 August. In a special ceremony, the Assembly presented the decrees to Louis on 13 August. The deputies believed the king would quickly accept the so-called August decrees and thought that news of them would reduce unrest throughout France.[4] Then they took up other constitutional questions, debating the outline and articles of a declaration of rights, again conceived as a way to calm the French by demonstrating the seriousness with which the deputies took their task to write a constitution. On 26 August, the deputies accepted an ultimately final version of the Declaration of the Rights of Man and Citizen. This document enshrined the sovereignty of the nation and the right of the people to participate in government, directly or through their representatives. But even as the deputies worked to calm the passions of the ordinary people, a group of center-right deputies began organizing to craft a constitution that would minimize the role popular influences would play in the new order.[5]

Deputies who favored a balanced constitution on the English model came to be called the *Monarchiens*. This group arose from the deputies who had led the moderates in the Third Estate: Mounier, the Dauphiné delegation, and their allies. One reason the group formed was the treatment Thouret had received when elected president of the Assembly at the beginning of August. Thouret had reliably sided with the Dauphinois deputies and he had opposed adopting the name "National Assembly" for the union of the orders. News of his election led to an eruption of unrest at the Palais Royal. Activists threatened to march on the Assembly to reverse what they saw as the triumph of the aristocrats. Thouret chose to

---

[3] Tackett, *Becoming a Revolutionary*, 171–75. Jones, *Reform and Revolution*, 181–86. See also G. Lefebvre, *The Great Fear*, trans. J. A. White (Princeton, 1982), esp. 157–58.

[4] Fitzsimmons, *Remaking of France*, 61–62.

[5] Margerison, *Pamphlets and Public Opinion*, 161–63. The Declaration of the Rights of Man and Citizen implied limitations on popular participation, as seen in Articles 6 and 14, where the French were assured their right to representation, not necessarily participation, in the legislative power.

prevent this by resigning. Mounier feared a precedent had been set and that Paris activists would continue to seek influence over the Assembly by threats of violence. He and his allies decided that a robust executive power would be necessary to maintain public order. Only a two-chamber house and a strong executive veto could prevent popular pressure from improperly influencing future assemblies' decisions.[6]

Mounier and his allies in the Third Estate saw themselves as patriots and supporters of the Revolution who recognized the essential sovereignty of the nation. They were concerned, though, that the Revolution was moving too quickly and that this rapid movement would alienate parts of the French population. They were deeply disturbed by popular unrest and feared a complete breakdown of law and order. In order to build a center-right constitution focused on a powerful king, they sought support from sympathetic conservative Noble and Clerical deputies. By the end of August or early September, the Monarchiens had formed a working alliance with conservative leaders like the abbé Jean-Sifrein Maury and Jacques Antoine Marie de Cazalès. This did not mean that these recalcitrants had decided to embrace the Revolution. Rather, they saw an opportunity to halt its forward motion so they could work toward their real goal, returning to the platform found in the king's declaration of 23 June.[7]

Mounier's alliance with the right in the Assembly meant that the centrist coalition that had proven so successful from May through July was breaking down. Gilbert du Motier, marquis of Lafayette, thought a division among the patriot deputies was dangerous and sought to reconcile them. He sponsored meetings between the more and less conservative members of the coalition and encouraged them to compromise, not least to prevent further deterioration of public order.[8] In particular, Lafayette sought compromise on the matter of the king's power to veto legislation sent him by future legislatures. Influential deputies met three times to discuss the veto, twice at Lafayette's home and once at the house of Thomas Jefferson, then in Paris acting as *chargé d'affaires* for the United States. Barnave, Duport, and Alexandre de Lameth argued in favor of the suspensive veto, one subject to possible override, but Mounier and his supporters would not budge in their

---

[6] Mounier, *Exposé*, 31–32. Margerison, *Pamphlets and Public Opinion*, 229 n. 43. On the Monarchiens, see Egret, *La révolution des notables;* Griffiths, *Le centre perdu.*

[7] Tackett, *Becoming a Revolutionary*, 185–87.

[8] Margerison, *Pamphlets and Public Opinion*, 165–66. Morris spoke often with Lafayette in June and July. See, for example, his discussion with Lafayette on constitutional matters of 28 July 1789. Morris, *Diary*, 164–65.

support for an unlimited veto.[9] Worse, the alliance of conservative and center-right deputies sparked unrest in the Palais Royal and an attempted march on the Assembly at the end of August. Menacing letters were sent to the president of the Assembly threatening revenge on any deputy who supported an absolute veto for the king. Rumor had it that proscription lists were being circulated containing the names of deputies who supported a royal veto.[10] After having made tremendous sacrifices in the August decrees and drafting the Declaration of Rights to establish their bona fides, the deputies faced threats to their lives and property.

In these disturbed circumstances, with threats to public order and with their own safety in mind, the deputies discussed the proper relationships between deputy and constituent and between Assembly and king. One difficulty with analyzing their discussion of these relationships is the amazing complexity of the debate, as deputy after deputy spoke at varying length, proposing model after model of how the king's veto power would function. The first three weeks of September also featured a series of debates on the permanence and basic unity of the legislative assembly and the frequency of elections. Their debates even touched on the critical question of whether or not the sitting executive – Louis XVI – would have the right to influence the constitution-writing process. Any attempt to understand the debates as a whole is made much more difficult by the fragmentary nature of the evidence available to us. During August and September of 1789 the debates of the National Assembly were still not officially recorded as spoken. We have to reconstruct the speeches from abbreviated newspaper accounts, from partisan *mémoires*, from incomplete accounts found in the diaries and letters of witnesses, and from printed versions compiled after the fact.

Given the complexity of the matters at hand and the incomplete record of these debates previously available, historians have arrived at very different conclusions from the same series of events. Historians have long portrayed the main division during the debate over the king's veto power as between those who wished to establish strong bulwarks against popular unrest by creating a robust executive power and those who thought it more

---

[9] Margerison, *Pamphlets and Public Opinion*, 166; Tackett, *Becoming a Revolutionary*, 189; L. Gottshalk and M. Maddox, *Lafayette in the French Revolution through the October Days* (Chicago, 1969), 227–30, 237–43.

[10] Margerison, *Pamphlets and Public Opinion*, 166–67. On the attempt to intimidate the deputies on 30–31 August, see A. C. Thibaudeau, *Biographie Mémoires: 1765–1792* (Paris, 1875), 97–99; Ferrières, *Mémoires*, 1: 222–27. See also Rouff, "Le peuple ouvrier de Paris," 484–505; Gottschalk and Maddox, *Lafayette*, 229–43; Alpaugh, *Non-Violence*, 67; Tackett, *Becoming a Revolutionary*, 190.

important to set up strong bulwarks against a return to ministerial despotism by creating a weak executive. In truth, both the Monarchiens and the center-left patriots who favored a suspensive veto feared popular disorder and wanted a strong executive, one that would share in the power delegated by the nation to their government. Where the two groups differed most was over the question of how disagreements between the executive and legislative powers would be managed, and how these inevitable disagreements could be resolved without causing public disorder. Only those who wished to deny the king a veto sought to create a truly weak executive, one that would be subordinate to the legislative assembly and be refused an equal share of the power delegated by the sovereign nation. As we will see, the main concern deputies had was to establish public order by restoring confidence in the government. Though they had differing ideas about how to accomplish their goal, they all agreed that forging the proper relationship between king and legislature was vital to establishing and maintaining public order.

On 31 August, in the shadow of threats against the deputies and an attempted march on the Assembly itself by Parisian activists, Lally-Tollendal delivered the Constitutional Committee's proposal for a two-chamber legislature and an unlimited royal veto. To justify a strong veto power, Lally-Tollendal argued that the king was a necessary and integral part of the legislative process, acting as a necessary shield against both the hasty actions of an impulsive legislature and against the encroachments on royal power that would result if the king could not protect his constitutional prerogatives. To give the executive power complete control over legislation or to exclude it entirely from its creation, he argued, could only result in tyranny. To support his claims, Lally-Tollendal used historical analogy. During the English revolution, when Parliament became a one-chamber house and not subject to a royal veto it had established despotism, he claimed, but the Glorious Revolution, involving the free decisions made by both houses of Parliament and accepted by the king, led to a stable political order.[11]

Lally-Tollendal proceeded to root discussion of the constitution in both history and the national will. He argued that the deputies had to respect the past they shared and that it would be a "grave error" to pretend that there had never been a settled system of government before their era. But having invoked a responsibility to the past, Lally-Tollendal then insisted that the deputies were not bound to blindly follow their ancestors. Instead, he gave

[11] AP 8: 514, 517.

the will of their constituents as expressed in the *cahiers* the definitive role in determining the outlines of the constitution to be written. He pointed out that the vast majority of their mandates demanded "imperatively" the "concurrence" and "concert of the orders and the king in the formation of the law and demand it as one of the bases of the constitution." Moreover, he continued, because their *cahiers* contained this instruction, the deputies had to act to establish this system "under pain of disobeying the nation and being disavowed" by their constituents, and of "inserting a clause that would be an infraction of the national will."[12] The deputies were not bound by the past, but they were accountable to their electors. To refuse the king a veto would be to refuse to listen to one's own electors, rendering the Assembly's actions illegitimate and invalid.[13]

Lally-Tollendal moved on to the relationship between the executive and legislative powers inherent in a good constitution. He noted the very different functions of the executive and legislative powers, and argued that the constitution must protect both powers from the impulsive demands of popular opinion. To combat such impulsion he introduced two features. First, he argued that there had to be a two-chamber legislature, and second, that the king needed a veto that could not be overridden. Lally-Tollendal began by noting that the very essence of the executive body was "unity, speed, motion," and that in contrast the legislative body had to be marked by "deliberation, slowness, stability." To maintain a unicameral body would be to risk "the constant danger of being led astray by eloquence, of being seduced by sophistry," dangers from inside the Assembly. A one-chamber house would be especially vulnerable, he argued, to the demands of the "public cry" that it would not dare ignore or resist. He thought that having a second chamber would help to avoid this problem, because it could suggest revisions to laws proposed by the popular house. If the two chambers could not agree, the matter would continue to be debated, slowing the process down and allowing for the law to reach such perfection as the human condition allowed.[14]

Lally-Tollendal also noted that with a one-chamber legislature there was a real danger that the king would not feel able to use his powers to protect

---

[12] Ibid., 515.
[13] Reference to the imperative mandate and the content of the *cahiers* in general by the Constitutional Committee ought to put paid to claims that the deputies had voted to abrogate their mandates while writing the constitution. Arguments in support of the absolute and suspensive vetoes relied on the will of the nation as expressed in the *cahiers*. Baker argues instead that the Monarchiens based their platform on the notion of the need to perfect an already existing constitution. Baker, *Inventing the French Revolution*, 258, 260, 273.
[14] AP 8: 516.

himself against it, fearing popular unrest. But in a system with two houses, the royal veto would seldom have to be used, as the debates between the houses would lead to laws the king would always be able to accept. With a one-chamber house, an absolute veto would be dangerous to use. With a two-chamber house, it would be used only in exceptional circumstances. Lally-Tollendal gave the example of England, in which the royal veto had been used only once in the eighteenth century because noisome laws had "expired between the two chambers, without having reached the throne." This practice was of particular use as it kept the king from appearing to be involved directly in politics and thus protected the dignity of the throne. The king would seldom have to veto a law, relying on the inability of the two houses to agree on bad legislation.[15]

The committee further proposed that the two houses have different compositions. The lower would be popularly elected, but the upper, while not replicating the old society of orders, would be made up of those who had proven themselves worthy of admission through their accomplishments. They would be older and wealthier than the members of the lower house, and would be chosen by the king. Lally-Tollendal then noted, almost in passing, that to give the king sole power to nominate these senators would violate the principle that the nation should choose its own representatives. With this principle in mind, he proposed that the provincial estates give the king a list from which the king could choose, and that the men he chose would to serve for life.[16] Thus, Lally-Tollendal introduced into the legislative body a group that would be accountable at least in part to the king, not the nation. Members of the senate, appointed for life, would not be accountable for their actions to the people and would establish a bulwark against popular pressure on the legislative assembly.

Even though the committee proposed a return to a divided legislature, the new proposal was hardly counter-Revolutionary. It did not envision a return to the society of orders or to the constitutional system Louis XVI had proposed in the Royal Session of 23 June. It contained plentiful safeguards meant to prevent a return to past abuses. The system was meant to allow for accountability of the government to the electorate, if sometimes only indirectly. Royal power would be substantially diminished. For example, in a departure from the consensus Third Estate deputies had reached in late June, the committee insisted that the king be denied initiative in proposing laws. Lally-Tollendal stated that the king could not have the power to propose laws out of a concern that the

[15] Ibid., 517.   [16] Ibid., 519.

executive would usurp the legislative power imperceptibly over time. In order to prevent diminishment of their powers, the legislature had to have a monopoly on proposing laws.[17] But as a counterweight, in order to protect his executive powers and the constitution itself, the king had to have the power to veto laws proposed by the legislature. Lally-Tollendal proposed for the king an unlimited veto (*veto illimité*), claiming that if the assembly could override his veto, the king did not truly hold part of the legislative power. If the king did not have a means to stop laws from being passed, then he would have no way to prevent usurpation of his powers or the confusion of powers, or even the overturning of the constitution and oppression of the people by the legislature. Moreover, Lally-Tollendal noted that since the power of the purse had been returned to the representatives of the people, there was be nothing to fear from an unlimited veto.[18] After all, the king could not rule without money.

Lally-Tollendal stated that without an absolute veto, there would be no monarchy:

> In the final analysis the question of whether the king will have a suspensive or unlimited veto is the question of whether or not there will be a king; for the will of the nation is that there will be a king, and the liberty of the nation requires a king, requires the king's prerogative, needs the sanction of the king. Finally, we do not fear to repeat . . . what count Mirabeau has said with his characteristic energy, that he would rather live in Constantinople than in France, if one can make the laws without the king's approval.[19]

For the Constitutional Committee, what separated freedom from tyranny was the right of the executive to veto laws passed by an elected assembly without fear that his veto would be overridden. The power of the

---

[17] In this we can see echoes of both Rousseau's fear that the main threat to a republic was encroachment by the executive power into the legislative power (in *The Social Contract*, book 3, sections 6, 10, and 18) and American debates over the correct balance of powers between the legislative and executive bodies. James Madison had written that "power is of an encroaching nature" and that measures had to be taken to protect the different powers from each other. In a hereditary monarchy the executive power was a major threat to the constitution, he wrote, though in a republic it was often the legislature that would undermine it (James Madison, *Federalist* 48 [1 February 1788]). Madison cites Jefferson's *Notes on Virginia*, which had been translated into French in 1786. Documents from the American debates were easily available to the deputies, with state constitutions translated from 1778 forward and the Federal Constitution from early 1789. D. Lacorne, *L'invention de la République: Le modèle americain* (Paris, 1991), 34, 78–79; H. Dippel, "Angleterre, Etats-Unis, France: Constitutionnalisme et souveraineté populaire," in R. Bourderon, ed., *L'an I et l'apprentissage de la démocratie: Actes du colloque organizé à Saint-Ouen les 21, 22, 23, 24 juin 1993 . . .* (Saint-Denis, 1995), 553–54. The American Founders and the French deputies drew on the same tradition of Classical education, relying on examples from Roman history to make their points. Lacorne, *L'invention de la République*, 49–50.

[18] AP 8: 521–22.   [19] Ibid., 522.

legislature to propose laws and control the purse would protect it from the king and his ministers. The existence of an upper house and of an absolute veto would protect the legislature against undue popular pressure, and it would protect the king from encroachments on his powers. Nevertheless, since the lower house held the power of the purse, the king would not be able to force a return to past abuses.

Mounier spoke next, further explaining the committee's proposal. He clarified that the king would not be able to veto constitutional acts. According to Mounier, the king would have a veto over legislation only once the constitution had been established. The committee recognized that the king could submit his opinions on the proposed constitution to the Assembly, but in the end, the king would have to accept the constitution when given to him. If the king refused, the Assembly could refuse new taxes or resort to its constituents for support, "because the nation certainly has the right to employ all necessary means to become free." This part of the proposal indicated a substantial change from the consensus held by deputies in late June, when it was assumed that the king would have to freely approve all aspects of the new constitution.

Mounier then drew the deputies' attention to specific articles in the proposed constitution concerning the relationship between deputies and their electors that bore the clear stamp of previous decisions taken by the Assembly. These included Article 27, which prohibited imperative mandates, and the statement in Article 55 that the legislative chambers could not deliberate in the absence of a quorum and that all decisions would be made on the vote of a simple majority.[20] The legislative assembly, not the king, would have the power to write laws and it would be able to defend itself in the future. The deputies would no longer require the traditional mandate to defend themselves against the king. Mounier wanted strong powers for the king in the future, but he also wanted the deputies to understand that they, not the king, would write the laws then, and that now they, not the king, would write the constitution.

The question of whether or not the king could veto laws proposed by the legislature ended up being the most controversial aspect of the committee's proposal. Debate on this issue ran off and on, interrupted by related constitutional issues, from 1 September until a final vote was held on 21 September. During the debates, the deputies discussed in great detail the relationship between the king and the Assembly and between both and

[20] Ibid., 523–24, 526.

the sovereign nation. They argued over simple words, like "sanction," and over broad philosophical ideas about representation. They also discussed the most practical issues: how to avoid a return to ministerial despotism and how to prevent a descent into anarchy. During the debate, deputies clustered around three ideas about what the royal veto power ought to be. The first group rallied around the proposal made by Lally-Tollendal. These deputies argued that the king ought to have an absolute right to veto legislation, with no possibility of a legislative or popular override. The unlimited or absolute veto was defended by the group of center-right Patriot deputies including Third Estate, Noble, and Clerical deputies known as the Monarchiens. It was also defended by deputies further to the right who did not believe the idea of national sovereignty that underpinned the committee's constitutional project.

A second group clustered around a suspensive veto to ensure that a king could not thwart the will of the nation. Advocates of the suspensive veto disagreed, though, on how a royal veto would be overridden. The first version, proposed by Third Estate deputies Jean-Baptiste Salle and Pétion on 1 September, conceived the king's veto as triggering a referendum in order to ascertain whose opinion better reflected the will of the nation, that of the king or that of the legislators. How this referendum would take place varied significantly according to its several proponents, but the key feature was that it would be up to the electors, not the deputies, to override the king's veto. A second version of the suspensive veto, that proposed by Thouret on 5 September, asked that the legislative assembly itself be the means by which the veto would be overridden. Supporters of this iterative veto disagreed over whether a royal veto would lead to snap elections or if there would be a delay until some number of regularly scheduled elections had passed. Nevertheless, the two versions of the suspensive veto had much in common. Both proposed that the ultimate decision to veto legislation could not be left in the hands of the king alone. The suspensive veto found support from deputies of the center and the center-left of the Assembly. Finally, the last, smallest, and most radical group clustered around the idea that there should be no royal veto power at all. Third Estate deputies like Sieyès and a still-unknown deputy from Arras named Maximilien Robespierre sought to exclude the king from the legislative process, arguing that the king was not an elected representative and could have no voice in matters that required representative status.[21] Even these deputies, though, disagreed as to what

---

[21] On Robespierre, see P. McPhee, *Robespierre: A Revolutionary Life* (New Haven, 2013); C. Haydon and W. Doyle, eds, *Robespierre* (Cambridge, 1999).

model to follow and some proposed that there be some kind of council of revision to prevent the legislative power straying from the will of the nation or being pressured by outside forces into adopting bad laws.

The Monarchiens were in favor of major constitutional changes. They rejected arguments that their ability to reform the constitution was limited to minor tinkering. They consistently argued that the king's powers arose from his status as a representative of the people, rather than from some personal privilege. But they wanted to establish a two-chamber legislature and an absolute veto in order to temper the ability of the people to pressure their deputies and the legislature to pressure the king. On 1 September, Malouet posed the king's veto as a service performed on behalf of the nation in order to guarantee that the legislature acted in the nation's best interests. According to Malouet, the veto "is a national right and a national prerogative, conferred on the chief of the nation by itself, in order to declare and guarantee whether or not a resolution made by its representatives is the expression of the general will." Like Lally-Tollendal, he found the basis for this role in the demands made by the French in the *cahiers* the deputies carried, not in some previous idea of a constitution. Malouet argued that the king, as an "integral part of the legislative body," could not be deprived of a power demanded for him by the nation in the instructions they had given their representatives. Moreover, Malouet noted that there were different kinds of representatives that filled different roles in a well-organized constitution. The king was a special kind of representative, one who combined with the representatives elected by the districts to express the presumed will of the nation. Malouet accepted that the king did not hold his powers by some kind of inherent right, but he denied that the deputies represented the nation adequately by themselves. Only the two bodies together represented the nation.[22] Later in the debate, responding to critics who had challenged the representative role of the king, Malouet agreed that "the king is a delegate of the nation . . . but the deputies chosen in each district are not the nation; they are also only delegates." Since neither the king nor the elected deputies adequately represented the nation alone, France expressed its will through the agreement of the king and the legislature.[23] Malouet's model of political representation marked an historic shift away from the traditional argument that the king alone represented the entire political body.

Mirabeau, though not a member of the group, eloquently laid out an argument almost identical to theirs. On 1 September, he argued that the

[22] AP 8: 536.   [23] Ibid., 586 (5 September 1789).

king was first and foremost a representative of the people. Mirabeau returned to the traditional argument that justified royal prerogative: the king drew his powers from his position as the sole representative of the entire nation. But Mirabeau took for granted the need for other representatives, elected representatives, to help the king find that national will. Mirabeau posed the main problem facing the nation as that of an aristocracy seeking to usurp the prerogatives of both the people and their king. Arguing that the "legislative power must be entrusted to representatives owing to the complete inability of the people to exercise it themselves"; that it was "in the nature of things that the choice of representatives does not necessarily fall to the most worthy"; and that the selection of representatives results in "a kind of aristocracy of fact which ... will become hostile both to the monarch, whom it will wish to equal, and to the people, whom it will always seek to hold down," there needed to be a power which would counterbalance the vanity of the representatives.[24] This power, the king, would act to represent the people's will and interests and prevent the legislature from becoming a new species of tyrant. Mirabeau also raised the delicate matter of the king's willingness to enforce laws that he had no role in creating. Mirabeau claimed that if the king had no role in making the laws he enforced, the deputies could expect him to act in "constant rebellion" against the will of the assembly. It was necessary that he consent to the laws he must enforce in order to ensure that he enforced them in good faith.[25] The king needed to be able to act in the name of the people to defend its interests as well as his own against the legislative body. The king would guarantee that the elected representatives acted in the public interest and his role in making the laws would guarantee that he himself would support them. Finally, he made explicit the link between a royal veto and the possibility of popular unrest. Mirabeau presented the king's veto as a way to correct the dangers of tyranny inherent in a representative government, and to prevent the "upheavals and dismemberments" that would occur if there were not some centralizing force.[26]

The Monarchiens likewise emphasized that an absolute veto would prevent popular unrest. Speaking on 2 September, Emmanuel-Henri-Louis d'Antraigues, deputy of the Nobles from Vivarais, argued that the royal veto was a means to make certain that the will of the assembly matched the will of the people. Given that the Declaration of the Rights

---

[24] H. G. Riquetti, comte de Mirabeau, *Discours de M. le comte de Mirabeau sur la sanction royale* (n.p., n.d.). Trans. by P. H. Beik, in Beik, ed., *The French Revolution* (New York, 1970), 99.
[25] Castellane, "Journal," 137.   [26] Mirabeau, *Discours*, 98.

of Man and Citizen enshrined the right to resist oppression, this check in the hands of the king would make popular revolt less likely because future assemblies would find it harder to pass oppressive laws.[27] The intent of the absolute veto was to influence the kind of legislation that would be proposed by the legislature. Fearing a royal veto, deputies would have to propose more moderate laws, and fearing a loss of popularity, the king would accept those laws that clearly were in the public interest. The two parties would have to work together to find laws they were both satisfied with. If the two parties could not agree, the ultimate veto, insurrection, would still belong to the nation.[28] Politics was to be carried out before the matter could reach a point of confrontation.[29] The king would remain in sole charge of the executive branch and act as a potent check on the legislative power, but he would not have the right to go against the will of the nation.

Supporters of a suspensive veto also grounded the king's veto power in the sovereignty of the nation. They agreed with the Monarchiens that a legislative assembly could err and posed the king's veto as a way to ensure that the will of the assembly was the same as the will of the nation. But they worried that the king, too, could make mistakes and wanted to make the king's veto a means for the nation itself to formally supervise the assembly's actions. They agreed with the Monarchiens that the king's veto would act as a way for the nation to express its will. But they posed a suspensive veto as a way for a disagreement between the executive and the legislature to be peacefully resolved, eliminating the need for the nation to rise up to protect its rights. Salle and his allies proposed that the nation be consulted directly in order to override a veto. On 1 September, Salle proposed the suspensive veto as "a kind of an appeal to the nation, which makes that nation intervene as a judge ... between the king and its representatives." While he recognized that it would be dangerous to arm the nation with such a potent weapon, he argued that the Revolution in the cities and in the

---

[27] AP 8: 543, 545. On the right to resist oppression, see M. Alpaugh, "The Right of Resistance to Oppression: Protest and Authority in the French Revolutionary World," *FHS* 39:3 (2016), 567–98.

[28] AP 8: 545. A. Viatte, *Le veto légilatif dans la Constitution des États-Unis et dans la Constitution française de 1791* (Paris, 1901), 84–85.

[29] A functional example of this could be seen in an English case alluded to by Lally-Tollendal in his speech: After 1707, the English monarchs had sought to influence Parliament as to the wisdom of the royal will before legislation was passed, rather than refusing consent. Djordje Rafajlovic argues that the royal veto fell out of use as the government came to be formed out of the majority party in Parliament. Any use of the veto would have clearly indicated a lack of faith in the majority party, and would have precipitated a constitutional crisis. D. Rafajlovic, *Veto ... son reflet historique et son importance politique actuellement* (Dillingen, 1951), 52, 55–56.

countryside had awakened in the people a sense of their rights and a love of liberty. But he drew a strong distinction between the sovereignty of the people and their ability to govern themselves. The people themselves could not legislate: that was the duty of their representatives. Salle praised the deputies for their sage deliberations in the Assembly, contrasting their behavior to the tumultuous single-chamber assembly unconstrained by an absolute veto imagined by the Constitutional Committee.[30]

Salle rather misleadingly referred to the suspensive veto as an *appel au peuple*, an "appeal to the people." He did not mean by this phrase an appeal to the people themselves, but to the electoral assemblies that sent deputies to the national legislative body.[31] Salle played skillfully on the notion that the *cahiers* produced by the electoral assemblies contained the basic principles of the new constitution. He went much further than the Monarchiens had in praising the *cahiers*. He also praised the local assemblies that had written the *cahiers*. Salle asked the deputies if their electoral assemblies had been sites of gross tumult and if the *cahiers* they had written did not carry "the germ of the best laws." Obviously, bodies capable of electing good deputies and writing wise *cahiers* were capable of meaningful work. Moreover, Salle argued that a suspensive veto in the form of a referendum to the electoral assemblies would prevent popular disorder. It would allow the people to display their opinions in a less confrontational manner than, for example, refusing to pay taxes or taking to the streets to protest against a royal veto. Pushing back against Lally-Tollendal's praise for the English constitution, Salle claimed that a national referendum would also guarantee that the legislative body would be free of the corruption found in England, where elected representatives acted against the interest of the nation. A suspensive veto would ensure that the deputies and the king alike acted in the interest of the common good.[32]

Salle accepted that the electoral assemblies were not part of the legislature and could not propose or modify the laws submitted to their scrutiny. To preserve simplicity and prevent unrest, the electoral assemblies could be restricted to a simple yes or no vote when considering a law vetoed by the king.[33] They would choose between two interpretations of the nation's will:

---

[30] AP 8: 529–31. On the veto as a referendum, see J. K. Wright "A Republican Constitution in Old Régime France," in M. Van Gelderen and Q. Skinner, eds., *Republicanism: A Shared European Heritage*, 2 vols. (Cambridge, 2002), 1: 305.

[31] This could potentially involve everyone who had voted in the primary electoral assemblies of 1789, an unprecedentedly large number of people. The deputies had not, however, decided the limits of the franchise and voting had proceeded very differently in different areas and in the different orders.

[32] AP 8: 531, 533. Salle most likely took this notion from Rousseau, *Social Contract*, book 3 sections 6, 10, 18.

[33] AP 8: 533–34.

that of the king and that of their legislature. This would prevent either from deviating from the general will. Salle worried that a veto that could not be overturned would lead to despotism as the king's "negative power would become a veritable positive power." He claimed that all despotic governments started out by obeying the law, but that they gained power by evading and bending it.[34] Only a veto that could be overridden would ensure that the king stayed within the bounds of his powers. Finally, Salle made a statement much like that of Lally-Tollendal on the rarity of an actual veto. Salle argued that the very threat of a suspensive veto would mean that the king would never have to use it. Future deputies would know that the laws they passed would be subject to a referendum if the king chose to veto them, and would thus act with wisdom and restraint, never passing laws the nation would not approve. The king would know that his veto would be subject to a referendum, and he would never abuse it by attempting to halt a law that had broad national support.[35] Thus Salle argued that the suspensive veto would have all of the benefits of the absolute veto, but would add on an additional layer of security. If the king were to use an absolute veto against the interests of the nation, the only recourse the French had was rebellion. But if a king used his suspensive veto the same way, the French would be able to overturn it in a peaceful and orderly manner.

Nevertheless, not all of the deputies agreed that the king derived his powers from the will of the nation. The most ardent royalists argued that the power of the king to veto legislation antedated any attempt by the deputies to write a constitution and was a part of the monarchy that could not be changed. These recalcitrant conservative deputies, mostly deputies who had refused to join in the National Assembly and who had used their mandates as a pretext to halt its activity, sought strong powers for the king and hoped for an aristocratic upper chamber in the legislature. Foremost among the orators of the recalcitrant conservatives was the abbé Maury. He spoke on 3 September in support of the king's already existing prerogatives and provided a stirring defense of royal power and privilege. He did not support broad constitutional changes or the crafting of a new constitution. Maury instead insisted that only abusive practices from the Old Regime needed to be rectified and that the acts of the

---

[34] Ibid., 532. Other deputies on the left worried that the absolute veto would lead to despotism. See L-P. Lofficial, "Lettres de Lofficial," *La nouvelle revue retrospective*, 7 (1897), 109; Palasne de Champeaux and Poulain de Corbion, "Lettres," 257.

[35] AP 8: 534. He was supported in his arguments by Pétion, who denounced the "dreadful" absolute veto. AP 8: 537.

Assembly were subject to revision according to their adherence to the old unwritten constitution.[36]

Like Lally-Tollendal, Maury argued that the king was an integral part of the legislative power, and that this role implied that he had the right to deny the acts of the legislative body the status of law.[37] Maury called the king a "co-legislator of the state . . . an integral part of the legislative body." He dismissed fears that the king would abuse his power, claiming that the committee's proposal contained sufficient means for the nation to resist a return to despotism. He noted that the permanence of the assembly and the responsibility of ministers to it would form a sufficient counterweight to any amount of royal power. Moreover, the power of a free press and of public opinion would act in concert to thwart any potential despot. Future deputies would thank the king for his veto when he used it to halt some unwise legislative project in the future.[38] But Maury claimed that the king held his powers by right, not as a power delegated to him by the nation. This opinion raised a great murmur in the hall, indicating that only a minority of the deputies supported his point of view.[39] Nevertheless, the abbé did not rely solely on an appeal to tradition to convince the deputies that they should support the committee's proposal. In addition, he proposed a maxim of political philosophy based on analysis of past events, meant to warn the deputies against overstepping the legitimate boundaries of their powers. The maxim, as he put it, was: "Whosoever, king or people, abuses authority, inevitably loses it."[40] According to Maury, history warned the deputies against overreaching their authority in an attempt to rein in a despotic king.

To prove his point, Maury invoked the specters of executive overreach and popular unrest. He began with the example of Louis XIV. According

---

[36] See P. H. Beik, "The Abbé Maury and the National Assembly," *Proceedings of the American Philosophical Society* 95: 5 (1951), 546–55. An abbreviated version of Maury's speech appears in AP 8: 552–3.

[37] AP 8: 552.

[38] *Le Point du jour*, 2: 290–91, 94. Jallet noted that Maury's speech was met with derisive applause when he invoked public opinion as being strong enough to halt any attempt by the king or his ministers to abuse the power of the absolute veto. J. Jallet, "Trois lettres de l'abbé Jallet," ed. D. Marié, *AHRF* 22 (1950), 348.

[39] AP 8: 553. Barère commented on 4 September that Maury was the best speaker in support of the absolute veto, but that the argument "appeared to have died on his lips." *Le Point du jour*, 2: 282–83.

[40] Ibid., 291; AP 8: 553. The point was made by Rousseau in his *Considerations on the Government of Poland and on Its Projected Reformation*, book 12 section 9: "Whoever dares to deprive others of their freedom almost always ends up by losing his own; this is true even of kings, and even truer of peoples." Trans and ed. V. Gourevitch, *Rousseau: The Social Contract and Other Later Political Writings* (Cambridge, 1997), 237. At this early stage of the Revolution, conservatives were still likely to use Rousseau's work to defend their projects.

to Maury, Louis XIV expanded royal power not because of some special merit on his part, but because the French felt a sense of shame following the excesses of the Fronde, a rebellion against royal authority that took place between 1648 and 1653. Their shame led them to allow Louis XIV to extend his powers far beyond their just limits without triggering a new rebellion.[41] Likewise, Maury used the English Civil War and Interregnum (1642–60) as an example of a legislature that had overreached, claiming, "the scaffold of Charles I established the power of his successor."[42] In the first case, a rebellion against the king's legitimate authority by aristocrats, parlements, and people led to an expansion of the king's power when the rebellion faltered. In the second, the legislative body's attempt to eliminate the monarchy led not just to a military dictatorship but to a return of the old system once the dictatorship faltered. Maury claimed that the British had struggled mightily to limit the powers of their kings. Like Lally-Tollendal, Maury claimed that they had only succeeded with the adoption of a balanced constitution following the Glorious Revolution. The century of stability in England that followed such a history of tumult, he claimed, proved the wisdom of their constitutional settlement: a two-chamber legislature and a king with an absolute veto.[43] Giving the king a strong veto would also prevent corruption within the assembly, he claimed, arguing that the executive power could not impartially enforce laws unless it had had some role in creating them. Should the king be formally excluded, he would be rendered dependent on the assembly, and would then be forced to use a tactic long enjoyed by kings, "to purchase the virtue of one faction in order to destroy the other."[44] In this he alluded to the Monarchien theme that a king who was excluded from the creation of the laws would act in constant rebellion against the body that made them, seeking to evade constraints to which he had not agreed.

After three days of open debate, Mounier rose on 4 September to defend the Constitutional Committee's proposal. He had a difficult task ahead of him. In addition to seeing off attempts to limit the veto power by allowing for a national referendum, Mounier had to argue against those who opposed any veto power (as we shall see). He had to reassure his colleagues that the committee's proposal did not ground the king's veto in preexisting prerogatives or in an ancient unwritten constitution that could override the will of the nation as expressed in the *cahiers*. Mounier defended the notion

---

[41] *Courrier de Versailles*, 3: 113.   [42] *Le Point du jour*, 2: 292; AP 8: 553.

[43] *Le Point du jour*, 2: 292–93. One should not miss the implicit criticism of Louis XVI in any praise, however veiled, of the Glorious Revolution.

[44] AP 8: 553.

of a representative system in which the nation chose deputies to act on its behalf. He agreed with defenders of a suspensive veto that the will of the deputies was not necessarily the same as the will of the nation, but he rejected their solution that the nation itself should act to guarantee that the legislatures adequately represented it.

According to Mounier, what the assembled deputies arrived at through their deliberations was "the legally presumed general will," not the general will itself. Given the possibility that future deputies might reach conclusions that differed from the general will, the king had a special role to play. The king would have two means to ensure that the decisions made by the deputies reflected the will of the nation: an absolute veto and the right to call for new elections. But the king did not hold these rights as personal prerogatives: he held them as the people's "first delegate," a representative much like the deputies themselves. Mounier emphasized that the nation had not given the right to act on their behalf to the deputies alone. Instead, they had charged, as expressed in the *cahiers,* the king and the assembly "act together to express the general will." Thus when the king refused his sanction, he was not acting to thwart the will of the nation. He was acting to ensure that the will of the assembly was the same as the general will.[45]

Mounier was also sensitive to claims that the king could use an unlimited veto to erode the constitution. Mounier insisted that the king could in no case force his will on the sovereign people. If the king persisted in vetoing a measure that had broad support in the nation, the people retained the right to impose their will on the king with a tax strike or through the terrible weapon of insurrection. But Mounier did not think this would happen. He argued, as had Antraigues on 2 September, that the existence of a powerful royal veto would have a moderating effect on legislation by encouraging the assembly to consider the rights of the people and the prerogatives of the king before submitting legislation for the king's approval. The king would seldom have to use his veto, and then only to protect the rights of the nation itself. In short, the royal veto would keep the deputies accountable to the nation by exposing their decrees to additional scrutiny before they became laws. Mounier also declared absurd the idea that a royal veto could be resolved by the nation itself. The only way to keep the legislative power fully in the hands of the people would be to create a system in which all deputies received binding mandates. He feared that this meant a return to the idea the Assembly had rejected in their

---

[45] AP 8: 561. On the proposed powers to veto legislation and to dismiss the legislature, see AP 8: 557, 561.

declaration of 8 July, that electoral districts could issue orders that bound the legislature itself. According to Mounier, such a system would cause chaos as each district imagined itself capable of commanding the whole nation.[46]

One way to balance the demands of those who wanted a suspensive veto and those who wanted an absolute one was to recognize, as Mounier had suggested, that it would be impossible for the king to persist in an unpopular veto without triggering an insurrection. On 4 September, Paul-Victor de Sèze developed the idea that an absolute veto could only ever be suspensive in practice. In line with his allies, Sèze posed the veto as a primary means of preserving public order and claimed that the suspensive veto was destined to stir unrest by involving the broad public in legislative matters, leading to anarchy. In contrast, the unlimited veto as proposed by the committee would prevent the legislature from making errors of judgment when crafting laws and would therefore help the king to preserve the peace.[47] Sèze emphasized that the king's negative power would be suspensive in fact, though not in name, because of the many and various means the people had to make their will known and, presumably, because the king would be certain to respect the will of the people insofar as it benefited the public good.[48] Demonstrating his acceptance of national sovereignty, Sèze noted that the king's veto opposed to "a fleeting will [i.e., that of the assembly] a permanent will [i.e., that of the king]," both of which were necessary parts of the general will. "The king," he noted, "represents the nation, and it is the nation itself that pronounces this veto."[49] Sèze's version of the absolute veto shared much with the suspensive veto and he in fact denied that there were important differences between the two proposals. Both parties sought a way for controversial matters to be settled without recourse to civil unrest, both sought a way to involve the king in legislative affairs and through him, to involve the will of the nation as arbiter in disputes between the king and the legislature.[50] The Monarchiens argued that the king could not and would not resist the will of the people if it were expressed with perseverance. They also argued that it was necessary for the king to have an absolute veto nonetheless to

---

[46] Ibid., 560–62.

[47] Sèze gave an abbreviated version of his speech on 4 September 1789, but had a longer version published. We include ideas from both versions in this analysis of Sèze's opinion. AP 9: 86. Such a seasoned journalist and political theorist as J.-P. Brissot found it impossible to make sense of Sèze's speech when he heard it given. *Le Patriote français*, 7 September 1789.

[48] AP 9: 89 (21 September 1789).   [49] AP 8: 564 (4 September 1789).

[50] Ibid. For a more developed version of this argument, see AP 9: 90. According to Lameth, Malouet made much the same point. Lameth, *Histoire*, 1: 133–34. See also Malouet, *Correspondance*, 113.

prevent the legislative power from infringing on royal prerogatives or leading the people into error. The absolute veto was meant to protect both the nation and the king from the legislature. It was not meant to protect the king from the nation.

But not everyone who defended a veto for the king was so focused on defending the people against their elected representatives. On 4 September, the abbé Henri Grégoire expanded on Salle's proposal for a suspensive veto by shifting from a defense of the electoral assemblies to an attack on the role of the king in a system with an absolute veto, questioning the wisdom of giving any one man so much power to interpret the national will. Moreover, he argued that use of an absolute veto would inevitably lead to public disorder. He began with a robust defense of the will of their constituents as found in the *cahiers*. In response to the Monarchiens' insistence that the absolute veto had been demanded in the *cahiers*, Grégoire claimed that accepting an absolute veto would violate the oath the deputies had sworn to faithfully represent their constituents. To grant the king an absolute veto, he argued, would far exceed the powers of the deputies as granted by their mandates. The deputies had not been given the power to end the liberty of their constituents.[51]

Grégoire agreed with the Monarchiens that the king did not hold the veto power as a right. The veto was a useful service to the nation meant to assure that the legislators did not fall into error and that only good laws were passed. Grégoire accepted the criticism that a single-chamber assembly might rush into unwise legislation or be pushed into it by popular opinion. He agreed with Lally-Tollendal that a unified assembly might make bad decisions. But for Grégoire, it was the certainty that the people would have the final say in any disagreement between the king and the legislature that would preserve public order. Grégoire attacked the idea that a king could be an infallible source of wisdom concerning the will of the nation, so much so that he should be granted a veto that could not be overridden. He asked if a single man could be "less susceptible to error or corruption, himself, than twenty-four million of his [countrymen]." He asked for proof that a king "is, if not infallible, at least more enlightened than the whole of the people," and he asked for the guarantee of "a constant succession of princes, of which the highest integrity, the most moderate, wise inclinations, will never come into collision with reason, such that their personal interests never offend the national interest." Grégoire followed

---

[51] AP 8: 556 (4 September 1789). On Grégoire, see A. Sepinwall, *The Abbé Grégoire and the French Revolution: The Making of Modern Universalism* (Berkeley and Los Angeles, 2005).

this attack on the wisdom of kings with an appeal to both general and historical examples that could easily be seen as insulting to the dignity of the sitting monarch: "Unhappily, kings are men, the truth reaches their thrones only with difficulty, withered by courtiers and often escorted by lies." Kings, as he said, were badly brought up for the most part and had "tumultuous" passions.[52]

Grégoire evoked the common fear of a king misled by bad advisors in a carefully oblique reference to the reign of Louis XVI and in particular the disastrous events of mid-July. He did this to show how an absolute veto would become in the hands of a weak king the veto of his ministers, ensuring a return to ministerial despotism. Though they had a good king now, he said, advised by ministers worthy of his confidence, this situation would not always obtain. With an absolute veto, at some point in the future "a weak king will be dominated by agents of power interested in invading the unlimited power of their master so that they could rule in his name." Nevertheless, Grégoire argued, it would not be in the hands of a weak king that the veto would be most dangerous, but in those of a strong and talented king. Grégoire chose the example of Louis XIV to illustrate his point. A future king like Louis XIV, "who did everything out of his own vanity, and always saw himself as better than his people," could use an absolute veto to invade the powers of the legislature and become a despot. When thinking about the constitution, he argued, they had to remember that they were building

> the foundations of a structure that can endure for centuries. The constitu-
> tion and the laws had to be independent of the moral qualities of the
> nation's chief; they had to be as invulnerable under a bandit-king, under
> a Nero, that is to say a Louis XI, as under a good prince, a Henry IV, that is
> to say, a king like Louis XVI.[53]

Grégoire argued against the absolute veto for the king on two fronts. First, past kings (and Louis XVI by implication) had been weak enough to be dominated by bad ministers, who had abused power to protect their own interests rather than acting in the public interest. Second, sooner or later a king determined to abuse his powers would take the throne and would use an absolute veto to expand his powers beyond their just bounds. Grégoire rejected arguments from the Monarchiens that informal means such as the pressure of public opinion, tax strikes, or even insurrection could make the king retract an absolute veto, noting that there was no

---

[52] AP 8: 566–67.   [53] Ibid., 566.

point in creating a strong veto only for "the pleasure of destroying it by violent means."[54] Given that the point of writing a new constitution was to preserve the rights of the French and restore public order, it was better to create a veto that could be overridden without resort to massive disobedience than to embrace one that would, sooner or later, require it.

By the end of the day on 4 September, deputies who supported an absolute veto and those who wished for a suspensive one agreed that a royal veto was necessary to protect the nation against its elected representatives. The more moderate partisans of the absolute veto had proposed something like what the supporters of the suspensive veto desired.[55] Nevertheless, the two positions remained distinct because the absolute veto left no formal avenue for overriding a veto and the suspensive veto did. This major difference between the two versions led to the most important exchange of the debate when, on 5 September, Thouret put forward a compromise proposal that featured a version of a suspensive veto that would preserve the dignity of the throne and Pétion responded that only a veto that featured a formal process by which it could be overridden would prevent disagreements between the king and the legislature from leading to public disorder. A careful analysis of the speeches these two deputies gave indicates that centrist deputies were working to fashion a political compromise, influenced by unrest in Paris and the provinces and the desire to establish lasting civil peace. Many historians have focused on Pétion's speeches and that given by Sieyès on 7 September (which we shall encounter) to the exclusion of that given by Thouret, and this has led to a misunderstanding of the debate. Without Thouret's speech criticizing the concept of an appeal to the people (and implicitly criticizing proposals by Salle, Pétion, and Grégoire given earlier in the debate) we can only arrive at an imperfect and misleading understanding of Pétion's conception of political representation as revealed in his speech of 5 September, one that overstates his desire for popular participation in the political process.

The Monarchiens argued that popular unrest provided an acceptable means for pushing a king to rescind his veto and worried that a referendum would cause the very unrest it was meant to prevent. Supporters of the suspensive veto worried that public unrest was a genie that could not be controlled and urged the Assembly to adopt a formal means to end disputes

---

[54] Ibid.

[55] Some witnesses were already convinced that the suspensive veto would win. See *Correspondance d'Anjou*, 303–04, 304 n. 1; Visme, "Journal," 142v. Lafayette had lobbied deputies consistently to support a suspensive veto. Gottshalk and Maddox, *Lafayette*, 229–56; Égret, *La révolution des notables*, 139–41.

between the king and legislature. Thouret and Pétion both crafted their proposals around the possibility of future popular unrest caused by disagreements between the executive and legislative powers. Examining their positions can help us better understand how the issue of keeping the king accountable to the nation hinged on a discussion of how to prevent civil disorder. Thouret wanted to avoid popular pressure on the king or the assembly. Instead, he focused on the power of public opinion to influence the king. He would exclude popular opinion, that of the uneducated masses, as unreasonable and deny it any role in the present or the future.[56] Pétion's proposed suspensive veto would rely on a referendum to electoral assemblies nationwide. It too would exclude popular opinion (and Paris's activists) at the present time. But he also argued that a suspensive veto would prepare the common man for possible inclusion in government affairs in the future, as disputes between king and legislature would educate citizens about their rights and the proper way to use their reason.

Thouret spoke at length on 5 September. He responded to those who supported the suspensive veto by offering a modified version of the absolute veto. Thouret proposed a two-pronged strategy to prevent popular pressure from influencing deputy opinions. First, it had to be understood that the king could not thwart the will of the people. The possibility of a prolonged disagreement between king and assembly had to be recognized and a means to arbitrate between them discovered. Thouret wanted public opinion to be that arbiter,[57] and suggested that given time, reasonable men would come to agree with either the king or the assembly, and that the king would not be able to resist the "force" of this opinion. If he tried, insurrection remained the right of the people.[58] Second, Thouret sought to minimize the appearance of confrontation between the deputies and the king in order to minimize the intrusion of passion and popular opinion into the debate. The king's veto was not to be defined. It was not absolute, as the king was not above the nation. It was not suspensive, because the people themselves did not have the power to arbitrate directly between king and assembly. Thouret claimed that the king and the assembly would naturally seek to avoid confrontation and, given time,

---

[56] For discussions of popular versus public opinion, see Margerison, *Pamphlets and Public Opinion*, 1–13; Chartier, *Cultural Origins*, 20–37; and Chisick, "Public Opinion and Political Culture in France," 48–77.

[57] *Courrier de Versailles*, 3: 136. On Thouret's ideas, see G. Glénard, *L'Exécutive et la Constitution de 1791* (Paris, 2010), 122–27. Many thanks to Michel Biard for introducing me to Glénard's work.

[58] *Courrier de Versailles*, 3: 136; *Le Point du jour*, 2: 313.

one or the other would always defer once it was clear what side public opinion was on. Nevertheless, Thouret noted that if the deputies did not wish to leave the veto undefined and the resolution mechanism informal, then a suspensive veto that lasted to the third following assembly would be best, as it would allow public opinion to clarify itself without the appearance of a direct contest between the king and the elected deputies. This would allow for the dignity of the throne to be preserved, as the king would still appear to be above politics and this approach would minimize the risk of popular unrest.[59]

Pétion spoke in response to Thouret's proposal. He disputed the main claim Thouret had made, that the system by which a veto could be overturned should be informal in order to avoid popular unrest. Pétion argued that any system that left it unclear what would happen in the case of disagreement between king and legislature would lead to the very unrest it was meant to prevent. The proper way to resolve a veto was to make it clear – very clear – that there was a formal resolution process. Pétion agreed with previous speakers that the frequency of irresolvable clashes between the king and legislature was likely to be exceedingly low, as both sides would seek to avoid such disputes.[60] But should such a stalemate arise Pétion wanted the resolution to be clear and certain. Neither the deputies nor the king, as interested parties, could have any say in the outcome of the dispute. Instead, since the judgment of the deputies and of the king was the issue at hand, the next rank down in the hierarchy of elected representatives would have the final say. At the next regularly scheduled election, each deputy would be given a yes/no instruction by their electors and would vote accordingly in the new legislature. Thouret had argued that allowing time to pass would allow for passions to dissipate and a rational decision to be made. Pétion argued instead that the very formality of the process would eliminate passion and allow for reasonable outcomes. No matter how sharply the king and the assembly disagreed, the people would not rise, as there would be no need. Instead of an indefinite standoff leading to public disorder, there would be a finite and relatively brief time of uncertainty followed by a decisive resolution.

Where the two deputies differed most, though, was over the effect that an attempt to resolve veto disputes outside the assembly would have. For Thouret, public opinion – by definition outside the assembly – needed

---

[59] See especially Mirabeau, *Courrier de Provence* (n.p., 1789), vol. 2: 399–405; Castellane, "Journal," 142.
[60] AP 8: 584.

time to resolve the dispute through discussion and debate and could do so without triggering popular involvement. Thouret worried that in the case of a national referendum the least educated citizens would be able to influence the decisions of their deputies without being able to comprehend the issues at hand. He worried that the least educated and least enlightened could even exercise a determining influence over the process.[61] To put the decision-making event in a specific place at a specific time ran the risk of the crowd taking part through simple intimidation. Given the conditions under which Thouret spoke, less than a week after deputies favoring an absolute veto were threatened with having their homes burned, less than a week after a march on the Assembly to intimidate deputies who might vote for a royal veto, we know that he was not speaking hypothetically. To propose excluding popular opinion from future disputes was to exclude the opinion of the Paris crowd from the current debate and to make decisions based on reason and the content of the *cahiers*, not according to what immediate decision would make a passionate crowd disperse.

Pétion also spoke in the shadow of Parisian unrest. He also sought to exclude unreasoned opinion from the process of resolving vetoes.[62] He assured the deputies that he did not wish to reopen a vetoed decree for popular debate – after all, who could have done a better job sorting through all of the issues than the deputies themselves? He recognized that an impasse between the assembly and the king would happen after careful political maneuvering on both sides. Both would marshal all the resources of rhetoric, reason, and persuasion in order to swing public opinion behind their position. But for Pétion, the possibility of crisis would occur after the process Thouret proposed had run its course. Once all of the possibilities had been talked through, if the king and the assembly could not agree, all that remained was for someone to make a final decision and end the stalemate. Since neither party involved in the disagreement could be relied on to make an unbiased decision, someone else had to make it. Why not the men who had chosen each individual deputy in the first place? According to Pétion, when the representatives could not agree, it was up to the nation to choose. But by this he meant the most educated men of each *bailliage*, not the average Frenchman.[63]

---

[61] *Courrier de Provence*, 2: 399–405.

[62] For a sharply different interpretation of Pétion's speech, see Friedland, *Political Actors*, 152–55.

[63] AP 8: 583; *Le Moniteur*, 1: 436. The deputies had yet to establish how deputies would be elected to the new legislature and it was unclear whether or not the system of indirect elections used to choose Third Estate deputies would persist. However, Pétion responded to Thouret's speech by denouncing those who would prevent the *bailliages* from being able to lift the veto, indicating that he meant

Pétion repeatedly stated that the only way to lift a veto was an appeal to the people, but he did not want the uneducated masses to actively participate.[64] Nevertheless, he *did* want them exposed to the process. This too was a tacit reference to the audience inside and the crowd outside the Assembly hall. According to Pétion, while the people would not be able to decide for themselves, they would be able to discuss the issues. Through exposure to higher-level debates they would be educated as to their rights, as to the stakes of the disputes, and as to the importance of their own development as reasoning citizens by the very process that excluded them. This education, Pétion claimed, would require a long process, but it was a process that was already taking place. Far from being doomed to act as slaves to their passions, uneducated Frenchmen were already learning to act reasonably to defend their rights. Why, he asked, should those so long enslaved be denied the right to educate and better themselves to the point where they could be trusted to act as citizens? Pétion accepted that allowing the people to be exposed to the real workings of government might stir up unrest. He agreed with Thouret that a suspensive veto that relied on frequent consultation of *bailliage* assemblies or snap elections immediately following a royal veto might lead to the very unrest the deputies sought to avoid. But Pétion also agreed with Lally-Tollendal's statement that the deputies were creating a system for use once matters had calmed down. A system that used recourse to electoral assemblies was not to be used when writing the constitution. It was a procedure to be used once the constitution had been implemented. Thus, Pétion reassured the deputies that while the rights of the people were to be respected, the average Frenchman (or more to the point, Parisian) was to have no direct influence over their current debates.[65]

Paul Friedland portrays the discussion of the king's veto powers and Pétion's speech in particular as key moments in the transition from a traditional concept of representation as "re-presentation" by which deputies simply manifested the will of their constituents to a modern concept of representation by elected representatives responsible for debating and arriving at decisions

---

for the bodies who had sent deputies to Versailles to act, not those lesser bodies that sent delegates to them. The electors who had sent Third Estate deputies to Paris had gone through three or four elections to reach their district assemblies and were almost entirely well-educated Third Estate elites. Given his later comments about how the least educated citizens would need more preparation before they could responsibly participate, we may determine that he meant to exclude the least educated Frenchmen from the process of resolving royal vetoes, at least in the short run.

[64] This is the theme most often repeated in contemporary accounts of his speech. See, for example, *Journal des débats*, issue 11; *Le Point du jour*, 2: 317; *Courrier de Versailles*, 3: 148.

[65] AP 8: 583–04. This is not to say that Pétion's language was not fiery. See especially *Le Moniteur*, 1: 436.

independently of the wishes of their constituents. He uses the defeat of Pétion's version of the suspensive veto to claim that the deputies rejected notions of political accountability by refusing to allow an appeal to the nation itself when resolving a veto.[66] His focus on imperative mandates and referenda ignores the long history of compromise and discussion within the Estates General. Moreover, an examination of the speeches made during the debate, and in particular that of Pétion on 5 September, shows that neither Thouret nor Pétion sought to exclude public (or "national") opinion from the process of resolving a dispute between the king and the legislature. Both sought to exclude *popular* pressure from the resolution of a stalemate between the king and the elected representatives. The live question in September of 1789 was that of how to craft a constitution such that the predictable disagreements between the king and the legislature would not devolve into the kinds of mass disorder or insurrection that had threatened to overwhelm France during the previous two months. Their thinking was much in line with constitutional thought in the new United States, or even the kingdom of Poland.[67] Supporters of a veto for the king, absolute or suspensive, were seeking ways to allow for the usual and predictable struggles between the executive power and the legislature to be resolved without the need for a new revolution. They were not seeking a mechanism to sever their ties to their electors.

The third position taken by deputies during the debate solved the question of how to prevent public disorder by denying the king a veto. If the king could not halt the work of the nation's elected representatives then there would be no reason for the people to rise up. Their arguments arose out of notions of national sovereignty and the idea of a separation of powers. They also arose out of the sense that the king was not an elected representative of the nation. Since only elected representatives could act as legislators, the king, unelected and unaccountable, had to be excluded from even an indirect, implied share of the legislative power. Though deputies defended this position for a variety of reasons, many historians have seen Sieyès's systematic and philosophical proposal of 7 September as the most important attempt to deny the king a veto.[68] In his speech, Sieyès

[66] Friedland, *Political Actors*, esp. 154–64.

[67] On Poland, see Lukowski, "'Machines of Government'"; Butterwick, "Political Discourses of the Polish Revolution"; Fiszman, *Constitution and Reform in Eighteenth-Century Poland.*

[68] See esp. Baker, *Inventing the French Revolution*, 244–51. Baker's ideas were anticipated to some extent by Viatte, who noted that those who opposed the veto did so out of a Rousseauist respect for a unified national will. Viatte also noted the similarities between their arguments and those found in the Virginia Constitution of 1776. Viatte, *Veto*, 87, 94. See also Carré de Malberg, *Contribution à la*

carefully defined the forms of political representation and accountability he saw as underpinning the new constitutional order, arguing (as had Pétion and Thouret on 5 September) that there were varying levels at which the French could be involved in the political process. He memorably characterized the French people as having different individual capacities, which led some to be more suited to manual work and others to the use of reason and thus the ability to rule. This led him to the principle that the electors had use their best reason to select those who would rule, and then leave those representatives to speak for the nation without interference or oversight, save the process of regular elections.[69]

The role Sieyès envisioned for the king derived from his understanding of the institutions necessary for a proper representative government. Sieyès was, by his own admission, in favor of increased centralization, wishing to impose uniform laws throughout France in order to prevent any possibility of a federation on the lines of the United States. All of these laws would be created by majority rule within the National Assembly and passed down to the electoral assemblies.[70] Neither the king nor the people would be involved in the creation of the laws. The informed reason assumed to be the characteristic of any electable deputy guaranteed that the legislature would rise above the vicissitudes of opinion to declare the general will. There was no point in giving the king a veto: his individual reason was no match to the collective wisdom of the people's representatives. Moreover, there was no point in appealing to the nation: the best thinkers were already in the nation's legislature and any appeal would be to those less capable of using their reason.

When Sieyès claimed that the nation could only speak through its representatives, he meant *elected* representatives. As the deputies to the National Assembly were the only *elected* representatives of the whole nation, the idea of an appeal to some other body, whether the king or the electoral assemblies, was unthinkable. The king was a representative of the nation, Sieyès admitted, but only in the sense that he reflected its wishes: he did not have the option of straying from the national will. To give the king a veto would be to include him in the legislative power, and to

---

Théorie générale de l'État, vol. 2: 258, n. 11; Forsyth, *Reason and Revolution,* 135; Sewell, *A Rhetoric of Bourgeois Revolution,* 58–60, 71–72. Bastid characterized the speech as part of Sieyès's larger strategic plan to prevent Mounier's ideas from passing into law. Bastid, *Sieyès et sa pensée,* 86.

[69] James Madison anticipated this argument in *Federalist* 10 (22 November 1787). I. Kramnick, "The 'Great National Discussion': The Discourse of Politics in 1787." *William and Mary Quarterly* 45: 1 (January 1988), 13.

[70] AP 8: 593–94.

include "individual wills" in what was properly a product of the general will, as found in the legislature. Sieyès felt that the exercise of any legislative power by the king was an invitation to the return of despotism.[71]

It is not clear, however, how much impact Sieyès's speech had at the time. One witness found it hard to follow Sieyès's points because of the high level of abstraction Sieyès used.[72] His proposal seems to have had no effect on the outcome of the debate. Moreover, Sieyès was not the only speaker who opposed a royal veto, and others used very different reasoning to arrive at the same conclusion. Much earlier in the debate, Third Estate deputy Claude-Alexis Cochard had claimed that to give the king an absolute veto would be to give him a share in the legislative power and the sovereignty of the nation, thereby voiding the social contract. Cochard warned the deputies that "this royal veto would totally annihilate your power," though he did not specify precisely how.[73] Robespierre also emphasized the functional sovereignty of the legislative body as rooted in its status as representative of the nation. The representatives of the nation were the only ones capable of making decisions binding on the nation, he argued. Once the nation met as a National Assembly, neither the electoral assemblies nor the king could exercise any kind of veto power.[74]

But not all of the deputies who resisted a royal veto relied on arguments like those of Sieyès, Robespierre, or Cochard that rooted opposition to the veto in a mechanistic notion of the exercise of sovereignty by elected representatives who in and of themselves adequately represented the nation. Indeed, many who opposed the veto seem to have derived their ideas on unicamerality and on the veto from American examples rather than from French *philosophes* or Sieyès's pamphlets. The historian Denis Lacorne notes that the deputies of 1789 were very interested in the various American state constitutions, all of which had been available for at least a decade. The state constitutions had first appeared translated into French in 1778, in *Affaires de l'Angleterre et de l'Amérique,* a newspaper linked to Benjamin Franklin. Louis-Alexandre, the duke of La Rochefoucauld, later a Noble deputy in the Estates General, had been the translator.[75] The French particularly admired the constitutions of

---

[71] Ibid., 592. Goupilleau felt that the aristocrats sought to undermine the "confidence that [the people] must have in their representatives . . . . The health of the state depends on this confidence; if [the aristocrats] destroy it, perhaps despotism will follow after anarchy." J. F. Goupilleau, Manuscript letters, B.M. Nantes, Collection Dugast-Matifeux, no. 98. Letter of "le [blank] septembre, 1789."
[72] Visme, "Journal," 145v.   [73] Delandine, *Mémorial historique,* 5: 84–85.
[74] AP 9: 79–83. Goupilleau noted that he was against the suspensive veto as there was, in his mind, no power above the sovereign people. Goupilleau, "le [blank] septembre, 1789."
[75] *Constitutions de Treize États-Unis de l'Amérique* (Paris, 1783). See Lacorne, *L'invention de la République,* 34, 78–79. See also Jourdan, *Nouvelle histoire,* 31–34.

Massachusetts and Pennsylvania (the latter they wrongly attributed to Franklin himself).[76] Supporters of a suspensive veto never ceased to praise America as an example (Mathieu-Jean-Félicité Montmorency-Laval, Jean-Nicolas Démeunier, Dupont de Nemours, La Rochefoucauld, and Lafayette among them). While some opponents of the veto, like Sieyès, wished to avoid American models as too closely linked to those colonies' own English past, other opponents of the veto derived their opposition directly from American precedents.[77]

These opponents of a royal veto used concrete historical examples taken from the American Revolution to support their claims rather than relying on abstract reason. Delandine was one such supporter of American forms. On 3 September, he countered arguments in favor of the absolute veto by noting that the English constitution itself was hardly perfect: "Let us not believe, gentlemen, that England has done all for the benefit of man, and that all we have to do is copy its example." He then quoted the American Declaration of Independence to support his claim that it was the threat of a royal veto that had forced the Americans to revolt. Continuing with the American example, Delandine referred to the Virginia Commonwealth constitution of 6 May 1776 and its lack of an executive veto as the model to be followed. He argued that the very concept of an executive veto implied the existence of an authority above the people, and that acceptance of a veto would mean the negation of national sovereignty. Even worse, Delandine claimed, a royal veto would violate the doctrine of separation of powers by giving the executive the right to interfere in the duties of the legislative.[78]

Nevertheless, deputies like Delandine who opposed a royal veto accepted that the representatives of the nation could make mistakes. They did not seek to set the future legislatures free from all constraints. First, they accepted that the future legislatures would be renewed by periodic elections, giving the electorate the opportunity to rid itself of deputies who did not live up to their ideal of an impartial legislator. Implicitly or explicitly, opponents of the royal veto power accepted the arguments made by its proponents that the legislative assembly might stray from the will of the people and they proposed mechanisms to make certain that the will of the assembly was the same as the will of the nation. While

---

[76] Lacorne argues advocates of a unicameral legislature were influenced by the 1776 constitution of Pennsylvania. Démeunier appears to have preferred the constitution of New Hampshire. On the other hand, Delandine favored the constitutions of Virginia and Pennsylvania from 1776. Lacorne, *L'invention de la République*, 80–82, 169.

[77] Ibid., 171.   [78] Delandine, *Mémorial historique*, 5: 55; AP 8: 546–47.

Delandine was adamantly set against an absolute veto, for example, he did admit that undue haste might lead to bad laws and proposed a mechanism for preventing bad outcomes: "That the representatives take a short delay to consult their constituents on a law that they hesitate to pass; it is a precaution that can be very wise, and the only that can be admitted by an enlightened nation." He then admitted that this delay might be rendered through a suspensive veto held by the executive, but one that lasted only until after the next elections had been held. The deputies themselves would have the final word.[79] Thus even an opponent of any veto at all found his way to supporting a suspensive veto, as long as it was resolved by the deputies sitting in the legislature in a formal and regular way.

Other deputies suggested creating a new body responsible for reviewing laws to ensure that they were in the public interest. On 7 September, several members proposed a "chamber of revision," which could review the decrees coming out of the legislative body to make sure there were no hasty moves or bad laws. This body would also try the crime of high treason. Witnesses noted that the proponents explicitly rooted their demand in the example of the American states.[80] This body would replicate some of the functions of the Parlement of Paris, under the guise of national sovereignty. Even Sieyès recognized that on occasion future legislators might act in haste and act in error. To prevent this, Sieyès proposed dividing the legislative body temporarily into three groups and giving each part a suspensive veto, with no veto for the king or popular referendum under any circumstances.[81] One witness to the debate found this proposal impractical, arguing that dividing the assembly in this way made for three suspensive vetoes rather than just one, entrusted to the king.[82] Opponents of any veto at all, too, came to see some kind of suspensive veto as necessary to prevent the legislature from acting in error.

Toward the end of the day on 7 September, Brulart de Sillery spoke, attempting to reconcile the competing plans of the deputies. Like the rest,

[79] Delandine, *Mémorial historique*, 5: 62. This practice appears to have been derived from the 1776 state constitution of Pennsylvania.

[80] *Correspondance d'Anjou*, 1: 319–20. An example of a "chamber of revision" can be found in the Pennsylvania state constitution of 1776 and one had been proposed and rejected in the Constitutional Convention of 1787. See J. P. Selsam, *The Pennsylvania Constitution of 1776* (Philadelphia, 1936), 199–201; Mintz, *Gouverneur Morris and the French Revolution*, 183.

[81] AP 8: 596–97. Patrice Gueniffey argues that the idea was that of the marquis of Condorcet, taken from American precedents and adopted by Sieyès. P. Gueniffey, "Constitution et intérêts sociaux: le débat sur les deux Chambres," in M. Troper and L. Jaume, eds. *1789 et l'invention de la Constitution* (Paris, 1994), 79.

[82] Visme, "Journal," 146r.

he wanted to ensure that the will of future legislative assemblies accurately represented the will of the nation, but he also wanted to ensure that there was no possibility for a return to ministerial despotism. He emphasized the sovereignty of the nation, but he wanted to ensure the king a meaningful role in the creation of laws. In his speech he supported the suspensive veto, which he saw as capable of providing the king a dignified role in the new constitution without allowing the vicissitudes of time and of royal ability to undermine the rights of the French people. First, like Grégoire, Sillery emphasized the problems of relying too heavily on the good will and capacities of individual monarchs. After a discussion of the history of France since 1614, one that Sillery characterized as "ten centuries of out-rages committed against the freedom of the French nation," Sillery noted that because of the Louis XVI's goodness and the strength of the National Assembly they had made great strides toward establishing a good constitu-tion and recovering their liberty. But history also showed Sillery how resilient the enemies of liberty could be. He referred to the corrupt officials and courtiers of the past as a many-headed threat to liberty, one that would be hard to destroy. He claimed that those who "seek to invade the authority of the throne by the different branches of executive power that they have usurped are many and strong." The plotters were currently in hiding because of the "patriotism" of the Assembly, but this "hydra" would return and without "the redoubtable shield of the National Assembly, the people have gained nothing and will fall back into slavery."[83]

According to Sillery, the Assembly had already met opposition in its attempts to rectify the failures of the Old Regime: "You have begun a great project; your resolve has already triumphed over the several obstacles that the enemies of the public good had sought out to oppose you."[84] One could hardly miss here the reference to the crises of 20 June–16 July 1789 and the role played by Artois and the Polignac faction. This was not the speech of a man in denial about the threat posed to the Revolution by the power of the executive branch, posed here as surrounded by a potentially tyrannous hydra that could only be temporarily vanquished, one which had already thrown obstacles in the way of the Assembly, one which would

---

[83] AP 8: 598–99. Henry IV, founder of the Bourbon line, had often been portrayed as vanquishing the "hydra" of anarchy. In the late 1780s, Louis XVI's aunts had commissioned a statue of Henry IV standing on a hydra's remains. J. B. Collins, "Dynastic Instability, the Emergence of the French Monarchical Commonwealth and the Coming of the Rhetoric of 'L'état,' 1360s to 1650s" in R. von Friedeburg and J. Morrill, eds, *Monarchy Transformed: Princes and Their Elites in Early Modern Western Europe* (Cambridge, 2017), 119; J. D. Draper and G. Scherf, *Augustin Pajou: Royal Sculptor, 1730–1809* (New York, 1997), 323–24.

[84] AP 8: 598.

always seek to subvert the constitution to serve its own ends. And yet, far from declaring that the king must be excluded from the legislative process, Sillery declared that for the liberty of the people to endure, the king had to be given a powerful weapon for himself with which to fight the hydra: the weapon of consent.

In order to convince the deputies that royal consent would be a powerful weapon against faction, Sillery used historical parallels to predict the future. Since the deputies had the liberty to establish the new constitution, they had to consider how a future king would interact with future assemblies, and they needed to realize that a king in name only would never respect the constitution of which he was the guardian:

> As for those who do not want any kind of royal veto, I have only one word to answer them.
>
> France is now governed by Louis XVI; but it has been governed by Louis XI. If future races feel a parallel misfortune, if this conqueror on his way back from a successful war returns to France at the head of a victorious army; if full of confidence in his legions he forgets that he only commands in the name of the law, would he not say, "Which one of my ancestors consented to and sanctioned such imperious laws? Which of them signed the act that established limits to my power? None? I can therefore choose . . . the model that suits me." If he is virtuous, he will choose Louis XVI; but if he is a tyrant, he will imitate Louis XI. France will lose its constitution and be plunged into a river of blood.[85]

The implication is hard to miss – no future king would feel bound by laws to which his ancestors had not freely assented. Only if the king felt that he had been involved in the legislative process would he feel bound by laws when he was strong and could do as he pleased. Sillery agreed with Grégoire concerning the character of monarchs: a hostile future king would not be contained by reason or an abstract sense of duty to remain faithful to the constitution. He could only be constrained by his respect for the traditions given him by his ancestors, who had freely accepted the new constitution and thus bound him by honor to accept it as well. This formulation contained an implied question for the deputies, one that the Monarchiens had encapsulated in the phrase "the dignity of the throne" but was too disrespectful of the king to be discussed publicly. How were the deputies to convince Louis XVI to respect the new order, once the current crisis had passed and he had the executive power fully in his hands?

---

[85] AP 8: 600–01. See Brulart de Sillery, "Journal," 498–500.

The only way they could expect him to respect the new state was to convince him that he had meaningfully participated in the creation of its laws.

But this weapon of consent could not be an absolute veto. As Sillery said, as if speaking directly to the king, "In giving you the veto, we have not wished to forge new chains for ourselves." The veto was to be used only for the common good. It was entirely possible that a future legislature might be mistaken when it passed a law, and it was the king's responsibility to examine the laws and to reject them if he thought them dangerous. But his veto could not be absolute, Sillery continued, explaining that the deputies represented the nation and the nation had chosen the king to be its chief. It had put the king as an intermediary between the nation and its deputies to protect the nation from laws that were against its interests. A royal veto would suspend a law until after the next regular elections. But if the newly elected representatives came to the same conclusions and again sent the suspended law to the king, he would have to approve it, as all sovereignty resided in the nation itself.[86] Thus Sillery argued that the king's consent to new laws would be necessary for any stable kind of constitutional settlement while admitting that the king did not have the right to deny the nation what it desired.

Sillery's speech demonstrates a central problem the deputies faced in limiting the king's powers. As a rule, during the debate deputies refused to openly state their reservations about Louis XVI's good will and how they intended to deal with the collapse of the royal administrative state. Nevertheless, there had been a major shift in the way the deputies saw the king. With memories of the July crisis in mind, deputies from the center-right to the far left feared a resurgent central executive authority, one that could use its powers not just to restore order, but to enforce the king's declarations of 23 June 1789. But the deputies also feared a descent into anarchy. The Revolutionaries had to discuss limiting royal power while worrying about the possibility that it might completely collapse if further undermined. It was this conundrum that the deputies faced as they sought to define the role of the executive power in the new constitution: How could they define the limits of executive power without provoking the sitting king into unwise action? How could they prevent unrest that might destroy any compromise reached? Insofar as it was possible, Louis XVI's recent actions as king – the Royal Session of 23 June, the dismissal of Necker and the reforming ministers – were left out of the discussion over

---

[86] Ibid., 496–97.

the extent of future royal power or were alluded to by euphemism and remote historical parallel.

The way forward suggested by Thouret and refined by Sillery was the suspensive veto with the appeal not being sent out to electoral assemblies directly but through the mechanism of regular elections. As Thouret had urged, the delay would be long enough for public opinion to take part. As Pétion had insisted, there would be a formal and predictable process. At the end of the day on 7 September, it seemed that the suspensive veto was the logical choice. But one hurdle remained before the deputies could reach agreement on the matter of the veto. The Constitutional Committee's proposal had envisioned a two-chamber legislature with the upper house having a veto over the lower house's proposals. Before the deputies decided how strong the king's veto would be, they had to decide if there would be an upper house, especially since the Monarchiens had emphasized how the presence of an upper house would mean that the king would seldom have to use his negative power. After a relatively brief debate, the vote was taken on 10 September. The deputies definitively rejected a return to the separate chambers of the old Estates General, with 490 votes for one chamber, 89 for two, and 122 giving no opinion. The unusually small number of votes cast indicated limited support from the privileged orders for the change. There would be a unitary legislature, and it would be much more important that the king have some form of powerful veto to prevent the assembly from straying too far from the will of the nation in its actions.[87]

In the meantime, something interesting was happening outside the Assembly, something that dovetailed nicely with the sentiment expressed by supporters of the suspensive veto that the king needed to have a strong but limited veto power. While the deputies put aside the matter of the veto until they had decided how many chambers their legislature would have, Jacques Necker worked behind the scenes to rally deputies behind the suspensive veto. On 7 September, Necker presented a project to the king at the Royal Council, proposing that the king accept a suspensive veto. On 11 September, Necker sent a letter to the Assembly asking that his project, as approved by the Royal Council, be read to the deputies. This request triggered a fascinating debate over whether or not the king had the right to ask that his opinions concerning constitutional acts be heard in the Assembly.

As it happened, the letter arrived after the debate over the veto had ended and the deputies were working on how to pose the question. The president

[87] AP 8: 607–08. Gueniffey, "Constitution et intérêts sociaux," 77–88.

announced that Necker had requested that his report be read to the Assembly, as it was relevant to the discussion. One of the secretaries went to read the report but was interrupted by Bon-Albert Brios de Beaumetz, Noble deputy from Arras. Given his support for the suspensive veto, we might expect him to have supported Necker's plan. Instead, Beaumetz reminded the deputies that the king did not have the right of initiative over laws and even less the right of initiative when it came to the constitution. Mirabeau then spoke. He said that the letter could not be read because the discussion had already been closed. If the king could ask for a matter to be reopened, then anyone in the kingdom had the same right and no matter would ever be closed.[88] Without a decision being taken on the letter, the deputies went back to phrasing the question for the upcoming vote. Then several deputies asked that the letter be read out of respect for the king. Mounier rose and clarified that in refusing to read the letter the Assembly was not taking away from the king his right to ask for modifications to be made to the constitution they sent him. Nevertheless, Mounier emphasized, the right to initiate laws or constitutional acts belonged to the Assembly and to the Assembly alone. The king had the right to accept or refuse the constitution, but he did not have the right to ask for or refuse to accept specific parts. Mounier argued that it was up to the Assembly to decide whether or not the king needed a veto, and that there was no reason to hear the king's opinion on the matter. In this, Mounier was entirely consistent with his position on 23 June 1789, when he had urged the deputies to refuse the king the right to impose his own constitution or insist that the deputies only discuss constitutional acts proposed by the king. After Mounier's speech, the debate continued with vigor, but in the end the matter was voted on and the Assembly decided not to read the report.[89]

Nevertheless, the contents of Necker's letter appear to have been already known by the deputies.[90] Necker had recommended that the king be given a suspensive veto, but not one subject to formal direct appeal to the electors. Instead, he suggested that a royal veto could be overridden by the legislature itself, but only after two sets of new regularly scheduled elections. In making this proposal, Necker appears to have carefully coordinated with a group of moderate

---

[88] AP 8: 600. Castellane, "Journal," 150; Visme, "Journal," 152r.

[89] Lally-Tollendal was among those who asked that the Necker's letter be read. AP 8: 601; Visme, "Journal," 152v; Mounier, *Exposé*, 53–54.

[90] Ferrières noted that everyone already knew what the letter said, and that its very appearance in the Assembly was as good as a public reading. Ferrières, *Mémoires*, 1: 231–32. See also Bailly, *Mémoires d'un témoin*, 2: 365. Brissot noted that Necker had published his opinion soon after he had sent it to the deputies. *Le Patriote français*, 14 September 1789; Visme, "Journal," 155v.

Patriot deputies in the Assembly, including the Lameth brothers, Barnave and Lafayette. Necker proposed to the king a system almost identical to that proposed by the deputy Thouret to the Assembly on 5 September.[91] This version of the veto was meant to be a powerful tool for the king, but it was also meant to be limited in order to be useful, so it would not incite insurrection or cause a tax strike, precisely the argument against the absolute veto deployed by supporters of a suspensive one.[92] Despite the uproar in the Assembly over his chosen method of expressing the king's wishes, Necker's opinion that the veto should be suspensive and last through two legislatures was known to the deputies as the opinion supported by the king. Despite the best efforts of Mounier and his allies to prevent Necker's opinion from being heard, the form Necker supported was in fact the form eventually adopted.

But first the deputies had to vote on whether or not the king should have a veto and on what kind it should be. After a fair amount of discussion about how to phrase the question, the deputies voted by a substantial margin to grant to grant the king a veto. They then voted 673–325 (with eleven votes spoiled) to make the veto suspensive rather than absolute.[93] The Third Estate and its allies had again mustered an overwhelming majority. The Assembly did not define what "suspensive" meant, and it remained to decide whether the veto would be resolved by the legislature itself or by an appeal to the electoral assemblies. Nevertheless, after 11 September and the appearance of Necker's letter, the idea of the veto as a national referendum vanished without a trace. Proposed forms of the veto came to differ only over how much time would intervene between attempts by the legislators to pass a law once vetoed by the king. The deputies had taken another step in the transformation of the Estates General into a true constituent assembly, as the deputies voted overwhelmingly to support the basic program found in their *cahiers*, vesting legislative power in the assembly but maintaining a role in it for the king. They had only to decide how powerful

---

[91] Égret, *La révolution des notables*, 153–54. On Necker's behind-the-scenes efforts to influence the veto debate see J. Égret, *Necker, Ministre de Louis XVI, 1776–1790* (Paris, 1975), 350–58.

[92] R. Bompard, *Le veto du Président de la République et la sanction royale* (Paris, 1906), 186–87. Ferrières thought that Necker had "believed it necessary to sacrifice royal prerogative in the interest of his own popularity." Ferrières, *Mémoires*, I: 231.

[93] AP 8: 612. Glénard surprisingly claims that the absolute veto would have won by a small margin had Necker not intervened. Glénard, *L'Exécutif et la Constitution de 1791*, 132–134.

that role would be. Deputies of the center had managed to arrange for the king to have a powerful weapon to defend both the nation and his own prerogatives from the possibility that the nation's deputies would deviate from the public good. But the sovereign nation, through its deputies, would have the final say in whether or not an act would pass into law.

CHAPTER 6

A Truly National Assembly

Here we examine the final steps the deputies elected to the Estates General of 1789 took to transform that traditional body into a national constituent assembly. We will examine three steps in detail, again relying on a broad array of sources to show how the decisions reached were shaped by the interplay between different developing political groups within the Assembly. First, as the summer of 1789 came to an end, the deputies sought to establish their power to craft France's new constitution as they saw best, guided by the wishes of their constituents, not by the will of the king. By the middle of September, the king had yet to accept the August decrees or the Declaration of the Rights of Man and Citizen. From 14 to 21 September, the deputies debated how to ensure that the king would accept the decrees without modification. As part of this discussion, the deputies broached the question of whether or not the king had the right to request changes to the constitution they were writing. They were careful not to cause unnecessary conflict between the king and the Assembly. When the deputies and their king had clashed during the summer unrest in Paris had followed, culminating in the taking of the Bastille on 14 July, the bloody murders of royal officials on 22 July, and the Great Fear throughout much of France in July and August. From late July through early September, the Assembly's debates over how to frame a constitution had featured discussions of the problem of public order. Rather than confront the king over his apparent unwillingness to approve the Assembly's decrees, the deputies returned to the tactic they had so successfully used on 1–2 and 13–16 July, sending gentle but insistent delegations to the king asking for his cooperation. Only when it became clear that the king was willing to accept the constitutional decrees without revision did the deputies reward him with a powerful suspensive veto over ordinary legislation. By denying the king the right to suggest changes to the constitution as they wrote it, they found a way to grant the king a significant role in the new system without giving him the ability to roll back the reforms they had made.

Next, we show how the eruption of the people of Paris into national politics in early October changed the relationship between the National Assembly and the king. Despite his apparent agreement with the Assembly, the king continued to delay acceptance of its constitutional acts. By the beginning of October, Louis had still not accepted and promulgated the August decrees or the Declaration of the Rights of Man and Citizen. He seemed unlikely to do so any time soon. Deputies in the Assembly demanded in increasingly strident terms that the king do so. This developing political stalemate dovetailed with increasing subsistence woes in Paris and controversy over the arrival of fresh troops in Versailles. The result was the explosive uprising in Paris and Versailles known to historians as the October Days. During the evening and night of 5 October, tens of thousands of protestors arrived in Versailles from Paris, demanding that the Assembly and the king do something about the scarcity of food and punish soldiers who had insulted the Revolution. The deputies were shocked by the intrusion of the common people into national politics. Nevertheless, they took advantage of the crisis to pressure Louis into accepting the constitutional acts they had sent him. Then it became apparent that the crowd was not interested in politics unless it brought them bread. In an effort to secure bread supplies, the crowd demanded that the king and his family accompany them to Paris. Faced with the king's imminent departure on 6 October, the Assembly declared itself inseparable from his person. The deputies declared that the public power consisted of the unity of the king and Assembly. In effect, they took the king under their protection. By this action, the Assembly claimed for itself the position of premier representative of the French nation, a position formerly held by the king himself.

The final step we examine here occurred soon after the October Days. Having established that they were competent to write a constitution and that the public power consisted of the king and the Assembly (with increasing emphasis on the power of the Assembly) the deputies moved to solve the financial crisis that had toppled the absolute monarchy. Beginning on 10 October, the deputies discussed using the vast wealth of the French Catholic Church to pay off the nation's debts and to provide security for new loans. After much debate, the Assembly decided to put the goods of the Church at the disposal of the nation. The state would become paymaster of the nation's clergy. The deputies' decision to take control of the Church's property had two major implications. First, it demonstrated that the National Assembly could examine and modify any institution in the kingdom, no matter how powerful or grounded in history. Second, this decision demonstrated convincingly that the era of the Estates General was over. No longer would each of the three Estates have exclusive areas of political responsibility. The Assembly would make its decisions by majority vote, even when the decisions focused on the privileges of a specific group in society. Though the vast majority of Clerical deputies voted against the measure, some claiming that the taking of Church property would violate property rights and presage future seizures, the motion still passed and was sent to Louis for his signature. The Clergy were accorded no special role in determining the fate of Church property.[1] With their vote on 2 November, the deputies finally lived up to the claims they had made in the Declaration of the National Assembly, that all decisions would be made by a majority of the deputies sitting in the common hall, with no veto between the National Assembly and the king.

When the deputies met on 12 September, they had yet to decide how the suspensive veto would work in practice. Would the veto be lifted by a national referendum or by the legislature itself? If the legislature could lift a veto, would a veto trigger snap elections so deputies could immediately overturn it? Could it be overruled by the next regularly elected legislature, or would the veto persist into a second or even third following legislature? Faced with these unresolved questions, the Noble deputy Louis-Michel Le Peletier, the marquis of Saint-Fargeau, proposed that the deputies take a brief detour to discuss the length of each future legislative term.[2] This would allow the deputies to better understand just how long a veto would last before a decree would pass into law without the king's approval. The Assembly adopted his suggestion and proceeded to discuss how long each session of the legislature would last. Without debate or controversy, the notion of a national referendum to resolve a veto was completely dropped. The king's veto would be lifted by the legislature itself. It only remained to choose how many regularly scheduled elections would be held before the deputies could overturn a royal veto.

The rapid and tacit resolution of one issue led to a sustained debate on a different matter. On 14 September, Barnave asked that any further discussion of the king's veto be put off until the deputies settled what the

[1] Eliminating the corporate personhood of the Catholic Church enabled the deputies to take control of its property without violating the Declaration of Rights and showed that the deputies were willing to risk undermining the natural right to property to defend the new regime.
[2] AP 8: 616.

king's role would be in writing the constitution. Barnave avoided taking too controversial a tack, however, and asked his question in a way that took the constituent power of the Assembly for granted. First, he pointed out that the deputies had yet to establish in statute how the decrees they passed would be brought to the king for promulgation. Then he noted that the deputies had not decided if the August decrees would be subject to the suspensive veto, as would laws passed by subsequent legislatures. It would be terrible, he said, if the August decrees were suspended, as they had been already been published and had met "universal joy." Barnave then laid a brilliant rhetorical trap. He moved that the Assembly decide whether or not the August decrees were constitutional acts or would require the king's sanction.[3] Barnave's motion brought to the front a serious problem. While the deputies had made the National Assembly France's functioning legislative body, the king continued to delay or avoid recognizing it as a true constituent assembly. As long as the king refused to sanction the Assembly's status, there was still a risk that the Revolution might founder and the Old Regime rise up again. Barnave had turned the debate over the veto into one on the Assembly's status as a constituent body.

As soon as Barnave had finished speaking, Monarchien and recalcitrant deputies rose up to defend the king and his honor. Lally-Tollendal noted that far from seeking to extend his prerogatives, the king had freely offered to limit them. Waving aside the king's delay in approving the August decrees, Lally-Tollendal noted that the Assembly itself had treated those decrees as subject to revision, sending them to committee for modification. If the king wished to examine the decrees and suggest modifications, he was doing no more than the Assembly had done. Lally-Tollendal decried the insult he found in the intimation that the king was up to no good. He asked "if it is in good faith that one can fear today the excesses and abuse of royal power? Where is the despot? Where are the minions of despotism? Where is the army? Moreover, where are the courtiers?" Lally-Tollendal suggested that the facts did not support any claim of malfeasance on the part of the executive. Instead, he argued that the threat to public order came from a new source, proposing a new variant on the trope of a good king badly advised. According to Lally-Tollendal, those who sought to harm France no longer tried to mislead the king. Instead, they sought to

---

[3] Ibid., 636. See also *Le Patriote français*, 16 September 1789, and *Journal de Paris*, 16 September 1789. Visme thought Barnave and his supporters hoped to use the matter of the veto as a lever to encourage the king to approve the 4 August decrees before recalcitrant Nobles and Clergy could have them revised. Visme, "Journal," 157r. See also Castellane, "Journal," 152–53.

mislead the Assembly by speaking ill of the monarch. The real threat now, he claimed, was not from an excess of executive vigor, but from too long a period of its weakness, from "the interruption of public revenues, the cessation of all justice, misery in the midst of abundance."[4] The real threat came from those who would further weaken the king. Virieu then asked that the deputies return to the order of business and discuss the duration of the king's veto. He argued that in order to calm the people it was necessary to establish the parameters of the king's powers, not enter into a dispute over whether or not the deputies exercised full constituent power.[5]

The recalcitrant Noble deputy Cazalès attacked Barnave's implied claim that the king could not interfere with constitutional acts. He argued that the Assembly should only discuss the first part of Barnave's motion, that of whether or not the deputies should delay debate over the royal veto until they had received the sanction of the August decrees. As for the second part of the motion, that of whether or not the king would be able to withhold his consent from constitutional acts, "one ought to leave over this question a religious veil (*un voile religieux*)"[6] That is, Cazalès wanted the deputies to discuss whether or not they should confront the king, but not discuss whether the king would be able to veto the constitution they were writing. The answer to the second question was a mystery best left hidden from public view. Cazalès here referred to the secret and even religious nature of the traditional system of royal government, but his point was novel in that the Assembly itself was invoked as the guardian of the mystery.

Mirabeau responded to Cazalès's speech, agreeing that a veil was draped over the king's ability to approve the constitution. But the great orator declared that "if the question of the validity of the constitution without the consent of the monarch has been left under a religious veil, it was not that the matter had not been decided, but that it had been judged useless and unseemly to openly declare a tacitly understood decision."[7] According to Mirabeau, the idea that the king's sanction was not necessary for the constitution was both true and dangerous.[8] It was true because, as Mounier had argued on 5 September, the king did not have the power to write a constitution, only to accept it. It was true because, as Mirabeau and Mounier had argued on 11 September, the king did not even have the right to initiate discussions of constitutional matters. But it was dangerous in

---

[4] AP 8: 637–38.   [5] Ibid., 638. See also *Le Point du jour*, 2: 374.

[6] *Journal de Paris*, 16 September 1789. Cazalès's intervention is critical to understanding the debate, but his remarks do not appear in the AP. This renders the following remarks of Mirabeau and Pétion cryptic. For Cazalès's speech, see also *Le Point du Jour*, 2: 374–75; *Courrier de Versailles*, 3: 283.

[7] *Journal de Paris*, 16 September 1789.   [8] *Le Point du Jour*, 2: 375.

two ways. First, too obviously pointing out the king's inability to make constitutional proposals risked alienating the king. Second, discussing whether or not the king could enter into discussions considering the constitution risked opening up too many questions about the extent of the king's powers all at once. Mirabeau had hardly been the voice of moderation thus far in the Assembly's debates, but he had been a consistent advocate of a strong king. Here he accepted that the king was indeed currently very weak. He urged the deputies to be prudent, arguing that it would be "unseemly" to humiliate the king without necessity.

Also responding to Cazalès, Pétion acknowledged that a religious veil existed, but he stated that the Assembly had the right to draw it away if necessary.[9] "The gentleman has told us that the Assembly wished to throw a religious veil over these grand questions and that the question is therefore out of order," Pétion said. But he denied that such matters should never be discussed. If the king refused to accept the August decrees, the deputies would have to discuss the matter. He argued against Mirabeau's claim that it was unseemly to discuss whether or not the king would have to accept the acts. The Constitutional Committee itself, Pétion noted, had earlier brought the matter of royal consent before the Assembly. Nevertheless, after defending his right to discuss the king's prerogatives, Pétion agreed with Mirabeau and Cazalès that "it was not a question of getting to the bottom of the [issue]." Pétion recommended that the deputies not enter into a formal discussion of the king's right to consent to the constitution. Instead, he urged the deputies to adopt the first half of Barnave's motion and delay sorting out the details of the suspensive veto until the king had sanctioned the August decrees.[10] The delay he recommended was implicitly meant to prevent a confrontation between the king and the Assembly, to prevent the lifting of the veil that concealed the king's weakness, to prevent alienating or humiliating the king. It was a call to allow for time to pass in order to resolve a brewing dispute between the Assembly and the king. It was a call to avoid stirring up the kinds of public unrest the deputies had witnessed in July and August. Pétion seemed to have adopted a page out of Thouret's playbook, allowing time for the problem to solve itself rather than demanding a rapid and formal resolution of a dispute between the king and the Assembly.

Mirabeau then spoke again and made the link between avoiding direct confrontation with the king and respect for the king explicit. He opened

---

[9] AP 8: 639. [10] Ibid.; *Le Point du jour*, 2: 376.

with the claim that he was far from upset that Barnave's motion had excited such strong feelings. To the contrary, he thought the matter was indeed worthy of such an uproar. Indeed, they had "thrown ... a religious veil over an acknowledged truth; but if that truth is attacked, it was necessary to lift the veil." That they did not raise a question out of respect for the king did not mean that they had yielded the point: "The religious veil must not prevent the National Assembly from explaining and manifesting a principle which is universal, and which must never suffer from circumstances."[11] Mirabeau indicated that the deputies had to preserve and demonstrate their respect for the king. But he also noted that such prudence had its limits: it could never stop the deputies from completing their work. Remarkably, deputies who had taken much different stances regarding the king and his powers came to the same conclusion. The staunch traditionalist Cazalès, the reforming monarchist Mirabeau, and the radical Pétion all agreed that the king had to be respected. All three argued that the king's exclusion from writing the constitution was so sensitive a matter that it should be kept from public view. It was imperative that the king not be humiliated during the process, that the executive power not be further weakened.

After much more discussion and a fair bit of tumult in the Assembly, Barnave agreed to divide his motion into two parts, separating discussion of the August decrees from the matter of whether or not the decrees were constitutional, avoiding the question of whether or not the king's approval was necessary for constitutional acts. He then agreed to drop the second half of his motion, allowing the matter to fall back under the veil. Nevertheless, the session remained disorderly. It came to an end only after a contested vote over whether or not the first half of Barnave's motion would be further discussed and then voted on. The Monarchien Clermont-Tonnerre, then president of the Assembly, declared the motion defeated in a voice vote. Barnave's supporters thought they had won and demanded that the vote be held again. The president felt insulted by the implied claim that he had behaved badly and refused to hold a new vote. After quite a bit of shouting and recriminations the matter was declared unfinished and the session ended without a decision having been made.[12]

The next day the Assembly returned to Barnave's proposal. In an attempt to win the point without forcing a vote, Le Chapelier suggested that the deputies not discuss Barnave's motion again and instead move on to constitutional questions that did not involve the veto power. This again

---

[11] AP 8: 639.   [12] *Journal de Paris*, 16 September 1789; *Courrier de Versailles*, 3: 286–87; AP 8: 640.

threw the Assembly into confusion. The deputies were unable to agree on whether or not Barnave's motion had been approved the night before, let alone whether or not they should resume debate over the veto power. During debate over whether or not to return to the day's business, Léon-Marguerite le Clerc, baron of Juigné, suddenly moved that the deputies declare the king's personal inviolability and the hereditary nature of the crown. This led to the vigorous and patriotic approval of Juigné's very traditional motion by universal acclamation. But then a question arose over whether or not the Spanish Bourbons would become eligible to inherit the throne. This led to much discussion of the part of the 1713 Treaty of Utrecht that prohibited the Spanish line of the Bourbon family from taking the French throne.[13]

Finally, Barnave's ally Adrien Duport suggested that the Assembly "throw a respectful veil over this matter" rather than making any decision about whether or not to endorse the exclusion.[14] Though he did not state it, we can take it that he thought the Assembly had the right to make a final decision in the matter, but out of respect for the king they ought to leave it undecided. In both cases where a veil had been invoked, the Assembly chose not to exercise a right that it claimed out of respect for the king and out of a desire to avoid stirring up unnecessary conflict between the king, the Assembly, and the people. The two previous standoffs between the Crown and the Assembly, those of 20–27 June and 11–16 July, had been resolved after the intervention of large crowds in Paris and Versailles in the first case and by a full-blown rebellion in Paris in the second. By seeking to keep matters concerning the limits of the king's powers beneath the veil, the deputies sought to prevent an overt standoff over the August decrees, preventing popular opinion from interfering in a dispute between the king and the Assembly. It was an important step toward creating a way for the king and Assembly to disagree without popular unrest being the result, a return to the tactic of 1 July when the Assembly had provided cover for the king rather than revealing his weakness. Instead of returning to Barnave's motion and making it clear that the Assembly and king were at a moment of impasse, the deputies voted to send the president to see the king and ask him to approve the August decrees. Then the Assembly moved on to other business.

---

[13] In the absence of survivors in Louis XVI's line, the crown would, by treaty, skip the Spanish line and go to the duke of Orléans and his descendants. See AP 8: 641–44; *Le Point du jour*, 2: 382–88; Ferrières, *Mémoires*, 1: 234. Louis XVI's closest male relatives, the Bourbons of Spain, would be excluded in defiance of the Salic Law.

[14] AP 8: 644.

On 18 September, the king responded to the Assembly's polite request that he sanction the August decrees with a series of observations about the decrees and suggestions about how to change them. Third Estate deputy Guillaume-François Goupil de Préfeln, always the king's man in the Assembly, proposed that the deputies form a committee to study Louis's response. Debate over what to do took up the rest of the session and was only resolved the following day. After several deputies attempted to formulate a respectful response that nonetheless asked the king to promulgate the August decrees, Duport finally hit the right tone. He asked that the president go to see the king and ask him to promulgate the decrees, while assuring the king that the deputies would treat his observations with "the greatest and most respectful consideration" when they undertook writing specific laws to put the decrees into effect. His motion, slightly reworded, was adopted with almost no dissent. The president duly approached the king, and reported back later in the session that the king had promised a reply by the following night. The king even assured the president that he could expect a "favorable" response to the request. When the Assembly met again on 21 September, the president read Louis's response. The king indicated that he would publish the decrees and that he intended to sanction the positive laws regarding them that the Assembly would create in the future.[15]

This rapid back-and-forth over the king's approval of the constitutional acts, so reminiscent of the solution found to the taking of the Abbaye prison on 30 June and the Assembly's attempts to convince Louis to recall Necker in mid July, demonstrated the existence of an informal system for resolving disputes between the Assembly and the king. In mid September, direct confrontation was avoided even as the deputies indirectly insisted on their right to move forward regardless of the king's decision. The deputies established their control of the constitution-writing process without forcing the king to acknowledge his defeat. By engaging in this oblique and resolutely polite confrontation with the king, the deputies sought to ensure his continued cooperation and to prevent the unrest in Paris sure to follow a disagreement between the Assembly and the king. It was a remarkable first step toward establishing a functional relationship between the newly powerful Assembly and the newly weakened monarch.

Flush with good feelings toward the king, the Assembly settled the form of the veto almost immediately after a second reading of the king's response. Clermont-Tonnerre only allowed a brief debate and the deputies

[15] AP 9: 28–31, 53. Fitzsimmons, *Remaking of France*, 66–67.

proceeded quickly to a decision. First, as had become their custom, the deputies sorted out the precise wording of the proposal. Then they voted: 10 abstained, 224 voted that the veto should only last until the next legislature was elected, and 728 voted that it should last until the legislature after the next. Each legislature would have to pass the measure, and only after the third passing would the decree be taken as signed, despite the king's protests.[16] Given that they had previously determined that each legislature would sit for two years, this meant at best a slightly longer than two-year-long period during which a vetoed law would be suspended. At worst, a law could take between four and six years to take effect over the king's resistance. This would certainly allow for public opinion to clarify itself as Thouret had proposed. It was a clear victory for those deputies who wanted a veto strong enough to curtail the excesses of a single-chamber legislature. It passed by an overwhelming majority, more than 70 percent of the votes cast, the latest in a series of major victories for the moderate Patriot platform, showing the unity of the reform party and the weakness of both the recalcitrant conservatives and the radicals.[17]

As Pétion had desired, a suspensive veto would lead to a discussion of laws vetoed by the king, a means to educate the people of their rights. But as the Monarchiens had wished, there would be no means for a wave of popular opinion to overwhelm the deputies and push them to make poor decisions.[18] As Alexandre de Lameth later wrote, "This decree was regarded as a means to conserve the dignity of the throne without compromising public liberty."[19] The king was ensured a role in the legislative body acting as a strong check on its powers. But his will was not the final word on legislation. While the form of the veto preserved the principle of national sovereignty, it also gave the king an enormous potential to influence the content of legislation, whether meant to protect his prerogatives as the Monarchiens wished or to ensure the king's willingness to enforce the laws, as Sillery had urged. The suspensive veto as adopted on 11 September and modified on 21 September offered something for all of the deputies from the old Society of Thirty. The acceptance of a suspensive veto denied the king a role as co-proprietor of the nation, but established a system in which the legislative and executive branches were theoretically equal parts of the

---

[16] AP 9: 54–55. Tackett argues that the president used his powers to prevent the radicals from speaking. Tackett, *Becoming a Revolutionary*, 94 n. 72.

[17] Glénard sees this as much more of a victory for the right. Glénard, *L'Exécutif et la Constitution de 1791*, 134, 146.

[18] For a different view, see Fitzimmons, *Night the Old Regime Ended*, 26.

[19] See Lameth, *Histoire*, 1: 143.

government. The new constitution featured a permanent, powerful legislative assembly. To go with it the deputies had created a permanent,
powerful executive.

While the decision to grant a suspensive veto seemed straightforward,
meant to preserve national sovereignty and to prevent the legislature from
rushing into error, it revealed a considerable change in the deputies'
attitude toward the king. In June, the deputies had declared that they
represented the nation, but they did so alongside the king as partners. They
had declared on 17, 20, and 23 June that they were responsible to the
nation, not to the king. They confirmed this stance in the midst of the great
disorder leading up to the taking of the Bastille. With this they signaled
that the National Assembly existed independently as part of the French
system of government, distinct from and equal to the king. In September,
they had clarified and elaborated on their earlier claims of equality with the
king, stating plainly that the nation was above both king and Assembly,
both of which were merely "*mandataires*" of the nation. Moreover, the
deputies came to the conclusion that the elected representatives of the
nation had two special responsibilities. First, they had to write the constitution according to what the nation willed (as seen in the *cahiers*), not
according to the king's wishes. Second, and this would apply to all future
legislatures, they had the task of interpreting the final will of the nation
when the king and the Assembly disagreed.

With these two decisions, the former tacitly understood and the latter
openly declared, the Assembly asserted for itself the powers of a constituent
assembly, its deputies bound to consider the will of their constituents but
not constrained by tradition or by past constitutions. In particular,
whether they wrote laws or wrote a constitution, they were not obliged
to obey the king, only to consult him. This was a major transformation,
giving the king a role in legislation somewhat like what the parlements had
held before the Revolution. The king's veto resembled the old parlementary right to remonstrate, to protest against features of new laws and ask
that changes be made. But the legislature, checked in its power by frequent
elections, would have the final say. It would always be able to force the
promulgation of new laws, much as the king had been able to force the
registration of laws in the Old Regime. Just as in the Old Regime, though,
it would be a burdensome process, allowing public opinion to weigh in.
The deputies had recognized that no system that failed to satisfy public
opinion could succeed, just as Brienne had stated when he dismissed the
Assembly of Notables in 1787. With their decision that the Assembly would
have the final word, the deputies transferred effective sovereignty from the

king to the legislature in the new constitution, subject to the proviso that ultimate sovereignty rested with the nation.

By narrowly defining the suspensive veto as a popular referendum and the absolute veto as a preservation of traditional monarchy, historians such as Halévi, Baker, and Friedland have elided much of the subtlety of the proposals made during the debates of September 1789. The majority of deputies supported a suspensive veto as a defensive measure, a means to prevent a return to ministerial despotism. This group included men like Lafayette, who favored a monarchy heavily influenced by American ideas, Thouret, who supported an absolute veto but was willing to support a suspensive veto under certain conditions, and skeptical reformers like Pétion. The version that had won the debate was that of Thouret, and it established the king as a powerful interpreter of the nation's will.[20] The suspensive veto, as proposed by Thouret and adopted by the Assembly, ensured that the king would retain a meaningful role in the new order. But the king and Assembly were not co-equal as legislators in the English sense. They remained co-equal powers in the American sense, as the American presidency cannot be seen as subordinate to Congress, despite the ability of the legislators to override the president's veto. But though the relationship between king and legislature resembled that of the United States in some ways, a hereditary king would always have more inherent power than an elected president. He would have the staying power to outlast multiple elected sessions and could steer events over long periods of time.

In practical terms, the new relationship among the Assembly, the king, and the nation developed slowly during September as the deputies sought the king's endorsement of the August decrees, the Declaration of the Rights of Man and Citizen, and later the constitutional framework of regular elections, a permanent one-chamber legislature, and a suspensive veto. Given that the deputies had reserved for themselves initiative in laws and the constituent power, they could not allow the king to take control of the process of writing the constitution. But they also did not wish to unduly and unnecessarily antagonize the king. Choosing to avoid direct confrontation just as they had during the mid-July crisis, the deputies pressed the king formally and politely to accept the constitutional acts. He responded by agreeing to do so, if his reservations would be taken into account in future legislation. The process seemed promising, almost a return to the days immediately after the taking of the Abbaye prison on

---

[20] Glénard claims that the outcome was much more ambiguous. Glénard, *L'Exécutif et la Constitution de 1791*, 145–47.

30 June when king and Assembly alike recognized the need cooperate to restore and maintain public order. But the rebirth of that early period of negotiation and compromise, backed by the new certainty that in time public opinion would convince the king or Assembly to back down, was cut short by events. Genial negotiation and compromise did not become regular features of the new relationship between king and Assembly.

Instead, in early October, the people of Paris intervened and changed the practical relationship among deputies, nation, and king. On 5 and 6 October, a large crowd marched from Paris to Versailles, invaded the National Assembly, and confronted the king at the royal chateau. After a night of uncertainty and some violence, the king agreed to return to Paris, there to take up permanent residence under the watchful eyes of his loyal subjects. This crowd action fundamentally changed the relationship between king, Assembly, and people by taking from the king any vestige of independence. Nevertheless, we cannot claim that the people of Paris rose up on 5 and 6 October to decisively side with the Assembly against a recalcitrant king. We cannot claim that the crowd demanded the king return to Paris in order to force him to accept the August decrees. There were three factors that led to the October Days, and the disagreement between king and Assembly was the least important of them. First and foremost was the ongoing scarcity of bread in Paris. Second was the arrival of a royalist contingent of soldiers, the Flanders Regiment, in Versailles. Third and least important was the king's ongoing reluctance to approve the August decrees and the Declaration of the Rights of Man and Citizen. These three issues were intertwined. The people of Paris saw their food shortages as a political issue related to aristocratic opposition to the Revolution. If there was a shortage of food in Paris, there had to be a political reason for it. Where previously the people had blamed only unnamed aristocrats, by the end of September some blame was beginning to stick to the king as well. The king's delay in sanctioning the constitutional acts was important because it signaled a stalemate at the top level of government and reinforced fears that no action would be taken to ensure Paris would be fed. The arrival of the Flanders Regiment implied that the king did not feel that the National Guard was sufficient to protect him and that he feared the people of Paris.[21]

The arrival of royal troops to the Paris region in late June and early July had contributed to unrest there and helped cause the explosive uprising of

[21] O. Hufton, "Women and Politics," in Hufton, *Women and the Limits of Citizenship in the French Revolution* (Toronto, 1992), 12. Andress, *French Revolution and the People*, 120.

mid July. Similarly, the arrival of the Flanders Regiment in early October transformed the nature of discontent in Paris. We lack clear evidence to explain why the king had summoned more troops to the region. The numbers arriving were far too small to put down a new insurrection in Paris. But the new troops had been summoned in mid September, around the time that Necker sent the National Assembly the king's reservations about the August decrees, making it appear that the two actions were related. It seems likely that the king brought the soldiers to Versailles to preserve his freedom of action. With loyal troops at his disposal, he would be able to hold out against demands by the Assembly that he accept the constitutional acts without modification. But this remains a speculative conclusion.

What we know with great certainty is that arrival of the new troops in Versailles was poorly managed and caused a public relations disaster. A banquet given by the King's Bodyguard and the Versailles National Guard for the arriving troops on 1 October led to claims that the troops closest to the king were more loyal to him than to the nation. The event could hardly have been more badly staged. While it was entirely traditional that officers of an arriving regiment be fêted, the king's appearance at the banquet, flanked by the queen and the royal children, was highly unusual. Ladies of the Court distributed white and black cockades to the soldiers and officers present, cockades meant to demonstrate loyalty to the king and queen. As they feasted, the men sang traditional royalist songs and cried out, "Long live the king" and "Long live the queen!" They did not call out, "Long live the nation!" The king, the ministers, and the Court were all deeply reassured by the apparent loyalty of the new troops. Their arrival certainly emboldened the king to seek concessions in his ongoing negotiations over the constitutional acts. During the next few days, news of the banquet spread in Paris and caused outrage there. Reports amplified and embellished the royalist atmosphere of the banquet. Accounts of the event in radical newspapers made it sound positively counter-Revolutionary. Rumor turned a banquet into an orgy, and the distribution of white and black cockades into the trampling of the national cockade underfoot. Officer's toasts in favor of the king were turned into cries against the Revolution and the nation.[22] Before the banquet, an uprising in Paris

[22] A. Mathiez, "Etude critique sur les journées des 5 et 6 octobre 1789," *Revue Historique* 68 (1898), 29; Gottschalk and Maddox, *Lafayette*, 321–23. Pétion and Grégoire referred to the banquet as an "orgy" in their speeches of 5 October 1789. *Le Moniteur*, 2: 9.

had been possible, given the ongoing shortages of bread. After the banquet, an uprising of some kind became almost inevitable.[23]

The events of 5 October in Paris began like any traditional protest about the price and scarcity of food. In this way, they were very different from those of 12–14 July, when the main concerns were Necker's dismissal and safety in the face of a possible royal attack on the city.[24] As usual in a protest focused on the supply of bread, women took the lead. When morning arrived, women from the main market in Paris beat drums and complained loudly about the lack of bread. They then joined up with working women from the nearby Saint-Antoine neighborhood, on the east side of the city near the site of the Bastille. The protestors gathered all of the women they met in the street and invaded houses to find more to join them. They marched to the nearby Hôtel de Ville around 8:00am, where they denounced the mayor, Bailly, and the leader of the National Guard, Lafayette. Women stormed the building, gathered up important papers, and threatened to burn them. They complained that the men of Paris and their representatives in the city government had failed to keep food prices stable. If the men could not ensure that Paris was adequately provisioned, it was up to the women to set matters straight.[25]

At this point, the protestors did not demand that the king come to Paris. Instead, they put pressure on the city government to ensure a supply of bread at acceptable prices. Though they carried weapons and used confrontational language, they sought less a change in government form than an end to the ongoing economic crisis. When the municipal authorities proved unwilling or unable to find bread for the city and satisfy the women's demands, the women moved on to the national authorities in Versailles.[26] The crowd that marched to Versailles on that rainy afternoon was unique both in size, with between six and seven thousand marching

---

[23] Mathiez, "Etude critique sur les journées des 5 et 6 octobre 1789," 265; Mathiez, "Etude critique sur les journées des 5 et 6 octobre 1789," *Revue Historique* 67 (1898): 280–81; Andress, *French Revolution and the People*, 121.

[24] D. Garrioch, "The Everyday Lives of Parisian Women and the October Days of 1789," *Social History* 24:3 (October, 1999): 231–49; Hufton, *Women and the Limits of Citizenship*, 16–17. Applewhite and Levy see the women's actions as much more radical. D. G. Levy and H. Applewhite, "Women and Militant Citizenship in Revolutionary Paris," in S. E. Melzer and L. W. Rabine, eds., *Rebel Daughters: Women and the French Revolution* (Oxford, 1992), 84–85. See also Alpaugh, *Non-Violence*, 69–70.

[25] Levy and Applewhite, "Women and Militant Citizenship," 83.

[26] Hufton, *Women and the Limits of Citizenship*, 13, 14–15. Shapiro claims that the revolt was aimed at the municipal government and that Lafayette and his allies redirected the crowd's anger toward royal inaction to consolidate their own power. Shapiro, *Revolutionary Justice in Paris: 1789–1790*, 91–92.

(almost entirely women), and in composition, as the women came from all over Paris, rather than being from one trade or one district.[27] They brought with them weapons of all kinds, from knives to pikes to cannon, indicating a willingness to escalate their protest to violence should their demands be ignored. But the marchers remained peaceful as they trudged through rain and mud to Versailles. Hours later, a second wave of some eighteen to twenty-four thousand Parisians followed the same route, a mixed crowd of men and women. It was accompanied by a twenty-thousand-strong contingent of the National Guard, reluctantly led by Lafayette.[28]

When the first wave of protestors arrived in Versailles it became clear that there was no leader directing the crowd. The marchers broke up into smaller groups, some going to the royal chateau where the women stood outside of the gates, some seeking shelter from a cold October rain wherever they could find it, and others going to the National Assembly. Hearing that a crowd had gathered outside of the chamber, the Assembly voted to allow a delegation in to address the deputies. Their spokesman, a hero of the taking of the Bastille named Stanislas-Marie Maillard, told the deputies that the women wanted bread, that they wanted the men of the Flanders Regiment punished for trampling the national cockade, and that they wanted to denounce an aristocratic plot to starve Paris into submission. He did not raise the matter of the king's failure to accept the August decrees or other constitutional acts. The Assembly responded to his demands by agreeing to ask the king to act quickly on matters of provisioning and by making available copies of the laws they had passed regarding the grain trade. The deputies had just voted to send Mounier to see the king and ask for the simple acceptance of the constitutional acts. The Assembly offered to allow six women to accompany him so they could present their requests to the king themselves.[29]

The six women accompanied Mounier on his trip through the crowd to the chateau, where they sat and waited for hours to meet with the king. Showing remarkable political acumen, Mounier turned the tumult in Versailles to the advantage of the Assembly. While he waited, Mounier warned members of Royal Council he saw walk by that the king could not be seen to be temporizing given the explosive nature of the situation. He urged them to adopt the strategy the deputies had developed over the

[27] Garrioch, "Everyday Lives," 244–45.
[28] On Lafayette's attempts to maintain order in Paris and his failure to convince the Paris National Guard to stay in Paris, see Gottschalk and Maddox, *Lafayette*, 330–40.
[29] AP 9: 346–48; *Le Moniteur*, 2: 11; Duquesnoy, *Journal*, 1: 401; Ferrières, *Mémoires*, 1: 307. Andress, *French Revolution and the People*, 122.

summer to calm the people of France. He told the king's ministers that the easiest way to calm the crowd would be to accept the Assembly's role as a constituent assembly. He argued that the crowd would see the decision by Louis to accept the Assembly's acts as a royal gift to the people, and that the king's display of generosity in accepting the acts would calm the crowd gathered just outside the chateau.[30] Where the king could not enforce his will, he could appear generous rather than weak.

In frantic discussions with his council during the afternoon, Louis had arrived at the same conclusion. When Mounier and the women finally had their audience with Louis, the king announced immediately that he accepted the August decrees and the Declaration of the Rights of Man and Citizen. He told the women that he would do what he could to ensure grain supplies would reach Paris. Mounier then pushed the king to write out his acceptance of the constitutional acts, so that he could show it to his fellow deputies when he returned to the Assembly. The king duly wrote out his acceptance of the August decrees and the Declaration of Rights. But accepting the constitutional acts did not calm the crowd. In fact, it was after the king had given in that the mood of the crowd seemed to worsen. As Mounier and the women left the chateau, they were hooted for having accepted the king's word that provisions would be sent to Paris. Women in the crowd shouted that they needed written promises from the king, like the written acceptance of the constitutional acts Mounier carried. For these women, at least, "the image of king as protector and provider was dissolving into the picture of an unreliable executive agent whose authority was limited at best, and who must be pinned down to signed contractual agreements."[31]

Mounier and his entourage had spent several hours at the chateau waiting for the king to see them. When Mounier returned with news of the king's acceptance of the constitutional acts he expected to find the Assembly still in session. Instead he found it adjourned and the hall filled with women. In his absence, the session had fallen apart. Most of the deputies had left. A woman had taken Mounier's place and other women sat on the deputies' benches, making mock proposals and voting mock

---

[30] J.-J. Mounier, *Faits relatifs à la dernière insurrection* (Paris, 1789), 17. Saint-Priest, who was present at the meeting with Mounier, later claimed that the National Assembly had used the tumult as a pretext to force acceptance of the Declaration of the Rights of Man and Citizen. Saint-Priest, *Mémoires*, 2: 14.

[31] Mounier, *Faits*, 16–17, 20; *Le Moniteur*, 2: 29. Lefebvre, *Coming of the French Revolution*, 199; Levy and Applewhite, "Women and Militant Citizenship," 83; Hufton, *Women and the Limits of Citizenship*, 9.

decrees. Mounier recovered his place and called the few remaining deputies to order. When announced that the king had accepted the constitutional acts, he was greeted with applause and cries of "Long live the king!" from the deputies. But the women asked Mounier how the king's acceptance of constitutional acts would help the poor in Paris find bread.[32] There was a fundamental mismatch between what Mounier had accomplished and what the market women wanted. Settlement of constitutional issues was not the main motive behind the women's march. They wanted their government – municipal, legislative and executive – to work together to relieve the suffering of Paris. The protestors focused their attention on the solution of local issues, not national or constitutional ones. Mounier's efforts to solve the standoff between the king and the Assembly by returning to the successful tactic of 1 July had succeeded. His attempts to calm the crowd had failed.

Later in the night, the second wave of protestors arrived, followed by the men of the National Guard. Only then, late in the night and early the next morning, did people in the crowd begin to call for the king to move to Paris. They had asked the Paris city government for solutions, and had not been satisfied. The National Assembly had failed them as well. The protestors moved up to the next level of authority. They focused their attention on the king. The leadership of women, vital to non-violent protest in Old Regime France, waned as they ceded initiative to the arriving men. Early in the morning of 6 October, the gates to the chateau's courtyard were forced and the crowd surged in. As the King's Bodyguard tried to maintain order, violence broke out. A seventeen-year-old journeyman and two of the King's Bodyguard were killed in brief fighting. A small group of women and men forced entry into the chateau itself and tried to find the queen. The queen fled to her husband's rooms. The National Guard was able to regain control of the public areas and soldiers cleared the halls of the chateau. But the crowd outside did not disperse and the situation remained extremely dangerous.

Louis had two choices, much the same as he had had on the night of 15 July. He could flee Versailles and set up his government somewhere else, or he could submit to the wishes of the crowd.[33] Lafayette urged the king to go to Paris, where Lafayette could assure his safety and that of the royal family. Cries rang out from the courtyard for the king to show himself, for

---

[32] Duquesnoy, *Journal*, 1: 402; Mounier, *Faits*, 20–21; Ferrières, *Mémoires*, 1: 316. Levy and Applewhite, "Women and Militant Citizenship," 84.

[33] Mathiez, "Etude critique sur les journées des 5 et 6 octobre 1789," 245; Lefebvre, *Coming of the French Revolution*, 200.

the queen to appear, for the king to return to Paris. Only when Louis appeared on the balcony and promised to free up grain supplies and to go to Paris did the mood of the crowd turn from murderous to festive.[34] The crowd had proceeded up the ladder of authority but had been dissatisfied at each rung. It was pleased only when the king publicly agreed to help them find grain and move his household back to Paris. Throughout the previous day and into the early morning there had been a fundamental mismatch between the demands of the assembled people and the actions of their representatives. The Assembly and the king chose to move forward with constitutional reform thinking that this would demonstrate that they were working to redress the nation's grievances. Even the king's promises to find grain were not enough. In the end, the only way to calm the crowd was for the king to take up residence in Paris, where his loyal people would surround him and make sure that he acted in their interest, not in the interests of the courtiers of Versailles.

As the deputies filed back into the Assembly hall later that morning for their regular meeting, they had yet to hear that the king planned to leave for Paris. Mounier announced that Louis had requested the Assembly move its session to the chateau where they could stay in constant contact with the king. He urged the deputies to do as the king had asked. But Mirabeau bristled at the suggestion that they relocate to the chateau, claiming that they would not be able to deliberate freely so close to the king himself. While the Assembly debated the issue, so reminiscent of their struggles on 20 and 23 June to establish the independence of the National Assembly from royal control, the king sent word that he and his family were going to relocate to Paris. Immediately after hearing the announcement, Mirabeau proposed that the deputies declare "that the king and the Assembly will be inseparable" and that the Assembly would also move to Paris. This would better allow the deputies to work with the king, Mirabeau argued, but it would also show that the deputies were choosing to go to Paris of their own accord, not because they had been forced to do so by the protestors. Remarkably, the Assembly found itself in the same position that Louis held in late June when facing unrest in Paris. Too weak to resist the demands of the crowd, the Assembly had to find at artful way to mask its weakness and prevent the spread of unrest nationwide.

Barnave spoke in support of Mirabeau's motion, noting that "it is certain that, in any case, they [the king and the Assembly] must not be

---

[34] Hufton, *Women and the Limits of Citizenship*, 11; Andress, *French Revolution and the People*, 122; Price, *Road from Versailles*, 106–07.

separated: the health and the peace of the kingdom, the unity of the public power and the inviolable fidelity that we owe to the king equally prescribe it." An unnamed deputy requested that they add the phrase "during the current session." The Assembly then accepted the modified proposal unanimously and sent a deputation of thirty-six deputies to inform the king. When the deputation returned, they brought with them a note from the king expressing his gratitude stating, "The wish of my heart is, you know, to never be separated from [the Assembly]." The deputies then voted to send a large delegation to accompany the king on his trip to Paris, and returned to the order of the day in order to show, in Mirabeau's words, that "the ship of state is not in danger, to signal forever this memorable day of concord [between the king and the Assembly]." Mirabeau urged the deputies to remain in session so that they would appear to be masters of the situation.[35] What other choice did they have?

Their decision to decree that the king and the Assembly were inseparable went far beyond a feeble attempt to preserve appearances. When the deputies voted unanimously never to separate from the king until the end of the present session, they in effect swore an updated version of the Tennis Court Oath. On 20 June, the Assembly had found itself threatened by an outside force that sought to regulate its meetings and control its agenda. By ordering the deputies not to meet, the king and his advisors had threatened the existence and independence of the National Assembly. Faced with an existential threat, the deputies had sworn to never separate until they had finished the constitution. On 23 June, after the Royal Session, the king had ordered them to disperse. Instead, the deputies of the National Assembly had defied the king and stayed in their seats. They had voted their own immunity from prosecution for their acts. They had declared that the king could not determine the conditions and rules under which they met. When the deputies had found themselves facing the crisis that followed Necker's dismissal, they voted to sustain their motions of 20 and 23 June. When the deputies voted never to separate from the king and accepted the king's promise never to separate from the National Assembly, the outside force that threatened the deputies came from Paris. The deputies once again voted not to separate until the constitution was finished (the meaning of their decision not to separate during the present session of Assembly) but in the updated version of their oath, they included the king himself. Henceforth, the unit of government was the *unity* of the public power, as Barnave had so memorably said. The fundamental

[35] For this and the previous paragraph, we rely on AP 9: 348–50; Mounier, *Faits*, 28–30; *Le Moniteur*, 2: 12; Duquesnoy, *Journal*, 1: 407; *Le Patriote français*, 7 October 1789.

unity in government was that of the king and the Assembly, both representatives of the sovereign nation. Where the deputies had once needed support
from the people against royal interference, they now undertook to defend
themselves and the king against the effervescent anger of the people they
represented.

The October Days led to profound changes in the course of the
Revolution. The crowd of women who invested the Hôtel de Ville on
5 October had claimed that men had failed to solve the subsistence
problems facing Paris. They had particularly harsh words for city leaders.
Given the failure of municipal authorities to solve their problems, the
women went to the national authorities to see what they could do. The
women seemed to believe that the national authorities could solve the
problems of grain supply if only they were willing to take action. By
marching to Versailles, the women hoped to change the political calculus
and force the deputies and the king to put the needs of Paris first, making
subsistence issues the order of the day. By their actions they helped to
create a new form of political actor, the militant citizen. As historians
Darline Gay Levy and Harriet Applewhite write, "For the *menu peuple*
[ordinary people] of Paris, especially for women, militant citizenship
would continue to mean at least a politics of intimidation, unrelenting
surveillance and control, practiced sometimes through legal means (like
petitioning or forming delegations within popular societies), but also in
insurrection." Radical journalists in Paris quickly created new meanings for
the militants' activities, divorcing them from traditional issues of subsistence. Journalists recast Parisians' militancy in "Rousseauian language,
legitimating insurrection as the arm of the sovereign nation, the most
authentic embodiment of the general will."[36] The marriage of popular
action with Rousseauian language created a rival conception of political
representation, one that would do much to radicalize the Revolution. The
October Days illustrated that the common people were unwilling to leave
politics to the politicians. Their success in bringing the king to Paris led to
the realization that ordinary people could force changes in national politics
through mass action. Neither the king nor the majority in the Assembly
accepted that popular opinion should have a regular role in the government. Nevertheless, after the October Days, the opinion of the Paris street
would have to be taken into account in every political decision, whether the
deputies or the king liked it or not. This new, democratic element was
unique for its time and truly revolutionary.

---

[36] Levy and Applewhite, "Women and Militant Citizenship," 85.

Moreover, there was a major change was in the way the deputies saw their relationship to the sovereign people, moving the majority to think through the implications of the principle that the law was a product of the general will. The Assembly found itself in an interesting bind. The king had accepted the constitutional acts because the people of Paris rose up, but their constitutional project envisioned an orderly process in which the voices of market women and most workingmen would only be heard indirectly if at all in national politics.[37] On 6 October, faced with an unruly crowd and the possibility that the king would move his residence, the deputies swore never to separate from his person. Where before they had chosen to defy the king in order to satisfy their electors and the nation, they now chose to defy the people of Paris, for the same reason. After the October Days, the deputies had to consider the possibility that the people of Paris would demand a more direct role in politics. They began to worry that Parisians might again invade the Assembly hall or the king's residence, demanding actions that could be unwise and might be impossible.

And so the deputies moved to criminalize political uprisings and to solidify control of the levers of power at all levels by good bourgeois citizens, those who had property or at least solid employment and thus had a stake in the new system. Given that the nation could now choose its own representatives, the nation would have to express its political will through those representatives, not through mass unrest. On 21 October, the deputies passed a decree that established how public order would be kept by civic authorities, including when and how elected civic authorities could declare martial law. Not long after, the Assembly decided to model voting rights on the system used in Paris to elect its deputies to the Estates General. Only those men who could prove that they paid taxes and had a stable residence would be able to vote. The decision to allow only men of means, however modest, to vote arose directly out of fears of popular unrest. Having lived through the October Days and having imagined them as a purely political event, whether as part of a conspiracy on the part of the duke of Orléans or on the part of unnamed aristocrats, the deputies wanted to deny the misuse of popular opinion by outside actors as a means to pressure the Assembly or the king.[38]

---

[37] This is not to say, as Friedland does, that the National Assembly sought to divorce itself entirely from the political demands and opinions of its electorate. Friedland, *Political Actors*, 11–13, 297–98; and, "Parallel Stages," 247–50.

[38] Hufton, *Women and the Limits of Citizenship*, 18; Andress, *French Revolution and the People*, 122–23; Shapiro, *Revolutionary Justice*, 94; Doyle, *Oxford History*, 2nd ed., 124. Urban workers would be most affected by the new restrictions. In the countryside, most men remained eligible to vote.

Convinced that the uprising had been political in nature, the deputies worked to prevent future uprisings in three ways. First, the deputies would ensure that no uprising would be needed to protect the rights of the nation by writing a just constitution. Second, the deputies would through law ensure that the nation's own resources were sufficient to put down rebellion without recourse to politically unreliable army units. Third, the need to improve security and prevent popular agitation allowed for a brief resurgence of the center-right in the Assembly as Lafayette tried once again to broker a deal between the members of the old patriot coalition. With Lafayette's rival Mounier gone, having fled back to Dauphiné in the aftermath of the October Days, it seemed that there was no one to thwart this push. But despite a weakening of the extreme left in the Assembly, compromised by their support of the marchers on 5–6 October, there was no long-term rapprochement between the center-left and the center-right in the Assembly. Lafayette's attempt to reunite the Patriot coalition failed.[39]

This did not mean, however, that the deputies abandoned their general plan to calm the people of France by increasing their confidence in the government. After the October Days, the National Assembly moved quickly to address the ongoing and worsening financial crisis that had fatally weakened the absolute monarchy and threatened the stability of the new order. The August decrees had created uncertainty in the countryside over what taxes, fees and dues still needed to be paid. The deputies were aware that the legitimacy of local authorities had been undermined and they were concerned with problems of public order throughout France.[40] By early October, tax receipts had ceased to come in. Credit markets had seized up. Voluntary gifts to the state called "patriotic donations" were not keeping up with expenses and it would take time for the expected "patriotic contribution" of 25 percent of income to provide significant revenue. Given that the deputies had solemnly declared there would be no bank-ruptcy, they absolutely had to find new means to secure the national debt and free up the possibility of new loans. There was little question about how the financial mess would be resolved. Everyone knew that the Church would be asked to pay. Such demands were hardly new, of course, having

---

[39] Shapiro, *Revolutionary Justice*, 94, 219–20.

[40] See, for example, the letter of 27 August 1789 from the judicial officials of the Auvergne to the local curés, asking them to clarify from the pulpit that the people were expected to pay the tithe and all other fees and dues until the National Assembly had passed specific laws concerning their redemption. Reprinted in the *Journal de Paris*, it was easily available to the deputies. *Supplement au no. 259 du Journal de Paris*, 16 September 1789.

surfaced in previous Estates General and appearing in perhaps one in every four of Third Estate *cahiers* in 1789.[41] It was only a question of how much the Church would pay and how it would pay it.

The debate over Church property unfolded over more than three weeks, beginning on 10 October, with discussion on several days before a final vote came on 2 November. The position of the left on the taking of Church property can be best seen in three speeches, those of Talleyrand and Mirabeau, given early in the debate, and that of the moderate Thouret, given on 23 October. It can also be seen in the remarkably blunt speech given by Le Chapelier on 2 November that expressed the concerns of the far left. The basic views of those who defended the Church's right to hold property and to exist as a special entity in French society were espoused with the greatest impact on the Assembly by Camus on 13 October, and by Boisgelin, the archbishop of Aix, and the abbé François-Xavier de Montesquiou-Fézensac on 31 October. We will survey here the major issues raised by the deputies so we may better understand their final decree. A careful study of deputy speeches shows that the decree was, as in so many debates during the early months of the Revolution, a compromise meant to gather as many votes as possible. But it was a compromise that attracted far fewer votes than had those we have studied so far.

The job of proposing to use the Church's property to fix the nation's finances fell to bishop Talleyrand, a man who knew as much about the ins and outs of Church finance as anyone. Talleyrand spoke on 10 October, giving form to what had been in the air around the deputies: the taking of Church property to pay down the national debt and stabilize the state's parlous finances.[42] Much as had his speech of 7 July on the binding mandates, his speech on Church property set the basic framework on which the following speeches hung. And, much as in July, his motion would fail to come to a vote, bypassed by his nominal allies. When Talleyrand took the podium the deputies already had a good idea of what he would say. Everyone knew, for example, that taxes were not coming in and that credit markets were frozen. They knew that the Clergy's renunciation of the tithe, made in August, would have drastic

---

[41] For the Estates General of 1576, see O. Ulph, "Jean Bodin and the Estates-General of 1576," *JMH* 19: 4 (1947), 294. For a recent discussion of the debate over Church property, see R. Dean, *L'Assemblée constituante et la réforme ecclésiastique, 1790* (Paris, 2014), 105–36. See also J. McManners, *The French Revolution and the Church* (New York, 1970), 26–29. Tackett, *Becoming a Revolutionary*, 198–207; D. Van Kley, *The Religious Origins of the French Revolution* (New Haven, 1996), 352–61; Shusterman, *French Revolution*, 61–65.

[42] *Journal de Paris,* 13 October 1789.

consequences for the Church's finances. Mirabeau had highlighted the worsening financial crisis in a speech on 26 September, comparing the deputies' hesitation in dealing with financial questions with the Roman Senate's debates over how to proceed while the grand bugbear Catalina executed a conspiracy to overthrow the republic. Mirabeau had denied that there was any grand conspiracy against France, instead posing the kingdom's finances as the existential threat. But, he claimed, the deputies were making the same mistake ancient Romans had. When faced with disaster, they debated.[43] On 10 October, Talleyrand proposed action.

Everyone knew the state had been burdened by great needs, Talleyrand announced, and that it would be necessary to use great means to fill them. As he put it, "Ordinary means have been used up, the people are pressured from all directions, the lightest additional burden ... would be insupportable." He recognized that funds were coming in from unusual sources, like the "patriotic donations" the Assembly had gratefully accepted, but pointed out that this money was destined merely to pay the "extraordinary needs" of the current year. It was necessary to rethink royal finance entirely, he claimed. The "extraordinary" needs of the state meant it would be necessary to have recourse to the goods of the Church to repair royal finances. The order of the Clergy, he continued, had long given proof of its "devotion to the public good," and one could readily expect its willingness to make "sacrifices that the extreme needs of the state solicit from its patriotism." Some operation to rework the finances of the Church was inevitable, he continued, simply because the Clergy's willingness to end the tithe had entirely ruined the livelihoods of some clerics. A reshuffling of the income from Church endowments was already necessary. It was now possible to rework Church finance in such a way that the clergy would be paid in a more equitable way. Whatever surplus was left after the basic needs of the Church had been paid for could be used to retire the national debt and to secure new loans necessary to save the state.[44]

In order to show that the nation could have recourse to the goods of the Church without violating the right to private property found in the Declaration of the Rights of Man and Citizen, Talleyrand sought to prove that the Church did not own property in the same way others did. The goods it used had never been given to the disposal of persons, he claimed, only for the fulfillment of duties. Moreover, he claimed, it was certain that the nation itself was the "protector of the will of the donors"

---

[43] Ferrières, *Mémoires*, 1: 171; AP 9; 196.   [44] AP 9: 398; *Le Point du jour*, 3: 273–74.

who had given property for the Church's use.[45] It was up to the nation to determine what to do with property that was no longer being used to support the public good as envisioned by its donors. If an endowment no longer funded the duties envisioned by the donors, Talleyrand argued, it could be shifted to other uses within the Church or given over to the public good. In addition, he claimed that donations to the Church were only meant to give the individual clerics a decent livelihood. The rest, the "excess," as he put it, was meant to be used to aid the poor and for the upkeep of churches.[46]

If there was a surplus beyond what was necessary to pay the clerics themselves, to aid the poor, and to maintain the buildings the Church needed, Talleyrand said, that surplus could be used for the public good. As he put it, the nation, "principally in a [time of] general distress," could "dispose of the goods" of various religious communities that must be suppressed, once the support of the individual clerics had been assured. The nation could "turn to its profit, in the current moment" the revenue of benefices without duties that were vacant and of such benefices that became vacant in the future, acting in the spirit of the intentions of the Church's benefactors. It could reduce the income of current holders of such benefices to a more modest sum as seemed appropriate. He thought actions like these would be no violation of the rights of property because they were consonant with the intentions of the donors. By these operations the Assembly could provide for the clergy and reduce the financial distress afflicting the nation.[47]

According to Talleyrand, the Church's property, its *rentes,* and endowments could be taken by the state, subject to the condition that the state pay all of the costs of the clergy, provide for the poor, and maintain necessary church buildings. He imagined this expropriation as a process, one in which religious houses for the regular clergy deemed "useless" would be wound down, in which "simple" benefices, those that had income but no duties, would gradually be extinguished, and the Church would cease to be the owner of large amounts of property in buildings, agricultural land, or forests. Nevertheless, the Clergy would be compensated for this taking. They would become the "first creditor" of the nation. The nation would guarantee a certain income to the Church, fixed to the price of wheat so the

---

[45] AP 9: 398.

[46] Ibid., 399. *Le Moniteur* noted that Talleyrand had argued the nation "can destroy those aggregations of [the Clergy] which might appear useless to society, and necessarily their goods would become the just portion of the nation." *Le Moniteur,* 2: 37.

[47] AP 9: 399.

value would not diminish over time. Perhaps the most important part of Talleyrand's speech involved this position for the Clergy as first creditor of the nation. The income to the Church would be secured and distributed before any other bills would be paid. The income would be put, "by a special privilege, under the guarantee of the nation," and would be paid from the "first revenues of the State."[48]

In a rather transparent attempt to rally support for his proposal among the more modest deputies from the Clergy, Talleyrand proposed that each curé be guaranteed an income of at least 1,200 *livres* a year, along with housing and a garden. An income of 1,200 *livres* a year would mean more money for most curés in France, many of whom subsisted on half that amount. The figure of 1,200 livres had appeared in the Paris general *cahiers* of the Clergy and Third Estate, indicating that this idea already had some support.[49] When Talleyrand finished the speech, he was warmly applauded. The Assembly ordered the speech printed and two copies given to each deputy, encouraging them to review it so a proper discussion of this major proposal could follow.[50] Despite the warm reception, though, support for the proposal was far from universal. Talleyrand's speech had thrown the deputies of the Clergy "into consternation," as Ménard de la Groye put it.[51] According to Ferrières, the proposal rallied the deputies of the Nobles and the Clergy against the "Revolutionaries and capitalists" who had proposed it.[52] The moderate Third Estate deputy René Maupetit noted that some deputies claimed the speech had been full of "false calculations and very important omissions."[53] It seemed certain that Talleyrand's motion would be fiercely contested.

The debate resumed before Talleyrand's proposal could be printed or distributed. Mirabeau spoke on 12 October and made a substitute motion. Gone was all of the careful phrasing and sugary words Talleyrand had used to sweeten the pill for his ecclesiastical colleagues. No mention was made of the Clergy having a special privilege when it came to state finances, nor was there any discussion of how the property of the Church would be used to resolve the current financial mess. If Talleyrand had besieged the deputies

---

[48] Ibid., 399–402; *Le Point du jour*, 3: 276, 278. Lameth thought that Talleyrand had included a reference to "privilege" in order to draw more deputies of the Clergy to support the motion, despite the risk that the Church would be kept as a separate body within the nation. Lameth, *Histoire* 1: 160–61.

[49] AP 9: 400; Chassin, *Les Élections et les cahiers*, 1: 308, 353.

[50] AP 9: 404; Delandine, *Mémorial historique*, 6: 159–60.

[51] Ménard de la Groye, *Correspondance*, 123.   [52] Ferrières, *Mémoires*, 1: 183.

[53] R. Maupetit "Lettres," edited by E. Queruau-Lamerie, *Bulletin de la Commission Historique et Archéologique de la Mayette*, 10: 19 (1903), 364.

with details, Mirabeau stunned them with simplicity. He avoided all discussion of finance and gave no reasons for the deputies to support his motion at all. He simply stated that all of the Church's goods belonged to the nation (the French verb is "*appartenir*"), subject to the provision that the nation must support the useful works of the Church. He then proposed that all curés be given an income of 1,200 livres a year and adequate housing. That was all. As he pointed out later in the debate, the whole point of his motion was its simplicity. He asked for the simple declaration that all lands belonged to the nation, he said, because this declaration itself would cause "a thousand useful reforms, and by this alone all obstacles will be overcome."[54] The abbé Grégoire then asked that further debate be halted, as the deputies had not yet received their copies of Talleyrand's printed proposal. The issue was initially put off, but given the Assembly's coming move to Paris it resumed the next day, 13 October.[55]

The debate that followed revolved around the issues Talleyrand and Mirabeau had raised. The deputies discussed the way in which the Church held its property, the justifications needed for the nation to take land from the Church, and above all the question of what kind of privilege the Church might have in the new French social order. Talleyrand had stated plainly that the Clergy as a body would have privileged access to state funds in the future, and that they were being asked to make a patriotic sacrifice. Mirabeau had responded with a motion that avoided a discussion of privilege at all. He denied that there was a need to ask the Clergy sacrifice its property since the property belonged to the nation in the first place.[56] This juxtaposition of reasons the nation could use Church land to pay its debts meant that the debate was not, as historians have long argued, simply one between progressive Revolutionaries and recalcitrant conservatives. It was also a fight between the center-left and the left over what the Revolution meant for the future reorganization of society.

In this jousting between the center and left, witnesses agreed that Thouret's speech on 23 October was the most important. His speech wove together aspects of Talleyrand and Mirabeau's motions, while using wording more palatable to moderate deputies. The conservative Third Estate deputy Duquesnoy recorded that Thouret seemed "to bring together all minds into a common opinion" as his "extreme moderation, wise principles and reasonable firmness conciliated all spirits."[57] In

---

[54] AP 9: 409, 640; *Le Point du jour*, 3: 299–30. Lameth saw Mirabeau's proposal as an "extension" of Talleyrand's proposal, not a rival proposal. Lameth, *Histoire*, 1: 162.

[55] AP 9: 409, 411.   [56] Ibid., 484 (23 October 1789), 640 (2 November 1789).

[57] Duquesnoy, *Journal* 1: 471.

underlining the influence Thouret's speech had on the Assembly, Ferrières noted that Thouret had previously appeared as a conservative, "once attached to the Court, even accused of belonging to the Polignac faction, promised the presidency by the aristocratic faction in the Assembly." These were great conservative *bona fides* and certainly ensured that the center-right in the Assembly would listen to what he had to say. After all, it was Thouret who had provided the path forward during the debate over the king's veto powers when he proposed an iterative version of the suspensive veto. This had allowed the king to retain a very important negative over legislation without taking the ultimate lawmaking power away from the Assembly.[58] One deputy who had heard Thouret's speech wrote that after 23 October the Assembly was no longer even discussing Talleyrand's motion.[59] Thouret had switched attention away from Talleyrand and Mirabeau and onto himself.

On 23 October, Thouret proposed a new substitute motion, stating that the goods of the Church "were at the disposal of the nation," rather than bluntly stating, as had Mirabeau, that they "belonged" to the nation. Thouret said that he did not wish to establish that the Church's goods belonged to the nation so much as to establish "the principle by which all these goods" are "essentially at the disposal of the nation."[60] In this he was closer to Talleyrand's proposal than to Mirabeau's, though he never suggested that all Church land must be sold immediately. What distinguished his speech was the attention he gave to the legal principle of "*mortemain*," by which corporations known as "moral bodies," such as the order of the Clergy, could hold property in perpetuity. Thouret denied that such corporations were identical to physical persons and insisted that their right to hold property only existed through the law. Since it was dependent on the civil law, not natural rights, it meant that the nation could declare such a corporation's goods at its disposal.[61] One witness reported that Thouret had "aggrandized and ennobled the question." He had acknowledged that the Church was the rightful owner of the properties it held, "but by the will of the nation." If the nation changed its will, "it could take back the property that it had ceded, but not given."[62] While the nation could destroy the fictive, moral person known as the "order of the

---

[58] Ferrières, *Mémoires*, 1: 185–86. *Journal de Paris* singled out Thouret's speech as very important and noted that the Assembly had voted to print it. *Journal de Paris*, 24 October 1789.
[59] Maupetit "Lettres," 366.   [60] AP 9: 487.
[61] Ibid., 485. This neatly sidestepped the Declaration of the Rights of Man and Citizen's guarantee of private property, as it was only guaranteed for legal persons.
[62] *Journal de Paris*, 24 October 1789.

Clergy," it would not destroy the actual Church or the men and women who were part of it. The properties simply needed to be declared at the disposal of the nation, not actually taken. As Thouret had put it, "The enjoyment of the properties can be provisionally left to those who currently possess them, up until the opportune moment for alienation arrives; and the administration of the domains will be usefully left for some time to the provincial assemblies."[63] Though deputies praised his powerful delivery and impressive reasoning there was later some confusion as to where Thouret stood on the issue. In the end, conservative deputies saw his wording as leaving room for continued Church ownership of ecclesiastical properties.[64] More radical deputies focused on how Thouret's argument expanded discussion of Church lands to include the king's property as well.[65] This element of confusion became important later in the debate, as we shall see.

Many deputies spoke out in favor of the Church's continuing ownership of property, though they did so in a variety of ways. Some focused on the very nature of property and claimed that if the Church's property could be seized on a whim of the National Assembly then no one's property was truly secure, despite the guarantees given in the Declaration of the Rights of Man and Citizen.[66] Others argued that the Church could not and did not own property, but that did not mean that the nation could take the property used by the Church at will. These deputies posed ownership as remaining in the hands of the donors, whose will had to be taken into account when disposing of the property they had given.[67] Others argued that the individual establishments were the proper owners, not the order of the Clergy or the Church as an institution.[68] They argued that any expropriation would have to be done according to canon or civil law, not according to a vote by the National Assembly.[69] Finally, a few deputies argued that the property did not belong to the nation or the Church at all, but to God Himself.[70]

---

[63] AP 9: 486–87.

[64] In his 30 October attack on Thouret's speech, Maury claimed Thouret left unclear who owned the properties used by the Church. Thouret responded that Maury's speech was "anti-patriotic" and clarified that he thought all Church goods belonged to the nation. AP 9: 610.

[65] Lameth, *Histoire*, 1: 163. *Le Point du jour*, 3: 435–36. Such a claim was not new: Jean Bodin had argued at the Estates General of 1576 that the king had only usufruct of his demesne and that the ultimate owners were the people. Ulph, "Jean Bodin and the Estates-General of 1576," 293.

[66] For example, Bonnai, the bishop of Clermont, AP 9: 484; Béthisy, the bishop of Uzès, AP 9: 490; Boisgelin, bishop of Aix, AP 9: 618.

[67] See Boisgelin, AP 9: 617.   [68] For example, Montlosier, AP 9: 415; *Le Point du jour*, 3: 316.

[69] For example, Boisgelin, AP 9: 625.

[70] For example, Beaumetz, AP 9: 629; *Journal de Paris* 3 November 1789.

Nonetheless, everyone who spoke in favor of the Church retaining ownership or custody of ecclesiastical properties acknowledged that the Clergy would make great sacrifices to save the nation from its financial woes.[71] Defenders of the Church focused on the principle that this was to be a voluntary gift, as had, they claimed, been established in 1560. Many defenders of the Church accepted that the nation had a right to make sure that the Church performed its duties well. Nevertheless, they proposed making a full survey of the Church's revenue, property, and liabilities prior to asking for access to Church wealth.[72] Even some who supported the idea that the nation could take the Church's property asked that the matter be discussed only after the true extent of the Church's ability to give was known.[73] In the end, those who defended the Church's property rights made the same kinds of proposals that deputies who sought to take or use the Church's wealth did. They too stated that simple benefices must be suppressed, that surplus religious houses and chapters should be closed, and that the curés be guaranteed a higher basic income.[74]

Many deputies spoke in favor of the Church's right to hold property, but three in particular had great impact.[75] The Parisian Third Estate deputy Camus, a specialist in church law, had led the charge to defend the Church on 13 October. His speech contained most of the elements other deputies highlighted in defense of the Church throughout the debate. Camus noted that given 1,300 years of possession, a "multitude" of laws, and "infinite" acts complicated any discussion of who owned what ecclesiastical property. Part of the problem, he said, was one of definition. Individual clergy were unable to own property, it was true. But if one accepted that the order of the Clergy was made up of a variety of corporations, from archbishoprics to monasteries, it became clear that these specific establishments owned particular properties. It was out of these smaller corporations that the Church was made. It was only in that sense, as an aggregate of property holders, that the Clergy or the Church could be said to own anything. Camus thought Mirabeau's motion had to be rejected or set aside. He urged the reform of the Church, not its destruction. They had, he pointed out, created a committee to discuss reforming

---

[71] For example, Béthisy, the bishop of Uzès. AP 9: 490.

[72] For example, abbé Montesquiou in *Journal de Paris* 13 October 1789; Camus in *Le Point du jour*, 3: 316–17.

[73] Lameth thought this was a general strategy for defenders of the Clergy. Lameth, *Histoire*, 1: 164–65. See, for example, Bureaux de Pusy, AP 9: 495; *Le Point du jour*, 3: 432.

[74] See Pellerin, AP 9: 518; Maupetit, "Lettres," 367.

[75] Maury made strong speeches, but he was dismissed as a beautiful speaker with corrupt character. Maupetit, "Lettres," 367.

the Church. They should wait until it had made its report before discussing how to dispose of the Church's excess wealth.[76] Camus's speech was well received on the right in the Assembly and it strongly influenced the arguments made by those who followed. One deputy went so far as to opine that Camus's election as president of the Assembly on 28 October had been possible because the Clergy supported his position on Church property.[77]

However, the two most influential speeches in favor of the Church's right to hold property came almost the end of the debate, on 31 October. In the first, Boisgelin, archbishop of Aix, rehearsed many of the basic points made by defenders of the Church earlier in the debate. To some, it appeared as a kind of grab bag of points that attacked the reasoning of deputies who wished to nationalize the Church's property. It took more than an hour to deliver and one witness remarked that Boisgelin had used out-of-date tone and delivery. Nonetheless, his speech had a strong impact on wavering deputies. Duquesnoy remarked that Mirabeau himself had taken part in the thunderous applause that greeted the end of the speech, saying *sotto voce* that "one applauds talent without adopting his opinions."[78]

Boisgelin attacked claims that the state could take Church property from a variety of directions. He addressed issues of natural rights, pointing out that those who had given property to the Church had property rights even if the Church did not, and that they had given property "when it had not been forbidden by law." Thus, he argued, the way in which the Church owned property was in its essence the same as the way its donors had held it. As he put it, "One cannot infringe on the law that upholds the gift without infringing on the law that upholds the ability to give." Taking Church property would require violating all kinds of contracts, made with "all kinds of citizens," contracts hallowed in law and in custom over long periods of time. After all, some of the dioceses and the lands given to the Church dated from the time of the Romans, long before the French monarchy. He also used more modern rights-based arguments, noting that consent was at the very basis of the Assembly's view of taxation. No one could be taxed without consent. But the Assembly was looking to tax the Church without its consent, he said, and was thinking of taking the

---

[76] AP 9: 415, 417.
[77] Duquesnoy, *Journal* 2: 14. Lameth felt it was because Camus had been a lawyer for the Church. Lameth, *Histoire,* 1: 173.
[78] *Journal de Paris,* 1 November 1789; Duquesnoy, *Journal,* 2: 9. See also Delandine, *Mémorial historique,* 6: 256. *Le Point du jour,* 4: 21.

property of the Church without its consent as well. Finally, he noted, some land had come into the hands of the Church through the labor of the clergy. Much Church property had been improved at the hands of clerics themselves. Boisgelin doubted that Assembly could deny the clergy the fruits of their own labor. He threw in other defenses, claiming that the benefice holders held mandates from their donors to do certain work, and that the *cahiers* of the deputies did not support taking Church property. Did the deputies, he asked, have the power to override the will of their constituents as expressed in the *cahiers*? He even referred to the Declaration of the Rights of Man and Citizen, claiming that its protections of property applied to Church lands as well. After all, he said, it was not as if the clergy were asking for special rights. They were simply asking to be treated as all other citizens were.[79]

Perhaps his most telling attack was on the notion that taking Church land was necessary to free up credit markets. He pointed out that the good credit of the state could hardly be founded on the unjust seizure of property. Such an action would undermine investors' confidence in the willingness of the state to fulfill its commitments. He pointed out that the credit of the nation was not based on material wealth alone, but on "justice and laws." If one did not have faith in those laws, no amount of goods would free up credit. One would have to revert to higher taxes in order to pay the state's bills and debts. Rather than seizing Church land, he said, the deputies ought to reform the financial system, impose taxes equally, and rely on a free gift given by the Clergy "by an operation without risk or danger, founded on a credit without limits," that of the good name of the Church. Of course, he admitted, the public had the right to ask the Clergy for sacrifices in a time of great need. He agreed that it was up to the National Assembly to determine what it was possible for the Church to give, agreeing that the nation would have oversight over Church finances. There would have to be a detailed accounting of Church property and liabilities. There would have to be reforms within the Church, with useless offices and establishments suppressed. But this all would be done with the consent of the Church and through regular civil and canon procedures, not as of right by the nation.[80]

By all accounts the most remarkable speech of the debate was given by the abbé Montesquiou, who had, according to one witness, erupted from obscurity with his brilliant performance, having previously failed to do so

[79] AP 9: 615–18; *Journal de Paris*, 1 November 1789.   [80] AP 9: 620, 622–25; *Le Point du jour*, 4: 21.

much as publish a pamphlet.[81] Witnesses were united in praising his delivery and persuasive reasoning. Duquesnoy listed him among the best speakers the Church had put forward in the debate. Delandine noted that Montesquiou spoke with "erudition allied to a great spirit."[82] Barère claimed that the abbé had spoken with great talent, refuting the main lines of argument deployed by those who would take the Church's property.[83] Montesquiou was the final speaker for the day on the subject, and he made the most of his opportunity.

Montesquiou rehearsed some of the same points heard before from defenders of the Church. He defended the right of the Church to own property, claiming that it had behaved for a long time like other property owners, paying taxes, buying and selling properties, and so on. One of his most telling blows was aimed at Thouret. He noted that Thouret had made the strongest argument in favor of taking the Church's property. If corporations only existed through the law, then indeed the nation could create them or destroy them. However, he wondered if the order of the Clergy had been created by law or had developed out of the "guaranteed facilities" of the law. Then he asked with great flourish, "I would like it if someone could cite one law which had established the grand ecclesiastical corporations." If there was no law by which they had been created, then Thouret's claims had no basis.

Montesquiou also attacked the idea that the clergy could be put on the state's payroll just like soldiers and administrators. He powerfully argued that the clergy were not men employed by the state to fulfill a specific function at a specific time. Clergy were "inseparably tied" to their role in society. They were bound forever to their role, he said. Finally, he approached claims that the Clergy should be taxed at a higher rate or that their property should be taken. When the state had previously taken property from the Church, it had always been with the Church's consent. It was by the Clergy that the "alienation" was made. This showed, Montesquiou claimed, that the nation had never had the right to take Church property. Moreover, it was up to the Church to suppress useless establishments or offices. The nation could point out the problems, but it was up to the Church to solve them. After all, the Assembly had recognized that there could be no taxation without consent. When he was done, his speech was thunderously applauded. One witness claimed it had been

---

[81] *Journal de Paris,* 1 November 1789.
[82] Duquesnoy, *Journal,* 2: 9; Delandine, *Mémorial historique,* 6: 256.   [83] *Le Point du jour,* 4: 13.

a success not just with defenders of the Church but with the whole Assembly.[84]

Montesquiou's speech was followed by several calls for a vote and a clear sense in the room that momentum in the debate had shifted away from the supporters of Mirabeau's motion.[85] Mirabeau, always an able politician, had sensed the shift. The Assembly had decided earlier in the day that a vote would be taken that afternoon. Rather than move to a vote on his motion, Mirabeau proposed delaying the matter until the next day. Mirabeau said that he wished for more deputies to be heard, that he wished to respond to abbé Montesquiou's speech, and that he worried about the logistics of taking a vote late in the session. But Mirabeau was more worried, as the well-informed Gouverneur Morris wrote in his diary, that his motion would fail if it came to a vote.[86] The Assembly adjourned the matter until the following Monday, 2 November.

When the debate resumed that day deputies from the so-called "Belgian Territories" spoke at length, as did other deputies in defense of or against Mirabeau's motion.[87] Major interventions were made by Beaumetz and Le Chapelier, the first seeking compromise and the second a decisive victory. Beaumetz sought a compromise by claiming that the lands belonged neither to the nation nor to the Church, but to God. Le Chapelier brushed this new argument aside, announcing that the deputies faced a critical moment. He claimed that all of the arguments made from history made it seem as if the nation could never change its laws or attempt to reform "vicious" institutions. When the country had been divided into orders, each of which had its own "dreadful veto," he said, of course it would have been foolish to declare the lands of the Church at the disposal of the nation. Such a move would have been at the mercy of the "uncertain" will of the king, and most of the proceeds would have ended up lining the pockets of courtiers. "But a new order of things has been established," he continued, "national assemblies are permanent and taxes can only be created by the representatives of the people; place in your constitution therefore this salutary principle: no corporation, no establishment may henceforth possess territorial goods; it is to the nation to dispose of them; it is up to her to support the corporations, the establishments of which she has need."[88]

---

[84] AP 9: 628; *Journal de Paris*, 2 November 1789.   [85] Duquesnoy, *Journal*, 2: 10.

[86] *Le Moniteur*, 2: 114, 118; Morris, *Diary*, 281. Morris had heard this from an aristocratic acquaintance.

[87] The Belgian Territories were lands in the north of France where the local Catholic church had never become part of the French Catholic hierarchy.

[88] *Le Point du jour*, 4: 29.

In a particular flourish, Le Chapelier noted that if the Clergy could make sacrifices, they still formed a political order in society and this threatened the ruin of the new constitution.[89] What the Clergy really wanted, Le Chapelier seemed to claim, was to resurrect the society of orders.[90] If the Clergy were given a veto over matters relating to the Church, the National Assembly would, in essence, accept what the king had attempted to dictate on 23 June. Immediately following his speech there were many calls for a vote and many calls to amend the motion. The deputies of the right thought they had a chance at victory and Cazalès asked that Mirabeau's motion be voted on without any additions or amendments. But the Assembly decided to hear amendments, including the center-right deputy Malouet's long amendment that amounted to a substitute motion. In it, he argued that the Assembly lacked the mandate to take the Church's lands, but he argued in favor of the idea that the nation had the right to oversee the use of Church lands and stated that the nation had the right to "dispose" of any surplus "for the pressing needs of the State." He also asked that the provincial assemblies be in charge of handling the affairs of any suppressed establishments. After he finished speaking, a large number of deputies demanded cloture.[91]

Mirabeau rose and claimed the priority of his motion and asked for a vote. As he read his motion out to the Assembly, though, he made modifications on the fly. Deputies interrupted to ask for the vote to be held by *appel nominal*, for the question to be divided, and for the motion to be tabled. Finally, after some two hours of delay and diversion, Mirabeau reworked his motion to include some of the principle ideas from various proposed amendments. The new version put the Church's property at the "disposal" of the nation, subject to the necessity of supporting the Church's ordinary functions. Curés were to be given 1,200 *livres* a year, with housing and a garden. Moreover, the decree put supervision of the disposal of Church properties in the hands of the provinces, not the National Assembly. The provinces would "oversee" and provide instructions for the use of Church property.[92] Mirabeau had changed his wording from a blunt assertion that the nation was the true owner of Church lands to Thouret's more equivocal phrase, that the properties were at the disposal of the nation. As the historian of the French church John McManners

---

[89] Ibid., 4: 31; Visme, "Journal," 223v.

[90] Dean, *L'Assemblée constituante et la réforme ecclésiastique*, 129.

[91] *Le Point du jour*, 4: 31; AP 9: 645, 648–49.

[92] AP 9: 649; *Journal de Paris*, 3 November 1789. The discussion was "long and tumultuous." Visme, "Journal," 224r; Brulart de Sillery, "Journal," AN KK 645: 361.

wrote, "'at the disposal of' does not necessarily mean 'belongs to,' and there was still a possibility that churchmen might retain ultimate ownership of their lands."[93]

Duquesnoy saw this move to Thouret's phrasing as a work of political genius. When Mirabeau had seen that he could not win a vote declaring the property belonged to the nation, he changed the wording to attract as many votes as possible. Many had rallied to the new version, Duquesnoy claimed, either from "fear that the question would not have passed otherwise," "or from the "fear of an uprising in the provinces" if the original wording had been used.[94] Some conservative deputies, even those who opposed the measure, thought at the time that some good would come of it. Ferrières wrote soon after the debate that if the decree were "well managed and applied with prudence" it could "result in a great help for the people." He thought that the final wording had been the result of resistance from provincial deputies, who would not "leave to be usurped by strangers that which makes up the resources of the villages and country-side." Far from being outraged by the treatment of the Church, he felt that the order of the Clergy was getting just what it deserved.[95] Ferrières later wrote that Mirabeau had only assured the passage of the motion by seizing on Thouret's delicate phrases. With the new wording Mirabeau had gained support from deputies "who were repelled by the open expropriation of the Clergy, not foreseeing or feigning not to foresee the consequences" of the decree.[96] Even Morris understood that the change in phrasing "[seemed] to have been adopted as conciliatory."[97] We should remember, too, that the center-right deputy Malouet had proposed on 2 November putting the Church's goods at the disposal of the nation, under the supervision of the provincial assemblies. Some deputies thought the compromise outcome meant that not all Church properties would be sold and the support of the local church would be left to the parishes.[98] Maupetit even reported to his constituents that their local church-run secondary school was safe, since the province would become responsible for its affairs.[99]

Nevertheless, the vote itself was unusually close for such a major structural issue. The votes over the naming of the National Assembly, over the

[93] McManners, *The French Revolution*, 27.

[94] Duquesnoy, *Journal*, 2: 14. Duquesnoy's copyist, Bernard, wrote to the prince of Salm-Salm that Mirabeau had taken up the wording on an amendment by Thouret himself. Duquesnoy, *Journal*, 2: 11.

[95] Ferrières, *Correspondance*, 187–88. For his later view that the whole thing had been a plot between Revolutionaries and capitalists, Ferrières, *Mémoires*, 1: 187.

[96] Ferrières, *Mémoires*, 1: 187. See also Duquesnoy, *Journal*, 2: 14.   [97] Morris, *Diary*, 281.

[98] Tackett, *Becoming a Revolutionary*, 204.   [99] Maupetit, "Lettres," 371.

binding mandate, over the royal veto: all had carried by overwhelming majorities, typically with 700 or more deputies voting in favor.[100] On 2 November, only the center-left and left of the Assembly supported the decree, with few defectors from the center-right. With 568 votes in favor, the Third Estate had peeled few votes from the other orders. One witness claimed only twenty curés had supported the motion, which is surprising on its face given that most curés would receive a raise in the new system. The curés seem to have rallied around the corporation of the Church and its ability to regulate its own financial affairs. (During the debate, a curé had asked if the Third Estate had invited clergy to join them in June of 1789 "only to make it easier to slit their throats.") Very few Nobles voted in favor. Forty deputies had voted in a way that rendered their opinions invalid and a fair number of deputies simply left the room before the vote was taken.[101] Out of the thousand or so deputies available to vote at the end of October, only 568 voted in favor. This is a tremendous drop in support of a reform pitched by the center-left and revealed a limit to what moderate deputies would accept. According to Tackett, the reduced majority caused real concern on the left in the Assembly while giving hope to the right.[102] A diminished majority meant that there would be challenges ahead as the Assembly continued its efforts to reform society, guided by the *cahiers* and the wishes of their constituents.

---

[100] The vote in favor of the National Assembly had been 490–91, an even larger majority.

[101] On the small number of Clergy supporting the decree, Duquesnoy, *Journal*, 2: 11 (Letter from Bernard, his copyist, to the prince of Salm-Salm); Ferrières, *Mémoires*, 1: 184.

[102] Tackett, *Becoming a Revolutionary*, 206–07.

Conclusion

The decree putting the goods of the Church at the disposal of the nation was a major act with far-reaching implications. As Barère announced in his newspaper, *Le Point du jour*, on 2 November the Assembly had definitively established itself as a tribunal before which all the institutions of society would be judged.[1] It had become a truly constituent body, one that could rid France of useless or pernicious institutions and establish those necessary for the public good. The political struggles of summer 1789 had determined who would lead the effort to reform France. The first phase had been a struggle between the Third Estate and conservatives in the Noble and Clerical orders over who would lead the Estates General. The second phase was the struggle between the king and the National Assembly to see who would establish the new constitutional order. Louis XVI had failed to see through essential reforms under his leadership. He had clumsily tried to block the National Assembly's efforts to build itself into a partner in reform, overtly through the dismissal of Necker in mid-July and covertly through his delays in accepting the August decrees, the Declaration of the Rights of Man and Citizen, and the other constitutional acts. The October Days had revealed the king's weakness for all to see. Only then did Louis yield the mantle of reform to his citizens as represented by their elected deputies (though, as it turned out, he did so in bad faith). It was the National Constituent Assembly's turn to enact the reforms necessary to save the nation.

Many historians have written about the long summer of 1789 and the rise of the National Assembly as a political force. We have innovated here in two major ways. First, we have examined the vital debates of 1789 in a new way. Where previous historians have relied on the imperfect record found in the *Archives Parlementaires*, supplemented by deputy memoirs written long after the events they describe, we have expanded the resource

[1] *Le Point du jour*, 4: 25.

base significantly. We have relied on multiple contemporary accounts of events and debates, showing that the accounts found in the *Archives Parlementaires* are insufficient to understand the development of the National Assembly as a political force. Second, relying on this expanded resource base, we have shown that the creation of the National Assembly as an independent legislative and constituent body happened in stages as the Patriot deputies faced resistance first from the privileged orders and then from the king himself. We have shown that more moderate deputies, men like Mounier, Malouet, Clermont-Tonnerre, Lally-Tollendal, and especially Thouret had much more impact on the decisions made during the early Revolution than older narratives of 1789 would have us believe. Working with the center-left, moderates were able to pass constitutional acts with strong majorities throughout the summer. As we saw in Chapter 6, the ability of the center to put together such majorities ran into difficulty following the October Days, when the Assembly moved to place the property of the Catholic Church at the disposal of the nation.

The deputies passed through several stages in their thinking about the extent of their powers and their relationship to the king and to the nation between May and November of 1789. The deputies worked hard, as deputies to the Estates General always had, to faithfully express the will of their constituents and to solve the problems that had led the king to call them. In response to the king's reluctance to embrace reform and to the spread and intensification of popular unrest in Paris and in the rest of France, the deputies slowly expanded the comprehensiveness of the reforms they proposed. They undoubtedly wished to include the king in the political process: after all, they wrote a monarchical constitution. However, faced with the king's hesitations and with the memory of the mid-July crisis clear in their minds, the deputies decided upon a limited monarchy, one in which the king would control the executive branch and have a strong veto power, but in which the constitution recognized the essential sovereignty of the nation. The king was reframed as a representative of the nation, no longer a God-given ruler. This new role for the king and the limitations on his power marked a profound change from the absolute monarchy and a major victory for the reformers.

In the first Chapter, we revised traditional narratives of the origins of the Revolution, showing how the Estates General was transformed from its traditional consultative form into a new legislative body in the public imagination. We discussed the three pretenders to status as political representatives in Old Regime France: the king, the Estates General, and the parlements. We saw how a long-defunct body, the Estates General, came to be envisioned as a representative body that would meet regularly, approve all taxes, and have a limited legislative role. In this, it came to embody all of the representative and legislative claims the parlements had made during the eighteenth century as well as the traditional claims to representative status held by the old Estates General itself. Out of the struggle between traditional political elites had come a new conception of political representation as the Estates General came to be seen as a body unlike the then-current provincial assemblies, the parlements, or the Estates General as it had met before. This change was not caused by the plans or intentions of any specific group, instead arising out of competition between the parlements and the king's ministers to see who could best make use of an emergent political force in the latter half of the eighteenth century, public opinion.

Public opinion had only become the main source for political legitimacy in France when the Crown sought support for a major package of financial reforms needed to save the state from bankruptcy. Though the sovereign courts claimed that they were legitimate representatives of the French because they best understood public opinion, it was only after the failure of the Assembly of Notables in 1787 that the Crown decided to fight the parlements on their own ground and rally public opinion behind the king's plans. As Collins writes, after Brienne's speech dismissing the Assembly of Notables, there was effectively an interregnum as Louis XVI had ceded leadership of France to public opinion.[2] The king's ministers and the parlements then fought a bitter pamphlet war, each side trying to discredit the other and rally public support for themselves. This did nothing but discredit both sides. The Crown's attempts to force through changes merely rallied public support behind the parlements. Finally, in an attempt to regain some control over the swirl of events, the Crown turned to a long-defunct body that could best be said to represent the will of the various orders and corporations of the nation, the Estates General. The contest then switched from a battle over who best understood public opinion to one over how the Estates General would be constituted. The decision of the Parlement of Paris to call for the forms of 1614 and the decision of the second Assembly of Notables to refuse a doubling of the Third Estate were political maneuvers in a contest to see who would have the most influence at the Estates General.

We saw in our analysis of the *cahiers de doléances* of 1789 the outlines of a future elected body that would adequately represent the various peoples

---

[2] Collins, *State in Early Modern France*, 2nd ed., 347.

and regions of France. Local electoral districts overwhelmingly demanded that the Estates General become a regularly called and consulted body. Freely elected deputies were to bring to the king the best possible information and to participate in the creation of legislation to solve the kingdom's problems. The long-term struggle between the Crown and the parlements and the short-term struggle between the privileged orders and the Third Estate in late 1788 and early 1789 had led to a new vision of the traditional body. The Estates General had inherited the pretensions to legislative power developed by the parlements in their struggles with the Crown in the eighteenth century.

In Chapter 2, we showed how events outside the Estates General itself had an impact on how the deputies behaved, and that the king's weak leadership helped push the Third Estate to declare itself the National Assembly. We learned that the deputies who came to Versailles in late April and early May 1789 to participate in the first Estates General held in over 170 years traveled through a disturbed landscape. The Crown's earlier attempts to force through its package of reform had led to open rebellion in major cities. Economic distress caused by a poor harvest, terrible weather, and an industrial recession had led to subsistence rioting. Regardless of their order or station in life, the deputies understood that the Estates General needed to work with the king to rescue France from a growing social, economic, and political crisis. Unfortunately, the deputies arrived in Versailles with instructions to demand meeting and voting in two very different ways. The Third Estate and its allies in the privileged orders came bearing instructions to organize the Estates General into a common body where all votes were taken by head. The majority of the Nobles and many of the Clergy arrived with orders to meet and vote only by order, maintaining a veto over any acts that would endanger their traditional rights and privileges. There was no obvious way to reconcile these two incompatible plans.

Louis XVI did little to broker a solution. A lack of leadership from the king allowed a stalemate to develop over how deputies would verify their credentials, by order or in common. From their first meeting on 6 May, the deputies of the Third Estate refused to declare themselves an active body unless the deputies verified their credentials in common. Their inaction made it impossible for the Estates General to do business. Over six weeks, this stalemate radicalized both the Third Estate and their opponents in the privileged orders. This period was key in the development of how the deputies understood the role of the Estates General, as they reconsidered its role and rights in what Tackett calls "the school of the Revolution."[3] Not until early June, almost a month after the first meeting of the Estates General, did Necker provide a blueprint for how to resolve the stalemate. By then it was too late to easily reconcile the Third Estate and the privileged orders. The Nobles voted to reject Necker's plan, saving the Third Estate the trouble. Neither side would yield.

After weeks of fruitless negotiations, the Third Estate decided on 10 June to act, alone if necessary, to make the Estates General a body in which the orders met in common and voted by head. In mid June, the Third Estate organized a roll call for all deputies, regardless of order, in the common meeting hall. No Nobles and only nineteen Clerics answered the call. On 15 and 16 June, the deputies of the Third Estate and their Clerical allies struggled to find an appropriate name for the active body of the Estates General, with many long and confusing titles proposed. Following an exhausting debate, the deputies agreed to call themselves the "National Assembly." They claimed for themselves the role of the active body of the Estates General. They declared that the orders of the Nobles and Clergy no longer had independent political standing. We innovated in showing how the declaration of the National Assembly was a compromise between different groups in the Third Estate, not the sole victory of the radical Breton deputies. This compromise was a tremendous step, but as we have seen, their actions did not go beyond the instructions the Third Estate deputies had been given by their constituents. They did not act to exclude the privileged orders or end the system by which deputies were identified with the order they represented. Most importantly, the deputies who declared the National Assembly on 17 June thought they had the support of the king and envisioned working with him as a partner to solve the nation's problems.

Chapter 3 showed how the Assembly's declaration of 17 June pushed the Revolution into a new phase, a struggle between the king and the National Assembly to see who would control the direction of reform. When the king and his ministers heard about the declaration of the National Assembly, they decided to suspend the meetings of the Estates General until after the king could make his will known. Briefly suspending meetings so the king could give guidance might have been a good idea much earlier, perhaps in mid-May as soon as the stalemate set in. By mid-June, after a prolonged struggle between the reformers and their opponents, the idea that the king could give orders to the National Assembly was a non-starter. When

---

[3] Tackett, *Becoming a Revolutionary*, 146.

deputies of the Third Estate found themselves locked out of their accustomed hall on 20 June, they moved to a nearby tennis court and swore an oath never to part until they had written a constitution. In a momentous step, spurred on by an admiring crowd and certain that the king had been misled, the National Assembly declared its independence as a political body within the French monarchy. Use of a broader resource base allowed us to show how important moderate voices were in the debates over the Tennis Court Oath. Despite its revolutionary character, the oath was not a victory for the radical deputies. Motions to move the Assembly to Paris or to denounce the king's advisors failed and center-right deputies like Mounier and his allies successfully urged the deputies to put their faith in the king.

We have also departed from earlier narratives of June 1789 by showing just how influential the king's actions were in pushing the National Assembly to claim its independence. On 20 June, the king's family and conservative figures at Court personally appealed to Louis, asking that he block the actions of the Third Estate. Necker had hoped that the Royal Council would approve a reforming line at the Royal Session and that the king would rally behind it. Between 20 and 23 June the conservative members of the Royal Council, reinforced by the king's brothers and the queen, won out. The platform the king put forth at his Royal Session on 23 June reflected their victory. Louis voided the declaration of a National Assembly and quashed its actions. He offered many important reforms, but he did not recognize the Estates General as a real legislative body, a true partner in governing. In response, the deputies of the Third Estate stayed in the Assembly hall after he dismissed them. They voted to persist in their actions of 17 and 20 June and refused the king the right to suspend or dismiss them. They interpreted the Royal Session as an outrageous attempt to impose the king's will on a co-equal body. They declared that the whole affair had been like a *lit de justice*, the traditional meeting at which the king forced his parlements to obey his orders. But, as Bailly wrote in his memoirs, with the summoning of the Estates General, the time of *lits de justice* was over.[4]

Louis had instructed the Estates General to meet separately by order the next day, 24 June, without the public present in the meeting halls. He deployed soldiers to police the meeting halls and enforce his will. Rather than enforce the royal will, the soldiers had shown sympathetic Clerical deputies how to join with the Third Estate in the main meeting hall,

---

[4] Bailly, *Mémoires d'un témoin*, 1: 183.

despite the king's clear command that they not do so. On 25 June, forty-seven Noble deputies arrived. A clear majority of the deputies had decided to meet in common. With disorder increasing in Paris and Versailles, the king had had few choices. On 27 June he asked the remaining deputies of the Nobles and Clergy to go sit with the rest of their fellows in the main hall. The deputies of the National Assembly were euphoric. It appeared that the king had endorsed their plan for how the body would meet, and they praised him for the sacrifices he had made. Whatever doubts the deputies had about the king seemed to vanish. The deputies of the National Assembly were eager to work with the king and their newly arrived colleagues to save France.

The arrival of the recalcitrant deputies in the main hall led to a new problem. More than a hundred deputies filed protests on 30 June against meeting as a National Assembly. They declared that their mandates forbade them to meet or vote in common. In Chapter 4, we reconstructed the resulting debate over deputy mandates in unprecedented detail, allowing us to show that, contrary to the accepted narrative, the deputies did not vote to void their mandates or sever their ties to their constituents. We saw that while the majority of the deputies recognized that the mandates conservative deputies had received were valid, they refused to accept that these mandates had any binding effect on the Assembly as a whole. Following Sieyès's motion on 8 July, the deputies decided by an overwhelming majority that no absent deputy or group of deputies could halt the working of the National Assembly, even as they decided that the Assembly had no power to void individual mandates. For months to come, deputies from the center-left to the far right would use their *cahiers* as justification for the proposals they made.[5] The National Assembly would remain in session, with the deputies guided by the will of their constituents as expressed in the *cahiers* they carried with them. In effect, the three orders sitting in common had voted to endorse the original declaration of the National Assembly. It was a tremendous victory for the Third Estate and its allies.

We also showed how the victory of the Third Estate and its privileged allies over their conservative opponents did not convince the king to accept the National Assembly and work with it to solve France's problems. From late June, Louis XVI had laid the groundwork to replace Necker and his

[5] See, for example, the debate on deputy mandates of 19 April 1790. R. H. Blackman, "A Mandate for Counter-revolution: Conservative Opposition in the National Constituent Assembly," *Proceedings of the Western Society for French History* (2012), 58–72; idem, "Did Cicero Swear the Tennis Court Oath?"

allies on the Royal Council with conservative ministers. From 22 June forward, Louis had issued orders to bring more soldiers to the vicinity of Paris. Louis hoped, in all probability, to impose his declaration of 23 June on a defiant National Assembly. On 8 July, the deputies asked Louis what his intentions were. Louis blithely responded that it was his responsibility to maintain public order. When news of Necker's dismissal reached Paris on 12 July, massive demonstrations broke out in his support. An attempt to impose order by force failed that same day, and the city slipped out of royal control. The electors of Paris quickly created a new city government. On 14 July, a crowd supported by mutinous soldiers took the Bastille, a medieval fortress that stood as a symbol of the king's authority in Paris. Paris had become a city in open revolt against the king's authority. The troops Louis had gathered to protect him and enforce his will proved completely unreliable. Almost by accident, the National Assembly had been saved.

The deputies had not been idle as the crisis mounted. On 13 July, facing the possibility of their arrest or worse, the deputies voted to persist in their decrees of 17, 20, and 23 June declaring the National Assembly a co-equal body with the king. Noble and Clerical deputies who had not been present on those days voted to support the decrees. Louis's attempt to restore his authority had inadvertently pushed Nobles and Clergy who previously refused to support the National Assembly into its arms. The collapse of the royal government in Paris and the spread of popular unrest pushed Louis to make a decision. Would he flee Versailles and attempt to restore his authority from somewhere else? Would he work with the National Assembly to restore order, despite his misgivings? Once he had been assured that the army could not protect his family on the road if he fled, Louis recalled Necker. Forced by circumstance, Louis recognized the National Assembly.

In Chapter 5, our use of a broader variety of sources allowed us to demonstrate that, in the aftermath of the mid-July crisis, the Assembly created a much more defensive constitution than they had envisioned in late June. The king's actions had led the deputies to consider the possibility that he was not a good-faith partner in reform. Facing threats to their life and liberty, they began discussing openly how the new constitutional system would prevent popular disorder that threatened anarchy and stop future kings from acting in bad faith to undermine or eliminate public liberty. Swamped with reports of increasing unrest in the countryside and in many cities, including Paris, the deputies did what they could to reassure the people of France that reform was coming and that the kingdom's problems would be solved. The August decrees and the Declaration of the Rights of Man and Citizen promised an end to the privileged social system of the old order. They were meant to reassure the people that their wishes, as expressed in the *cahiers*, would be acted on and that that unjust or pernicious institutions would be ended.

In late August and throughout September, the deputies worked to establish the new constitutional order. They had to clearly lay out the boundaries between the legislative and executive powers. We added a new dimension to discussion of the constitutional debates by showing how central the issue of public order was to deputy arguments about what kind of veto power the king should have. The *cahiers* had envisioned that the Estates General would work with the king to craft the law, either endorsing what the king proposed or asking the king's approval for what it had decreed. The king's behavior in the mid-July crisis had pushed deputies to reconsider their relationship to the executive power. There was a clear majority that favored a veto of some kind and rooted that veto in the king's power as a chosen representative of the nation. A center-right group of deputies, the Monarchiens, sought solve the problems of public disorder and government collapse by creating a strong executive limited by a written constitution and checked by a powerful two-house legislative body. To strengthen the king's hand, they wished to give him a veto that could not be overridden. Deputies on the far right supported them even though they disagreed with Monarchien claims that the nation was sovereign and had the right to rise up should the king attempt to thwart its will. Opposing the absolute veto were two groups: first, those who wanted the veto subject to override, whether by a national referendum or by the legislature itself; second, a much smaller group who argued that a true separation of powers required that the king have no veto at all.

Deputies of the center quickly rallied around a suspensive veto that could be lifted by the legislature itself. On 5 September, Thouret proposed a veto that could be lifted by the legislature after two regularly scheduled elections, and on 7 September, Necker gained the king's approval for a similar veto. On 11 September, Necker sent a letter to the Assembly stating that the king favored a suspensive veto. The appearance of the letter triggered a debate over whether or not the king could take the initiative in writing the constitution, something Mounier and his allies strongly disputed. In the end, the letter was not read, on the basis that it was the Assembly's task to write the constitution without the king's input. In the middle of a debate over the royal veto, the deputies declared that they alone had the right to craft the constitution. Nevertheless, it was clear enough to the deputies what the king wanted. The Assembly voted overwhelmingly for a suspensive veto, a victory for moderate Patriot deputies who wished for a powerful executive and also wanted guarantees that executive power could not be abused.

In Chapter 6 we followed three major developments that signaled the Assembly's transition from a body that held a theoretical role in governing into one that enjoyed and acted on its powers. We continued our novel discussion of how important matters of public order were to the deputies as we showed them struggling with how to persuade Louis to accept constitutional acts without revision. The key issue was the king's reluctance to accept the August decrees, the Declaration of the Rights of Man and Citizen, and other constitutional acts that the deputies crafted during September. To maintain public order, or at least keep it from worsening, the deputies had to prevent the appearance of serious disagreement between the king and the Assembly. A clever attempt by Barnave to delay discussion of the king's veto power until he had accepted the August decrees allowed the deputies to consider how dangerous it would be to clearly state that the Assembly had the power to write the constitution without the king's assistance. Only when Louis agreed to accept the constitutional acts, assured that the deputies would take his comments into account when writing future legislation, did the deputies grant the king a strong suspensive veto, ensuring that the king would remain an active part of the legislative process. In giving the king a strong veto, the deputies clearly indicated that they wanted a monarchical constitution with a powerful executive and that they intended to work with Louis to maintain public order.

The deputies' careful attempts to create mechanisms for peaceful resolution of differences between the Assembly and the king never had time to bear fruit. The king continued to delay real acceptance of the August decrees and the other constitutional acts. As September turned to October, the deputies of the left and center-left were losing patience with him. Unrelated problems of provisioning Paris dovetailed with political problems in Versailles to cause the October Days, the march of tens of thousands of women and men from Paris to Versailles. They demanded an adequate food supply for Paris, punishment for soldiers who had failed to show adequate respect for the nation and the Revolution, and the return of the king and his family to Paris. This eruption of popular unrest and the intervention of market women into national politics led the Assembly to declare itself inseparable from the king, and the public power in France to be the unity of the king and the Assembly. The king accepted the constitutional acts on 5 October. From 6 October forward, when the deputies took the king under their protection with this decree, the Assembly undeniably held the initiative in crafting the constitution as well as normal legislation.

We are now back to where we began this conclusion, the Assembly's decision on 2 November to place to goods of the Church at the disposal of the nation. Whereas on 6 October the deputies had declared themselves, with the king, to be the unit of public power, on 2 November they made it clear that the Assembly would act as it saw fit, guided by public opinion and the content of the *cahiers* they carried, to reform France as necessary to solve the immense problems it faced. As we have mentioned, Collins argues that an interregnum began in 1787 with the Crown's recognition of public opinion as the body that could legitimate government action. He claims that the interregnum ended with the declaration of the National Assembly on 17 June 1789.[6] We have shown instead that the interregnum ended on 2 November, with the vote to place the Church's property at the disposal of the nation. This is when the Assembly definitively moved from a body that aspired to write a constitution to one that had established the foundation for one; from a body that claimed certain powers to one that used them.

The creation of a sovereign National Constituent Assembly was the outcome of a long process, and it was the beginning of a new phase in the Revolution. The deputies had created a functioning legislature under very trying conditions, as the remnants of the absolutist state collapsed around them. They had made a credible start in establishing a constitutional monarchy around which the people of France could rally. From 1789–91 they reformed the state at every level, establishing everything from a new court system to a new division of France into electoral districts. They enjoyed broad public support for their many reforms. What caused their project to fail? The constitutional monarchy would only last until 10 August 1792, when a new Revolution toppled the king and the constitutional order established in the summer of 1789. Perhaps the roots of this failure can be found in the many and deep reforms to the Catholic Church the deputies made in 1790, reforms that had their root in the decision to place Church property at the disposal of the nation.[7] While the outcome of the debate over Church property did not create the hard right as a political force, it was the first move toward the great political division over religious reform that would prove such a motor of radicalization in the Revolution.

---

[6] Collins, *State in Early Modern France*, 2nd ed., 347.   [7] Doyle, *Oxford History*, 2nd ed., 138–46.

Much more important, though, was the Louis XVI's attitude toward the Revolution. The king's position regarding the Revolution was poorly understood after 6 October. While Louis consistently signed decrees sent to him by the Assembly and even declared his loyalty to the new constitution the following February, he had secretly declared himself against the reforms sweeping France. Before 6 October, Louis had engaged in debate with the Assembly, suggesting via his ministers matters to be addressed (such as Necker's letter to the Assembly concerning the suspensive veto) and his opinion on actions taken by the Assembly (such as his suggestions concerning the August decrees). After 6 October, the king no longer cooperated with the Assembly in good faith. He played a double game. He secretly denounced the Revolution to his Bourbon cousin, the king of Spain. He maintained an independent and clandestine foreign policy through agents in exile. He pursued a duplicitous charade of cooperation while he secretly (and fitfully) pursued two political goals, an escape from Paris to regain his freedom of action and the implementation of his declaration of 23 June.[8] This refusal of the king to act in good faith was to have tremendous consequences.

Nevertheless, had the deputies of the center-left and left found a way to work with the deputies of the center-right, the overwhelming majorities these groups brought together in the Assembly might have pushed the king to cooperate despite his misgivings. But there would be no reconciliation between center-right and center-left. As fall turned to winter the center-right largely ceased to exist. Much of the Monarchien leadership fled Versailles in the aftermath of the October Days. Mounier, Lally-Tollendal, and La Luzerne, all former presidents of the Assembly, found reasons to return home. Other center-right deputies, men like Antraigues and Virieu, moved further to the right, abandoning their earlier willingness to compromise. With the departure of some center-right deputies who had supported the Revolution and the conversion of others to recalcitrant royalism, the right in the Assembly risked becoming only a voice of rejection. The disappearance of the link the Monarchiens had provided between Revolutionaries and their conservative opponents limited the ability of the deputies to come to consensual decisions. It left true reactionaries such as Maury, Cazalès, and the André Boniface Louis de Riqueti, vicomte of Mirabeau (younger brother of count Mirabeau) to be spokesmen of the right in the Assembly.

---

[8] Hardman, *Louis XVI* (1993), 174; Price, *The Road from Versailles*, 108–09. See also T. Tackett, *When the King Took Flight* (Cambridge, 2004).

This evacuation of the center-right led to the perception that the conservative deputies were somehow alien to the Revolution and thus to the nation. Only with this discrediting of the right in the Assembly could Sieyès's claim that the privileged orders were alien to the nation, made in *What Is the Third Estate?*, become true. These two problems, the failure of the king to act in good faith and the hollowing out of the center-right, helped radicalize the Revolution as moderate Patriot deputies lost ground to those on the left who denounced aristocratic resistance to the Revolution and questioned the king's commitment to the new regime. It would take time for the new constitutional order to take form and for the benefits of its new structures and principles to be felt. As the Assembly continued to reform France according to the wishes of its citizens, networks developed on the right to support resistance to the Revolution. Deputies on the far left came to see counterrevolutionary conspiracies everywhere. But worst of all, the king had little faith in the system he was supposed to lead.

Select Bibliography

Primary Sources

Newspapers

Journal des débats et des décrets (ed. by deputy J.-F. Gaultier de Biauzat)
Journal des États généraux convoqués par Louis XVI . . . .
Journal de Paris (ed. by deputy D.-J. Garat)
Le Courrier de Versailles (ed. by deputy A.-J. Gorsas)
Le Courrier français
Le Patriote français (ed. by future deputy J.-P. Brissot)
Le Point du jour (ed. by deputy B. Barère)
Lettres de Mirabeau à ses commettans/Courrier de Provence (ed. by deputy H.-G. Mirabeau)
Mercure de France
Réimpression de l'ancien Moniteur: Le Moniteur universel
Révolutions de Paris

Unpublished Primary Sources

Deputy witnesses:
Brulart de Sillery, Charles-Alexis, marquis de. *Journal de l'Assemblée des Etats-Généraux*. Archives Nationales, KK 641, 642, 645.
Castellane, Boniface-Louis-André, comte de. Manuscript notes. Bibliothèque Nationale de France, Nouv. acq. fr. 4121.
Goupilleau, J. F. Manuscript letters. Bibliothèque Municipale de Nantes, Collection Dugast-Matifeux, no. 98.
Pellerin, Joseph-Michel. *Journal de la Tenue des Etats Généraux de 1789*. Bibliothèque Municipale de Versailles, ms 823 F.
Visme, Laurent de. *Journal des Etats généraux*. Bibliothèque Nationale de France, Nouv. acq. fr. 12938.

Published Primary Sources

Deputy witnesses

Alquier, Charles-Jean-Marie. Excerpts from letters. In H. Perrin de Boussac, *Un témoin de la Révolution et de l'Empire: Charles-Jean-Marie Alquier.* Paris, 1983.

Anonymous. "Correspondance d'un député de la noblesse avec la marquise de Créquy," ed. B. d'Agours, *Revue de la Révolution. Documents inédits* 2 (1883), 1–8, 33–41, 65–74, 97–104, 139–43.

Bailly, Jean-Sylvain. *Mémoires d'un témoin de la Révolution,* eds. Berville and Barrière, 3 vols. Paris, 1821–22.

Banyuls de Montferré, Raymond-Antoine de. Excerpts from letters written with his fellow deputy, Michel de Coma-Serra and sent to their electors. In Jean Capeille, *Histoire de la maison des chaveliers de Banyuls de Montferré.* Céret, 1923.

Barère, Bertrand. *Mémoires,* ed. Hippolyte Carnot, 4 vols. Paris, 1842. (In English, *Mémoires,* trans. De V. Payen-Payne, 4 vols. London, 1896.)

Biron, Armand-Louis de Goutault, duc de. *Lettres sur les Etats-Généraux de 1789,* ed. R. de La Lande. Paris, 1865.

Boissy d'Anglas, François-Antoine. "Lettres inédites sur la Révolution française," ed. René Puaux, *Bulletin de la Société de l'histoire du Protestantisme français* 75 (1926), 282–99, 425–35.

Bouchette, François-Joseph. *Lettres de François-Joseph Bouchette (1735–1810),* ed. Cammille Looten. Lille, 1909. Appears in *Annales du Comité Flamand de France* 29 (1908–09).

Boullé, Jean-Pierre. "Correspondance de Boullé," in "Ouverture des Etats généraux de 1789," Albert Macé, ed. *Revue de la Révolution* 14 (1889), 26–32, 42–51, 82–92, 114–23.

Buzot, François-Nicolas-Léon. *Mémoires sur la Révolution française,* ed. M. Guadet. Paris, 1823.

Camusat de Belombre, Nicolas-Jean. "Le journal de Camusat de Belombre, député du Tiers de la ville de Troyes," ed. Henri Diné. *AHRF* 37 (1965), 257–69.

Colaud de La Salcette, Jacques-Bernardin. "Lettres de Colaud de La Salcette," *Bulletin de la Société départmentale d'archéologie et de statistique de la Drôme* 69 (1944), 137–56.

Coma-Serra, Michel de. Excerpts from letters written with his fellow deputy, Raymond-Antoine de Banyuls de Montferré, and sent to their electors appear on pp. 450–60. In Jean Capeille, ed., *Histoire de la maison des chaveliers de Banyuls de Montferré.* Céret, 1923.

Correspondance de MM. les députés des Communes de la province d'Anjou, avec leur commettans, Relativement aux États-Généraux tenans à Versailles en 1789, 2 vols. Angers, 1789.

Costa de Beauregard, Marie-Charles, marquis de. *Le roman d'un royaliste sous la Révolution. Souvenirs de Cte de Virieu.* 2nd ed. Paris, 1892.

Creuzé-Latouche, Jacques-Antoine. *Journal des Etats Généraux de début de l'Assemblé nationale, 18 mai-29 juillet 1789*, ed. Jean Marchand. Paris, 1946.

Crillon, Francois-Félix-Dorothée Des Balbes de Berton, comte de. *Lettre du Cte de Crillon, député de la noblesse du bailliages de Beauvais, à ses électeurs, protestant contre l'arrêté de la noblesse en faveur du vote par ordre*. N.p., 30 May 1789.

Delandine, Antoine-François. *Mémorial historique des Etats généraux*, 6 vols. N.p., 1789.

Duquesnoy, Adrien-Cyprien. *Journal d'Adrien Duquesnoy*, ed. R. de Crèvecoeur, 2 vols. Paris, 1894.

Ferrières-Marçay, Charles-Elie, marquis de. *Correspondence inédite (1789, 1790, 1791)*, ed. Henri Carré. Paris, 1932.

Mémoires, 2 vols. 2nd ed. Paris, Badouin Frères, 1822–25.

Gaultier de Biauzat, Jean-François. *Gaultier de Biauzat, député du Tiers état aux Etats généraux de 1789. Sa vie et correspondance*, ed. Francisque Mège, 2 vols. Clermont-Ferrand, 1890.

Gauville, Louis-Henri-Charles, baron de. *Journal du Baron de Gauville*, ed. Edouard de Barthélemy. Paris, 1864.

Jallet, Jacques. *Journal inédit de Jallet, Curé de Chérigné, député du clergé du Poitou, aux États-Généraux de 1789*, ed. J. J. Brethé. Fontenay-le-Comte, 1871.

"Trois lettres de l'abbé Jallet," ed. D. Marié. *AHRF* 22 (1950), 326–49.

Lally-Tolendal, Trophime-Gérard, comte de. *Pièces justificatives, contenant différentes motions de M. le comte de Lally-Tolendal*, n.p., n.d.

Lameth, Alexandre-Théodore-Victor, comte de. *Histoire de l'Assemblée constituante*, 2 vols. Paris, 1828–29.

Lévis, Pierre-Marc-Gaston, duc de. "Lettres du duc de Lévis, 1784–1795," ed. duc de Lévis-Mirepoix, *La Revue de France* 4 (1929), 227–74, 425–44; 5 (1929), 258–95, 418–42, 614–49.

Lofficial, Louis-Prosper. "Lettres de Lofficial," ed. Lerous-Cesbron, *La Nouvelle revue retrospective* 7 (1897), 73–120, 169–92.

Malouet, Pierre-Victor. *Correspondance de Malouet avec les officiers municipaux de la ville de Riom, 1788–89*, ed. François Boyer. Riom, n.d.

Mémoires, ed. Baron Malouet, 2 vols. Paris, 1868.

Maupetit, Michel-René. "Lettres de Michel-René Maupetit, député à l'Assemblée nationale constituante, 1789–91," ed. Queruau-Lamerie. *Bulletin de la Commission Historique et Archéologique de la Mayette*, 2ème sér., 17 (1901): 302–27, 439–54; 18 (1902): 133–63, 321–33, 447–75; 19 (1903): 205–50, 348–78.

Ménard de la Groye, François-René. *Correspondance (1789–1791)*, ed. Florence Mirouse. Le Mans, 1989.

Mounier, Jean-Joseph. *Exposé de ma conduite dans l'Assemblée nationale et Motifs de mon retour en Dauphiné*. Paris, 1789.

Faits relatifs à la dernière insurrection. Paris, 1789.

Palasne de Champeaux, Julien-François and Jean-François-Pierre Poulain de Corbion. "Lettres des députés des Côtes-du-Nord aux Etats généraux et à l'Assemblée nationale constituante," ed. D. Tempier, *Bulletin et mémoires de la Société d'émulation des Côtes-du-Nord* 26 (1888), 210–63; 27(1889), 21–63.

Pellerin, Joseph-Michel. *Correspondance inédite de J.-M. Pellerin . . . : 5 mai 1789—29 mai 1790 . . ..* Paris, 1883.

Périsse-Duluc, Jean-André. Excerpts of his letters to J. B. Willermoz. In Alice Joly, *Un mystique lyonnais et les secrets de la franc-maçonnerie, 1730–1824.* Macon, France, 1938.

Pétion de Villeneuve, Jerôme. *Mémoires inédits de Pétion.* Paris, 1866.

Poncet-Delpech, Jean-Baptiste. *La première année de la Révolution vue par un témoin,* ed. Daniel Ligou. Paris, 1961.

"Documents sur les premiers mois de la Révolution," ed. Daniel Ligou, *AHRF* 38 (1966), 426–46, 561–76.

Prieur, Pierre-Louis. *Notes et Souvenirs inédits de Prieur de la Marne,* ed. Gustave Laurent. Paris, 1912.

Rabaut-Saint-Étienne, Jean-Paul. *Ouvres de Rabaut-Saint-Étienne, précédées d'une notice sur sa vie,* ed. J.-A.-S. Collin de Plancy, 2 vols. Paris, 1826.

Robespierre, Maximilien. *Correspondance,* ed. Georges Michon, 2 vols. Paris, 1926–41.

Rousselot, Claude-Germain. *Correspondance de l'Abbé Rousselot, Constituant, 1789–1795,* ed. Anne-Marie Malingrey. Besançon, 1992.

Thibaudeau, Antoine Claire. *Biographie Mémoires: 1765–1792.* Paris, 1875.

Toulongeon, François-Emmaneul, vicomte de. *Histoire de la France depuis la Révolution,* 7 vols. Paris, 1801.

Vallet, Claude-Benjamin, abbé. *Mémoire de sieur Vallet, curé de Saint-Louis de Gien sur-Loire.* N.p., n.d.

Other witnesses:

Garonne, Allesandro Galante. *Gilbert Romme.* Paris, 1971. Contains excerpts of letters sent by Gilbert Romme to various.

Jefferson, Thomas. *The Papers of Thomas Jefferson,* ed. Julian Boyd, vol. 15 (27 March 1789 to 30 November 1789). Princeton, NJ, 1958.

Writings, ed. Merrill D. Peterson. New York, 1984.

Morris, Gouverneur. *The Diary and Letters of Gouverneur Morris,* ed. Anne Cary Morris, 2 vols. New York, 1888.

A Diary of the French Revolution, 1789–1793, ed. Beatrix Cary Davenport, 2 vols. Boston, 1939.

Mousset, Albert. *Un témoinage de la Révolution, le comte de Fernan Nuñez, ambassador d'Espagne à Paris, 1787–91.* Paris, 1923.

Saint-Priest, François-Emmanuel Guignard, comte de. *Mémoires: Régnes de Louis XV et de Louis XVI,* ed. baron de Barante, 2 vols. Paris, 1929.

Young, Arthur. *Travels in France during the Years 1787, 1788, and 1789.* London, 1792.

Collections:

Aulard, F. V. A., ed. *Récit des séances des députés des communes, depuis le 5 mai 1789 jusqu'au 12 juin suivant.* Paris, 1895.

Baker, K. M., ed. *The Old Regime and the French Revolution.* Chicago, 1987.

Beik, P. H., ed. *The French Revolution.* New York, 1970.

Brette, A. *Recueil de documents relatifs à la convocation des États Généraux de 1789,* 4 vols. Paris, 1894–1915.

Chassin, C.-L. *Les Élections et les Cahiers de Paris en 1789,* 4 vols. Paris, 1888.

Lefebvre, G., and A. Terroine, eds. *Recueil de documents relatifs à séances des Etats Généraux de 1789.* Tome I: vol. 1, *Les Préliminaires—La Séance du 5 May*; vol. 2, *La Séance du 23 Juin.* Paris, 1953 and 1962.

Mavidal, M. J., and M. E. Laurent, eds. *Archives parlementaires de 1787 à 1860, première série (1787 à 1799).* 2nd ed., 82 vols. Paris, 1867–1913.

Reuss, R., ed. *L'Alsace pendant la Révolution française,* vol. 1, *Correspondance des députés à l'Assemblée nationale (Année 1789).* Paris, 1880.

Roberts, J. M., ed. *French Revolutionary Documents,* vol. I. New York, 1966.

Stewart, J. H., ed. *A Documentary Survey of the French Revolution.* New York, 1951.

Secondary Sources

Alpaugh, M. *Non-Violence and the French Revolution.* Cambridge, 2014.

Andress, D. *1789: The Threshold of the Modern Age.* New York, 2009.

ed. *Experiencing the French Revolution.* Oxford, 2013.

The French Revolution and the People. New York and London, 2006.

ed. *The Oxford Handbook of the French Revolution.* Oxford, 2015.

Applewhite, H. B. *Political Aignment in the French National Assembly, 1789–1791.* Baton Rouge, LA, 1993.

Baker, K. M., ed. *The French Revolution and the Creation of Modern Political Culture,* vol. 1, *The Political Culture of the Old Regime.* Oxford, 1987.

Inventing the French Revolution. Cambridge, 1990.

Bastid, P. *Sieyès et sa pensée.* Paris, 1939.

Beik, P. H. "The Abbé Maury and the National Assembly," *Proceedings of the American Philosophical Society* 95: 5 (1951), 546–55.

Bell, D. A. *The Cult of the Nation in France: Inventing Nationalism, 1680–2000.* Cambridge, MA, 2003.

Bercé, Y.-M. *The Birth of Absolutism.* Trans. Richard Rex. New York, 1996.

Biard, M. and R. Dupuy. *La Révolution française, 1787–1804.* 3rd ed. Paris, 2016.

Blackman, R. H. "Representation without Revolution: Political Representation as Defined in the General Cahiers de doléances of 1789," *FH* 15:2 (June 2001), 159–85.

"What Does a Deputy to the National Assembly Owe His Constituents? Coming to an Agreement on the Meaning of Electoral Mandates in 1789." *FHS* 34:2 (Spring 2011), 205–41.

"What's in a Name? Possible Names for a Legislative Body and the Birth of National Sovereignty during the French Revolution, 15–16 June 1789." *FH* 21:1 (March 2007), 22–43.

"What Was 'Absolute' about the 'Absolute Veto'? Ideas of National Sovereignty and Royal Power in September 1789." *Proceedings of the Western Society for French History* 32 (2004), 123–39.

Bompard, R. *Le Veto du Président de la République et la sanction royale.* Paris, 1906.

Bonney, R. "Absolutism: What's in a Name?" *FH* 1:1 (March 1987), 93–117.

Bradby, E. D. *The Life of Barnave,* 2 vols. Oxford, 1915.

Brasart, P. *Paroles de la Révolution.* Paris, 1988.

Brette, A. "Les cahiers de 1789 considéré comme mandats impératifs." *Révolution française* 31 (1896), 123–39.

Campbell, P. R., ed. *The Intellectual Origins of the French Revolution.* New York, 2007.

Campbell, P. R. *Power and Politics in Old Regime France.* London and New York, 1996.

Carré de Malberg, R. *Contribution à la Théorie générale de l'État,* 2 vols. Paris, 1920–22.

Chartier, R. *The Cultural Origins of the French Revolution.* Trans. Lydia Cochrane. Durham, NC, 1991.

Chaussinand-Nogaret, G. *The French Nobility in the Eighteenth Century.* Trans. William Doyle. Cambridge, 1985.

Mirabeau. Paris, 1982.

Chisick, H. "Public Opinion and Political Culture in France during the Second Half of the Eighteenth Century," *English Historical Review* CXVII 470 (February 2002), 48–77.

Collins, J. B. *From Tribes to Nation: The Making of France, 500–1799.* New York, 2002.

"Noble Political Ideology and the Estates General of Orléans and Pointoise: French Republicanism." *Historical Reflections/Réflexions Historique* 27:2 (2001), 219–40.

The State in Early Modern France, 2nd ed. Cambridge, 2009.

Crook, M. *Elections in the French Revolution.* Cambridge, 1996.

Dean, R. *L'Assemblée constituante et la réforme ecclésiastique, 1790.* Paris, 2014.

Desan, S., L. Hunt, and W. M. Nelson, eds. *The French Revolution in Global Perspective.* Ithaca, NY, 2013.

Dippel, H. "Angleterre, Etats-Unis, France: Constitutionnalisme et souveraineté populaire." In R. Bourderon, ed., *L'an I et l'apprentissage de la démocratie: Actes du colloque organisé à Saint-Ouen les 21, 22, 23, 24 juin 1993 . . . .* Saint-Denis, France, 1995, 537–60.

Doyle, W. *Aristocracy and Its Enemies in the Time of the French Revolution.* Oxford, 2009.

The Origins of the French Revolution, 2nd. ed. Oxford, 1990.

The Oxford History of the French Revolution, 2nd ed. Oxford, 2002.

"The Parlements of France and the Breakdown of the Old Regime, 1771–1788."
French Historical Studies 6:4 (Fall 1970), 415–58.

Venality: The Sale of Offices in Eighteenth-Century France. Oxford, 1996.

Edelstein, M. *The French Revolution and the Birth of Electoral Democracy*. Surrey, 2014.

Égret, J. *The French Prerevolution, 1787–1788*. Trans. W. D. Camp. Chicago, 1977.

Necker, Ministre de Louis XVI. Paris, 1975.

La révolution des notables: Mounier et les monarchiens, 1789. Paris, 1950.

Farge, A. *Subversive Words: Public Opinion in Eighteenth-Century France*. Trans. R. Morris. University Park, PA, 1994.

Félix, J. *Louis XVI et Marie-Antoinette: un couple en politique*. Paris, 2006.

Fitzsimmons, M. "New Light on the Aristocratic Reaction in France," *FH* 10:4 (1996), 418–31.

The Night the Old Regime Ended: August 4, 1789 and the French Revolution. University Park, PA, 2002.

"Privilege and the Polity in France, 1786–1791," *AHR* XCII (1987), 269–95.

The Remaking of France: The National Assembly and the Constitution of 1791. Cambridge, 1994.

Ford, F. *Robe and Sword*. Cambridge, MA, 1962.

Forrest, A., and M. Middell, eds. *The Routledge Companion to the French Revolution in World History*. London and New York, 2016.

Forsyth, M. *Reason and Revolution: The Political Thought of the Abbé Sieyès*. Leicester, 1987.

Friedland, P. "Parallel Stages: Theatrical and Political Representation in Early Modern and Revolutionary France." In C. Jones and D. Wahrman, eds., *The Age of Cultural Revolutions*. Berkeley and Los Angeles, 2002, 218–50.

Political Actors. Ithaca, New York, 2002.

Furet, F. *Interpreting the French Revolution*. Trans. E. Forster. Cambridge, 1981.

Revolutionary France 1770–1880. Trans. A. Nevill. Oxford and New York, 1992.

Furet, F., and R. Halévi, *La Monarchie républicaine*. Paris, 1996.

Furet, F., and M. Ozouf, eds. *A Critical Dictionary of the French Revolution*. Trans. A. Goldhammer. Cambridge, MA, 1989.

Garrioch, D. "The Everyday Lives of Parisian Women and the October Days of 1789," *Social History* 24:3 (October 1999), 231–49.

Gauchet, M. *La Révolution des pouvoirs: La souveraineté, le peuple et la représentation, 1789–1799*. Paris, 1995.

Gershoy, L. *Bertrand Barère: A Reluctant Terrorist*. Princeton, 1962.

Glénard, G. *L'Exécutif et la Constitution de 1791*. Paris, 2010.

Godechot, J. *The Taking of the Bastille*. Trans. J. Stewart. New York, 1970.

Gottschalk, L., and M. Maddox. *Lafayette in the French Revolution: Through the October Days*. Chicago, 1969.

Gough, H. *The Newspaper Press in the French Revolution*. London and New York, 1988.

Griffiths, R. *Le centre perdu: Malouet et les "Monarchiens" dans la Révolution française*. Grenoble, 1988.

Gruder, V. R. *The Notables and the Nation: The Political Schooling of the French, 1787–88.* Cambridge, MA, 2007.

Gueniffey, P. "Constitution et intérêts sociaux: le débat sur les deux Chambres." In M. Troper and L. Jaume, eds., *1789 et l'invention de la Constitution.* Paris, 1994, 77–88.

Le nombre et la raison. Paris, 1993.

Guilhaumou, J. *L'avènement des porte-parole de la Republique (1789–1792).* Paris, 1998.

Habermas, J. *The Structural Transformation of the Public Sphere.* Trans. T. Burger. Cambridge, MA, 1991.

Hampson, N. *Prelude to Terror: The Constituent Assembly and the Failure of Consensus, 1789–1791.* Oxford, 1988.

Will & Circumstance: Montesquieu, Rousseau and the French Revolution. Norman, Oklahoma, 1983.

Hanson, P. *Contesting the French Revolution.* Chichester, 2009.

Hardman, J. *The Life of Louis XVI.* New Haven, 2016.

Louis XVI. New Haven, 1993.

Louis XVI: The Silent King. London and New York, 2000.

Overture to Revolution: The 1787 Assembly of Notables and the Crisis of France's Old Regime. Oxford, 2010.

Hayden, J. M. *France and the Estates General of 1614.* Cambridge, 1974.

Henshall, N. *The Myth of Absolutism: Change and Continuity in Early Modern European Monarchy.* London and New York, 1992.

Holt, M. P. "Attitudes of the French Nobility at the Estates-General of 1576." *Sixteenth Century Journal* 18:4 (Winter 1987), 489–504.

Horn, J. *The Path Not Taken: French Industrialization in the Age of Revolution, 1750–1830.* Cambridge, MA, 2006.

Hufton, O. *Women and the Limits of Citizenship in the French Revolution.* Toronto, 1992.

Hutt, M. G. "The Curés and the Third Estate: the Ideas of Reform in the Pamphlets of the French Lower Clergy in the period 1787–1789." *Journal of Ecclesiastical History* VIII (1957), 190–220.

Hyslop, B. *A Guide to the General Cahiers of 1789.* New York, 1968.

French Nationalism in 1789 According to the General Cahiers. New York, 1968.

Jainchill, A. *Reimagining Politics after the Terror: The Republican Origins of French Liberalism.* Ithaca, NY, 2008.

Jones, P. M. *Reform and Revolution in France: The Politics of Transition, 1774–1791.* Cambridge, 1995.

Jourdan, A. *Nouvelle histoire de la Révolution.* Paris, 2018.

Kaiser, T., and D. Van Kley, eds. *From Deficit to Deluge: The Origins of the French Revolution.* Stanford, 2011.

Kates, G. *The French Revolution: Recent Debates and New Controversies,* 2nd ed. New York and London, 2006.

Kettering, S. *French Society, 1589–1715.* New York and London, 2001.

Koselleck, R. *Critique and Crisis.* Cambridge, MA, 1988.

Lacorne, D. *L'invention de la République: Le modèle americain.* Paris, 1991.

Lamarque, P. "La naissance de 'l'Assemblée nationale'," *Dix-Huitième Siècle*, 20 (1988), 111–18.

Lefebvre, G. *The Coming of the French Revolution.* Trans. R. R. Palmer. Princeton, 2005.

The Great Fear. Trans. J. A. White. Princeton, 1982.

Lemay, E. H. *Dictionnaire des Constituants,* 2 vols. Oxford, 1991.

La Vie quotidienne des députés aux États Généraux 1789. Paris, 1987.

Levy, D. G., and H. Applewhite, "Women and Militant Citizenship in Revolutionary Paris." In S. E. Melzer and L. W. Rabine, eds., *Rebel Daughters: Women and the French Revolution.* Oxford, 1992, 79–101.

Linton, M. *Choosing Terror: Virtue, Friendship, and Authenticity in the French Revolution.* Oxford, 2013.

Lucas, C. "The Crowd and Politics between the Ancien Regime and Revolution in France," *JMH* 61 (1989), 421–57.

ed. *The French Revolution and the Creation of Modern Political Culture,* vol. 2, *The Political Culture of the French Revolution.* Oxford, 1988.

Luttrell, B. *Mirabeau.* Carbondale, IL, 1990.

Major, J. R. *The Estates General of 1560.* Princeton, 1951.

From Renaissance Monarchy to Absolute Monarchy: French Kings, Nobles, and Estates. Baltimore, 1994.

Representative Government in Early Modern France. New Haven, 1980.

Representative Institutions in Renaissance France, 1421–1559. Madison, 1960.

"The Third Estate in the Estates General of Pontoise, 1561." *Speculum* 29:2 (April 1954), 460–76.

Margerison, K. *Pamphlets and Public Opinion.* West Lafayette, IN, 1998.

Markoff, J. *The Abolition of Feudalism.* University Park, PA, 1996.

Mathiez, A. "Etude critique sur les journées des 5 et 6 october 1789." *Revue historique,* LXVII (1898), 241–81; LXVIII (1898) 258–94; LXIX (1899), 41–58.

McMahon, D. *Enemies of the Enlightenment.* Oxford, 2001.

McPhee, P., ed. *A Companion to the French Revolution.* New York, 2013.

Liberty or Death: The French Revolution. New Haven, 2016.

Robespierre: A Revolutionary Life. New Haven, 2013.

Mintz, M. M. *Gouverneur Morris and the French Revolution.* Norman, OK, 1970.

Mousnier, R. "The Fronde." In R. Forster and J. Greene, eds., *Preconditions of Revolutions in Early Modern Europe.* Baltimore, 1970, 131–59.

The Institutions of France under the Absolute Monarchy, 1598–1789, 2 vols. Vol. 1 trans. B. Pierce; vol. 2 trans. A. Goldhammer. Chicago, 1979, 1984.

La monarchie absolue en Europe de ve siècle à nos jours. Paris, 1982.

Nathans, B. "Habermas's 'Public Sphere' in the Era of the French Revolution," *FHS* 16:3 (Spring 1990), 620–44.

Palmer, R. R. *The Age of Democratic Revolution,* vol. I: *The Challenge.* Princeton, 1959.

Patrick, A. "The Second Estate in the Constituent Assembly, 1789–1791," *JMH* 62: 2 (June 1990), 223–52.

Pimenova, L. "Analyse des cahiers de doléances: l'exemple des cahiers de la Noblesse," *Mélanges de l'Ecole de Rome* 103 (1991), 85–101.

Popkin, J. *Revolutionary News: The Press in France, 1789–1799.* Durham, NC, 1990.

Popkin, J., and D. Van Kley. *The Pre-Revolutionary Debate,* section 5 of The French Revolution Research Collection, Colin Lucas, general editor. Oxford, 1990.

Price, M. *The Road from Versailles.* New York, 2003.

Rafajlovic, D. *Veto ... son reflet historique et son importance politique actuallement.* Dillingen, 1951.

Robin, R. *La société française en 1789: Semur-en-Auxois.* N.p., 1970.

Rouff, M. "Le peuple ouvrier de Paris aux journées du 30 juin et du 30 août 1789," *La Révolution française* 63 (1912), 430–54, 481–505.

Sepinwall, A. *The Abbé Grégoire and the French Revolution: The Making of Modern Universalism.* Berkeley and Los Angeles, 2005.

Sewell, W. *A Rhetoric of Bourgeois Revolution.* Durham, NC, 1994.

Shapiro, B. M. *Revolutionary Justice in Paris: 1789–1790.* Cambridge, 1993.
   Traumatic Politics: The Deputies and the King in the Early French Revolution. University Park, PA, 2009.

Shapiro, G., and J. Markoff et al. *Revolutionary Demands: A Content Analysis of the Cahiers de Doléances of 1789.* Stanford, 1998.

Shusterman, N. *The French Revolution: Faith, Politics and Desire.* London and New York, 2014.

Stone, B. *The French Parlements and the Crisis of the Old Regime.* Chapel Hill, 1986.

Sutherland, D. M. G. *The French Revolution and Empire: A Quest for Civic Order.* Oxford, 2003.

Swann, J. *Provincial Power and Absolute Monarchy: The Estates General of Burgundy, 1661–1790.* Cambridge, 2003.

Swann, J., and J. Félix, eds. *The Crisis of the Absolute Monarchy: France from Old Regime to Revolution.* The Proceedings of the British Academy, no. 184. Oxford, 2013.

Tackett, T. *Becoming a Revolutionary: The Deputies of the French National Assembly and the Emergence of a Revolutionary Culture (1789–1790).* Princeton, 1996.
   The Coming of the Terror in the French Revolution. Cambridge, MA, 2015.
   "Nobles and the Third Estate in the Revolutionary Dynamic of the National Assembly, 1789–90." In G. Kates, ed., *The French Revolution: Recent Debates and New Controversies,* 2nd ed. New York, 2006, 131–64. Originally published in *AHR* 94 (April 1989), 271–301.
   Priest and Parish in Eighteenth-Century France. Princeton, 1977.
   Religion, Revolution, and Regional Culture in Eighteenth Century France. Princeton, 1986.
   "Use of the <<Cahiers de doléances>> of 1789 for the Analysis of Regional Attitudes." *Mélanges de l'École française de Rome* 103 (1991), 27–46.

Taylor, G. V. "Revolutionary and Nonrevolutionary Content in the *Cahiers* of 1789: An Interim Report." *FHS* 7 (1972), 497–502.

Thompson, E. *Popular Sovereignty and the French Constituent Assembly, 1789–1791.* Manchester, 1952.

Tilly, C. *The Vendée.* Cambridge, MA, 1964.

Troper, M. "Le titulaire de la souveraineté." In J.-P. Cotten, R. Damien, and A. Tosel, eds., *La Répresentation et ses crises.* Besançon, 2001, 155–73.

Ulph, O. "Jean Bodin and the Estates-General of 1576," *JMH* 19: 4 (1947), 289–96.

Van Kley, D., ed. *The French Idea of Freedom: The Old Regime and the Declaration of Rights of 1789.* Stanford, 1994.

The Religious Origins of the French Revolution. New Haven, 1996.

Viatte, A. *Le veto légilatif dans la Constitution des États-Unis et dans la Constitution française de 1791.* Paris, 1901.

Wick, D. *A Conspiracy of Well-Intentioned Men: The Society of Thirty and the French Revolution.* New York, 1987.

"The Court Nobility and the French Revolution: The Example of the Society of Thirty," *Eighteenth Century Studies,* 13 (Spring 1980), 263–84.

Wright, K. "A Republican Constitution in Old Régime France." In M. Van Gelderen and Q. Skinner, eds., *Republicanism: A Shared European Heritage,* 2 vols. Cambridge, 2002, vol. 1: 289–306.

Index

CPSIA information can be obtained
at www.ICGtesting.com
Printed in the USA
LVHW022337140820
663230LV00010B/322